# Captured by the Indians

15 Firsthand Accounts, 1750–1870

*Edited by* **Frederick Drimmer**

*Dover Publications, Inc., New York*

Published in Canada by General Publishing Company, Ltd., 30 Lesmill Road, Don Mills, Toronto, Ontario.

Published in the United Kingdom by Constable and Company, Ltd., 10 Orange Street, London WC2H 7EG.

This Dover edition, first published in 1985, is an unabridged and corrected republication of the work first published by Coward-McCann, Inc., New York, in 1961 under the title *Scalps and Tomahawks: Narratives of Indian Captivity.*

Manufactured in the United States of America
Dover Publications, Inc., 31 East 2nd Street, Mineola, N.Y. 11501

**Library of Congress Cataloging in Publication Data**

Main entry under title:

Captured by the Indians.

Reprint. Originally published: Scalps and tomahawks. New York: Coward-McCann, 1961.

1. Indians of North America—Captivities. I. Drimmer, Frederick.
E85.C274   1985      973'.0497               85-4542
ISBN 0-486-24901-8

**For Andrew and Amelia**

May these true tales
of adventures with the Indians
amaze and enthrall you
as they did so many readers
who came before you

# CONTENTS

# INTRODUCTION

FOR many minutes now, the long dark gun barrels slanting from the loopholes of the besieged cabin had been silent. The warriors crouching in the bushes wondered: Have the palefaces used up their powder and shot so soon? A young Indian, eager to make a name for himself, decided to find out. He screamed and jumped up—once, twice, three times. Each time he exposed himself only briefly, but his glistening, brightly painted body presented a tempting target.

No one in the cabin fired.

Instantly, with a wild whoop of triumph, the naked warriors rushed for the cabin and rammed their musket butts against the narrow door. The bars that braced it gave way and it swung open. The cabin was crowded with trembling children and women. In front of them stood their men, tight lipped; they had only knives and axes in their hands. The Indians howled joyfully and plunged inside.

In a moment the men had been shot and hacked to pieces, and the scalps ripped from their heads. One or two men were saved, to provide the Indian village with a sacrifice and a day's wild frolic, or to be held for ransom or adopted into the tribe. The weak, the wounded, the old of both sexes were killed and mutilated. The young women and the older children, particularly the boys, were spared;

# Captured by the Indians

these, too, were to be taken home and adopted. Hastily the Indians stripped the dead of their belongings and searched the cabin for other booty. Then, brandishing their tomahawks to enforce silence, they hurried their prisoners off into the woods.

Many a captivity among the Indians began with an incident like this. Often the white prisoner lived with the Indians for the rest of his life. But sometimes, after waiting months or even years, a prisoner might make his escape. Or he might be ransomed, or else a treaty of peace was signed and the Indians were obliged to give up their prisoners. The experiences these captives recounted when they got home were astonishing, and they were frequently urged to put them in a book.

Quite a number of them did. They told of massacres and raids on wagon trains, of which sometimes they were the sole survivors, and of being dragged long distances through the wilderness with the tomahawk always waiting if they fell behind. They spoke of running the gauntlet, of being adopted into Indian tribes in curious rituals, and of scalp dances and captives tortured to death. They told how they had hunted the bear and the buffalo with the Indians, and fought in bloody conflicts between different tribes. They told of Indian love and marriage, of witchcraft, and of sages and sorcerers who brought eerie gods to life. No one had ever heard or read tales quite like these before.

"There is nothing in English, or in any other language, that surpasses these narratives of Indian captivities in vividness or in the bare statement of physical suffering and of mental torment," George Parker Winship has observed in the *Cambridge History of American Literature.* As true stories of strange adventure and perilous escape, also, they do not have many rivals. Thousands and thousands of readers have thrilled to the experiences of young James Smith and his wise old Indian brother, Tecaughretanego, during the French and Indian War, to Alexander Henry's narrow escapes from the bloodthirsty allies of Chief Pontiac, to John Rodgers Jewitt's adventures among the head-hunting Nootkas of the Northwest Coast, and the other narratives that are brought together in this book. For our ancestors, these remarkable tales had all the suspense and romance that the historical novel, the science-fiction tale, and the detective story hold for us today, with one important difference—these stories were *real,* and the same dangers and tragedies could befall the reader, for there were still hostile Indians on the prowl somewhere in the land. A large number of the captivity narratives were reprinted time and again, in both the United States and Europe. Some were among the great best sellers of their day.

As the Indian settled on reservations, exchanging the role of the threatening, hostile raider for that of the peaceful farmer and herdsman, the captivity narratives began to die out and disappear. Today these wonderful tales are all but lost. Except for an occasional reprint by a scholarly press, you can find them only in the rare-book rooms and special collections of our great libraries. This is a shame, for they were not written for scholars but for everyone, and they are as rich in human interest and excitement as they ever were. The intimate firsthand pictures they paint of life on the frontier, the warfare between red man and white, and the customs of the Indian in the days of scalps and tomahawks are a fascinating personal record of a vanished age. This book has been designed to "rescue" some of the most interesting and unusual of these narratives and place them within the reach of the modern reader.

Each of the captives in this book tells of things that he saw with his own eyes. All relate their stories in the first person. About half of these narratives were written by the captives themselves, some of whom were persons of no mean literary skill. The rest were related by the captives to editor-writers, much as is done today by people who have had a remarkable experience but lack the ability to set it down in writing. Occasionally there is a note of exaggeration or romanticizing in the narratives, but by and large they bear the stamp of truth. They have been accepted as authentic since their earliest publication, and have frequently been used as sources by historians and anthropologists.

At least two of the captives who tell their stories here were condemned to be burned at the stake, but made almost miraculous escapes. Three were so badly wounded that the Indians left them for dead. One was ransomed. Most of the rest married into the Indian band that took them captive, were adopted by the Indians, or else were destined for adoption when they won their way to freedom.

Adoption of prisoners was a practice among the Indians from ancient times, and a very useful one. Many of the tribes or bands were constantly fighting with one another, and war with them was war to the death. No one was spared, either young or old, for the victor saw every member of the conquered band as a part of its potential fighting power. Starvation and disease claimed their victims, too. Adoption was the remedy, and the Indians sometimes practiced it on a large scale. In 1722, for example, the Iroquois Confederacy, whose strength had been sapped by decades of warfare, adopted an entire tribe, the Tuscaroras. When the whites appeared upon the scene, the Indians adopted them, too.

It was a custom that the prisoner belonged to the first Indian who laid hands on him. If more than one Indian claimed him, all might own him in common. If a disagreement arose about who had prior right to a captive, it might be settled by killing him on the spot. This was almost the fate of one of our captives, Thomas Brown.

The lot of a prisoner could vary greatly, depending on the character and wishes of his captor, who might treat him as a friend and brother or as a hated enemy or a slave. If an Indian "master," as he was called, did not want to adopt his prisoner, he might allow him to be ransomed, or sell him to a white nation that was allied with the tribe. In the French and Indian Wars, which lasted, on and off, from 1689 to 1763, large numbers of English colonists were captured by

Indian raiders allied with the French, and were sold to the French Canadians, who often used them as servants, adopted them, or attempted to convert them. Usually the Indian captor's wish was paramount in disposing of a captive. During the American Revolution, Daniel Boone was taken prisoner by the Shawnee chief Blackfish, who adopted the celebrated frontiersman as his son after rejecting a handsome offer from the British lieutenant governor of Detroit to purchase him.

James Smith, who tells his story in this book, was captured and adopted by the Caughnawaga Indians in the French and Indian War (as the last of the French and Indian Wars is commonly called). The ceremony by which he was initiated into the tribe was typical. He was plunged up to his middle in a stream and then three young squaws rubbed him briskly. Later an old chief told him that by this ritual every drop of white blood had been washed out of him. "You are adopted into a great family," the chief said, "and now received with great solemnity in the place of a great man. You are now one of us by an old strong law and custom."

Experience taught Smith that the old Indian meant what he had said. Thereafter Smith was treated exactly as though he had been born into the tribe. It is interesting to observe that a captive was usually adopted in the place of someone who had died or been killed in war. He was given not only the name, but also the privileges and responsibilities of the person whose place he took—was expected to be a husband to the dead man's wife and a father to his children. Sometimes a party of warriors would set out with the express aim of taking a white captive to replace a deceased member of their family or clan. This was how John Tanner, the "white Indian" whose story is told in this book, came to begin his thirty-year stay among the Ottawas and Ojibways.

Anyone reading early accounts of captivity among the Indians is struck by the fact that female prisoners do not appear to have been abused by the Indians in the eastern section of the country. Mary Rowlandson, who was taken captive in Massachusetts by the Wampanoags and Narragansetts in King Philip's War, in 1676, observed, "I have been in the midst of those roaring lions and savage bears that feared neither God nor man, nor the devil, by night and day, alone and in company, sleeping all sorts together, and yet not one of them ever offered the least abuse of unchastity to me in word or action."

Isabella McCoy, captured in 1747 by the St. Francis Indians, reported that "nothing like insult or indecency did they ever offer her during the whole time she was with them." General James Clinton, who took part in the punitive expedition the Americans made against the Iroquois in New York in 1779, summed it up when he wrote, "Bad as the savages are, they never violate the chastity of any women their prisoners."

One observation on this subject is particularly curious. The anonymous author of *A Narrative of the Capture of Certain Americans at Westmoreland,* writing in 1780 about a war party of Iroquois who had captured a man, woman, and child in Pennsylvania and then allowed the woman and child to go free, commented, "I don't remember to have heard an instance of these savages offering to violate the chastity of any of the fair sex who have fallen into their hands; this is principally owing to a natural inappetency in their constitution." Actually, it was a custom for the braves to make elaborate preparations before going on the warpath, and these included the practice of continence and rites of purification. To abuse a female captive would have weakened the Indians' "medicine." Moreover, a woman's body was generally held to belong to herself alone, and this principle was extended to white women brought back to live with the tribe. As Francis Parkman noted, a young woman who would not marry an Indian husband was treated with "a singular forbearance." On the other hand, at a somewhat later period, numerous cases of violation were reported by white women captured by Indians west of the Mississippi.

White captives, particularly if they were very young when they were taken prisoner, became greatly attached to the families into which they were adopted, and to the Indian way of life. The Indians were usually affectionate toward their children, rarely punishing them, and an Indian mother would treat an adopted white child as her own. Although squaws had many tasks to perform, they were seldom the drudges that they are described as being, and in an Indian village they often enjoyed more companionship, fun, and independence than did their white sisters dwelling along the frontier. The white woman captive who married an Indian and reared a half-breed family might become more an Indian than a white in her habits and outlook as the years went by. Thus it is not too surprising that, when offered an opportunity to return to the whites, many captives were not greatly delighted at the prospect. Often they did not remember any other life before their capture, and they were reluctant to leave the Indians. This was the case with one captive who tells his story here. When John Tanner returned to his own people he had forgotten his native language and even his name.

In 1764, at the close of Pontiac's War, Colonel Henry Bouquet led an army against the Ohio Indians and compelled them to sign a treaty of peace. He has described how heartbroken the Indians were when they were obliged to give up their captives. The Indians (presumably the women) shed "torrents of tears" over them, Bouquet observed, and begged him to take good care of them. They visited the captives all the time they were in camp, bringing them corn, skins, horses, and any other possessions that had been bestowed upon them while they were among the Indians. When the army marched off toward Fort Pitt, some of the Indians begged and obtained permission to accompany their former captives and hunted for them and brought them food along the way. White children who had lived with the Indians for a long while seemed to regard being restored to their parents as the start of a new captivity.

"But it must not be denied," Bouquet noted, "that there were even some grown persons who shewed an unwillingness to return. The Shawanese were obliged to bind several of their prisoners and force them along to the camp; and some women, who had been delivered up, afterwards found means to escape and run back to the Indian towns. Some, who could not make their escape, clung to their savage acquaintance at parting, and continued many days in bitter lamentations, even refusing sustenance."

With all these marks of deep affection that Indians and captives showed each other, it is still a bitter fact that the Indian put to the tomahawk all but a small proportion of those who fell into his power. Not a single one of the fifteen survivors who tell their stories in this volume fails to mention others he knew who were killed by the Indians. Death at the hands of the Indians was an ever-present threat to many Americans who lived on the frontier.

It is impossible to make a reliable estimate of the total number of whites who were slain by Indians, but it must have been staggering. A leading Kentuckian wrote to the Secretary of War in 1790 that in the seven years after the end of the Revolution fifteen hundred people had been killed in Kentucky or on the routes leading to it. One of these unfortunates was Abraham Lincoln, grandfather of the sixteenth

President, who was named for him. "He was killed by Indians, not in battle but by stealth, when he was laboring to open a farm in the forest," was the caustic comment of his famous grandson. Thomas Lincoln, then just a boy—he was to be the father of the President— was saved when his elder brother shot an Indian who was about to tomahawk him.

Although there were many tragedies and near-tragedies like these, the white man and the Indian were not always at war. Often they lived fairly close together in friendship and peace. The French, in particular, maintained a warm relationship with the Indians of New France and often took Indian wives. In the first major warfare in which the Indians took part, the French and Indian Wars, they did not fight as enemies of the whites but as allies of opposing nations— the Canadian tribes on the side of the French, and the Iroquois on the side of the English.

When serious trouble erupted between the white man and the Indian, its cause could usually be summed up in a single word: land. The number of settlers was always increasing and they kept pressing westward, hungry for more and better land. Frequently the Indian's best hunting grounds were taken from him by treaties that he signed but did not understand, or frontiersmen moved in on his territory without his consent. Officials treated him arrogantly and traders cheated and robbed him without mercy. Treaties were also broken or rewritten to suit the needs of the swelling white population or of special interests, and the Indian was pushed toward and across the Mississippi.

As the Indian's hunting grounds shrank, so did his numbers. It has been estimated that in 1492 there were about 900,000 Indians north of Mexico. By 1870, when most of the tribes had been forced to settle on reservations, their numbers had been reduced to about 300,000. They had lost their four-hundred-year-long struggle to preserve their way of life—which, for many of the Indians, meant life itself.

During frontier days the Indian dwelling north of the Rio Grande still lived in the Stone Age. He had some of the savage customs that primitive man has had around the world. One of the most barbarous of these was the taking of scalps as trophies of victory in combat. His earlier custom was to take the head itself, or occasionally other parts of the body. An old Dutch account speaks of the Mohawks carrying home leg and arm bones after a foray, and Mary Jemison, taken captive in the French and Indian War, speaks of seeing fragments of burnt bodies hanging on a pole in a Shawnee village on the banks of the Ohio. Thomas Brown, a colonial soldier, was horrified to see his captain's head mounted on a pole by Indians in the service of the French. The colonists speedily learned to pay the Indians back by cutting off their heads and displaying them publicly. They also learned to take scalps as efficiently and routinely as the Indians did.

The operation of scalping held a morbid fascination for the captives of the Indians, and they mention it frequently in their narratives. Because so many varying statements are made about scalps and scalping, it is worth examining into what the Indians' practices actually were.

Through the ages different peoples have ascribed magic powers to the hair, and the Indian was one of them. He believed that the scalp was mystically connected with a person's fate. He is said to have burned cuttings or combings of his own hair because he feared that they might fall into an enemy's hands and voodooistically be used to bewitch or injure him. His scalp lock—if he wore one—was a symbol of life to him.

Various tribes had their own special ways of dressing the hair, and the scalp lock took different forms among different groups. Among the Sioux it was usually a small, finely plaited hair braid which hung from the back of the head. A Pawnee warrior cut his hair close to the head, but left a roach or ridge in the middle, extending from the front to the crown of the head. Here the scalp lock was separated and treated with fat and paint, so that it formed a stiff curve, like a horn. The brave carefully decorated his scalp lock with ornaments that symbolized his boldest acts and triumphs in war. The scalp lock personified the man and his manliness.

Some authorities believe that scalping began on the East Coast, others that it also developed independently among the Plains Indians. It apparently was practiced only in a few fairly restricted areas until the coming of the white man. When the French were at war with the British, they paid their Indian allies a bounty for British scalps. The British offered the friendly Iroquois a price for the scalps of Indians in the service of the French. During the Revolution and the War of 1812, and in later Indian wars, the Americans entered the scalp-buying market. Each side, of course, expressed abhorrence for the taking of scalps when it was done by the other. With the white man's help scalping spread across the continent, although it never became a universal custom among the Indians, as is popularly supposed.

Scalping was a brutal, painful experience, but it did not always cause death. Sarah Ann Horn, who lived in northern Mexico in 1839, spoke to a man who had been scalped by a Comanche. He told her that the Indian had first made an incision around his head, then stood on his shoulders and tore the scalp off as he would the skin from a slaughtered sheep. Usually the victim lay face down and the victor knelt on him, perhaps pressing his knee into his back. He would seize the victim's hair in his left hand and, with a scalping knife held in his right, make a swift cut around the head. Then he would pull hard at the scalp (or scalp lock if the victim was an Indian) and jerk it off with the skin attached. Occasionally he might use his teeth to help. Frequently, but not always, a section of scalp about three inches in diameter was taken. Some elderly Blackfeet told John C. Ewers that Indians who survived scalping wore caps to cover their bald spots. It was not uncommon, among the Plains Indians, to scalp an enemy and then spare his life and send him back to his people as an insult and an act of provocation. However, the enemy was often killed, and the entire scalp was removed. In the collection of the Museum of the American Indian in New York City there is a very large scalp— complete with the ears of the victim!

Not every brave who brought in a scalp was the one who had subdued the victim. To obtain full credit for the trophy, the warrior had to have his claim confirmed by others present when he took the scalp. Among many Indians, the custom was to stretch the scalp within a hoop and paint it on the skin side. Usually when the war party reached home victorious there would be a scalp dance performed by the women, who carried the trophies on poles in the celebration.

The scalp might be treated in different ways, depending on tribal custom and the wishes of the warrior who had taken the trophy. Some scalps might be kept by the individual, or they might be made a part of the Indian band's "medicine" or collection of sacred objects. A scalp might be offered up to the gods or the spirit of the person from whom it was taken, or it might simply be destroyed. If the warrior had taken a large enough scalp he might use some of the hair to decorate his shirt, his leggings, or the bridle of his horse. The Apalachees are reported to have decorated their bows with the scalps of De Soto's followers.

More than scalping, the white who was taken prisoner feared torture or death at the stake. Not every tribe tortured captives, but the savage finesse of some of those that did was legendary. There are few scenes that surpass in vivid horror the ones that Nelson Lee, John Knight, John Slover, and other survivors describe here of how their comrades were put to death. The torture of George Washington's old friend, Colonel William Crawford, who led a militia expedition against the Sandusky Indians of Ohio in 1782, was remembered by both Indians and whites for many years along the frontier. Indians often made a cult of torture, and young and old, male and female, took part in it. The squaws had a special reputation for ferocity.

What little can be said in extenuation of these practices is suggested by the statements of some of the captives whose experiences are reported in this book. For example, Charles Johnston remarks about a war dance that he witnessed: "On these occasions it is their practice to repeat the injuries inflicted on them by their enemies the whites: to tell how their lands were taken from them—their villages burnt—their cornfields laid waste—their fathers and brothers killed—their women and children carried into captivity." An Indian chief, otherwise friendly, became so infuriated by the recital of these wrongs that he attacked Johnston and two other prisoners. John Tanner relates that when he was being led through a Shawnee village a young woman came toward him crying and struck him on the head, because some of her friends had been killed by Americans. The Indian had his grievances against the whites. To him, one American or Englishman was like another, and all were held responsible for the misdeed of one. Given the provocation and the opportunity, he often exacted the last full measure of revenge.

There was cruelty on both sides. Indians massacred whites, but whites massacred Indians. By Indian standards, Colonel Crawford, mentioned above, deserved a cruel death: he had marched against the Indian towns, and his militiamen, if they had found any Indians, would probably have slaughtered them indiscriminately. In fact, the militia had done just that some months earlier. A band of them, out to take vengeance upon the Ohio Indians for raiding along the frontier, came to the town of Gnadenhutten, which was inhabited by peaceable Christian Delawares, converted by Moravian missionaries.

Ninety-six unsuspecting Indian men, women, and children were herded into a few houses. Meek and unprotesting, the Indians sang hymns and said their prayers while they were butchered with axes and clubs by the militiamen. "Even now a just man's blood boils in his veins at the remembrance," said Theodore Roosevelt, hardly an Indian partisan. "It is impossible not to regret that fate failed to send some strong war party of savages across the path of these inhuman cowards to inflict on them the punishment they so richly deserved."

To the captive of the Indians, one of their most horrifying practices was cannibalism. Human flesh has been eaten by primitive groups of people all over the world, and the custom was occasionally observed among the Indians. In fact, the word cannibalism itself is derived from the name of a West Indian tribe, the Caribs, who were man eaters. Cannibalism, in most places, was a religious ritual based on the principle that "you are what you eat." Usually the Indian would eat the flesh of an enemy because he believed that with it he would absorb the strength, the courage, and other manly qualities of the victim. The flesh of an enemy who had died a cowardly death was carefully avoided, as a rule.

Cannibalism, then, was a rite of warfare, like the purification rituals the warrior performed to gain power and the favor of the spirit world in battle. The heart was considered the most desirable part of the body, and usually it was eaten by the warriors. Sometimes it was torn from the body of the victim while he was still alive. The warm blood of the enemy was also drunk, as Alexander Henry relates in his account of the Chippewa massacre at Michilimackinac. Other parts of the body might be given to the women and children and eaten raw or roasted. Among the Iroquois the torture of an enemy is said to have almost always ended in cannibalism, and they were reputed to have acquired a taste for human flesh.

There are cases on record of starving Indians who ate human flesh —John Tanner mentions one in his narrative. This sort of cannibalism, practiced on members of one's own tribe, was regarded with great horror by the Indians, and might be punished with death.

The hostile Indian, like his captive, has vanished; both continue to live on only in the pages of books. I wish I had been able to keep more of them alive in this one, but there was not room for all the captivities I should have liked to include. Those I have selected are the ones I considered the most interesting and dramatic of hundreds I have read, but I had to omit others equally good. Variety was one of my touchstones: these narratives cover a wide range of time and they involve different tribes and sections of the country. I have tried to strike a balance between captives who had a good experience with the Indian and those who had an unfortunate one. Necessarily the greater number hated their captors. If a person's relatives or friends had been killed by Indians and the recollection was still fresh in his mind, even kind treatment might seem harsh and cruel to him.

There are seven full-length books here, all considerably condensed, and eight shorter pieces. This volume is intended for the popular reader, not the historian or scholar, who has access to the originals. Thus, although I have tried to preserve the spirit and tone of the old narratives, I have revised them freely to improve their readability. Paragraph length and sentence structure have been changed and minor errors corrected, archaic language has been modernized and indirect discourse occasionally made direct. However, the facts, ideas, and opinions, like most of the words, are those of the original writers.

Where I felt that notes were needed to explain the places, personalities, events, or details in a narrative, I have added them; they will be found at the end of the book. I have not attempted to clarify every allusion, particularly those that are explained in standard dictionaries and encyclopedias. The source of each narrative, and the date of its first publication, so far as I could ascertain it, are given in these notes or in the introduction to the narrative.

Preparing a book as large in scope as this one takes a long time, but the assistance of wise, informed people helps to shorten it. Although she will deny it altogether, my wife, Evelyn, helped greatly with perceptive advice and unfailing aid and comfort. So did Lurton Blassingame, my agent, with his faith in this project. Many persons and organizations assisted by answering questions, supplying information, or making available needed books and documents. I owe a special debt of gratitude to:

The Honorable Michael V. DiSalle, Governor of the State of Ohio; William Kaye Lamb, Dominion Archivist, Public Archives of Canada; Frank H. H. Roberts, Jr., Director, and Dr. William C. Sturtevant, of the Bureau of American Ethnology, Smithsonian Institution; Frederick R. Goff, Chief of the Rare Book Division, the Library of Congress; G. Glenn Clift, Assistant Director and Editor of the Kentucky Historical Society; The Museum of the American Indian; Frederick Hall of the Ayer Collection, Newberry Library, Chicago; James J. Heslin, Director of the New York Historical Society; Erwin C. Zepp, Director of the Ohio Historical Society; John Melville Jennings, Director of the Virginia Historical Society; John D. Cushing, Assistant Librarian of the New England Historic Genealogical Society; John R. Cuneo of Westport, Connecticut, military historian and author of a recent biography of Robert Rogers; Ruth Adams, Reference Librarian of the Westport Public Library; John J. Hallahan, Librarian of the Norwalk Public Library, Norwalk, Connecticut; the United States Coast Guard; Columbia University Library; the Chamber of Commerce of Mackinaw City, Michigan; and the New York Public Library and the Sterling Memorial Library of Yale University, both of which were of inestimable aid to me.

—FREDERICK DRIMMER

# Captured
# by the Indians

# Prisoner of the Caughnawagas

## JAMES SMITH

FORT DUQUESNE *stood on the forks of the Ohio River, where the Monongahela meets the Allegheny. (Pittsburgh stands there today.) Manned by French troops, the fort was a spearhead pointed at the rich Ohio valley, which the British regarded as their own. In 1755 Major-General Edward Braddock massed two thousand English troops and American militia for a full-scale assault on the French stronghold.*

*To bring supplies to Braddock's forces, the colonists began to cut a road through the wilderness. One of the road builders was an eighteen-year-old Pennsylvania youth named James Smith. Riding along the road, Smith was captured by Indian marauders in the service of the French. He was a prisoner at Fort Duquesne when the French and Indians returned with their spoils and captives after Braddock's defeat.*

*Smith lived for five years among the Caughnawagas, a branch of the Mohawks friendly to the French. Adopted into the tribe, he was treated like a brother. Most of his captivity was spent in Ohio. He acquired a profound understanding of Indian customs and psychology, and a deep respect for the Indians themselves. In 1759 he accomplished his escape by stealing away from the Caughnawaga town.*

*Returning to Pennsylvania, Smith settled in his old home in Franklin*

*County, married, and took to farming. His reputation as an Indian expert was widespread, and when the Indians began to attack along the frontier in 1763, his fellow colonials turned to him for help. He quickly organized a company of Rangers and dressed them, painted them, and taught them to fight like Indians. Their success in defending the settlements was notable. Smith took part in later campaigns against the Indians, and during the Revolutionary War won a colonelcy.*

*Smith was one of the first white men to explore southern Kentucky and Tennessee. He settled in Kentucky in 1788, and later represented Bourbon County in the State Legislature. Always a religious man, he spent much of his time as a missionary to the Indians in his later years. In the War of 1812, at the age of seventy-five, he offered to place his experience at the disposal of his country and he published a treatise on Indian warfare. He died about two years later.*

*A rebel and a man of indomitable courage, Smith was cast in the same rugged, heroic mold as his fellow Kentuckian, Daniel Boone. His contemporaries knew him as a reader and a thinker, a taciturn man with strong convictions. He waited until almost forty years after his escape from the Indians to write his memoirs, basing them on a journal he had kept while a captive of the Caughnawagas. The following selection is taken from* An Account of the Remarkable Occurrences in the Life and Travels of Col. James Smith, *Lexington, Kentucky, 1799.*

In May 1755, the province of Pennsylvania agreed to send out three hundred men to cut a wagon road from Fort Loudon to join Braddock's road near the Turkey Foot or three forks of Yohogania. My brother-in-law, William Smith, Esquire, of Conococheague, was appointed commissioner in charge of these road cutters.

Though I was at that time only eighteen years of age, I had fallen violently in love with a young lady who, I believed, possessed a large share of both beauty and virtue. But I decided I must leave her and go out with this company of road cutters to see the outcome of the campaign. I expected that sometime in the course of the summer I should return to the arms of my beloved.

We went on with the road without interruption until near the Allegheny Mountain. Then I was sent back to hurry up some provision wagons that were on the way after us. Finding the wagons were coming on as fast as possible, I returned up the road towards the Allegheny Mountain in company with one Arnold Vigoras.

About four or five miles above Bedford, three Indians had made a blind of bushes, stuck in the ground as though they grew naturally. Here they concealed themselves about fifteen yards from the road. When we came opposite them, they fired upon us and killed my fellow traveler. Their bullets did not touch me, but my horse made a violent start and threw me. The Indians immediately ran up and took me prisoner.

The one that laid hold of me was a Canasatauga, the other two were Delawares. One of them could speak English, and asked me if there were any more white men coming behind me.

"Not any near, that I know of," I told him.

Two of these Indians stood by me whilst the other scalped my comrade. We then set off and ran at a smart rate through the woods for about fifteen miles. That night we slept on the Allegheny Mountain, without fire.

The next morning the Indians divided the last of their provision, which they had brought from Fort Duquesne, and gave me an equal share—about two or three ounces of mouldy biscuit. This and a young ground hog about as large as a rabbit, roasted and also equally divided, was all the provision we had until we came to Loyal-Hanna Creek, which was about fifty miles. A great part of the way we came through exceedingly rocky laurel thickets, without any path.

When we came to the west side of Laurel Hill, they gave the scalp halloo, which is a long yell or halloo for every scalp or prisoner they have. The last of these scalp halloos was followed with quick and sudden shrill shouts of joy and triumph. We were answered by the firing of a number of guns on Loyal-Hanna Creek, one after another, quicker than one could count, by another party of Indians. As we advanced near this party they increased their repeated shouts of joy and triumph, but I did not share their excessive mirth.

When we came to this camp, we found they had plenty of turkeys and other meat there. I had never before eaten venison without bread or salt, yet, as I was hungry, it relished very well. There we stayed that night, and the next morning the whole of us marched on our way for Fort Duquesne. The following night we joined another camp of Indians, with nearly the same ceremony, attended with great noise and joy among all except one.

The next morning we continued our march. In the afternoon we came in full view of the fort, which stood on the point near where Fort Pitt now stands. We made a halt on the bank of the Allegheny and the Indians repeated the scalp halloo. It was answered by the firing of all the firelocks in the hands of both Indians and French who were in and about the fort, and also the great guns. This was followed by the continued shouts and yells of the different savage tribes collected there.

As I was unacquainted with this mode of firing and yelling of the savages, I concluded that there were thousands of Indians there, ready to receive General Braddock. But, what added to my surprise, I saw numbers running toward me, stripped naked, excepting breechclouts, and painted in the most hideous manner with various colors—red, black, brown, blue, etc.

As they approached, they formed themselves into two long ranks, about two or three yards apart. I was told by an Indian that could speak English that I must run betwixt these ranks and they would flog me all the way. If I ran quickly, it would be so much the better, as they would quit when I got to the end of the ranks.

There appeared to be a general rejoicing around me. I could find nothing like joy in my breast, but I started the race with all the resolution and vigor I was capable of. I was flogged the whole way. When I got near the end of the lines, I was struck with something that appeared to me to be a stick, which caused me to fall to the ground.

Recovering my senses, I endeavored to renew my race. As I arose, someone cast sand in my eyes, which blinded me, so that I could not see where to run. They continued beating me most intolerably, until I was at length insensible. Before I lost my senses, I remember my wishing them to strike the fatal blow. I thought they intended killing me, but were too long about it.

The first thing I remember was my being in the fort, amidst the French and Indians, and a French doctor standing by me, who had opened a vein in my left arm. The interpreter asked me how I did. I told him I felt much pain. The doctor then washed my wounds and the bruised places of my body with French brandy. As I felt faint and the brandy smelt well, I asked for some inwardly. But the doctor told me, by the interpreter, that it did not suit my case.

When they found I could speak, a number of the Indians came

around me and questioned me. They threatened me with a cruel death if I did not tell the truth.

The first question they asked me was: "How many men are there in the party coming from Pennsylvania to join Braddock?"

I told them the truth—that there were three hundred.

The next question was: "Are they well armed?"

I told them they were all well armed (meaning the arm of flesh), for they had only about thirty guns among the whole of them. If the Indians had known this, they would certainly have gone and massacred all of them. Therefore I could not in conscience let them know the defenseless situation of these road cutters.

I was then sent to the hospital and carefully attended by the doctors, and recovered quicker than I expected.

Some time after, I was visited by the Delaware Indian already mentioned, who was at the taking of me. Though he spoke bad English, I found him to be a man of considerable understanding. I asked him if I had done anything that had offended the Indians, which caused them to treat me so unmercifully. He said no, it was only an old custom, like saying how do you do. After that, he said, I would be well used.

I asked him if I should be permitted to remain with the French. He said no—and told me that as soon as I recovered I must not only go with the Indians, but must be made an Indian myself.

"What news from Braddock's army?" I asked.

He said the Indians spied on them every day. He showed me, by making marks on the ground with a stick, that Braddock's army was advancing in very close order, and that the Indians would surround them, take to the trees, and (as he expressed it) "shoot um down all one pigeon."

Shortly after this, on the 9th day of July, 1755, in the morning I heard a great stir in the fort. As I could then walk with a staff in my hand, I went out and stood upon the wall. The Indians were in a huddle before the gate, where there were barrels of powder, bullets, flints, etc., and everyone was taking what he needed. I saw the Indians also march off—likewise the French Canadians and some regulars. I estimated them to be about four hundred, and wondered that they attempted to go out against Braddock with so small a party. I was then in high hopes that I would soon see them flying before the British troops, and that General Braddock would take the fort and rescue me.

I remained anxious to know the outcome of this day. In the afternoon I again observed a great noise and commotion in the fort. Though at that time I could not understand French, I found it was the voice of joy and triumph, and feared they had received what I called bad news.

I had observed some of the old-country soldiers speak Dutch.[1] As I spoke Dutch I went to one of them and asked him what was the news. He told me a runner had just arrived who said Braddock would certainly be defeated. The Indians and French had surrounded him and were concealed behind trees and in gullies, and kept a constant fire upon the English, who were falling in heaps. If they did not take to the river and make their escape, the runner had said there would not be one man left alive before sundown.

Sometime after this I heard a number of scalp halloos and saw a company of Indians and French coming in. They had a great many bloody scalps, grenadiers' caps, British canteens, bayonets, etc., with them. They brought the news that Braddock was defeated.

After that another company came in which appeared to be about one hundred, and chiefly Indians. It seemed to me that almost every one of this company was carrying scalps. After this came another company with a number of wagon horses and also a great many scalps. Those that were coming in and those that had arrived kept up a constant firing of small arms and also the great guns in the fort. This was accompanied with the most hideous shouts and yells from all quarters, so that it appeared to me as if hell had broken loose.

About sundown I beheld a small party coming in with about a dozen prisoners, stripped naked, with their hands tied behind their backs and their faces and part of their bodies blacked. These prisoners they burned to death on the bank of the Allegheny River opposite the fort.

I stood on the fort wall until I beheld them begin to burn one of these men. They had him tied to a stake and kept touching him with firebrands, red-hot irons, etc. He screamed in a most pitiful manner, the Indians in the meantime yelling like devils. As this scene was too shocking for me to behold, I retired to my lodgings.

When I came in, I saw Russel's *Seven Sermons*. They had brought this book from the field of battle and a Frenchman had made a present of it to me. From the best information I could receive there were only seven Indians and four French killed in this battle—and five hundred British lay dead in the field, besides those that were killed in the river on their retreat.

The morning after the battle I saw Braddock's artillery brought into the fort. The same day I also saw several Indians in British officers' dress, with sash, half-moon, laced hats, etc., which the British then wore.

A few days after this the Indians demanded me and I was obliged to go with them. I was not yet well able to march, but they took me in a canoe up the Allegheny River to an Indian town on the west branch of the Muskingum, about twenty miles above the forks. This town, called Tullihas, was inhabited by Delawares, Caughnawagas, and Mohicans.

The day after my arrival a number of Indians collected about me, and one of them began to pull the hair out of my head. He had some ashes on a piece of bark, in which he frequently dipped his fingers in order to take the firmer hold. And so he went on, as if he had been plucking a turkey, until he had all the hair clean out of my head, except a small spot about three or four inches square on my crown. They cut this off with a pair of scissors, excepting three locks, which they dressed up in their own mode. Two of these they wrapped round with a narrow beaded garter made for that purpose, and the other they plaited at full length and then stuck full of silver brooches.

After this they bored my nose and ears, and fixed me up with earrings and nose jewels. They ordered me to strip off my clothes and put on a breechclout, which I did. Then they painted my head, face and body in various colors. They put a large belt of wampum on my neck, and silver bands on my hands and right arm.

Next, an old chief led me out in the street and gave the alarm halloo, *"Coo-wigh!"* several times, repeated quickly. At this, all that were in the town came running and stood round the old chief, who held me by the hand in their midst.

At that time I knew nothing of their mode of adoption, and had seen them put to death all they had taken. As I never could find that they saved a man alive at Braddock's defeat, I did not doubt they were about to put me to death in some cruel manner.

The old chief, holding me by the hand, made a long speech very loud, and handed me to three young squaws. They led me by the hand down the bank into the river until the water was up to our middle.

The squaws made signs to me to plunge myself into the water. I did not understand them. I thought the result of the council was I should be drowned, and these young ladies were the executioners. All three took violent hold of me. For some time I opposed them with all my might, which occasioned loud laughter among the multitude on the bank of the river.

At length one of the squaws resorted to speaking a little English (for I believe they began to be afraid of me) and said, "No hurt you!" At this I gave myself up to their ladyships, who were as good as their word. Though they plunged me under water and washed and rubbed me severely, I could not say they hurt me much.

These young women then led me up to the council house, where some of the tribe were ready with new clothes for me. They gave me a new ruffled shirt, which I put on, a pair of leggings done off with ribbons and beads, a pair of moccasins, and garters dressed with beads, porcupine quills, and red hair—also a tinsel-laced cloak.

They again painted my head and face with various colors, and tied a bunch of red feathers to one of the locks they had left on the crown of my head, which stood up five or six inches. They seated me on a bearskin and gave me a pipe, tomahawk, and polecat-skin pouch which contained tobacco and dry sumach leaves, which they mix with their tobacco—also flint, steel, and spunk, a kind of dry wood they use as tinder.

When I was seated, the Indians came in dressed and painted in their grandest manner. They took their seats and for a considerable time there was a profound silence. Everyone was smoking, but not a word was spoken among them. Finally one of the chiefs made a speech which was delivered to me by an interpreter.

"My son, you are now flesh of our flesh and bone of our bone. By the ceremony which was performed this day, every drop of white blood was washed out of your veins. You are taken into the Caughnawaga nation and initiated into a warlike tribe. You are adopted into a great family, and now received with great solemnity in the place of a great man. You are one of us by an old strong law and custom.

"My son, you have nothing to fear. We are under the same obligation to love, support and defend you that we are to love and defend one another. You are to consider yourself as one of our people."

I did not believe this fine speech, but since that time I have found there was much sincerity in it. From that day I never knew them to make any distinction between me and themselves in any respect whatever. If they had plenty of clothing, I had plenty; if we were scarce of provisions, we all shared one fate.

After this ceremony was over, I was introduced to my new kin, and told that I was to attend a feast that evening, which I did. And as the custom was, they gave me a bowl and wooden spoon, which I carried with me to the place, where there was a number of large brass kettles full of boiled venison and green corn. Everyone advanced with his bowl and spoon and had his share given him. After this, one of the chiefs made a short speech, and then we began to eat.

The name of one of the chiefs in this town was Tecanyaterighto, alias Pluggy, and the other Asallecoa, alias Mohawk Solomon. As Pluggy and his party were to start the next day to war, to the frontiers of Virginia, the next thing to be performed was the war dance and their war songs.

All those who were going on this expedition collected together and formed. An old Indian began to sing and timed the music by beating on a drum. The warriors began to move forward as well-disciplined troops would march to the fife and drum. Each warrior had a tomahawk, spear or war club in his hand, and they all moved regularly towards the east, the way they intended to go to war. At length they all stretched their tomahawks towards the Potomac and gave a hideous yell. Then they wheeled quickly about and danced back in the same manner.

Next came the war song. In performing this, only one sang at a time, in a moving posture, with a tomahawk in his hand, while all the other warriors were engaged in calling aloud "He-uh, he-uh!" They constantly repeated this while the war song was going on. When the warrior that was singing had ended his song, he struck a war post with his tomahawk, and with a loud voice told what warlike exploits he had done and what he now intended to do. This was answered by the other warriors with loud shouts of applause. Some who had not before intended to go to war were so excited by this performance that they took up the tomahawk and sang the war song, which was answered with shouts of joy, as they were then initiated into the present marching company.

The next morning this company collected at one place, with their heads and faces painted with various colors, and packs upon their backs. They marched off all silent, except the commander, who was in front and sang the traveling song. It began in this manner: *"Hoo caughtainte heegana."* Just as the rear passed the end of the town, they began to fire in their slow manner, from the front to the rear, which was accompanied with shouts and yells from all quarters.

Shortly after this I was given a gun and went out on a long hunting trip with Mohawk Solomon and some of the Caughnawagas. After some time we came upon some fresh buffalo tracks.

I had observed that the Indians were upon their guard, and afraid of an enemy, for until now they and the southern nations had been at war. As we were following the buffalo tracks, Solomon seemed to be upon his guard. He went very slowly, and would frequently stand and listen.

We came to where the tracks were very plain in the sand.

"They are surely buffalo tracks," I said.

"Hush, you know nothing. May be buffalo tracks, may be Catawba," Solomon answered.

He went very cautiously until we found some fresh buffalo dung. He smiled. "Catawba cannot make so."

He then stopped and told me an odd story about the Catawbas. He said that once the Catawbas came near one of the Caughnawaga hunting camps, and at some distance from the camp lay in ambush. In order to decoy the Caughnawagas out, the Catawbas sent two or three warriors in the night, past the camp, with buffalo hoofs fixed on their feet, so as to make artificial tracks.

In the morning those in the camp followed these tracks, thinking they were buffalo, until they were fired on by the Catawbas, and several of them killed. The others fled, collected a party and pursued the Catawbas.

But the wily Catawbas had brought with them rattlesnake poison, collected from the bladder at the root of the snakes' teeth. They had also brought small reeds, which they made sharp at the end and dipped in this poison. They stuck these in the ground among the grass, along their own tracks, in such a position that they might stick into the legs of the pursuers. When the Catawbas found that a number of the enemy were lame, being artificially snake bit, and they were all going back, the Catawbas turned upon the Caughnawagas and killed and scalped all that were lame.

When Solomon had finished this story and found I understood him, he concluded: "You don't know Catawba. Velly bad Indian, Catawba. All one devil Catawba."

Our hunting party encamped on a creek. One day I was told to take the dogs with me and go down the creek—perhaps I might kill a turkey. Since it was in the afternoon, I was also told not to go far from the creek, and to take care not to get lost.

When I had gone some distance down the creek I came upon fresh buffalo tracks. I had a number of dogs with me to stop the buffalo and decided I would follow them and kill one.

A little before sundown, I despaired of catching up with the buffalo. I was then thinking how I might get to camp before night. The buffalo had made several turns, and if I took the track back to the creek, it would be dark before I could get to camp. Therefore I thought I would take a near way through the hills, and strike the creek a little below the camp.

But it was cloudy weather and I was a very young woodsman: I could find neither creek or camp. When night came on, I fired my gun several times and hallooed, but received no answer.

Early the next morning the Indians were out after me. As I had with me ten or a dozen dogs, and the grass and weeds were rank, they could readily follow my track. When they came up with me they appeared to be in a very good humor.

I asked Solomon if he thought I was running away.

"No, no," he said, "you go too much clooked."

On my return to camp they took my gun from me. For this rash step I was reduced to a bow and arrows for nearly two years.

We were out on this tour about six weeks. When we returned to the town, Pluggy and his party had arrived, and brought with them a considerable number of scalps and prisoners from the South Branch of the Potomac. They also brought with them an English Bible, which they gave to a Dutch woman who was a prisoner. As she could not read English, she made a present of it to me, which was very acceptable.

I remained in this town until sometime in October, when my adopted brother, Tontileaugo, who had married a Wyandot squaw, took me with him to Lake Erie.

On this route we had no horses with us, and when we started from the town all the pack I carried was a pouch, containing my books, a little dried venison, and my blanket. I had then no gun, but Tontileaugo, who was a first-rate hunter, carried a rifle and every day killed deer, raccoons or bears.

Tontileaugo could not speak English. I had to make use of all the Caughnawaga I had learned even to talk very imperfectly with him. I found I learned to talk Indian faster this way than when I had those with me who could speak English.

As we proceeded down the Canesadooharie waters, our packs increased by the skins that were daily killed, and became so very heavy that we could not march more than eight or ten miles per day.

At the mouth of Canesadooharie, we came to a large camp of Wyandots, where Tontileaugo's wife was, and we stayed here for some time. At length a party of us left for our winter hunt. There were eight men and thirteen squaws, boys, and children in our company, and all embarked in a large birch-bark canoe. This vessel was about four feet wide, three feet deep, and five and thirty feet long. In spite of its size four men could carry it several miles from one landing place to another, or overland from the waters of Lake Erie to the Ohio.

Proceeding up the Canesadooharie a few miles, we went on shore to hunt. To my great surprise the Indians carried the vessel up the bank, turned it bottom up, and converted it to a dwelling house. Then we kindled a fire before us to warm ourselves by and cook. With our baggage and ourselves in this house we were very much crowded, yet our little house turned off the rain very well.

We kept moving and hunting up this river until we came to the falls. Here we remained some weeks, and killed a number of deer, several bears, and a great many raccoons.

While we remained here, I left my pouch with my books in camp, wrapped up in my blanket, and went out to hunt chestnuts. On my return my books were missing. I asked the Indians if they knew where they were. They told me they supposed the puppies had carried them off. I did not believe them. I thought they were displeased at my poring over my books and had destroyed them.

After this I went out after chestnuts again. On my return I beheld a new erection: two white oak saplings that were forked about twelve feet high and stood about fifteen feet apart. They had cut these saplings at the forks and laid a strong pole across. The posts were shaved very smooth and painted in places with vermilion.

I could not conceive the use of this piece of work and concluded it was a gallows. I thought I had displeased them by reading my books and they were going to put me to death.

The next morning I observed them bringing their skins all to this place and hanging them over this pole to preserve them from being injured by the weather. This removed my fears. They also buried their large canoe in the ground, which is the way they preserve this sort of a canoe in the winter season.

As we had at this time no horses, everyone got a pack on his back and we marched east about twelve miles and encamped. The next morning we proceeded on the same course about ten miles to a large creek that empties into Lake Erie.

Here the Indians made their winter cabin. They cut logs about fifteen feet long and laid these upon each other, driving posts in the ground at each end to keep the logs together. The posts they tied together at the top with bark. By this means they raised a wall fifteen feet long and about four feet high. In the same manner they raised another wall opposite this, about twelve feet away. Then they drove forks in the ground in the center of each end and laid a strong pole from end to end on these forks. From these walls to the poles they set poles instead of rafters, and on these they tied small poles in place of laths. A cover was made of linden bark, which will strip even in winter.

At the end of these walls they set up split timber, so that they had timber all round, excepting a door at each end. At the top, in place of a chimney, they left an open place. For bedding they laid down the same kind of bark, and spread bearskins on it. From end to end of this hut along the middle there were fires, which the squaws made of dry split wood. The squaws stopped with moss the holes or open places that appeared. At the door they hung a bearskin. Notwithstanding the winters are hard here, our lodging was much better than I expected.

It was sometime in December when we finished this winter cabin. When we got into this comparatively fine lodging, another difficulty arose: we had nothing to eat.

While the hunters were all out, exerting themselves to the utmost of their ability, the squaws and boys (in which class I was) were scattered out, hunting red haws, black haws, and hickory nuts. As it was too late in the year, we did not succeed in gathering haws, but we had tolerable success in scratching up hickory nuts from under a light snow. After our return the hunters came in. They had killed only two small turkeys, which were but little among twenty-one persons. But all was divided with the greatest justice—everyone got their equal share.

The next day the hunters turned out again, and killed one deer and three bears. One of the bears was very large and remarkably fat. The hunters carried in meat sufficient to give us all a hearty supper and breakfast.

The squaws and all that could carry turned out to bring in meat. Everyone had their share assigned them. My load was among the least, but I was not accustomed to carrying in this way. I got exceedingly weary.

"My load is too heavy," I told them. "I must leave part of it and come for it again."

They made a halt and only laughed at me. Taking part of my load, they added it to a young squaw's, who had had as much before as I carried.

This kind of reproof had a greater tendency to excite me to exert myself in carrying without complaining than if they had whipped me for laziness.

After this the hunters held a council and concluded that they must have horses to carry their loads and would go to war even in this severe season in order to bring in horses. It was agreed that Tontileaugo and three others should stay and hunt, and the other four go to war.

After the departure of these warriors we had hard times. Though we were not altogether out of provisions, we were brought to short allowance. At length Tontileaugo had considerable success, and we had meat brought into camp sufficient to last ten days.

Tontileaugo then took me with him some distance from the winter cabin to try his luck there. We carried no provisions with us; he said we would leave what was there for the squaws and children, and we could shift for ourselves.

We went south up the waters of the creek and encamped about ten or twelve miles from the cabin.

It was still cold weather. There was a crust upon the snow, which made a noise as we walked and alarmed the deer. We could kill nothing, and went to sleep without supper. The only chance we had, under those circumstances, was to hunt bear holes, as the bears, about Christmas, search out a lodging place where they lie about three or four months without eating or drinking.

Early the next morning we went on. When we found a tree scratched by a bear's climbing up, and a hole in the tree sufficiently large to admit the bear, we felled a sapling or small tree against or near the hole. It was my business to climb up the sapling and drive out the bear, while Tontileaugo stood ready with gun and bow.

We went on in this manner until evening without success. Finally we found a large elm scratched, and a hole in it about forty feet up. There was a tree that grew near the elm and extended up near the hole. But this tree leaned the wrong way, so that we could not lodge it to advantage.

Tontileaugo got a long pole and some dry rotten wood which he tied in bunches with bark. Then he tied the rotten wood to his belt, and to one end of the pole he tied a hook and a piece of rotten wood which he set fire to. He began to climb the tree, reaching this hook from limb to limb and gradually moving the pole up as he proceeded.

When he got opposite the hole he put dry wood on fire into it with the pole. The bear snuffed. Tontileaugo came speedily down. He took his gun and waited for the bear to come out. When it finally appeared he attempted to take sight with his rifle, but it was too dark.

Setting the rifle down by a tree, Tontileaugo instantly bent his bow, took hold of an arrow, and shot the bear a little behind the shoulder.

I was also preparing to shoot an arrow, but he called to me to stop, as there was no occasion. And with that the bear fell to the ground.

Being very hungry, we kindled a fire. We opened the bear, took out the liver, wrapped some of the caul fat round and put it on a wooden spit which we stuck in the ground by the fire to roast. Then we skinned the bear, got on our kettle, and had both roast meat and boiled, and also sauce to our meat. I found it delicious. After I was fully satisfied I went to sleep.

Tontileaugo awoke me. "Come, eat hearty," he said. "We have got meat plenty now."

The next morning we cut down a linden tree, peeled bark and made a snug little shelter facing the southeast, with a large log betwixt us and the northwest. We made a good fire before us and scaffolded up our meat at one side. When we had finished our camp we went out to hunt. We searched two trees for bears, but to no purpose. As the snow thawed a little, in the afternoon Tontileaugo killed a deer, which we carried with us to camp.

We remained here about two weeks, and in this time killed four bears, three deer, several turkeys, and a number of raccoons. We packed up as much meat as we could carry and returned to our winter cabin. On our arrival there was great joy, as the Indians were all in a starving condition, the three hunters that we had left having killed very little. All that could carry a pack rushed to our camp to bring in meat.

Sometime in February the four warriors returned. They had taken two scalps and six horses from the frontiers of Pennsylvania. The hunters could then scatter out a considerable distance from the winter cabin and encamp, kill meat and pack it in upon horses. So after this we commonly had plenty of provision.

In this month we began to make sugar. As some of the elm bark will strip at this season, the squaws, after finding a tree that would do, cut it down and with a crooked stick, broad and sharp at the end, took the bark off the tree. Of this bark they made vessels that would hold about two gallons each; they made above one hundred of these vessels. In the sugar tree they cut a notch, sloping down, and at the end of the notch stuck in a tomahawk. In the place where they had stuck the tomahawk, they drove a long chip, in order to carry the sap out of the tree. Under this they set their vessel to receive it.

For carrying the sap they also made bark vessels that would hold about four gallons each. They had two brass kettles that held about fifteen gallons each, and other smaller kettles in which they boiled the sap.

The way that we commonly used our sugar, while encamped, was to put it in bear's fat until the fat was almost as sweet as the sugar itself. In this we dipped our roasted venison.

About this time some of the Indian lads and myself were employed in making and attending traps for catching raccoons, foxes, wildcats, etc. As the raccoon is a kind of water animal that frequents the runs or small water courses almost the whole night, we made our traps here. Laying one small sapling on another, we drove in posts to keep them from rolling. The upper sapling we raised about eighteen inches, and set it so that, on the raccoon's touching a string or small piece of bark, the sapling would fall and kill it. Lest the raccoon should pass by, we laid brush on both sides of the run, only leaving the channel open.

The fox traps we made nearly in the same manner, at the end of a hollow log or opposite a hole at the root of a hollow tree, and put venison on a stick for bait. We had it so set that when the fox took hold of the meat the trap fell. While the squaws were employed in making sugar, the boys and men were engaged in hunting and trapping.

About the end of March we began to prepare for moving into town, in order to plant corn. When all things were ready we moved back to the falls of the Canesadooharie.

We had brought with us on horseback about two hundredweight of sugar, a large quantity of bear's oil, skins, etc. The canoe we had buried at the falls was not large enough to carry all this. Therefore we were obliged to make another one of elm bark.

While we remained here a young Wyandot found my books and the Indians collected together. I was a little way from camp and saw the crowd but did not know what it meant. They called me by my Indian name.

"Scoouwa! Scoouwa! Scoouwa!" they called.

I ran to see what was the matter. They showed me my books and said they were glad they had been found, for they knew I was grieved at the loss of them.

As I could then speak some Indian, especially Caughnawaga (for both that and the Wyandot tongue were spoken in this camp), I thanked them for the kindness they had always shown to me, and also for finding my books. They asked if the books were damaged. I told them not much. They then showed how the books had lain all winter in a deerskin pouch, in the best manner to turn off the water.

This was the first time that I felt my heart warm towards the Indians. Though they had been very kind to me, I had detested them on account of the barbarity I beheld after Braddock's defeat. Neither had I ever before pretended kindness, or expressed myself in a friendly manner. But now I began to excuse the Indians on account of their want of information.

When we were ready to embark, Tontileaugo would not go to town with the others. He had decided to go up the river and hunt, and asked me if I wanted to go with him. I told him I did. We packed up some sugar, bear's oil bottled up in a bear's gut, and some dry venison, and went up the Canesadooharie about thirty miles and encamped.

In the woods here we found some stray horses—a stallion, a mare, and a young colt—that were quite wild. Tontileaugo one night concluded that we must run them down. I told him I thought we could not accomplish it. He said he had run down bears, buffaloes and elks; and in the great plains, with only a small snow on the ground, he had run down a deer. He thought that in one whole day he could tire or run down any four-footed animal except a wolf. He had heard the Wyandots say I could run well, and now he would see whether I could or not.

I told him I never had run with the Wyandots more than seven or eight miles at one time.

"That was nothing," he said. "We must either catch these horses or run all day."

We left camp early in the morning, stripped naked except for breechclouts and moccasins. At sunrise we saw the horses and started after them. About ten o'clock I lost sight of both Tontileaugo and the horses, and did not see them again until three o'clock in the afternoon. They passed where I was, and I fell in close after them. I endeavored to keep ahead of Tontileaugo, and after some time I could hear him behind me calling *"Chakoh, chakoanaugh"*—"Do your best." We pursued on, and after some time Tontileaugo passed me. About an hour before sundown we despaired of catching these horses and returned to camp, where we had left our clothes.

Tontileaugo then decided he would do as the Indians did with wild horses when out at war. This is to shoot them through the neck under the mane, and above the bone, which will cause them to fall and lie until the Indians can halter them, and then the horses recover again. This he attempted to do. But the mare was very wild and he could not get close enough to shoot her in the proper place. However, he shot her anyhow. The ball passed too low and killed her. As the stallion and colt stayed at this place, we caught them and took them to camp.

After about two weeks we moved on to Lake Erie and encamped again. While we were here, Tontileaugo went out to hunt. When he was gone, a Wyandot came to our camp. I gave him a well-roasted shoulder of venison which I had by the fire and he received it gladly.

When Tontileaugo came home, I told him about the Wyandot and the roasted venison.

"That was very well," he said. "And I suppose you also gave him sugar and bear's oil to eat with his venison?"

"I did not. The sugar and bear's oil were down in the canoe and I didn't want to go for them."

"You have behaved just like a Dutchman. Don't you know that when strangers come to our camp we ought always to give them the best that we have?"

I acknowledged that I was wrong. He said that he could excuse this as I was but young, but I must learn to behave like a warrior and do great things, and never be guilty of such selfish behavior.

It was not far to Sunyendeand, the Wyandot town to which the other members of our party had gone. In this town there were French traders who purchased our skins and fur, and we all got new clothes, paint, tobacco, etc.

After I had got my new clothes, and my head done off like a red-headed woodpecker, I, in company with a number of young Indians, went down to the cornfield to see the squaws at work. They asked me to take a hoe. I did, and hoed for some time. The squaws applauded me as a good hand at the business.

When I returned to the town, the old men, hearing of what I had done, chided me and said that I was adopted in the place of a great man, and must not hoe corn like a squaw. They never had occasion to reprove me for anything like this again, as I never was extremely fond of work.

The Indians, on their return from the winter hunt, bring in with them large quantities of bear's oil, sugar, dried venison, etc. At this time they have plenty, and do not spare eating or giving. Thus they use up their provisions as quickly as possible. They have no such thing as regular meals, breakfast, dinner or supper. If anyone would go to the same house several times in one day, he would be invited to eat of the best.

With them it is bad manners to refuse to eat when it is offered. If they will not eat, it is interpreted as a symptom of displeasure, or that the persons refusing to eat are angry with those who invited them.

Towards the last of this time, which was in June, 1756, they were all engaged in preparing to go to war against the frontiers of Virginia. When they were equipped, they went through their ceremonies and sang their war songs. Then they all marched off, from fifteen to sixty years of age. Some boys only twelve years old were equipped with their bows and arrows and went to war. None were left in town but squaws and children, except myself, one very old man, and another about fifty years of age, who was lame.

After the warriors left, we had neither meat, sugar, or bear's oil left. All we had to live on was corn pounded into coarse meal or small hominy. This they boiled in water till it appeared like well-thickened soup, and they ate it without salt or anything else.

The warriors did not return as soon as they expected and at length we were in a starving condition. There was but one gun in the town and very little ammunition. The old lame Wyandot concluded that he would go hunting in a canoe and take me with him, and try to kill deer in the water.

Traveling up the Sandusky a few miles, we turned up a creek and encamped. As we were to hunt in the night we had lights prepared, and also a piece of bark and some bushes set up in the canoe, in order to conceal ourselves from the deer. A little boy that was with us held the light, I worked the canoe, and the old man, who had his gun loaded with large shot, fired when we came near the deer. In this manner we killed three deer in part of one night. We ate heartily, and in the morning returned to relieve the hungry and distressed.

When we came to town the children were crying bitterly on account of pinching hunger. We delivered what we had taken, and though it was but little among so many it was divided according to the strictest rules of justice. We immediately set out for another hunt, but before we returned a part of the warriors had come in and brought with them a quantity of meat. These warriors had divided into different parties and all struck at different places in Augusta County. They brought with them a considerable number of scalps, prisoners, horses, and other plunder.

When the prisoners were to run the gauntlet, I went and told them how to act. One, John Savage, was a middle-aged man, or about forty years old. After telling him what he had to do, I fell into one of the ranks with the Indians, shouting and yelling like them. As they were not very severe on him, when he passed me I hit him with a piece of pumpkin. This pleased the Indians much but hurt my feelings.

About the time these warriors came in, the green corn was beginning to be of use. We had either green corn or venison, and sometimes both, which was comparatively high living. When we could have plenty of green corn or roasting ears the hunters became lazy and spent their time in singing and dancing. They appeared to be fulfilling the Scriptures in taking no thought of tomorrow and living in love, peace and friendship together, without disputes. In this respect they shame those who profess Christianity.

Sometime in October, another adopted brother, older than Tontileaugo, came to pay us a visit at Sunyendeand, and he asked me to take a hunt with him on the Cuyahoga. I consulted with Tontileaugo, and he told me that our old brother, Tecaughretanego, was a chief, and a better man than he was. As Tecaughretanego was going to a part of the country I had never been in, I agreed to go with him.

I went with Tecaughretanego to the mouth of a little lake, where he met with the company he intended going with, which was composed of Caughnawagas and Ottawas. Here I was introduced to a Caughnawaga sister, who was married to a Chippewa, and others I had never before seen. My sister's name was Mary, which they pronounced "Maully."

I asked Tecaughretanego how it came that she had an English name.

"It is the name the priest gave her when she was baptized," he said. "There are a great many of the Caughnawagas and Wyandots that are a kind of half Roman Catholics. As for myself, the Indians' old religion is better than this new way of worshipping God."

This company had four birch canoes and four tents. We were kindly received, and they gave us plenty of hominy and wild fowl, boiled and roasted. Until December, 1756, we kept moving on the rivers and hunting. Then we buried the canoes and marched to a large pond called Beaver Creek. Here we wintered in the tents of the Ottawas.

Near this pond, beaver was the principal game. Before the waters froze up, we caught a great many with wooden and steel traps. After that we hunted the beaver on the ice. In some places here the beavers built large houses to live in, and in other places they had lodgings in the banks.

Where the beavers lodged in the ground we had no chance of hunting them on the ice, but where they had houses we went with clubs and handspikes and broke all the hollow ice, to prevent them from getting their heads above the water under it. Then we broke a hole in the house and they made their escape into the water. They

cannot live long under water and so were obliged to go to some of
those broken places to breathe, and the Indians put in their hands,
caught them by the hind leg, hauled them on the ice and tomahawked
them. Sometimes they shot them in the head, when they raised it
above the water.

I asked the Indians if they were not afraid to catch the beavers
with their hands.

"No," they said. "The beaver is not much of a biting creature. Yet
if we catch it by the forefoot it will bite."

In conversation with Tecaughretanego, I happened to be talking of
the beavers' catching fish.

"Why do you think that the beaver catches fish?" he asked.

I told him that I had read in a book that the beaver makes dams
for the convenience of fishing.

He laughed. "The man that wrote that book knew nothing about
the beaver. The beaver never eats flesh of any kind, but lives on the
bark of trees, roots, and other vegetables."

In order to make certain of this, when we killed a beaver I carefully examined the intestines, but found no sign of fish. I afterwards
made an experiment on a pet beaver which we had, and found that
it would eat neither fish nor flesh. Therefore I acknowledged that the
book I had read was wrong.

One day I went out beaver hunting with Tecaughretanego and some
others but we did not succeed. On our return we saw where several
raccoons had passed while the snow was soft. We all made a halt
and looked at the raccoon tracks. At a distance, the Indians saw a
tree with a hole, and told me to go and see if the raccoons had gone
into it. If they had, I was to halloo, and the Indians would come and
take them out. When I went to that tree I found the raccoons had
gone past. Their trail led to another tree. I proceeded to examine that
and found they had gone up it. I began to halloo. There was no
answer.

Now it began to snow and blow most violently. I returned and
proceeded after my companions. For some time I could see their
tracks. But the old snow was only about three inches deep, with a
crust upon it, and the present driving snow soon filled up the tracks.

As I had only a bow, arrows, and tomahawk with me, and no way
to strike fire, I was in a dismal situation. The air was dark with snow,

and I had little more prospect of steering my course than I would in the night.

At length I came to a hollow tree with a hole at one side that I could go in at. I went in and found that it was a dry place. The hollow was about three feet in diameter and high enough for me to stand in. There was also a considerable quantity of soft, dry rotten wood around this hollow. I concluded that I would lodge here, and would go to work and stop up the doorway of my "house."

I stripped off my blanket (which was all the clothes I had, excepting a breechclout, leggings and moccasins). Then I went out and with my tomahawk fell to chopping at the top of a fallen tree that lay nearby. Carrying the wood back, I set it on end against the opening, until I had it three or four feet thick all around, excepting a hole I had left to creep in at. I had a block prepared that I could haul after me, to stop this hole. I also put in a number of small sticks, that I might more effectually stop it on the inside.

When I went in, I took my tomahawk, and cut down all the dry, rotten wood I could get, and beat it small. With it I made a bed like a goose nest or hog bed, and with the small sticks stopped every hole until my house was almost dark. I stripped off my moccasins and danced in the center of my bed for about half an hour, in order to warm myself.

The snow, meanwhile, had stopped all the holes, so that my house was as dark as a dungeon, though I knew it could not yet be dark out of doors. I coiled myself up in my blanket, lay down in my little round bed, and had a tolerable night's lodging.

When I awoke, all was dark—not the least glimmering of light was to be seen. Immediately I recollected that I was not to expect light in this new habitation; there was neither door nor window in it. As I could hear the storm raging, and did not suffer much cold, I concluded I would stay in my nest until I was certain it was day.

When I had reason to believe it surely was day, I arose and put on my moccasins, which I had laid under my head. I then endeavored to find the door. I had to do this by the sense of feeling, which took me some time. At length I found the block. It was heavy and a large quantity of snow had fallen on it, so at the first attempt I could not move it. I felt terrified. Among all the hardships I had sustained, I had never known before what it was to be thus deprived of light.

I went straightway to bed again, wrapped my blanket round me, and lay and mused awhile, and then prayed to Almighty God to direct and protect me as He had done heretofore.

I once again attempted to move away the block. My effort proved successful; it moved about nine inches. A considerable quantity of snow fell in from above, and I immediately received light. I found a very great snow had fallen, above what I had ever seen in one night. I was so happy at obtaining the light that all my other difficulties seemed to vanish. I belted my blanket about me, got my tomahawk, bow and arrows, and went out of my den.

I was now in tolerable high spirits, though the snow had fallen above three feet deep. The only guide I had by which to steer my course to camp was the trees: the moss generally grows on the northwest side of them if they are straight. I proceeded on, wading through the snow. About twelve o'clock I came upon the creek that our camp was on.

When I came in sight of the camp there was great joy. All the Indians came round me. No questions were asked, and I was taken into a tent, where they gave me plenty of fat beaver meat, and then asked me to smoke.

When I had finished, Tecaughretanego desired me to walk out to a fire they had made. I went out and they all collected round me, both men, women, and boys. Tecaughretanego asked me to give them a particular account of what had happened from the time they left me. I told them the whole of the story and they never interrupted me; but when I made a stop, the intervals were filled with loud acclamations of joy.

When all this was done, Tecaughretanego made a speech to me in the following manner.

"Brother, you see we have prepared snowshoes and were almost ready to go after you when you appeared. As you had not been accustomed to hardships in your country to the east, we never expected to see you alive. Now we are glad to see you. We do not blame you for what has happened. We blame ourselves because we did not think of this driving snow filling up the tracks until we came to camp.

"Brother, your conduct hath pleased us much! You have given us evidence of your fortitude, skill and resolution. We hope you will go on to do great actions, as it is only great actions that can make a great man."

I told Tecaughretanego that I thanked them for their care of me and the kindness I always received. I told him that I always wished to do great actions, and hoped I never would do anything to dishonor those with whom I was connected.

About two weeks after this there came a warm rain and took away the snow. Then we engaged in making wooden traps to catch beavers, nearly in the same manner as the raccoon traps already described.

One day I was looking after my traps when suddenly I became aware that night had fallen and a maze of beaver ponds blocked my way to camp. I could find no suitable lodging place, I had neglected to take flint and steel with me, and the weather was very cold. The only way to keep myself from freezing was to exercise. I danced and hallooed the whole night with all my might.

The next day I made my way back to camp. Though I had suffered much more than the other night I stayed out, the Indians had not been so much concerned, as they thought I had the means to make fire. When they knew how it was, they did not blame me. They said that old hunters frequently were trapped in this place. After applauding me for my fortitude, they said they now had plenty of beaver skins and would purchase me a new gun at Detroit, as we were to go there the next spring. Then, if I should chance to be lost in dark weather, I could make fire, kill provision, and return to camp when the sun shone.

Two years before, by going astray near the waters of the Muskingum, I had lost repute and been reduced to the bow and arrow. Now, by staying out two nights here, I had regained my credit.

Sometime in February we scaffolded up our furs and skins and moved about ten miles in quest of a suitable place to make sugar, and encamped on the headwaters of Big Beaver Creek. We had some difficulty in moving, as we had a blind Caughnawaga boy about fifteen years of age to lead. This country is very brushy and we frequently had to carry him. We also had my Chippewa brother-in-law's father with us, who was thought by the Indians to be a great conjuror. His name was Manetohcoa. This old man was so decrepit that we had to carry him upon a bier—and pack all our baggage on our backs.

One night, about the time we were done making sugar, a squaw raised an alarm. She said she had seen two men with guns in their hands upon the bank on the other side of the creek, spying on our tents.

The Indians supposed these were Mohawks in the service of the British. At once the squaws were ordered to slip quietly out some distance into the bushes. All of us who had guns or bows were to squat in the bushes near the tents. If the enemy rushed up, we were to give them the first fire, and let the squaws have an opportunity of escaping.

I got down beside Tecaughretanego.

"Do not be afraid," he whispered. "I will speak to the Mohawks. They speak the same tongue that we do and they will not hurt the Caughnawagas or you. They will kill all the Chippewas and Ottawas they can and take us along with them."

This news pleased me well, and I heartily wished for the approach of the Mohawks.

Before we withdrew from the tents the Indians carried old Manetohcoa to the fire and gave him his conjuring tools—dyed feathers, the shoulder blade of a wildcat, tobacco, etc. While we were in the bushes, Manetohcoa was in a tent at the fire, conjuring away to the utmost of his ability. At length he called aloud for us all to come in. We quickly obeyed.

The old man told us he had gone through the whole of his ceremony, expecting to see a number of Mohawks on the flat bone when it was warmed at the fire. Instead, the pictures of two wolves only had appeared.

"You must not be angry with the squaw for giving a false alarm," he said. "She went out and happened to see the wolves but she got afraid and imagined they were Indians with guns in their hands. You can all go to sleep, for there is no danger."

And that was just what we did.

The next morning we went to the place and found wolf tracks; there was no sign of moccasin tracks. If there is any such thing as a wizard, I think Manetohcoa was as likely to be one as any man. The Indians believed what he told them as if it had come from an oracle. Otherwise they would not, after an alarm like this, have all gone to sleep in such an unconcerned manner.

This appeared to me the most like witchcraft of anything I beheld while I was with the Indians. I scrutinized their proceedings in business of this kind, yet I generally found that their pretended witchcraft was either trickery or mistaken notions whereby they deceived themselves. Before a battle they spy the enemy's motions carefully, and when they find that they have the greatest prospect of success, the old men pretend to conjure or tell what the outcome will be. They do this in a figurative manner, which will bear something of a different interpretation, and it generally comes to pass nearly as they foretold. Therefore the young warriors generally believed these old conjurors, which had a tendency to excite them to push on with vigor.

Sometime in March, 1757, we began to move back to the forks of the Cuyahoga. On our way we camped at a large pond to rest ourselves and to kill ducks and geese.

While we remained here I went with a young Caughnawaga about fifteen or seventeen years of age, Chinnohete by name, to gather cranberries. As he was at some distance from me, three Chippewa squaws crept up undiscovered and ran toward him. But he nimbly escaped and came to me apparently terrified.

"What are you afraid of?" I asked him.

"Did you not see those squaws?"

"I did—and they appeared to be in a very good humor. Why are you afraid of them?"

"The Chippewa squaws are very bad women, and have a very ugly custom among them. When two or three of them catch a young lad that is betwixt a man and a boy out by himself, if they can overpower him they will strip him to see whether he is coming on to be a man or not. That was what they intended when they crawled up and ran so violently at me. I am very glad that I escaped!"

I agreed with Chinnohete in condemning this as a bad custom and an exceedingly immodest action for young women to be guilty of.

At the forks of the Cuyahoga we found that the skins we had scaffolded were all safe. Though this was a public place and Indians frequently had passed, there was nothing stolen. It is seldom that Indians do steal anything from one another. They say they never did until the white people came among them and taught some of them to lie, cheat, steal, and swear.

I remember that Tecaughretanego, when something displeased him, said, "God damn it!"

"Do you know what you have said?" I asked him once.

"I do"—and he mentioned one of their degrading expressions which he supposed to have the same meaning.

"That doesn't bear the least resemblance to it—what you said was calling upon the Great Spirit to punish the object you were displeased with."

He stood for some time amazed. "If this be the meaning of these words, what sort of people are the whites? When the traders were among us these words seemed to be intermixed with all their discourse. You must be mistaken. If you are not, the traders applied these words not only wickedly, but oftentimes very foolishly.

"I remember once a trader accidentally broke his gun lock and called out aloud, 'God damn it!' Surely the gun lock was not an object worthy of punishment by Owaneeyo, the Great Spirit."

We took up our birch-bark canoes which we had buried here, and found that they were not damaged by the winter. Then we all embarked, and arrived safely at the Wyandot town, nearly opposite Fort Detroit,[2] on the north side of the river. Here we found a number of French traders, every one very willing to deal with us for our beaver. We bought ourselves fine clothes, ammunition, paint, tobacco, etc., and, according to promise, the Indians purchased me a new gun.

We had parted with only about one-third of our beaver. At length a trader came to town with French brandy. We purchased a keg of it, and held a council about who was to get drunk and who was to keep sober. I was invited to get drunk but I refused. Then they told me that I must be one of those who were to take care of the drunken people. I did not like this, but of two evils I chose that which I thought was the least.

I fell in with those who were to conceal the arms and keep all dangerous weapons out of the way of the drinking club and try, if possible, to keep them from killing each other. This was a very hard task. Several times we hazarded our own lives and got ourselves hurt in preventing them from slaying each other. Before they had finished the keg, nearly one-third of the town was introduced to this drinking club. They could not pay their part, as they had already disposed of all their skins, but that made no difference—all were welcome to drink.

After the Indians were done with this keg, they bought from the traders a kettle full of brandy which they divided out with a large wooden spoon. Then they bought another, and another, and never quit while they had a single beaver skin. When the trader had got all our beaver, he moved off to the Ottawa town, about a mile above the Wyandot town.

When the brandy was gone and the drinking club sober, they appeared much dejected. Some of them were crippled, others badly wounded, a number of their fine new shirts torn, and several blankets were burned. A number of squaws were also in this club, and neglected their corn planting.

We could now hear the effects of the brandy in the Ottawa town. They were singing and yelling in the most hideous manner, both night and day. Their frolic ended worse than ours. Five Ottawas were killed and a great many wounded.

About the first of June, 1757, in the Wyandot, Potawatomi and Ottawa towns the warriors were preparing to go to war. A great many Chippewas came down from the upper lakes to join them. After singing their war songs and going through their usual ceremonies, they marched off against the frontiers of Virginia, Maryland and Pennsylvania, singing the traveling song and firing their guns slowly.

By the middle of June, the Indians were almost all gone to war, yet Tecaughretanego remained in town with me. In former years, when they were at war with the southern nations, he had been a great warrior and an eminent counselor. But he had all along been against this war, and strenuously opposed it in council. He said, "If the English and French have a quarrel, let them fight their own battles themselves. It is not our business to meddle in their affairs."

Before the warriors returned we were very scarce of provision. Though we did not commonly steal from one another, during this time we stole anything that we could eat from the French living about Detroit. We felt it was just for us to do so because they supported their soldiers, and our squaws, old men and children were suffering on account of the war, as our hunters were all gone.

Sometime in August the warriors returned and brought in with them a great many scalps, prisoners, horses and plunder. The common report among the young warriors was that they would entirely subdue the *Tulhasaga* or "Morning Light inhabitants"—that is, the English.

About the first of November a number of families, including my own, prepared to go on their winter hunt. Leaving the town, we coasted round the lake and hunted together. Then we went our separate ways. In my party were Tecaughretanego, Tontileaugo, their families, and two families of the Wyandots.

Cold weather was now approaching. We began to feel the effects of having extravagantly and foolishly spent the large quantity of beaver we had taken in our last winter's hunt. We were all nearly in the same circumstances—scarcely one had a shirt to his back. Each of us had an old blanket which we belted round us in the day and slept in at night, with a deer or bear skin under us for our bed.

When we came to the falls of Sandusky, we buried our birch-bark canoes as usual, at a large burying place for that purpose a little below the falls. At this place the river falls about eight feet over a rock. With much difficulty we pushed up our other canoes. Some of us went up the river and the rest traveled by land with the horses, until we came to the great prairies that lie between the Sandusky and the Scioto.

At this place we met with some Ottawa hunters and agreed with them to take what they call a ring hunt. We waited until we expected rain was near falling and then we kindled a large circle of fire on the prairie. At this time a great number of deer lay concealed in the grass in the day and moved about in the night. As the fire burned in towards the center of the circle, the deer fled before it. The Indians were scattered at some distance before the fire and shot them down at every opportunity, which was very frequent as the circle became small. When we came to divide the deer there were above ten to each hunter, all killed in a few hours.

The rain did not come that night to put out the outside circle of the fire, and as the wind arose the flames spread over the whole prairie. This put an end to our ring hunting this season, and upon the whole we received more harm than benefit by it. We then moved from the north end of the glades and encamped.

About the time the bucks quit running, Tontileaugo, his wife and children, Tecaughretanego, his son Nunganey and myself left the Wyandots. Crossing the Scioto River, we proceeded to a large creek, the Olentangy. Here we made our winter hut, and had considerable success in hunting.

After some time one of Tontileaugo's stepsons offended him, and he gave the boy a moderate whipping. This much displeased his Wyandot wife. She acknowledged that the boy was guilty of a fault, but thought that he ought to have been ducked, which is their usual chastisement. She said she could not bear to have her son whipped like a servant or slave. She was so displeased that when Tontileaugo went out to hunt she got her two horses and all her effects (in this country the husband and wife have separate property) and moved back to the Wyandot camps that we had left.

When Tontileaugo returned, he was much disturbed to hear of his wife's departure. He said he would never go after her on his own account, but he was afraid she would get lost, and his children, whom she had taken with her, might suffer. Tontileaugo went after his wife and they patched up the quarrel. He never returned. Tecaughretanego, his son (a boy about ten years of age), and myself were left alone all winter.

Tecaughretanego had been a first-rate warrior, statesman and hunter. Though he was now nearly sixty years of age, he was yet equal to the common run of hunters, but subject to rheumatism. Now he became lame and could scarcely walk out of our hut for two months.

I had considerable success in hunting and trapping. Though Tecaughretanego endured much pain and misery, he bore it with wonderful patience. He would often endeavor to entertain me with cheerful conversation. Sometimes he would applaud me for my skill and activity—and at other times he would take great care in giving me instructions concerning the hunting and trapping business. He would also tell me that if I failed of success we would suffer very much, as we were about forty miles from anyone we knew of.

Tontileaugo left us a little before Christmas, and from then until sometime in February we always had plenty of bear meat, venison, etc. I killed much more than we could use, but, having no horses to carry in all I killed, I left part of it in the woods.

In February there came a snow, with a crust. When I walked on it, it made a great noise which frightened away the deer. As bear and beaver were scarce here, we got entirely out of provision.

I hunted two days without eating anything. Having had very short allowance for some days before, I felt faint and weary as I returned late in the evening.

When I came into our hut, Tecaughretanego asked: "What success?"

"Not any," I told him.

He commanded Nunganey, his little son, to bring me something to eat. He brought me a kettle with some bones and broth. I thought the victuals had a most agreeable relish. It was only fox and wildcat bones, which had lain about the camp and been picked over by the ravens and turkey buzzards. These Nunganey had collected and boiled, until the sinews that remained on the bones would strip off. I speedily finished my allowance, such as it was.

"How do you feel now?" Tecaughretanego asked.

"Much refreshed."

He handed me his pipe and pouch. "Take a smoke."

I did so.

"Brother," Tecaughretanego said, "as you have lived with the white people, who have stocks of cattle and barns filled with grain, you have not had the same advantage as we Indians of knowing that the Great Being above feeds his people in due season. We are often out of provisions and yet are wonderfully supplied—so frequently that it is evidently the hand of the great Owaneeyo that doth this.

"I know you are now afraid we will all perish with hunger, but you have no reason to fear this. Owaneeyo sometimes suffers us to be in want in order to teach us our dependence upon him, and to let us know that we are to love and serve him.

"Brother, be assured that you will be supplied with food just in the right time, but you must go to sleep and rise early in the morning and go hunting. Be strong and exert yourself like a man, and the Great Spirit will direct your way."

The next morning I went out. I saw deer frequently. But the crust on the snow made a great noise and they were always running before I spied them so I could not get a shot. I became intolerably hungry and I decided to run off to Pennsylvania, my native country.

As the snow was on the ground, and Indian hunters almost the whole of the way before me, I had but a poor prospect of making my escape. My case appeared desperate. If I stayed here I thought I would perish with hunger. If I met with Indians they could but kill me.

I went on as fast as I could walk. When I got about ten or twelve miles from our hut, I came upon fresh buffalo tracks. Following these, in a short time I came in sight of the animals as they were passing through a small glade. I ran with all my might, and got ahead of them. Then I lay in ambush and killed a very large cow. I immediately kindled a fire and began to roast meat, but could not wait till it was done—I ate it almost raw.

When my hunger was abated I began to be tenderly concerned for my old Indian brother and the little boy. I made haste and packed up what meat I could carry, secured what I left from the wolves, and returned homewards.

I had scarcely thought of the old man's speech while I was almost distracted with hunger. Now, returning, I reflected on my hardheartedness and ingratitude in attempting to run off and leave the venerable old man and little boy to perish with hunger. The old man's speech had proved remarkably true.

As it was moonlight, I got home to our hut without difficulty. The old man was in his usual good humor. He thanked me for my exertion.

"Sit down, you must certainly be fatigued," he said. "Nunganey, make haste and cook."

"I will cook for you," I said. "Let the boy lay some meat on the coals for himself"—which he did, but ate it almost raw, as I had.

I immediately hung on the kettle with some water, cut the beef in thin slices, and put them in. When it had boiled awhile, I started to take it off the fire.

"Let it be done enough," the old man said, in as patient and unconcerned a manner as if he had not missed a single meal. "Nunganey, eat no more beef now, lest you hurt yourself. Sit down, and after some time you may sup some broth."

Reluctantly Nunganey obeyed.

When we were all refreshed, Tecaughretanego spoke again. He reminded me that Owaneeyo is the great giver—he supplies our wants in time of need and we must receive his gifts with thankfulness.

Such speeches from an Indian may be thought altogether incredible by those who are unacquainted with them. But when we reflect on the Indian war, we may readily conclude that they are not an ignorant or stupid sort of people, or they would not have been such fatal enemies. Besides, Tecaughretanego was no common person, but was among the Indians as Socrates in the ancient heathen world—equal to him, if not in wisdom and learning, yet perhaps in patience and fortitude.

We remained here until April, 1758. At this time Tecaughretanego had recovered enough to walk about. We made a bark canoe, embarked, and went down the Olentangy some distance. But the water was low and we were in danger of splitting our canoe upon the rocks. Tecaughretanego decided we should go ashore and pray for rain.

After we encamped, Tecaughretanego made himself a sweat house. He stuck a number of hoops in the ground, each forming a semicircle, and covered this all around with blankets and skins. He then prepared hot stones, which he rolled into the hut. Then he went into it with a little kettle of water in his hand. This water was mixed with a variety of herbs which he had cured and carried in his pack—they afforded a fragrant perfume.

When he was in, he told me to pull down the blankets behind him. Then he began to pour water upon the hot stones and to sing aloud. He stayed in this very hot place about fifteen minutes. All this he did in order to purify himself before he would address the Supreme Being.

Coming out of his sweat house, Tecaughretanego began to burn tobacco and to pray. He began each petition with *oh, ho, ho, ho,* which signifies an ardent wish. I observed that all his petitions were only for immediate blessings. He began his address by thanksgiving.

"O Great Being! I thank thee that I have obtained the use of my legs again—that I am now able to walk about and kill turkeys, etc., without feeling exquisite pain and misery. I know that thou art a hearer and a helper, and therefore I will call upon thee.

*"Oh, ho, ho, ho!* Grant that my knees and ankles may be well, that I may be able not only to walk but to run, and to jump logs, as I did last fall.

*"Oh, ho, ho, ho!* Grant that on this voyage we may frequently kill bears as they may be crossing the Scioto and Sandusky.

*"Oh, ho, ho, ho!* Grant that we may kill plenty of turkeys along the banks, to stew with our fat bear meat.

*"Oh, ho, ho, ho!* Grant that rain may come to raise the Olentangy about two or three feet, that we may cross in safety down to the Scioto, without danger of our canoe being wrecked on the rocks. And now, O Great Being! thou knowest how matters stand—thou knowest that I am a great lover of tobacco. Though I know not when I may get any more, I now make a present of the last I have unto thee, as a free burnt offering. Therefore I expect thou wilt hear and grant these requests, and I, thy servant, will return thee thanks and love thee for thy gifts."

During the whole of this scene I sat by Tecaughretanego. As he went through it with the greatest solemnity, I was seriously affected by his prayers. I remained composed until he came to the burning of the tobacco. I knew that he was a great lover of it, and when I saw him cast the last of it into the fire, it excited in me a kind of merriment and I smiled unconsciously. Tecaughretanego observed me. He was displeased.

"Brother," he said, "I have somewhat to say to you, and I hope you will not be offended when I tell you of your faults. You know that when you were reading your books in town, I would not let the boys or anyone disturb you. But now, when I was praying, I saw you laughing. I do not think that you look upon praying as a foolish thing—I believe you pray yourself. Perhaps you think my manner of prayer foolish. If so, you ought to instruct me in a friendly manner, and not make sport of sacred things."

I acknowledged my error, and he handed me his pipe to smoke in token of friendship and reconciliation, though at that time he had nothing to smoke but red willow bark. He said he believed that Owaneeyo would hear and help everyone that sincerely prayed to him.

A few days after Tecaughretanego had gone through his ceremonies and finished his prayers, the rain came and raised the creek a sufficient height. We passed in safety down to the Scioto, and then on to the carrying place.[3] From here we went down the Sandusky, and in our passage we killed four bears and a number of turkeys.

Tecaughretanego appeared fully persuaded that all this came in answer to his prayers—and who can say with any degree of certainty that it was not so?

Shortly after this we arrived at Detroit, where we remained that summer. In May we heard that General Forbes, with seven thousand men, was preparing to carry on a campaign against Fort Duquesne. Upon receiving this news, the French commander at Detroit sent off a number of runners to urge the different tribes of Indian warriors to hasten to the defense of Fort Duquesne.

Sometime in July, 1758, the Ottawas, Chippewas, Potawatomis and Wyandots rendezvoused at Detroit and marched off to Fort Duquesne to prepare for the encounter with General Forbes. The common report was that they would serve him as they did General Braddock and obtain much plunder. They met his army near Fort Ligonier and attacked them, but were routed. They said that Forbes's men were beginning to learn the art of war, and that there were a great number of American riflemen along with the redcoats, who scattered out, took to the trees, and were good marksmen; therefore the Indians were obliged to retreat.

When they returned from the battle to Fort Duquesne, the Indians decided to go to their hunting. The French tried to persuade them to stay and fight another battle. The Indians said if it was only the redcoats they had to do with, they could soon subdue them, but they could not withstand *Ashalecoa,* or the Great Knives, which was the name they gave the Virginians. They then returned home to their hunting, and the French evacuated the fort. General Forbes took possession of it without further opposition late in the year 1758 and began to build Fort Pitt.

That year we hunted up the Sandusky and down the Scioto, taking nearly the same route that we had the last hunting season. We had considerable success, and returned to Detroit sometime in April, 1759.

Shortly after this, Tecaughretanego, his son Nunganey and myself went by canoe to Caughnawaga, a very ancient Indian town about nine miles above Montreal. About the first of July I heard of a French ship at Montreal that had English prisoners on board, in order to carry them overseas and exchange them. Stealing away from the Indians, I got on board. But General Wolfe had blocked the St. Lawrence, and we were all sent to prison at Montreal. Here I remained four months. Sometime in November we were all sent to Crown Point [4] and exchanged.

Early in 1760 I came home to Conococheague, and found that my people could never ascertain whether I was killed or taken, until my return. They received me with great joy, but were surprised to see me so much like an Indian both in my gait and gesture.

Upon enquiry, I found that my sweetheart had been married a few days before I arrived. I must leave my feelings on this occasion for those of my readers to judge who have felt the pangs of disappointed love. It is impossible now for me to describe the emotion of soul I felt at that time.

# Death in the Snow

## THOMAS BROWN

**O**N *September 19, 1759, a scouting patrol of seven British light infantrymen prowled around the Indian town of Caughnawaga, near the enemy citadel of Montreal. Their guide was a young Massachusetts soldier named Thomas Brown. After learning all they could, the party headed back home across Lake Champlain in a small sailboat. They had just swung around a point of land when they found themselves under the guns of a French brig. The enemy gave chase and quickly overtook them. On Isle aux Noix, the next morning, the prisoners shivered in the cold as they were stripped by the Indians and dressed in their fashion.*

*For Tom Brown, the entire experience was disastrously familiar. Less than three years before he had been captured by Indians not far from that very spot. He had seen with his own eyes—and felt with his own flesh—how terrible the fate of an Indian captive could be.*

*Fortunately for Brown, this time his captivity was short and less painful. Within a few months he was released and returned to his regiment.*

*Early in 1760, Brown got his discharge and went home. His story,* A Plain Narrative of the Uncommon Sufferings and Remarkable Deliverance of Thomas Brown, *was written soon afterward and published in Boston. Demand was heavy for this brief and bloody tale. The French strongholds of Crown Point, Ticonderoga, and Quebec had recently fallen, and Montreal was about to fall—the long war with the French and Indians had reached its final climax, and people in the British colonies were eager to read the adventures of this young combat veteran. Three editions of his book were sold out that year.*

*Tom Brown's story attracted special interest because he had been a Ranger, fighting under the command of Major Robert Rogers, the daring soldier-adventurer whose name looms so large in the history of the period. Rogers was a controversial figure most of his life, and Brown contributed his drop of acid to the controversy—he quietly accused Major Rogers of deserting his wounded on the field of battle. Although Brown did not know it, Rogers had actually carried off most of his wounded. Only a few were left behind—they were either overlooked in the dark or else they may have appeared more dead than alive.*

*Of these, poor Tom Brown had been one.*

I was born in Charlestown, near Boston, in New England, in 1740, and was apprenticed by my father to Mr. Mark White of Acton. In May, 1756, I enlisted in Major Rogers' Corps of Rangers, in the company commanded by Captain Spikeman. We marched to Albany, where we arrived the first of August, and from there to Fort Edward. I was out on several scouting patrols, on one of which I killed an Indian.

On the eighteenth of January, 1757, we marched on a patrol from Fort William Henry. Major Rogers himself headed us. All of us were volunteers. Coming to the road leading from Ticonderoga to Crown Point, we saw about fifty sleighs on Lake Champlain, which was frozen over. The major thought it proper to attack them and ordered us all—about sixty in number—to lie in ambush. When they were close enough we were ordered to pursue them.

I happened to be near the major when he took the first prisoner, a Frenchman. I singled one out, too, and followed him; some fled one way and some another, but I soon caught up with my man and took him prisoner. We captured seven in all—the rest escaped, some to Crown Point and some to Ticonderoga, where they had come from. When we had brought the prisoners to land, the major questioned them. They informed him that there were thirty-five Indians and five hundred regulars at Ticonderoga.

It was a rainy day, so we made a fire and dried our guns. The major thought it best to return to Fort William Henry by the same path we had come, as the snow was very deep. We marched in Indian file and kept the prisoners in the rear, in case we should be attacked.

We went on in this order about a mile and a half. As we were going up a hill, and the center of our line was at the top, a party of about four hundred French and thirty or forty Indians opened fire on us before we had even seen them. The major ordered us to advance.

At the first volley from the enemy I received a wound through the body. When I was able, I went to the rear, to the prisoner I had taken on the lake. I knocked him on the head and killed him—we did not want him to give information to the enemy.

As I was going to take shelter behind a large rock, an Indian started up from the other side of it. I threw myself backward into the snow. It was very deep and I sank so low that I broke my snowshoes. In a moment I had pulled 'em off, but I was obliged to let my shoes go with them. One Indian threw his tomahawk at me, and another was just about to seize me, but I was lucky enough to escape and get to the center of our men.

Hiding behind a large pine, I loaded and fired at every opportunity. After I had discharged my gun six or seven times, a ball came and cut it off just at the lock. About half an hour later, I received a shot in my knee. I crawled to the rear again and, as I was turning about, received a shot in my shoulder.

The engagement lasted, as near as I could guess, five and one-half hours and, as I learned afterward, we killed more of the enemy than there were of us. By this time it had grown dark and the firing ceased on both sides. Taking advantage of the night, the major escaped with the well men without telling the wounded his plans, so they could not inform the enemy, who might pursue him before he was out of their reach.

Captain Spikeman, a man named Baker, and myself, all very badly wounded, had made a small fire. After sitting about it for half an hour, we looked round and could not see any of our men. Captain Spikeman called to Major Rogers but received no answer, except from the enemy at some distance. We concluded our people had fled. All our hope of escape vanished now. We were so badly wounded that we could not travel; I could just barely walk, the others could scarcely move. We decided to surrender to the French.

Just as we came to this decision I saw an Indian coming towards us over a small stream that separated us from the enemy. I crawled away from the fire so that I could not be seen, though I could see what happened there.

The Indian came to Captain Spikeman, who was not able to resist, and stripped him and scalped him alive. Baker, who was lying by the captain, pulled out his knife to stab himself. But the Indian prevented him and carried him away.

Seeing this frightful tragedy, I made up my mind to crawl into the woods if possible and die there of my wounds. But I was not far from Captain Spikeman and he saw me.

"For God's sake," he begged me, "give me a tomahawk so I can put an end to my life!"

I refused him, and exhorted him as well as I could to pray, as he could not live many minutes in that deplorable condition on the frozen ground, covered with snow. He asked me to let his wife know —if I lived to get home—the dreadful death he died.

I traveled on as well as I could. As I was creeping along, I found one of our people dead. I pulled off his stockings—he had no shoes— and put them on my own legs.

By this time the enemy had made a fire and had a large number of sentries out on the Rangers' path. I was obliged to creep completely round them before I could get into the path again. Just before I came to it I saw a Frenchman behind a tree. He was within ten yards of me, but the fire was shining right on him and prevented him from seeing me. About every quarter of an hour they cried out in French, "All is well!" While the man that was so near me was calling out, I took the opportunity to creep away, so that he did not hear me and I got back into our path.

I had no shoes, and the snow and cold put my feet into such pain that I soon could go on no longer. I sat down by a brook and wrapped my feet in my blanket. But my body became very cold from sitting still. I got up and crawled along in this miserable condition the rest of the night.

The next day, about eleven o'clock, I heard the shouts of Indians behind me and I supposed they had seen me. Within a few minutes four of them came running towards me. I threw off my blanket, and fear and dread quickened my pace for a while. But I had lost so much blood from my wounds that my strength soon gave out.

When the Indians were within ten or fifteen yards they cocked their guns and called me to stop. I refused, hoping they would fire and kill me on the spot; I preferred this to the terrible death Captain Spikeman had died.

The savages soon came up with me, but instead of scalping me they took me by the neck and kissed me. On searching my pockets they found some money. They were so fond of it that they almost killed me in trying to see who could get the most. Then they took some dry leaves and put them into my wounds, and turned about and ordered me to follow them.

When we came near the main body of the enemy the Indians gave a live-shout, as they call it when they bring in a prisoner alive (different from the shout they give when they bring in scalps, which they call a dead-shout). The other Indians ran to meet us. One of them struck me across the side with a cutlass; he cut through my clothes, but did not touch my flesh. Others ran against me with their heads.

I asked if there was an interpreter among them.

"I am one," a Frenchman cried.

"Is this the way you treat your prisoners—let them be cut and beaten to pieces by the Indians?" I asked.

The interpreter told me to come to him, but the Indians would not let me—one held me by one arm and another by the other. A difference arose among the four Indians that had captured me and they began to fight. Seeing this, their commanding officer came and took me away. He brought me to the interpreter.

This fellow drew his sword and pointed it to my breast. "Tell the truth," he ordered, "or I will run you through. How many men are there in your scouting party?"

"Fifty," I told him.

"Where did they go?"

"You have so many men that I suppose you can tell better than I," I replied.

"You tell me wrong," he said. "I know of more than one hundred of your men that were slain."

I told him we had lost but nineteen in all.

"There were that many officers," he said, and he led me to a body. It was Lieutenant Kennedy. I saw that he had been severely tomahawked by the Indians. The interpreter asked me if he was an officer and I told him he was a lieutenant. Then he took me to another, who I told him was an ensign. From them he led me to Captain Spikeman, who was lying in the place I had left him. The Indians had cut off his head and fixed it on a pole.

I begged for a pair of shoes and something to eat. The interpreter told me I should have what I needed when I got to Ticonderoga, which was only a mile and a quarter off, and then delivered me to the four Indians who had captured me. The Indians gave me a piece of bread and put a pair of shoes on my feet.

About this time Robert Baker, mentioned above, was brought where I was. Though we were in such a distressed condition we were extremely glad to see each other. He told me of five other Rangers that had been taken prisoner.

Now we were ordered to march on toward Ticonderoga. Baker replied that he could not walk. An Indian pushed him forward, but he could not go, and he sat down and cried. At this, an Indian took him by the hair and was going to kill him with his tomahawk. I was moved with pity for him. Weak as I was, I took his arms over my shoulders and was able to get him to the fort.

Upon our arrival we were immediately sent to the guardhouse. About half an hour later we were brought before the commanding officer. He questioned us separately through his interpreter and then sent us back to the guardhouse. The interpreter came and told us that we were to be hanged the next day because we had killed the seven prisoners we had taken on the lake. Afterwards he was so kind as to tell us this was done only to terrify us.

About an hour later a doctor and his mate came and dressed our wounds, and the commanding officer sent us a quart of claret. We lay on the floor without blankets all night.

The next day I was put into the hospital. I remained here till the nineteenth of February, when the Indians insisted on having me to bring to their home and broke into the hospital. But the sentinel called the guard and turned them out. After this the commanding officer persuaded them to let me stay till the first of March. By that time I was able to walk about the fort and I was quartered with the interpreter.

One day, while I was in the interpreter's lodging, ten or twelve Indians came in with scalps they had taken, to have a war dance.

They set me on the floor, put seven of the scalps on my head, and danced round me. When the dance was over they lifted me up in triumph. After they put me down, I went and stood by the door. Suddenly two of the Indians began to dance a live-dance, and one of them threw a tomahawk at me. Fortunately I had been watching him and I dodged the weapon.

I lived with the interpreter till the first of March, when General Rigaud came to the fort with about sixteen hundred men in order to make an attack on Fort William Henry. Their plan was to scale the walls and I saw them making scaling ladders for this purpose.

The day before they marched the general sent for me.

"Young man," he said, "you are a likely fellow. It's a pity you should live with such an ignorant people as the English. You had better live with me."

I told him I was willing to live with him.

"You shall," he answered, "and go with me wherever I go."

"Perhaps you will have me go to war with you."

"That is just the thing I had in mind. I want you to guide me to Fort William Henry and show me where I can scale the walls."

I told him I was sorry that a gentleman should ask such a thing of a youth, or try to draw him away from his duty.

He said that he would give me seven thousand livres on his return. But I replied that I was not to be bought with money, to be a traitor to my country and help in destroying my friends.

He smiled. "In war you must not even show consideration for your father or mother."

When he found that he could not persuade me with all the alluring promises he had made, he ordered me back to the fort. Then he had two other prisoners brought before him. To them he made the same proposals he had to me, and they consented.

The next day I went into the room where these men were and asked them if they had been with the general. They said they had, and that they were to have seven thousand livres apiece as a reward for their services.

"Is that the value of your fathers and mothers, and of your country?" I asked them.

"We are obliged to go."

"The general cannot force you. If you take part in this attack, you had better not return among your own people. If you do, and Baker and I live to get home, we will do everything we can to see you hanged."

At this time a smith came and put irons on my feet. But the general gave each of those two men a blanket, a pair of stockings and shoes. They were taken out of the guardhouse and marched with the French as guides.

The general did not succeed. He only burnt our bateaux, etc., and returned to Ticonderoga. Nor did the two poor fellows ever have their reward. Instead, they were sent to the guardhouse and put in irons.

Soon after this I was taken out of irons and went to live with the interpreter again. On the twenty-seventh of March the Indians came and took me with them, to go to Montreal. They tied my arms with a rope and set me to draw a large sled loaded with provisions.

By the time we got to Crown Point I was so lame that I could not walk. The Indians went ashore and built a fire, and then told me I must dance. I obeyed rather than be killed.

When we set out again I knew I could not draw the sled much further and I did not know how to get rid of it. A strange fancy came into my head. I invited three squaws to sit on my sled and then I pleasantly told them I wished I was able to draw 'em.

All this delighted the Indians. They freed me of the sled and gave it to other prisoners. They stripped me of all my clothes and gave me a blanket. And the next morning they cut off my hair and painted me like one of themselves. With needles and Indian ink they pricked on the back of my hand the form of one of the scaling ladders which the French had made to carry to Fort William Henry. I understood they were vexed with the French because of their failure to capture it.

We traveled about nine miles on Lake Champlain. When the sun was two hours high we stopped and the Indians made a fire. Then they took one of the prisoners that had not been wounded, and were going to cut off his hair as they had done mine. He foolishly resisted them, so they prepared to burn him. But the commanding officer prevented it at this time. However, the next night they made a fire, stripped him and tied him to a stake. The squaws cut pieces of pine, like skewers, and thrust them into his flesh, and set them on fire. Then the Indians began to whoop and dance round him.

My captors ordered me to do the same. Love of life obliged me to obey, for I could expect no better treatment if I refused. With a bitter and heavy heart I pretended that I was merry. They cut the poor man's cords, and made him run backwards and forwards. I heard him cry to heaven for mercy. Finally, in extreme anguish and pain, he pitched himself into the flames and died.

From there we traveled without anything worthy of notice happening till we came to an Indian town about twenty miles from Montreal. When we were about a gun's shot from the town the Indians gave as many live-shouts as they had prisoners and as many dead-shouts as they had scalps. The men and women came out to meet us and stripped me naked. After this they pointed to a wigwam and told me to run to it. They beat me with sticks and stones all along the way.

Next day we reached Montreal, where I was brought before Governor Vaudreuil and questioned. Afterwards I was taken into a French merchant's house.

I lived at the merchant's house for three days. On the third night two of the Indians that had captured me came in drunk and asked for me. The merchant's wife called me into the room. When I came in, one of the savages began to dance the war dance about me, and I could see that he intended to kill me. As he lifted his hand to stab me, I caught hold of it with one of mine and I knocked him down with the other. Then I ran up into the garret and hid.

The lady sent for some neighbors to clear the house of her unwelcome guests, and they came and turned them out. It was a very cold night. One of the Indians, being excessively drunk, fell down near the house. In the morning he was found frozen to death.

It was not long before the other Indians came to the house. When they found their brother was dead, they said I had killed him. Gathering a number of their people together with guns, they surrounded the house and demanded me of the lady, saying I should die the most cruel death.

The lady told me what the Indians were up to. "There are some large casks of wine in the cellar," she said. "Go and hide under them."

I did as she advised. Soon I heard the Indians searching the house. They even came down into the cellar, but they did not find me. Then the good-hearted lady asked a Frenchman to tell the Indians that he had seen me outside the city and that I was running away. They were soon out after me in every direction.

It was only a question of time before the Indians would discover they had been deceived and return and find me. The merchant had come home by now and, like his wife, he took pity on me. Getting his carriage, he covered me with a blanket and drove me about five miles outside the city, to a village where his wife's father lived. Here I went into hiding.

After a while the Indians gave up their futile search and returned to the merchant's house. They hunted through it again. When they still could not find me they were certain that the merchant had hidden me somewhere. They appealed to the Governor to have me delivered up to them so they could kill me for killing their brother. By way of threat, they added that if I was not surrendered to them, they would turn and be against the French.

The Governor investigated the matter and assured the Indians that I was innocent. They were satisfied now and said that they would not kill me, but that I was their captive and they wanted me to live with them.

The Governor told them where I was and they came and took me with them to Montreal again and dressed me like an Indian.

My Indian master's home was on the Mississippi, and on the first of May we set out to go there. The party had two other English prisoners with them. For several days the Indians treated me very badly, but then it wore off. We went in bark canoes till we came to Lake Sacrament [Lake George], the first carrying place. Here we hoisted our canoes and carried them overland to the next water.

We continued our journey till we came to the Ohio, where General Braddock was defeated. At this place the Indians seized one of the prisoners, ripped open his belly with a knife and took one end of his guts and tied it to a tree. Then they whipped the miserable man round and round till he died. They obliged me to dance while they had their sport with the dying man.

Finally, on the twenty-third of August—having passed over thirty-two carrying places since we had left Montreal—we reached the Mississippi. Here I was ordered to live with a squaw, who was to be my mother. I stayed with her through the winter, and hunted, dressed leather, etc.

In the spring a French merchant came from Montreal, bringing his goods in bark canoes. When he was ready to return he needed hands to help him and he persuaded my mistress to let me go with him. After we got to Montreal, I was sent to work on his father-in-law's farm. All I received for my labor was food and clothing. I fared no better than a slave.

The family often tried to persuade me to be of their religion and made many attractive promises if I would. Wanting to see what change this would make in their conduct towards me, one Sunday morning I came to my mistress and said:

"Mother, will you give me good clothes if I will go to Mass?"

"Yes, son," she answered. "As good as any in the house."

She did indeed, and I rode to church with two of her daughters. They gave me directions how to behave, telling me I must do as they did. When we came home I sat at the table and ate with the family, and every night and morning I was taught my prayers. Thus I lived for more than a year.

At the next house there was an English lad, also a prisoner. One day we decided to run away together through the woods and try to get home to our families. But we did not know how to obtain provisions for the journey. Finally I was allowed a gun to kill pigeons, which were very plentiful here. I shot a number, split and dried them and concealed them in the woods.

We set out separately on a Sunday morning. After meeting at an appointed place, we began our journey towards Crown Point.

We traveled for twenty-two days. For the last fifteen we had no food except roots, worms and the like. We were so weak and faint that we could scarcely walk. At last, my companion gave out and could go no further. He asked me to leave him, but I would not. I went and found three frogs and divided them between us.

The next morning he died. I sat down by him. At first I intended to make a fire and eat his flesh and, if no help came, to die with him. But finally I came to this resolution: I would cut as much flesh off his bones as I could and tie it up in a handkerchief, and then continue my journey as well as I could. I did this and then I buried my companion and left.

I got three frogs more the next day. Being weak and tired, about nine o'clock I sat down, but could not eat my friend's flesh. I expected to die soon myself and began to commend my soul to God.

Suddenly a partridge alighted very close to me. I thought it surely must have been sent by Providence. I was so weak that I could not hold out my gun, but I rested a little and then I was able to bring it to bear on the partridge and kill it.

While I was eating it, two pigeons came so near that I killed 'em both. After I had fired, I heard a gun at a distance. I fired again and was answered twice. This aroused me; I got up and traveled as fast as I could towards the report of the guns, and about half a mile off I saw three Canadians. I went to 'em and pretended to be a Dutchman, one of their own regulars, that was lost in the woods. They brought me to Crown Point.

Upon my arrival I was put in irons and locked in the guardhouse. After ten or twelve days the commanding officer sent me back to Montreal in a bateau under a guard of twelve soldiers, and I was returned to my master. He was very angry when he saw me and threatened to kill me for stealing his gun when I ran away, but after a while he was calmed down.

Here I lived and worked as before till the nineteenth of November, 1758, when I was released and returned to Albany. My misfortunes were not over yet, for during the following year I was captured by the Indians again and taken to Canada, where I served the same master as before. It was not until January, 1760—after an absence of three years and almost eight months—that I was able to return in peace to my father's house.

*"O! that man would praise the Lord for His goodness, and for His wonderful works to the children of men!*

*"Bless the Lord, O my soul!"*

# Massacre at Michilimackinac

## ALEXANDER HENRY

**A** *PREMATURE attempt to share in the fur trade of Canada, directly on the conquest of the country, led the author of the following pages into situations of some danger and singularity." So begins Alexander Henry's account of his adventures as a fur trader, explorer, hunter, and prisoner of the Chippewas. It includes his eyewitness report on the massacre at Fort Michilimackinac—one of the bloodiest episodes in the history of the Northwest.*

*Fort Michilimackinac stood on the south shore of the Straits of Mackinac, which separate Lake Huron from Lake Michigan. The fort was an important military post and a center of the fur trade in the days when Canada was New France. Here the traders prepared their outfits to go deeper into Indian country, and here the returns in fur were collected, sorted, and embarked for Montreal. The soft, slurred accents of the French Canadian boatmen and* coureurs de bois *mingled with the dialects of Chippewas and Ottawas as canoes were loaded and unloaded on the beach, and tobacco and gunpowder traded for pelts in the stores of the fort.*

*Then a new, alien tongue was heard, and the faces of Indian and Canadian alike grew dark. In 1760 New France fell to the redcoats, and English traders raced into the fur country. One of the first was*

*Alexander Henry, an alert and enterprising young merchant. Henry, born in Brunswick, New Jersey, in 1739, had been a supplier to the British during the recent campaign against Montreal.*

*Setting up shop at Michilimackinac, Henry and his clerks were soon carrying on a brisk trade. The French and the Indians swallowed their hatred for their former enemies, but the Indians could not keep it down. Only the timely arrival of British troops saved Henry's life.*

*Two years passed in smoldering quiet. Then, in May, 1763, the famed "Conspiracy of Pontiac" exploded. Chief Pontiac led his Ottawas and their allies against the British at Detroit. This was a signal for violence to flare up all along the frontier. Before the onslaught of the Indians, outpost after outpost crumbled. One of these was Fort Michilimackinac. The French Canadians, remembering their long wars with the English, stood by with arms folded as the tomahawk struck and struck again.*

*Miraculously, Alexander Henry survived. When peace was restored, he went back to trading at Michilimackinac. After making and losing several fortunes in the Northwest, he settled in Montreal, where he became a rich and respected merchant.*

*Over the years Henry had jotted down notes of his experiences and adventures. Finally, at the age of seventy, he gave in to the temptation to tell it all. His fine book,* Travels and Adventures in Canada and the Indian Territories Between the Years 1760 and 1776, *appeared in 1809. In the frontispiece we see old Henry, still bright-eyed and firm of chin—still the "handsome Englishman," as the Indians had called him.*

*Henry died in 1824. Michilimackinac lived on, though greatly changed. Today, on the original site, is Mackinaw City, a resort village. Here there is a rebuilt stockade of the fort where Alexander Henry's extraordinary adventure began in 1763, when he returned from a visit to his good friend, M. Cadotte.*

When I reached Fort Michilimackinac I found several other traders who had arrived before me from different parts of the country. They declared the mood of the Indians to be hostile to the English, and even feared an attack. M. Laurent Ducharme distinctly informed the commandant, Major Etherington, that a plan was afoot for destroying him, his garrison and all the English in the upper country.

But the commandant believed this and other reports to be without foundation, proceeding from ill-disposed persons with a tendency to do mischief. He expressed much displeasure against M. Ducharme and threatened to arrest the next person who should bring a story of the same kind.

The garrison, at this time, consisted of ninety privates, two sub-alterns and the commandant; [1] the English merchants were four in number. Thus strong, few were concerned about the Indians, who had no weapons but small arms.

Meanwhile the Indians, from every quarter, were daily assembling in unusual numbers, but with every appearance of friendship. They visited the fort and disposed of their furs in such a manner as to set almost everyone's fears at rest. For myself, I took the liberty of observing to Major Etherington that no confidence ought to be placed in them and that I was informed no less than four hundred lay around the fort.

The major only laughed at my timidity; and it is to be confessed that if this officer neglected fair warning on his part, so did I on mine . . . .

Shortly after my first arrival at Michilimackinac in the preceding year, a Chippewa named Wawatam had begun to come often to my house, showing me strong marks of personal regard. Wawatam was about forty-five years of age, of an excellent character among his nation, and a chief.

After this had continued for some time, he came on a certain day with his whole family, bringing a large present of skins, sugar and dried meat. Laying these in a heap, he informed me that some years before he had, according to the custom of his nation, gone off alone into the wilderness and observed a fast. By this he hoped to obtain from the Great Spirit protection through all his days.

On this occasion the Great Spirit had given him a dream in which he adopted an Englishman as his son, brother and friend. From the moment he first beheld me, he had recognized me as the person the Great Spirit had pointed out to him for a brother. He hoped I would not refuse his present, and said he should forever regard me as one of his family.

I could do no otherwise than accept the present and declare my willingness to have so good a man as this appeared to be for my friend and brother. I offered a present in return, and Wawatam accepted it. Thanking me for the favor which he said that I had rendered him, he left me and soon after set out on his winter's hunt.

Twelve months had now elapsed, and I had almost forgotten my "brother." Then, on the second day of June, Wawatam came again to my house, visibly melancholy and thoughtful. He told me he had just returned from his wintering ground. I asked after his health.

Without answering my question, he said he was very sorry to find me at Michilimackinac, and wished me to go to the fort at Sault de Sainte-Marie the next morning, along with him and his family.

Wawatam also asked whether or not the commandant had heard bad news, adding that during the winter he had been frequently disturbed with *the noise of evil birds*. He suggested there were numerous Indians near the fort, many of whom had never shown themselves within it.

Crediting much of what I heard to the peculiarities of the Indian character, I did not pay Wawatam's entreaties and remarks all the attention they deserved. I answered that I could not think of going to the Sault so soon, but would follow him there later. Finding himself unable to persuade me, he withdrew.

Early the next morning he came again, bringing his wife and a present of dried beef. He expressed, a second time, his fears because of the numerous Indians round the fort, and earnestly pressed me to consent to an immediate departure for the Sault. As a reason for this request, he assured me all the Indians intended to come that day to the fort, to demand liquor of the commandant, and he wished me to be gone before they should grow intoxicated.

I had made much progress in the Chippewa language, but the Indian manner of speech is so figurative that only a perfect master can follow it entirely. Had I been further advanced I think I should have gathered from my friend's remarks the design of the enemy, and been enabled to save others as well as myself.

As it was, I turned a deaf ear to everything. Wawatam and his wife, after long but ineffectual efforts, departed alone with mournful faces, and not before they had each let fall some tears.

Later that day the Indians came in great numbers into the fort. They purchased tomahawks and frequently desired to see silver armbands and other valuable ornaments I had for sale. These ornaments they did not purchase, but, after turning them over, left them, saying they would call again the next day. Their motive, as it afterward appeared, was to discover where I kept them so they might lay their hands on them quickly in the moment of pillage.

At night I turned over in my mind the visits of Wawatam. Though they were calculated to excite uneasiness, nothing induced me to believe serious mischief was at hand.

The next day, the fourth of June,[2] was the King's birthday. The morning was sultry. A Chippewa came to tell me his nation was going to play at baggatiway with the Sauks, another Indian nation, for a high wager. He invited me to witness the sport, adding that the commandant was to be there and would bet on the Chippewas. Disturbed by this news, I went to the commandant and argued that the Indians might have some sinister end in view. The commandant only smiled at my suspicions.

Baggatiway, called by the Canadians *le jeu de la crosse,* is played with a ball and a bat, curved and terminating in a sort of racket. Two posts are planted in the ground at a considerable distance from each other, as a mile or more. Each party has its post, and the game consists in throwing the ball up to the post of the adversary.

I did not go to see the match, which was to be played outside the fort, but employed myself in writing letters. Even when a fellow-trader, Mr. Tracy, called upon me, saying that a canoe had just arrived from Detroit and I should go with him to the beach to inquire the news, I still remained to finish my letters, promising to follow in a few minutes. He had not gone more than twenty paces from my door when I heard an Indian war cry, and a noise of general confusion.

Going instantly to my window, I saw a crowd of Indians within the fort, furiously cutting down and scalping every Englishman they found.

I had in the room a fowling piece loaded with swan shot. This I immediately seized and held for a few minutes, waiting to hear the drum beat to arms. In this dreadful interval I saw several of my countrymen fall, and more than one struggling between the knees of an Indian who, holding him in this manner, scalped him while yet living.

The game of baggatiway is attended with much violence and noise. Nothing could be less liable to excite premature alarm than that the ball should be tossed over the pickets of the fort, nor that, having fallen there, it should be followed, on the instant, by all engaged in the game, all eager, all struggling, all shouting. This was the stratagem by which the Indians had obtained possession of the fort.[3] To be still more certain of success, they had persuaded as many as they could to come outside the pickets, particularly the commandant and garrison.

No resistance was made to the enemy. Realizing my own unassisted arm could do little against four hundred Indians, I thought only of seeking shelter. Amid the slaughter which was raging, I observed many of the Canadian inhabitants of the fort calmly looking on, neither opposing the Indians nor suffering injury. From this I conceived a hope of finding security in their houses.

Between the yard door of my own house and that of M. Langlade, my neighbor, there was only a low fence, over which I easily climbed. At my entrance, I found the whole family at the windows, gazing at the scene of blood before them. I addressed myself immediately to M. Langlade, begging that he would put me into some place of safety, until the heat of the affair should be over.

*"Que voudriez-vous que j'en ferais?"* M. Langlade looked for a moment at me, then turned again to the window, shrugging his shoulders. He felt he could no nothing for me.

This was a moment for despair. But, the next, a Pani Indian woman, a slave of M. Langlade's, beckoned me to follow her. She brought me to a door, which she opened, telling me that it led to the garret, where I must go and conceal myself. I joyfully obeyed her directions, and she, having followed me up to the garret door, locked it after me and with great presence of mind took away the key.

This shelter obtained, if shelter I could hope to find it, I was anxious to know what might still be passing without. Through an opening which afforded a view of the area of the fort, I beheld the ferocious triumphs of the barbarian conquerors. The dead were scalped and mangled, the dying were writhing and shrieking under the knife and tomahawk. From the bodies of some, ripped open, their butchers were drinking the blood, scooped up in the hollow of joined hands, and quaffed amid shouts of rage and victory.

I was shaken, not only with horror but with fear. The sufferings which I witnessed I seemed on the point of experiencing.

No long time elapsed before, everyone being destroyed who could be found, there was a general cry of "All is finished!" At the same instant I heard some of the Indians enter the house in which I was.

The garret was separated from the room below only by a layer of single boards. I could therefore hear everything that passed.

The Indians no sooner came in than they inquired whether any Englishman was in the house. M. Langlade replied that he could not say, he did not know of any. In this answer he did not exceed the truth, for the Pani woman had not only hidden me by stealth, but kept my secret and her own. M. Langlade added that they might see for themselves. Saying this, he brought them to the garret door.

The state of my mind will be imagined. Some delay was occasioned by the absence of the key, and a few moments were thus allowed me to look around for a hiding place.

In one corner of the garret I saw a heap of vessels of birch bark used in maple sugar making. The door was unlocked and opening and the Indians ascending the stairs before I had completely crept into a small opening at one end of the heap.

An instant after, four Indians entered the room, all armed with tomahawks and all besmeared with blood.

I could scarcely breathe, but I thought the throbbing of my heart made a noise loud enough to betray me. The Indians walked in every direction about the garret, and one of them approached me so closely that had he put forth his hand he must have touched me. Still, I remained undiscovered.

After taking several turns in the room, during which they told M. Langlade how many they had killed and how many scalps they had taken, the Indians returned downstairs. I heard the door locked for the second time.

There was a feather bed on the floor; exhausted by the nervous strain, I threw myself down on this and fell asleep.

At dusk I was awakened by a second opening of the door. The person that entered was M. Langlade's wife, who was much surprised at finding me. She advised me not to be uneasy, observing that the Indians had killed most of the English, but that she hoped I might myself escape. I begged her to send me a little water to drink, which she did.

I was unable to discover a resource from which I could hope for life. A flight to Detroit had no probable chance of success. The distance was four hundred miles, I was without provisions, and the road lay through Indian countries where the first man I should meet would kill me. To stay where I was, threatened nearly the same outcome. As before, worn out with anxiety, I fell asleep.

The respite which sleep afforded me was put to an end by the return of morning. At sunrise I heard the family stirring and, afterward, Indian voices informing M. Langlade they had not found me among the dead and supposed me to be concealed somewhere.

M. Langlade appeared by this time acquainted with the place of my retreat, no doubt informed by his wife. The poor woman declared to her husband, in French, that he should no longer keep me in his house but deliver me up to my pursuers, or the Indians might revenge it on her children.

M. Langlade resisted, at first, but soon allowed her to prevail. He informed the Indians that I was in his house and he would put me into their hands. Then he began to ascend the stairs, the Indians following upon his heels.

I now resigned myself to the fate with which I was menaced. I arose from the bed and presented myself full in view to the Indians who were entering the room. They were all in a state of intoxication and entirely naked except about the middle.

One of them, named Wenniway, whom I had previously known, and who was upward of six feet in height, had his face and body covered with charcoal and grease, only that a white spot encircled either eye. This man seized me with one hand by the collar while in the other he held a large carving knife as if to plunge it into my breast. His eyes meanwhile were fixed steadfastly on mine.

After some seconds of the most anxious suspense he dropped his arm, saying, "I won't kill you!" He added that he had lost a brother whose name was Musinigon, and I should be adopted into the tribe in his place and be called after him.

A reprieve, upon any terms, placed me among the living. But Wenniway ordered me downstairs, and informed me I was to be taken to his cabin. There and everywhere the Indians were mad with liquor; death again was threatening, and not as possible only, but as certain. I mentioned my fears to M. Langlade, begging him to point out the danger to my Indian master. M. Langlade did not withhold his compassion, and Wenniway consented that I should remain where I was until he found another opportunity to take me away.

Thus far secure, I went back up my garret stairs to place myself out of the reach of drunken Indians. I had not remained there more than an hour when I was called to the room below. An Indian was there who said Wenniway had sent him to fetch me and I must go with him out of the fort.

This man I had seen before. In the preceding year I had allowed him to take goods on credit, for which he was still in my debt. Some short time previous, I had upbraided him with want of honesty. "I will pay you before long!" he had said. This speech now came fresh into my memory and led me to suspect the fellow had formed a design against my life. I communicated the suspicion to M. Langlade, but he gave for answer, "You are not now your own master, and must do as you are ordered."

The Indian directed that I should undress myself, declaring my coat and shirt would become him better than me. Having obeyed his order, no alternative was left me than to go out naked or to put on his clothes, which he freely gave me in exchange. His motive for stripping me of my own apparel was that it might not be stained with blood when he should kill me.

I was now told to proceed, and my captor followed me close until I had passed the gate of the fort. Then I turned toward the spot where I knew the Indians to be encamped. This did not suit my enemy, who drew me violently in the opposite direction. Here, finding I was approaching the bushes and sand hills, I determined to proceed no further. I told the Indian I believed he meant to murder me and he might as well strike where I was.

He replied with coolness that my suspicions were just and he meant to pay me in this manner for my goods. At the same time he produced a knife and held me in a position to receive the blow.

Both this and what followed were the affair of a moment. By some effort too sudden to be remembered I stopped his arm and gave him a sudden push, releasing myself from his grasp. Then I ran toward the fort with all the swiftness in my power. The Indian followed me. I expected every moment to feel his knife.

I succeeded in my flight and entered the fort. Wenniway was standing in the midst of the area, and to him I hastened for protection. Wenniway told the Indian to leave. But the Indian kept pursuing me round him, making several strokes at me with his knife and foaming at the mouth with rage at his repeated failure.

At length Wenniway drew near to M. Langlade's house. The door was open. I ran in, and the Indian abandoned the pursuit.

Preserved so often and so unexpectedly, I returned to my garret with a strong inclination to believe that through the will of an overruling power no Indian enemy could do me hurt. But new trials were at hand.

At ten o'clock in the evening, I was roused from sleep and once more asked to descend the stairs. Major Etherington, Mr. Bostwick and Lieutenant Lesslie were in the room below.

These gentlemen had been taken prisoner while looking at the game outside the fort and immediately stripped of all their clothes. They were now sent into the fort under a guard of Canadians, because the Indians had resolved on getting drunk and the chiefs feared the prisoners would be murdered if they continued in the camp. Lieutenant Jemette and seventy soldiers had been killed, and but twenty Englishmen were still alive. These were all within the fort, together with nearly three hundred Canadians belonging to the canoes, etc.

Since there were so many of us, I and others proposed to Major Etherington that we should make an effort to regain possession of the fort and hold it against the Indians. We consulted the Jesuit missionary about this plan, but he discouraged us. He pointed out that if the Indians should get the upper hand again, we could expect no mercy from them, and that we could place little dependence upon our Canadian auxiliaries. Thus the fort and the prisoners remained in the Indians' hands—though through the whole night the prisoners and Canadians were in actual possession, and the Indians were outside the gates.

The greater part of that night was passed in mutual condolence, and my three fellow-prisoners shared my garret. In the morning I was called down by my master, Wenniway. He led me to a small house within the fort, where I found the trader Mr. Ezekiel Solomons, an Englishman from Detroit, and a soldier, all prisoners. With these I remained in painful suspense. At ten o'clock in the forenoon an Indian arrived and marched us to the lake side, where a canoe was waiting for us.

Our voyage would have commenced immediately, but one of the Indians who was to be of the party was absent. There was a long delay, during which we were exposed to a keen northeast wind. An old shirt was all that covered me, and I suffered much from the cold.

M. Langlade came down to the beach and I asked him for a blanket, promising, if I lived, to pay him any price he pleased. The answer I received was that he could let me have no blanket unless there were someone to be security for the payment. For myself, he observed, I had no longer any property in that country. I had no more to say to M. Langlade.[4]

Presently seeing another Canadian, John Cuchoise, I addressed to him a similar request, and was not refused. Naked as I was, but for the blanket I must have perished.

At noon, our party was all collected. The Indians in the canoe were seven in number, the prisoners four. A paddle was put into each of our hands, and we were made to use it.

We were bound for the Isles du Castor [Beaver Islands], in the mouth of Lake Michigan, and we should have crossed the lake, but a thick fog came on. The Indians deemed it safer to keep the shore close under their lee. We therefore approached the lands of the Ottawas and their village of L'Arbre Croche on the opposite side of the tongue of land on which the fort is built. Every half hour the Indians gave their war whoops, one for every prisoner in their canoe.

In this manner, we reached Wagoshense, eighteen miles from Michilimackinac. An Ottawa appeared upon the beach, who made signs that we should land. As we approached, the Ottawa asked the news, and kept the Chippewas in conversation till we were within a few yards. At this moment a hundred men rushed upon us from the bushes and dragged the prisoners out of the canoe amid a terrifying shout.

No sooner were we on shore than the chiefs of the party advanced and gave us their hands. They told us they were our friends, and Ottawas, whom the Chippewas had insulted by destroying the English without consulting with them. They added that the Chippewas had been carrying us to the Isles du Castor only to kill and devour us.

It was not long before we were embarked in the canoes of the Ottawas. The same evening they relanded us at Michilimackinac and marched us into the fort. The Chippewas were confounded at beholding the Ottawas espouse a side opposite to their own.

The Ottawas, who had accompanied us in sufficient numbers, took possession of the fort. We were lodged in the house of the commandant and strictly guarded.

Early the next morning a council was held. The Chippewas complained much of the conduct of the Ottawas in robbing them of their prisoners. They alleged that all the Indians, the Ottawas alone excepted, were at war with the English; that Pontiac had taken Detroit; the king of France had awoke and repossessed himself of Quebec and Montreal; and the English were meeting destruction not only at Michilimackinac but in every other part of the world. They urged the Ottawas to join in 'the war. The speech was followed by large presents, part of the plunder of the fort.

The Indians rarely make their answers till the day after they have heard the arguments offered, and the council was therefore adjourned. We, the prisoners, whose fate was in controversy, were unacquainted with this transaction and therefore enjoyed a night of tolerable tranquillity. The council was resumed at an early hour in the morning, and after several speeches we were sent for and returned to the Chippewas.[5]

The Chippewas, as soon as we were restored to them, marched us to a village below the fort and put us into a lodge. It was already the prison of fourteen soldiers, tied two and two, each with a rope about his neck.

I was left untied, but I passed a night full of wretchedness. My bed was the bare ground, and I was again reduced to an old shirt, as my blanket had been taken from me among the Ottawas. For two days I had eaten nothing.

I confess that in the canoe, with the Chippewas, I was offered bread —but bread with what accompaniment! They had a loaf which they cut with the same knives they had employed in the massacre—knives still covered with blood. The blood they moistened with spittle and, rubbing it on the bread, offered this to their prisoners, telling them to eat the blood of their countrymen.

Toward noon Menehwehna, the war chief of the village of Michilimackinac, and Wenniway were seated in the lodge. My friend and brother, Wawatam, suddenly came in. In passing by, he gave me his hand, but went immediately toward the chief and sat down. Uninterrupted silence prevailed, while each smoked his pipe. Then Wawatam arose and left, saying to me as he passed, "Take courage!"

An hour elapsed, during which several chiefs entered and preparations appeared to be making for a council. At length Wawatam reentered the lodge, followed by his wife. Both were loaded with merchandise, which they carried up to the chiefs and laid in a heap before them. Some moments of silence followed. Then Wawatam spoke.

"Friends and relations," he began, pointing to myself, "see there my friend and brother among slaves—himself a slave! You all know that long before the war began I adopted him as my brother. Because I am your relation, he is therefore your relation, too. How, being your relation, can he be your slave?

"On the day the war began you were fearful lest, on this very account, I should reveal your secret. You requested, therefore, that I would leave the fort and cross the lake. I did so after you, Menehwehna, gave me your promise you would protect my friend, delivering him safely to me.

"The performance of this promise I now claim. I come not with empty hands to ask it. I bring these goods to buy off every claim which any among you may have on my brother."

Wawatam ceased. The pipes were again filled. After they were finished, a further period of silence followed. Then Menehwehna arose.

"My relation and brother," said he, "what you have spoken is the truth. I promised to take care of your friend. We accept your present, and you may take him home with you."

Wawatam thanked the chiefs and, taking me by the hand, led me to his lodge, which was a few yards away. My entrance appeared to give joy to the whole family, which consisted of the wife of my friend, his two sons, of whom the eldest was married, and whose wife and daughter completed the list. Food was immediately prepared for me, and I now ate the first hearty meal since my capture. I found myself one of the family and, but for my fears as to the other Indians, I felt as happy as the situation could allow.

The next morning I was alarmed by a noise in the prison lodge. Looking through the openings of the lodge in which I was, I saw seven dead bodies of white men dragged forth. I was informed that a certain chief, having been absent when the war began, was desirous of showing the Indians he approved of what they had done, and had gone into the prison lodge and with his knife put these seven men to death.

Shortly after, the Indians took the fattest of the bodies, cut off the head and divided the whole into five parts. These were put into five kettles hung over as many fires. A message came to our lodge for Wawatam to take part in the feast.

Wawatam obeyed the summons, taking with him his dish and spoon.

After about half an hour he returned, bringing in his dish a human hand and a large piece of flesh. He did not appear to relish the repast, but told me it always had been the custom, among all the Indian nations when returning from war, to make a war feast from among the slain. This, he said, inspired the warriors with courage in attack.

On the ninth of June a general council was held. It was agreed to move to the island of Michilimackinac, about six miles away, because it could be more easily defended than the fort in the event of an attack by the English. The Indians had begun to entertain fears of want of strength.

The camp was broken up and we embarked, taking with us the prisoners still undisposed of. We reached the island in safety, and the women were not long in erecting our lodges. In the morning there was a muster of the Indians, at which there were found three hundred and fifty fighting men.

In the course of the day a canoe arrived from Detroit with ambassadors who tried to persuade the Indians to return with them to the assistance of Pontiac. But fear was now the prevailing passion. A guard was kept during the day and a watch by night, and alarms were very frequently spread. Had an enemy appeared, all the prisoners would have been put to death, and I suspected that as an Englishman I should share their fate.

Several days had now passed when, one morning a continued alarm prevailed. Two large canoes from Montreal were in sight. All the Indian canoes were immediately manned, and those from Montreal were surrounded and seized.

In the canoes was a large proportion of liquor. This threatened disturbance among the Indians, even to the loss of their dearest friends. Wawatam owned he could not resist joining in the debauch. That I might escape all mischief, he requested that I would accompany him to a thickly wooded mountain in the middle of the island, where I was to remain hidden till the liquor should be drunk.

We ascended the mountain and my friend left me there. Two days passed without the return of Wawatam, and without food. At length the sound of a foot reached me and he appeared. He made many apologies for his long absence, the cause of which was an unfortunate excess in the enjoyment of his liquor. On returning to the lodge, I was cordially received by the family.

A few days later, Menehwehna came to the lodge. After the usual ceremony of smoking, he observed that Indians were daily arriving from Detroit, some of whom had lost relations or friends in the war and would certainly retaliate on any Englishman they found. He advised that I should be dressed like an Indian, so that I might hope to escape all future insult.

I could only consent to the proposal. My head was shaved, except for a spot on the crown, and my face was painted red and black. A shirt was provided for me painted with vermilion mixed with grease. A large collar of wampum was put round my neck, another suspended on my breast. Both my arms were decorated with large bands of silver above the elbow, besides several smaller ones on the wrists, and my legs were covered with a kind of hose made of scarlet cloth. Over all, I was to wear a scarlet blanket and on my head a large bunch of feathers.

I parted, not without regret, with my long hair, which I fancied to be ornamental; but the ladies of the family and the village appeared to think my person improved and now condescended to call me handsome, even among Indians.

In the Indian village at this time much scarcity of food prevailed. We were often for twenty-four hours without eating. In the morning when we had no victuals for the day before us, the custom was to black our faces with grease and charcoal and exhibit, through resignation, a temper as cheerful as if in the midst of plenty. However, we soon left the island in search of food. At the Bay of Boutchitaouy, distant eight leagues, we found plenty of wild fowl and fish.

At the bay my guardian's daughter-in-law was taken in labor of her first child. She was immediately removed out of the common lodge, and a small one, for her separate accommodation, was erected by the women in less than half an hour.

The next morning we heard she was very ill. The family was much alarmed because cases of difficult labor are very rare among Indian women. Wawatam requested me to accompany him into the woods, and informed me that if he could find a snake he should soon secure relief to his daughter-in-law.

We speedily obtained a small garter snake. Holding it fast while it coiled round his arm, Wawatam cut off its head, catching the blood in a cup. He carried home the blood, mixed it with water and administered two tablespoonfuls. Within an hour the patient was delivered of a fine child. Wawatam declared that the remedy was one that never failed.

The next day we left the bay. The young mother, in high spirits, assisted in loading the canoe, barefooted and knee-deep in the water.

The medical information, diseases and remedies of the Indians often engaged my curiosity, and I shall take this occasion to introduce a few particulars about them.

The Indians are in general free from disorders. Inflammations of the lungs are among their most ordinary complaints, and rheumatism still more so, especially with the aged. Their mode of life, in which they are so much exposed to the wet and cold, sleeping on the ground and inhaling the night air, accounts for their liability to these diseases. The remedies on which they most rely are emetics, cathartics and the lancet, but especially the last. Bleeding is so favorite an operation among the women that they never lose an occasion of enjoying it, whether sick or well. I have sometimes bled a dozen women in a morning as they sat in a row along a fallen tree, beginning with the first—opening the vein—then proceeding to the second—and so on, having three or four individuals bleeding at the same time.

In most villages this service was required of me, and no persuasion of mine could ever induce a woman to dispense with it.

Our next encampment was on the island of Saint-Martin, off Cape Saint-Ignace. Here we fished for sturgeon with great success; and here, in the enjoyment of a plentiful supply of food, we remained until the twentieth of August. The autumn being at hand, Wawatam proposed going to his wintering ground. The move was a subject of the greatest joy to myself, on account of the frequent insults to which I still had to submit from the Indians of our band. At our wintering ground we were to be alone, for the Indian families separate in the winter and reassociate in the spring and summer.

In preparation, our first business was to sail for Michilimackinac. There, we procured from a Canadian trader, on credit, some trifling articles, together with ammunition and two bushels of maize. This done, we steered for Lake Michigan. At L'Arbre Croche we stopped on a visit to the Ottawas. The chief, the same who took me from the Chippewas, behaved with great kindness, presenting me with a bag of maize.

Next we proceeded to the mouth of the river Aux Sables, on the south side of the lake, about a hundred and fifty miles from Fort Michilimackinac. On our voyage, we passed several deep bays and rivers, where we killed many wild fowl and beaver.

To kill beaver, we used to go several miles up the rivers before the approach of night, and, after the dusk came on, let the canoe drift down the current without noise. The beaver, in this part of the evening, came abroad to procure food or materials for repairing their lodges. As they were not alarmed by the canoe, they often passed within gunshot.

While we hunted I enjoyed a personal freedom of which I had been long deprived, and became as expert in the Indian pursuits as the Indians themselves.

On entering the river Aux Sables, Wawatam took a dog, tied its feet together, and threw it into the stream, uttering a long prayer to the Great Spirit, begging his blessing on the chase and his aid in the support of the family through the dangers of a long winter. Our lodge was fifteen miles above the mouth of the stream. The principal animals which the country afforded were the stag or red deer, the common American deer, the bear, raccoon, beaver and marten, all of which we hunted through the months of cold and snow.

Raccoon hunting was my more particular and daily employment. I usually went out at dawn and seldom returned till sunset. By degrees I became familiarized with this kind of life, and had it not been for the idea that I was living among savages—or if I could have forgotten that I had ever been otherwise—I could have enjoyed as much happiness as in any other situation.

One evening, on my return from hunting, I found the fire put out and the opening in the top of the lodge covered over with skins to exclude as much light as possible. I observed that the ashes had been removed from the fireplace, and dry sand was spread where they had been. Soon after, a fire was made outside, and a kettle hung over it to boil.

I supposed that a feast was in preparation. I supposed so only, for it would have been indecorous to inquire into the meaning of what I saw. No person among the Indians would take such a liberty. Good breeding requires that the spectator should patiently await the result.

As soon as the darkness of night had arrived, the family, including myself, were invited into the lodge. I was requested not to speak, as a feast was about to be given to the dead, whose spirits delight in uninterrupted silence.

As we entered, each was presented with his wooden dish and spoon, after which we seated ourselves. The door was shut and we remained in perfect darkness.

The master of the family was the master of the feast. Still in the dark, he asked everyone, by turn, for his dish and put into each two boiled ears of maize. Then he called upon the spirits of his deceased relations and friends, beseeching them to assist him in the chase, and to partake of the food he had prepared for them. When he had ended, we proceeded to eat our maize, which we did in silence. The maize was not half boiled, and it took me an hour to consume my share. I was requested not to break the spikes, as this would be displeasing to the departed spirits.

When all was eaten, Wawatam made another speech and the ceremony ended. A new fire was kindled, with fresh sparks from flint and steel and, the pipes being smoked, the spikes were carefully buried in a hole made in the ground for that purpose within the lodge. Then the whole family began a dance, with Wawatam singing and beating a drum. The dance continued the greater part of the night, to the great pleasure of the lodge. This feast was on the first of November.

On the twentieth of December, we took an account and found that we had a hundred beaver skins, as many raccoons, and a large quantity of dried venison. All of this was secured from the wolves by being placed upon a scaffold.

A hunting excursion into the interior of the country was resolved on. Early the next morning the bundles were made up by the women for each person to carry. The bundle given to me was the lightest, and those carried by the women the largest and heaviest.

On the first day of our march we advanced about twenty miles and then encamped. Being somewhat fatigued, I could not hunt, but Wawatam killed a stag not far from our encampment. The next morning we moved our lodge to the carcass. Here we remained two days, drying the meat. The method was to cut it into slices of the thickness of a steak and then hang it over the fire, in the smoke. On the third day we moved on, marching till two o'clock in the afternoon.

While the women were busy erecting and preparing the lodges, I took my gun and strolled away, telling Wawatam that I intended to look for some fresh meat for supper. He answered that he would do the same, and we both left the encampment, going in different directions.

The sun being visible, I entertained no fear of losing my way. But, in following several tracks of animals, I proceeded a considerable distance. It was not till near sunset that I thought of returning. The sky had become overcast, and I was left without the sun for my guide. I walked as fast as I could, always supposing myself to be approaching our encampment, till it became so dark that I ran against the trees.

I became convinced that I was lost, and I was alarmed to think I was in a country entirely strange to me, and in danger from strange Indians. With the flint of my gun I made a fire and then lay down to sleep. In the night it rained hard. I awoke cold and wet. As soon as light appeared, I recommenced my journey, sometimes walking and sometimes running, not knowing where to go, bewildered and like a madman.

Toward evening I reached the border of a large lake of which I could scarcely discern the opposite shore. I had never heard of a lake in this part of the country and felt myself further than ever from my destination. To retrace my steps appeared to be the most likely means of saving myself. I determined to turn my face directly from the lake and keep this direction as nearly as I could.

A heavy snow began to descend and night soon came on. I stopped and made a fire and, stripping a tree of its sheet of bark, lay down under it to shelter myself from the snow. All night the wolves howled around and, to me, seemed to be acquainted with my misfortune.

Amid the most distracted thoughts, I finally was able to fall asleep. It was not long before I awoke. I felt refreshed, and I wondered at the terror to which I had yielded. I thought I must have lost my senses—otherwise I could never have suffered so long without remembering the lessons I had received from my Indian friend for use in difficulties of this kind. These were that, generally, the tops of pine trees lean toward the rising of the sun; that moss grows toward the roots of trees, on the side which faces the north; and that the limbs of trees are most numerous and largest on the side which faces the south.

I decided to guide myself by these marks, convinced that I would sooner or later reach Lake Michigan this way. At break of day I began my march. I had not eaten anything since leaving our encampment. I had my gun and ammunition with me and was therefore not concerned about obtaining food. The snow was about half a foot deep.

My eyes were now busy upon the trees. When their tops leaned different ways I looked to the moss or to the branches and, by connecting one with another, I found the means of traveling with some degree of confidence. At four o'clock in the afternoon the sun, to my inexpressible joy, broke from the clouds and I had no further need of examining the trees.

Going down the side of a lofty hill, I saw a herd of red deer approaching. Desirous of killing one of them for food, I hid myself in the bushes. A large one came near, and I took aim. But my gun missed fire because the priming was wet. The animals walked along without taking the least alarm.

Having reloaded my gun, I followed them and took aim a second time. But now a disaster of the heaviest kind had befallen me. On attempting to fire, I found that I had lost the cock of my gun.

Of all the sufferings which I had experienced, this seemed to me the most severe. I was in a strange country and did not know how far I had to go. I had been three days without food; I was now without the means of procuring either food or fire. Despair almost overpowered me. But I soon resigned myself into the hands of that Providence whose arm had so often saved me, and returned on my track in search of the lost part of my gun. My search was in vain. I resumed my course, wet, cold, and hungry, and almost without clothing.

The sun was setting fast when I descended a hill, at the bottom of which was a small lake, entirely frozen over. Drawing near, I saw a beaver lodge in the middle, offering some faint prospect of food. But I found it already broken up.

While I looked at it, it suddenly occurred to me that I had seen it before. Turning my eyes round the place, I discovered a small tree which I had myself cut down in the autumn when, in company with my friends, I had taken the beaver.

I was no longer at a loss, but knew both the distance and the route to the encampment. I had only to follow the course of a small stream of water, which ran from the encampment to the lake on which I stood.

An hour before, I had thought myself the most miserable of men. Now I leaped for joy and called myself the happiest.

The whole of the night and through all the following day I walked up the rivulet and at sunset reached the encampment. I was received with the warmest expressions of pleasure by the family, by whom I had been given up for lost after a long and vain search for me in the woods.

For some days I rested and regained my strength. After this I began to hunt again. The snow had now fallen, and I was certain that I could always find my way back by following my tracks.

In January I happened to observe that the trunk of a very large pine tree was much torn by the claws of a bear, both in going up and down. I saw that there was a large opening in the upper part, near which the smaller branches were broken. From these signs and the circumstances that there were no tracks on the snow, there was reason to believe a bear lay concealed in the tree.

Returning to the lodge, I communicated my discovery. It was agreed that all the family should go together to assist in cutting down the tree, the girth of which was not less than eighteen feet. The women at first opposed the undertaking, because our axes were only of a pound and a half weight and not well adapted to so heavy a labor. But the hope of finding a large bear and obtaining a great quantity of oil from its fat at length prevailed.

In the morning we surrounded the tree, both men and women, as many at a time as could conveniently work at it. Here we toiled like beavers till the sun went down. This day's work carried us about halfway through the trunk. The next morning we renewed the attack, continuing it till about two o'clock in the afternoon, when the tree fell to the ground.

For a few minutes everything remained quiet, and I feared that all our expectations were disappointed. But as I advanced to the opening a bear of extraordinary size came out. Before she had proceeded many yards I shot her.

The bear being dead, my assistants approached. All, but particularly my old mother (as I used to call her), took the animal's head in their hands and stroked and kissed it several times, calling her their relation and grandmother. They begged a thousand pardons of the bear for taking away her life and requested her not to lay the fault upon them, since it was an Englishman that had put her to death.

This ceremony was not of long duration. If it was I that killed their grandmother, they were not themselves behindhand in what remained to be performed. The skin being taken off, we found the fat in several places six inches deep. This loaded two persons, and the flesh parts were as much as four persons could carry. In all, the carcass must have exceeded five hundredweight.

As soon as we reached the lodge, the bear's head was adorned with all the trinkets in the possession of the family, such as silver armbands and wristbands and belts of wampum. They then laid the beast upon a scaffold set up for it within the lodge. Near the nose was placed a large quantity of tobacco.

The next morning, preparations were made for a feast to the spirit of the bear. The lodge was cleaned and swept. The head of the bear was lifted and a new blanket which had never been used before, spread under it.

The pipes were now lit and Wawatam blew tobacco smoke into the nostrils of the bear, telling me to do the same and thus appease the anger of the bear on account of my having killed her. I endeavored to persuade him that she no longer had any life, and assured him that I did not fear her displeasure. But I could see that he was far from convinced.

At length the feast was ready. Wawatam commenced a speech resembling his address to the spirits of his relations and departed companions. But it had this peculiarity, that he deplored the necessity of men to destroy their *friends* thus. He represented, however, that the misfortune was unavoidable, since without doing so they could not live. The speech ended, we all ate heartily of the bear's flesh. Even the head itself, after remaining three days on the scaffold, was put into the kettle.

It is only the female bear that makes her winter lodging in the upper parts of trees, a practice by which her young are secured from the attacks of wolves and other animals. She brings forth her cubs in the winter season and remains in her lodge till they have gained some strength.

The male always lodges in the ground, under the roots of trees. He takes to this habitation as soon as the snow falls, and remains there till it has disappeared. Excepting for a short part of the season, the male lives constantly alone.

The fat of our bear was melted down and the oil filled six porcupine skins. A part of the meat was cut into strips and fire-dried. Then it was put into the vessels containing the oil, where it remained in perfect preservation until the middle of summer.

February, in the country where I was, is called the Moon of Hard or Crusted Snow, for now the snow can bear a man, or at least dogs, in pursuit of animals of the chase.

At this season the stag is very successfully hunted. His feet break through at every step and the crust upon the snow cuts his legs, with its sharp edges, to the very bone. He is consequently an easy prey. It frequently happened that we killed twelve in the short space of two hours. By this means, we were soon in possession of four thousand pounds of dried venison. This was to be carried on our backs, along with all the rest of our wealth, for seventy miles, the distance to the lake shore at which we had left our canoes in the autumn. It was our next business to perform this journey.

Our venison and furs were to be disposed of at Michilimackinac, and it was now the season for carrying them to market. The women prepared our loads. On the morning of departure we set off at daybreak and continued our march till two o'clock in the afternoon. Where we stopped we erected a scaffold, on which we deposited the bundles we had brought and returned to our encampment, reaching it in the evening. In the morning we carried fresh loads which we deposited with the rest, and we returned a second time in the evening. We repeated this till all was forwarded one stage. Then, moving our lodge to the place of deposit, we carried our goods with the same patient toil a second stage; and so on, till we were not far from the shores of the lake.

When we arrived here, we turned our attention to sugarmaking, which belongs to the women, the men cutting wood for the fires and hunting and fishing. In the midst of this we were joined by several lodges of Indians, most of whom were of the family to which I belonged and had wintered near us. The lands belonged to this family, and it had therefore the exclusive right to hunt on them. This is according to the custom of the people, for each family has its own lands. I was treated very civilly by all the lodges.

A short time after the arrival of our friends an accident occurred which filled all the village with anxiety and sorrow. A little child belonging to one of our neighbors fell into a kettle of boiling syrup. It was instantly snatched out, but with little hope of its recovery.

So long as it lived, a continual feast was observed. This was made to the Great Spirit and Master of Life, that he might be pleased to save and heal the child. At this feast I was a constant guest and often found difficulty in eating the large quantity of food which, on such occasions, is put upon each man's dish. The Indians accustom themselves both to eat much and to fast much with facility.

Several sacrifices were also offered. Among these were dogs, killed and hung upon the tops of poles, with the addition of blankets and other articles. These, also, were given to the Great Spirit.

The child died. To preserve the body from the wolves, it was placed upon a scaffold. Here it remained till we went to the lake, on the border of which was the burial ground of the family.

On our arrival there, in the beginning of April, I attended the funeral. The grave was large, and the inside was lined with birch bark. On the bark the body of the child was laid, and with it an axe, a pair of snowshoes, a small kettle, several pairs of common shoes, its own strings of beads, and—because it was a girl—a carrying belt and a paddle. The kettle was filled with meat.

All this was again covered with bark. At about two feet nearer the surface, logs were laid across and these again covered with bark, so that the earth could not fall upon the corpse.

Before the burial the mother cried over the dead body of her child and took a lock of hair from it for a memorial. While she did this I tried to console her by offering the usual arguments—that the child was fortunate in being released from the miseries of this present life, and that it would be restored to her in another world, happy and everlasting. She answered that she knew it, and that the lock of hair would help her recognize her daughter, for she would take it with her. She was referring to the day when some pious hand would place this little relic in her own grave, along with her carrying belt and paddle.

I have frequently inquired into the ideas and opinions of the Indians in regard to a future life, and always found that they were somewhat different in different individuals.

Some suppose their souls remain in this world, invisible to human eyes but capable of assisting their friends in moments of distress and danger.

Others suppose the spirit is sent to a distant world or country in which it receives reward or punishment according to the life it has led. Those who have lived virtuously are transported to a place abounding with every luxury, with deer and all other animals of the woods and water, where the earth produces all its sweetest fruits in their greatest perfection. On the other hand, those who have violated or neglected the duties of this life are removed to a barren soil, where they wander up and down among rocks and morasses and are stung by gnats as large as pigeons.

While we remained on the border of the lake a watch was kept every night. The Indians were fearful of an attack from the English, to avenge the massacre of Michilimackinac. Their immediate grounds for this worry were the constant dreams the more aged women were having about it. I tried to persuade them that nothing of the kind would take place, but their fears were not to be subdued.

On the twenty-fifth of April we embarked for Michilimackinac. At La Grande Traverse we met a large party of Indians. Like ourselves, they appeared to fear that they would be destroyed by the English. Questions were continually put to me whether I knew of any plan to attack them. They believed I had a foreknowledge of events and was informed by dreams of all things doing at a distance.

When I said I knew nothing, they suspected me of a desire to conceal my knowledge. On this account I told them, at length, that I knew there was no enemy to harm them, and that they might proceed to Michilimackinac without danger. I declared that if ever my countrymen returned to Michilimackinac, I would recommend them to their favor on account of the good treatment I had received from them. Encouraged, they embarked the next morning.

On the twenty-seventh we landed at the fort, which now contained only two French traders. Wawatam and myself settled our stock, and I found my share was a hundred beaver skins, sixty raccoon skins and six otter, of the total value of about one hundred and sixty dollars. With these earnings I purchased clothes and laid in a good stock of ammunition and tobacco. To the latter I had become much attached during the winter. It was my principal recreation after the chase, for my companions in the lodge were unaccustomed to pass the time in conversation. Among the Indians, the topics of conversation are but few, limited for the most part to the deeds of the day, the number of

animals they have killed and of those which escaped, and other incidents of the chase.

Eight days had passed when there arrived a band of Indians. They
had assisted at the siege of Detroit, and came to muster recruits for
that service. I was informed that as I was the only Englishman in the
place, they proposed to kill me, to give their friends a mess of English
broth to raise their courage.

This news was not of the most agreeable kind, and I requested
Wawatam to take me to the Sault de Sainte-Marie, at which place
I knew the Indians were peaceably inclined. M. Cadotte, the interpreter, was married to a Chippewa woman and enjoyed a powerful
influence over their conduct. They considered him their chief, and
he was not only my friend, but a friend to the English.

Wawatam consented at once. Leaving Michilimackinac in the night,
he transported myself and all his lodge to Point Saint-Ignace, on the
opposite side of the strait. Here we remained till daylight, and then
went into the Bay of Boutchitaouy, where we spent three days fishing
and hunting. Leaving the bay, we made for the Isle aux Outardes,
where we were obliged to put in, on account of a shift in the wind.
We proposed sailing for the Sault the next morning.

But, when the morning came, Wawatam's wife complained she
was sick, adding she had had bad dreams, and knew that if we went
to the Sault we should be destroyed. To have argued against the in-
fallibility of dreams would have been extremely unadvisable. I should
have appeared guilty not only of want of faith but also of want of
feeling for the possible calamities of a family which had done so much
for me. I was silent; but the disappointment seemed to seal my fate.

No prospect opened to console me. To return to Michilimackinac
could only ensure my destruction. To remain at the island was to
brave almost equal danger, since it lay in the route along which the
Indians from Detroit were hourly expected to pass on their mission.
I did not doubt that they would take advantage of the solitary situation of the family to carry out their plan to kill me.

I passed all that day on the highest part of a tall tree, from which
the lake on both sides of the island lay open to my view. Here I
might hope to learn the approach of canoes and be warned in time to
conceal myself.

On the second morning, I discovered a white sail coming from
Michilimackinac, much larger than those usually employed by the

Indians. I therefore hoped it might be a Canadian canoe on its voyage to Montreal, and I might be able to prevail upon the crew to take me with them and thus release me from all my troubles.

Descending the tree, I went to the lodge with my tidings and schemes of liberty. The family congratulated me on so fair an opportunity of escape. At this time a boy came into the lodge, informing us the canoe was bound to the Sault de Sainte-Marie. It was manned by three Canadians, and was carrying home Madame Cadotte.

My hopes of going to Montreal being now gone, I resolved on accompanying Madame Cadotte. She cheerfully consented to take me.

I did not leave the lodge without the most grateful sense of the many acts of goodness I had experienced in it, nor without the sincerest respect for the virtues of its members. All the family accompanied me to the beach, and the canoe had no sooner put off than Wawatam commenced an address to the Great Spirit, beseeching him to take care of me, his brother, till we should next meet. We had proceeded too great a distance to hear his voice before Wawatam ceased his prayers.

Being no longer in the society of Indians, I laid aside their dress, putting on that of a Canadian: a blanket coat over my shirt and a handkerchief about my head, hats being very little worn in this country.

On the second morning of our voyage we perceived several canoes behind us. As they approached, we ascertained them to be the fleet bound for Detroit, of which I had been so long in dread. It amounted to twenty sail.

Coming up to us, they surrounded our canoe. An Indian challenged me as an Englishman and his companions supported him, declaring that I looked very like one. I affected not to understand any of the questions which they asked me, and Madame Cadotte assured them that I was a Canadian whom she had brought on his first voyage from Montreal.

The following day saw us safely landed at the Sault, where I experienced a generous welcome from M. Cadotte. There were thirty warriors at this place, restrained from joining in the war only by M. Cadotte's influence.

Here, for five days, I was once more in possession of tranquillity. On the sixth, a young Indian came into M. Cadotte's, saying that a canoe full of warriors had just arrived from Michilimackinac; that they had inquired for me and he believed their intentions to be bad. Nearly at the same time a message came from the good chief of the village, desiring me to conceal myself until he should discover the views and temper of the strangers.

A garret was a second time my place of refuge. It was not long before the Indians came to M. Cadotte's. My friend immediately informed Mutchikiwish, their chief, who was related to his wife, that he had heard they intended mischief against myself. Mutchikiwish frankly acknowledged they had had such a design. But he added that, if displeasing to M. Cadotte, it should be abandoned. He stated that their errand was to raise a party of warriors to return with them to Detroit and it had been their intention to take me with them.

M. Cadotte proceeded to assemble all the chiefs and warriors of the village. These, after deliberating for some time, sent for the strangers, to whom both M. Cadotte and the chief of the village addressed a speech. I was declared to be under the immediate protection of all the chiefs, by whom any harm I might suffer would be avenged. The ambassadors were told that they might go back as they had come—none of the young men of this village were foolish enough to join them.

A moment after, a report was brought that a canoe had just arrived from Niagara. As this was a place from which everyone was anxious to hear news, a message was sent to these fresh strangers, requesting them to come to the council.

The strangers came and were seated. A long silence followed. Finally one of them took up a belt of wampum [6] and addressed the council:

"My friends and brothers, I have come with this belt from our great father, Sir William Johnson.[7] He desired me, as his ambassador, to tell you he is making a great feast at Fort Niagara; his kettles are all ready, his fires lit. He invites you to partake of the feast with your friends, the Six Nations,[8] which have all made peace with the English. He advises you to do the same. Otherwise you cannot fail to be destroyed, for the English are on their march with a great army. Before the fall of the leaf they will be at Michilimackinac, and the Six Nations with them."

This speech greatly alarmed the Indians of the Sault, and after a short consultation they agreed to send deputies to Niagara. This was a project highly interesting to me, since it offered me the means of leaving the country. I suggested this to the chief of the village, and he promised I should accompany them.

It was proposed to set forward on the voyage with very little loss of time. But the occasion was too important not to call for more than human wisdom, and preparations were made for solemnly invoking the GREAT TURTLE.[9]

The first thing to be done was the building of a large wigwam. Within this was placed a tent for the use of the priest and reception of the spirit. Five pillars of five different species of timber about ten feet high were set in a circle about four feet in diameter, and bound together at the top. Over this edifice were spread moose skins. On one side a part was left unfastened to admit the priest.

The ceremonies commenced at the approach of night. To give light within the wigwam several fires were kindled round the tent. Nearly the whole village assembled in the wigwam. It was not long before the priest appeared, almost naked. As he approached the tent the skins were lifted to allow his creeping under them on hands and knees.

His head was scarcely within when the massy edifice began to shake. The skins were no sooner let fall than the sounds of numerous voices were heard beneath them; some yelling, some barking as dogs, some howling like wolves. In this horrible concert were mingled screams and sobs. Articulate speech was also uttered, but in a tongue unknown to the audience.

These confused and frightful noises were followed by silence. Now we heard the voice of a new character in the tent. This was low and feeble, resembling the cry of a puppy. All the Indians clapped their hands for joy, exclaiming that this was the Chief Spirit, the TURTLE, the spirit that never lied! Other voices they had previously hissed, recognizing them to belong to evil spirits.

For half an hour, a succession of songs were heard in different voices. From his entrance till these songs were finished, we heard nothing in the voice of the priest; but now he addressed the multitude, declaring the presence of the GREAT TURTLE and the spirit's readiness to answer questions.

The chief of the village put a large quantity of tobacco into the tent. Then he desired the priest to inquire whether the English were preparing to make war upon the Indians, and whether there were at Fort Niagara a large number of English troops.

These questions having been put by the priest, the tent shook violently. A terrific cry announced the departure of the TURTLE.

A quarter of an hour elapsed in silence. Then the voice of the spirit was again heard. The language of the GREAT TURTLE was unintelligible to every ear except that of his priest.

The spirit, we were now informed by the priest, had during his short absence crossed Lake Huron and proceeded as far as Fort Niagara, at the head of Lake Ontario, and thence to Montreal. At Fort Niagara, he had seen no great number of soldiers. But, on descending the Saint Lawrence, he had found the river covered with boats filled with soldiers in number like the leaves of the trees. They were coming to make war upon the Indians.

The chief had a third question. "If the Indians visit Sir William Johnson, will they be received as friends?"

"Sir William Johnson," said the spirit (and after the spirit, the priest), "will fill their canoes with presents—with blankets, kettles, guns, gunpowder and shot, and large barrels of rum."

At this there was a clapping of hands. A hundred voices exclaimed, "I will go, too! I will go, too!"

Individuals were now permitted to inquire about their absent friends and the fate of the sick. I observed the answers allowed of much latitude of interpretation.

I yielded to the promptings of my own anxiety for the future. Having made my offering of tobacco, I inquired whether I should ever revisit my native country. The tent shook as usual, after which I received this answer:

"Take courage and fear no danger, for nothing will happen to hurt you. You will reach your friends and country in safety."

I was so grateful I presented an extra offering of tobacco.

On the 10th of June, I embarked with the Indian deputation of sixteen men. The wind blowing very hard, we put ashore at Point aux Grondines. While the Indians erected a hut, I made a fire. As I was gathering wood, an unusual sound caught my attention. I cast my eyes on the ground and discovered a rattlesnake two feet from my naked legs. The reptile was coiled, its head raised considerably above its body.

I hastened to the canoe to procure my gun, but the Indians begged me to desist. They followed me to the spot with their pipes and tobacco pouches in their hands. I found the snake still coiled.

The Indians surrounded it. All addressed it by turns, calling it their "grandfather," but keeping at some distance. They filled their pipes, and now each blew the smoke toward the snake, who appeared to receive it with pleasure. After remaining coiled and receiving incense for half an hour, it stretched itself along the ground in visible good humor. At last it moved slowly away. The Indians followed it, beseeching it to take care of their families during their absence and to open the heart of Sir William Johnson, so that he might fill their canoe with rum.

Early the next morning we proceeded. Soon the wind increased and the Indians, alarmed, frequently called on the rattlesnake to come to their assistance. The waves grew high and it blew a hurricane; we expected every moment to be swallowed up. One of the chiefs took a dog and, tying its forelegs, threw it overboard, calling on the snake to preserve us and satisfy its hunger with the dog. But the wind still increased. Another chief sacrificed another dog, with some tobacco, beseeching the snake not to avenge upon the Indians the insult he had received from myself. He assured the snake I was absolutely an Englishman, and of kin neither to him nor to them.

An Indian observed that if we were drowned it would be for my fault alone, and I ought myself to be sacrificed to appease the angry manito; nor was I without fear that if the situation became worse this would be my fate. Happily for me, the storm at length abated.

On the 18th of June we crossed Lake Aux Claies, which appeared to be upward of twenty miles in length. At its further end we came to the carrying place of Toronto. Here the Indians obliged me to carry a burden of more than a hundred pounds weight. The day was very hot and the woods and marshes abounded with mosquitoes; but the Indians walked at a quick pace, and I could by no means see myself being left behind. The whole country was a thick forest, through which our only road was a footpath, or what is termed in America an *Indian path*.

Next morning at ten o'clock we reached the shore of Lake Ontario. Here we were busy two days making canoes out of the bark of the elm tree, in which we were to transport ourselves to Niagara. For this purpose the Indians first cut down a tree, made a lengthwise incision, and then stripped off the bark in one entire sheet about eighteen feet in length. Next the Indians closed its ends by sewing the bark together. After a few ribs and bars had been introduced, the architecture was finished. In this manner we made two canoes, of which one carried eight men and the other nine.

On the 21st, we encamped in the evening four miles short of Fort Niagara, which the Indians would not approach till morning.

At dawn the Indians were awake and presently assembled in council, still doubtful as to the fate they were to encounter. I assured them of the most friendly welcome. At length, after painting themselves with the most lively colors, in token of their peaceable views, and after singing the song they use on going into danger, they embarked and made for the north side of the strait of Niagara; the fort is on the south. A few minutes after, I crossed over to the fort. Here I was received by Sir William Johnson in a manner for which I have ever been gratefully attached to his person and memory.

# An Inch of Ground to Fight On

## MAJOR MOSES VAN CAMPEN

MOSES VAN CAMPEN was past eighty in 1838, when he sent
Congress a petition for a pension, accompanied, we are told, by the
memoir that follows. In it he recounts the main facts of his seven
years' service in the War of the Revolution—including his two cap-
tures by the Indians, the murder of his father and brother, and the
grisly revenge he took with tomahawk and scalping knife on their
slayers. The old warrior's petition was granted—but not before he had
furnished more prosaic proof for his claim than this extraordinary
story of valor and hardship.

Van Campen was born in New Jersey in 1757, the son of a farmer.
Soon afterward the family moved to Pennsylvania, settling on Fishing
Creek. Here young Van Campen was "nurtured in the school of the
rifle and tomahawk," as he was fond of saying in later years. Indians,
then friendly, were among his teachers.

In 1775 the clouds of war glowed red on the frontier. The Iroquois
in New York and many of the western tribes, in the pay of the British,
became a serious menace to the border settlements. Van Campen took
an active part in organizing and drilling a militia company near his
home. The patriots worked hard to perfect themselves in traditional
European methods of warfare and in Indian methods as well. Often

*their target was a life-size figure of an Indian, chalked out on a tree,
at which the militiamen would throw the hatchet, aiming at a point
between the eyes. A nail in a tree was an excellent practice target for
marksmen who would later be aiming at the buttons of red coats.
In 1777 Van Campen began his active duty as an orderly sergeant
in a militia regiment defending the Pennsylvania frontier. He served
until 1783.*

*After the war Van Campen married a daughter of the Widow
M'Clure, near whose house he had built a fort in '81. For a while
he managed the M'Clure estate. Then he moved to New York, settling
in the town of Angelica, in Allegany County. Here he worked as a
land surveyor and became in time a judge and county treasurer.*

*Van Campen was often visited by Indians from nearby Caneadea
Reservation, on the Genesee, who were curious to see this doughty
enemy of former times. One of them was Chief John Mohawk, who
called and paid his respects almost fifty years after Van Campen had
tomahawked him. Van Campen did not recognize him until the old
Indian permitted him to run his hand along the copper-colored shoulder under the clothing. "Yes," said Van Campen, "you are John
Mohawk—that's my mark."*

*Van Campen outlived most of his contemporaries, to become a
revered and, as the years went by, an increasingly lonely figure at
patriotic celebrations. A portrait of him, made at age ninety, shows
a very old but still alert and forceful face: nose massive, chin strong,
eyes bright and piercing. He died in 1849.*

My first service was in the year 1777, when I served three months
under Colonel John Kelly, who stationed us at Big Isle, on the West
Branch of the Susquehanna. In March, 1778, I was appointed lieutenant of a company of six-months' men. Shortly afterward, I was ordered by Colonel Samuel Hunter to proceed with about twenty men
to Fishing Creek, which empties into the North Branch of the Susquehanna about twenty miles from Northumberland, to build a fort about
three miles from its mouth, for the reception of the inhabitants in
case of an alarm from the Indians.

In May, when my fort was nearly completed, our spies discovered
a large party of Indians making their way towards it. The neighboring
residents had barely time to flee to the fort for protection, leaving
their goods behind. The Indians soon made their appearance. Having

plundered and burnt the houses, they attacked the fort, and kept a steady fire upon us during the day. At night they withdrew, burning and destroying everything in their route. What loss they sustained we could not ascertain, as they carried off all the dead and wounded. From the marks of blood on the ground it must have been considerable.

The inhabitants that took shelter in the fort had built a yard for their cattle at the head of a small flat a short distance from the fort. One evening in June, just as they were milking them, my sentinel called my attention to some movement in the brush. I soon discovered Indians making their way to the cattle yard.

There was no time to be lost. I immediately selected ten of my sharpshooters and, under cover of a rise of land, got between the milkers and the Indians. On ascending the ridge we found ourselves within pistol shot of them. I fired first and killed the leader. The Indians ran off at once, and a volley from my men did no further execution. In the meantime the milk pails flew in every direction, and the best runner got to the fort first.

As the season advanced, Indian hostilities increased. Notwithstanding the vigilance of our scouting parties, which were constantly out, houses were burnt and families murdered.

In the summer of 1778 the great massacre of Wyoming occurred.[1] After this the governors of Connecticut, New York and Pennsylvania petitioned Congress to adopt speedy measures for the protection of the western frontier. The subject was referred to a committee of Congress and General Washington. The committee recommended that the war should be carried into the enemy's country and a company of rangers raised for the defense of the frontier.

In 1779 General Sullivan was sent with an army into their country. The provisions for the supply of the army were purchased in the settlements along the waters of the Susquehanna and deposited in storehouses. I was appointed, under the title of quartermaster, to superintend this business. About the middle of July, by means of boats, I had collected all the provisions at Wyoming, where General Sullivan and his army were waiting for them.

About the last of July our army moved toward Tioga Point, while a fleet of boats ascended the river parallel with the army. We reached Tioga Point early in August. Here we halted for General Clinton to join us with his brigade, which came by way of the Mohawk River, and so into Lake Oswego.

During this time the Indians were collecting in considerable force at Chemung, a large Indian village about eleven miles distant. As they became very troublesome neighbors, General Clinton contemplated an attack upon them, but wished to ascertain their numbers and situation, and selected me for that dangerous enterprise. I prepared myself an Indian dress—breechcloth, leggings, and moccasins. My cap had a good supply of feathers and I was painted in Indian style. I set off with one man, dressed in the same manner.

We left the camp after dark and proceeded with much caution until we came to the Chemung, which we supposed would be strongly guarded. We ascended the mountain, crossed over it and came in view of their fires.

Having descended the mountain, we waited quietly until they lay down and got to sleep. We then walked around their camp and counted the fires and the number of Indians at some of the fires, thus forming an estimate of their number, which I took to be about six or seven hundred. Then we returned.

After making my report to the general early next morning, I went to my tent, spread my blanket, and had a refreshing sleep. In the afternoon Major Adam Hoopes, one of the general's aides, requested me to wait upon the general. I obeyed. The latter requested, as I had learnt the way to Chemung, that I would lead the advance guard. He had selected General Edward Hand, of the Pennsylvania line, to make them a visit with eleven hundred men. I accepted the service and we took up our line of march after sundown.

When we came to the Narrows I halted, according to order, until the main body came up. Then the general ordered us to enter the Narrows, observing, "Soldiers, cut your way through." We did so and entered the Indian village and camp at daybreak, but found that the birds had flown. We halted a few minutes for our men to refresh, set fire to their village and, having discovered from their trail that they had gone up the river, followed it about two miles.

Here our path lay up a narrow ridge called Hogback Hill, which we remarked seemed formed by nature for an Indian ambuscade. Accordingly, every eye was fixed on the hill.

As we began to ascend, we saw the bushes tremble. Immediately rifles were pointed at us and we received a deadly fire, by which sixteen or seventeen of the advance guard were killed or wounded.

We that were unhurt sprang under cover of the bank and for a moment held our fire. Six or seven stout fellows rushed out with tomahawk and knife to kill and scalp our comrades. It was now our turn to fire. Every shot accounted for one.

General Hand now came on at quick step, advanced within fifteen or twenty yards of them, and ordered his men to fire and then charge them at the point of the bayonet. They were soon routed and put to flight. We returned with our dead and wounded the same night to our former camp.

We had no further opportunity of coming to a brush with them until we were joined by our whole force under General Clinton. We were opposed by the enemy's whole force, consisting of Indians, British and Tories, to whom we gave battle a little below Newtown Point [Elmira, New York]. Our loss was trifling.

On the return of the army I was taken with camp fever and was removed to the fort I had built in '78, where my father was living. In the course of the winter I recovered my health.

My father's house had been burnt in '78 by the party which attacked the fort, and he requested me to go with him and a younger brother to our farm, about four miles distant, to make preparations for building another and raising some grain. Very little fear was entertained of trouble from the Indians this season, as they had been so completely routed the year before. We left the fort about the last of March, accompanied by my uncle and his son, about twelve years old, and one Peter Pence.

We had been on our farms about four or five days when, on the morning of the 30th of March, we were surprised by a party of ten Indians. My father was lunged through with a war spear, his throat was cut and he was scalped, while my brother was tomahawked, scalped, and thrown into the fire before my eyes.

While I was struggling with a warrior, the fellow who had killed my father drew his spear from his body and made a violent thrust at me. I shrank from the spear and the savage who had hold of me turned it with his hand so that it only penetrated my vest and shirt. They were then satisfied with taking me prisoner, as they had the same morning taken my uncle's little son and Pence, though they had killed my uncle. The same party, before they reached us, had touched on the lower settlements of Wyoming and killed a Mr. Upson and taken a boy prisoner of the name of Rogers.

We were now marched off up Fishing Creek. In the afternoon of the same day we came to Huntingdon, where the Indians found four white men at a sugar camp. Fortunately they discovered the Indians and fled to a house; the Indians only fired on them and wounded a Captain Ransom.

The Indians continued their course till night, when they encamped and made their fire. We, the prisoners, were tied and well secured, five Indians lying on one side of us and five on the other.

In the morning they pursued their course and touched the head-waters of Hemlock Creek. Here they found one Abraham Pike, his wife and child. Pike was made prisoner, but they painted his wife and child and told her, *"Joggo, squaw"*—"Go home." They continued their course that day, and encamped the same night in the same manner as the previous.

It came into my mind that sometimes individuals performed wonderful actions and surmounted the greatest dangers. I then decided that these fellows must die and thought of the plan to kill them.

The next day I had an opportunity to communicate my plan to my fellow-prisoners. They treated it as a visionary scheme for three men to attempt to kill ten Indians. I spread before them the advantages that three men would have over ten when asleep. I said that we would be the first prisoners that would be taken into their towns and villages after our army had destroyed their corn, and that we should be tied to the stake and suffer a cruel death; however, we had now an inch of ground to fight on, and if we failed it would only be death, and we might as well die one way as another.

That day passed away and, having encamped for the night, we lay as before. In the morning we came to the river and saw their canoes, which they had descended the river in and then run upon Little Tunkhannock Creek, so called. We crossed the river and they set their canoes adrift.

I renewed my suggestion to my companions to slay the Indians that night, and urged they must decide the question. They agreed to make the trial.

"But how shall we do it?" was their question.

"Disarm them. Then let each of us take a tomahawk and come to close work at once. There are three of us. If we plant our blows with judgment, three times three will make nine, and the tenth one we can kill at our leisure."

They agreed to disarm them and, after that, one of us would take possession of the guns and fire at the one side, and the other two take tomahawks on the other side and slay them. I observed that would be a very uncertain way; the first shot fired would give the alarm, and they might defeat us. But in the end I had to yield to their plan. Peter Pence was chosen to fire the guns, Pike and myself to tomahawk.

That night we cut and carried plenty of wood to give the Indians a good fire. Then we were tied and laid in our places. After I was laid down, one of the savages had occasion to use his knife. He dropped it at my feet. I turned my foot over it and concealed it. Finally they all lay down and fell asleep.

About midnight I got up and found them in sound sleep. I slipped to Pence, who rose. I cut him loose and handed him the knife. He did the same for me, and I in turn took the knife and cut Pike loose. In a minute's time we disarmed them.

Pence took his station at the guns. Pike and myself, with our tomahawks, took our stations; I was to tomahawk three on the right wing, and Pike two on the left.

That moment Pike's two awoke and were about to get up. Here Pike proved a coward. He lay down.

It was a critical moment. I saw there was no time to be lost. Their heads turned up fair. I killed them in a moment, and turned to my lot as per agreement. As I was about to strike the last on my side of the fire, Pence shot and did good execution.

There was only one at the off-wing that Pence's ball did not reach; his name was Mohawk, a stout, bold, daring fellow. In the alarm he jumped off about fifteen yards from the fire. He saw it was the prisoners that made the attack and, giving the war whoop, he darted to take possession of the guns. I was as quick to prevent him. The contest was then between him and myself. I raised my tomahawk, but he turned quickly and jumped from me.

I followed him and struck at him. But, missing his head, my tomahawk struck his shoulder, or rather the back of his neck. He pitched forward and fell. At the same time my foot slipped and I fell by his side. We clinched; he caught me around my neck, while I caught him with my left arm around the body and gave him a close hug. At the same time I felt for his knife but could not reach it.

In our scuffle my tomahawk dropped out of his shoulder. My head was under the wounded shoulder and I was almost suffocated with his blood. I made a violent spring and broke from his hold. We both rose at the same time and he ran. It took me some time to clear the blood from my eyes. My tomahawk got covered up and I could not find it in time to overtake him. He was the only one of the party that escaped.[2]

Pike had been powerless throughout the assault. Now I saw that he was trying to pray and Pence was swearing at him, charging him with cowardice and saying he ought to have fought. We were masters of the ground, and in possession of all their guns, blankets, coats, etc.

I turned my attention to scalping the Indians. Recovering the scalps of my father, brother and others, I strung them all on my belt for safekeeping.[3]

We remained there till morning. Then we built a raft, as our camp was near the bank of the river, about fifteen miles below Tioga Point. We got all our plunder on it and set sail for Wyoming, the nearest settlement.

Before long our raft began to give way and we made for land. We lost considerable property, though we saved our guns and ammunition. Traveling on land, we reached Wyalusing late in the afternoon. At the narrows we discovered smoke below and a raft lying at the shore. We were certain that a party of Indians had passed us in the course of the day and had halted for the night.

There was no alternative for us but to fight them or go over the hill. The snow on the north side was deep; on the other hand, we knew from the appearance of the raft that the party must be small, and we had two rifles each. My only fear was of Pike's cowardice.

To know the worst, we agreed that I should ascertain their number and give the signal for the attack. I crept down the side of the hill and came so near as to see their fires and packs, but saw no Indians. I concluded they had gone hunting for meat, and that this was a good opportunity for us to make off with their raft to the opposite side of the river.

I gave the signal. My comrades came and threw their packs on to the raft, which was made of small, dry pine timber. With poles and paddles we drove her briskly across the river, and had got nearly out of reach of shot when two of the Indians came in. They fired, but their shots did no injury, and we soon got under cover of an island and went several miles.

We had waded deep creeks through the day, and the night was cold. We landed on an island and found a sinkhole in which we made a fire. After warming ourselves, we were alarmed by a cracking in the crust of the snow.

Pike supposed the Indians had got on to the island, and was for calling for quarter. To keep him quiet, we threatened him with death.

The stepping grew plainer and seemed coming directly to the fire. I kept watch and soon a noble raccoon came under the light. I shot it.

Pike jumped up. "Quarter, gentlemen—quarter, gentlemen!" he called out.

I took my game by the leg and threw it down to the fire.

"Here, you cowardly rascal," I cried, "skin that and give us a roast for supper."

The next night we reached Wyoming. There was much joy to see us. We rested one day and, as it was not safe to go to Northumberland by land, we procured a canoe and with Pence and my little cousin we descended the river by night. Before day we came to Fort Jenkins, where I found Colonel Kelly and about one hundred men encamped outside the fort.

Colonel Kelly informed me that he had buried my father and uncle as well as my brother, who was so burnt that a small part of him only was to be found. He likewise informed me that my mother and her children were in the fort and it was thought that I also had been killed. Colonel Kelly then went into the fort to prepare her mind to see me. I took off my belt of scalps and handed them to an officer to keep.

Human nature was not sufficient to stand the interview. She had just lost a husband and a son, and one had returned to take her by the hand—one, too, that she supposed was killed.

The day after, I went to Sunbury, where I was received with joy. My scalps were exhibited, the cannons were fired, etc. Before my return a commission had been sent me as ensign of a company to be commanded by Captain Thomas Robinson. This was, as I understood, a part of the quota which Pennsylvania had to raise for the Continental line.

The summer of 1780 was spent in the recruiting service; our company was organized and was retained for the defense of the frontier. In February, 1781, I was promoted to a lieutenancy, and entered upon the active duty of an officer by heading scouting expeditions. As Captain Robinson was no woodsman or marksman, he preferred that I should encounter the danger and head the scouting parties. We kept up a constant chain of them around the frontier settlements, from the North to the West Branch of the Susquehanna. In the spring of 1781 we built a fort on the widow M'Clure's plantation, called M'Clure's fort, where our provisions were stored.

In the summer of 1781 a man was taken prisoner in Buffalo Valley, but made his escape. He came in and reported there were about three hundred Indians on Sinnemahoning, hunting and laying in a store of provisions, and that they would divide into small parties and attack the whole chain of the frontier at the same time, on the same day. Colonel Samuel Hunter selected a company of five, including myself, to reconnoiter.

We carried with us three weeks' provisions, and proceeded up the West Branch with much caution and care. Reaching the Sinnemahoning, we made no discovery except old tracks. Then we marched up the Sinnemahoning so far that we were satisfied it was a false report, and we turned back. A little below the Sinnemahoning, near night, we saw smoke. We discovered there was a large party of Indians, how many we could not tell, but we determined to attack them.

As soon as it was dark we primed our rifles, sharpened our flints, and examined our tomahawk handles. All was now ready, and we waited with great impatience till they lay down. The time came, and with the utmost silence we advanced, trailing our rifles in one hand and the tomahawk in the other.

The night was warm. We found some of them rolled in their blankets five or ten yards from their fires. Having got amongst them, we first handled our tomahawks. They rose like a dark cloud. We now fired our shots and raised the war yell. They took to flight in the utmost confusion, few taking time to pick up their rifles. We were masters of the ground and all their plunder, and took several scalps.

It was a party of twenty-five or thirty, who had been as low down as Penn's Creek and had killed and scalped two or three families. We found several scalps of different ages which they had taken, and a large quantity of domestic cloth, which was carried to Northumberland and given to the distressed who had escaped the tomahawk and knife.

In the latter part of March, at the opening of the campaign in 1782, we were ordered by Congress to our respective stations. I marched Robinson's company to Northumberland, where Mr. Thomas Chambers joined us, who had been recently commissioned as an ensign of our company. We halted at Northumberland two or three days for our men to wash and rest; from here Ensign Chambers and myself were ordered to Muncy, Samuel Wallis's plantation, to rebuild Fort Muncy, which had been destroyed by the enemy. We reached that station and built a small blockhouse for the storage of our provisions.

About the 10th or 11th of April, Captain Robinson arrived with four gentlemen. I was ordered to select twenty or twenty-five men with these gentlemen, and to proceed to Bald Eagle Creek, to the place where a Mr. Culbertson had been killed by Indians.

On the 15th of April we reached the place and encamped for the night. In the morning we were attacked by eighty-five Indians. It was a hard-fought battle. Three of our men made their escape; I think we had nine killed and the rest of us were made prisoners.

We were stripped of all our clothing excepting our pantaloons. When they took off my shirt they discovered my commission; our commissions were written on parchment and carried in a silk case hung with a ribbon in our bosom. Several got a hold of it, and one fellow cut the ribbon with his knife and succeeded in obtaining it.

They took us a little distance from the battleground and made us sit down in a small ring. The Indians formed another around us in close order, each with his rifle and tomahawk in his hand. Then they brought up five Indians we had killed, and laid them within their circle. Each of us reflected for himself that our time would probably be short. As for myself, I looked back upon the year '80 and the party of Indians I had killed, and thought that if I was discovered to be the person responsible, my case would be a hard one.

Their prophet or chief warrior made a speech. I was informed afterwards by the British lieutenant who belonged to the party that he was consulting the Great Spirit about what to do with the prisoners —whether to kill us on the spot or spare our lives. He came to the conclusion that there had been blood enough shed; as to the men they had lost, it was the fate of war, and we must be taken and adopted into the families of those whom we had killed.

We were then divided amongst them. Packs were prepared for us, and we crossed the river in bark canoes. We then made our way to the waters of the Genesee River. After two days' travel down the Genesee we came to a place called the Pigeon Woods, where a great number of Indian families had come to catch young pigeons.

Here we met a party of about forty warriors on their way to the frontier settlements. They encamped some little distance apart and the warriors of the two parties held a council at our camp. I soon perceived that I was the subject of their conversation. I was seized and dragged to the other camp, where the warriors were sitting on one side of a large fire. I was seated alone on the opposite side.

Every eye was fixed upon me. I perceived they were gathering around in great numbers. In a short time a man pressed through the crowd. He came to me and sat down. I saw he was a white man, painted and in Indian dress. He examined me on the situation of the frontiers, the strength of our forts, the range of our scouting parties, etc.

After he got through, he observed that there was only one besides himself there that knew me.

"Do you know me, sir?" said I.

"I do. You are the man that killed the Indians."

I thought of the fire and the stake. But he said that he was a prisoner and a friend. He told me that his name was Jones,[4] and he had been taken prisoner in the spring of '81 in Bedford County. He said that he would not expose me, and if I could pass through undiscovered and be delivered up to the British, I would be safe; if not, I would have to die at the stake.

The next morning we moved down the river. Two days afterwards we came to the Caneadea village, the first on the Genesee River, where we were prepared to run the Indian gauntlet. The warriors don't whip—it is the young Indians and squaws. They meet you in sight of their council house, where they select the prisoners from the ranks of the warriors, bring them in front and, when ready, the word *joggo* is given. The prisoners start, the whippers follow after, and if they outrun you, you will be severely beaten.

I was placed in front of my men. The word was given and we started.

Being young and full of verve, I led the way. Two young squaws came running up to join the whipping party and, when they saw us start, they halted and stood shoulder to shoulder with their whips. When I came near them I bounded and kicked them over. We all came down together. There was considerable kicking amongst us, so much so that they showed their underdress, which appeared to be of a beautiful yellow color. I had not time to help them up.

It was truly diverting to the warriors. They yelled and shouted till they made the air ring.

We halted at that village for one day and then went to Fort Niagara, where I was delivered up to the British. I was adopted, according to the Indian custom, into the family of Colonel Butler,[5] then the commander of the British and Indians there. I was to take the place of his son, Captain Butler, who was killed late in the fall of 1781 by the Americans. As his adopted son I was confined to a private room and not put under a British guard.

My troubles soon began. The Indians were informed by the Tories that knew me that I had been a prisoner before and had killed my captors. The Indians were outraged. They went to Butler and demanded me, offering to bring in fourteen prisoners in my place.

Butler sent an officer to examine me on the subject. He came and informed me of the heavy accusations their Indians had made against me and said that his colonel wished to know the facts.

I observed, "Sir, it is a serious question to answer. I will never deny the truth. I have been a prisoner before and killed the party that took me, and returned to the service of my country. But, sir, I consider myself a prisoner of war of the British, and I presume you will have more honor than to deliver me up to the savages. I know what my fate would be. And please to inform your colonel that we have it in our power to retaliate."

He left me. In a short time he returned and stated that there was no alternative for me to save my life but to abandon the rebel cause and join the British standard; that I should take the same rank in the British service as I had in the rebel service.

I replied, "No, sir, no. Give me the stake, the tomahawk, or the knife before a British commission. Liberty or death is our motto."

Some time after, a lady came to my room with whom I had been well acquainted before the Revolution—we had been schoolmates. She was then married to a British officer, a captain of the Queen's

Rangers, and he came with her. She said that she had been to Colonel Butler, and she was authorized to make me the same offer as the officer had done.

I thanked her for the trouble she had taken for my safety, but told her that I could not accept the offer. She observed how much more honorable it would be to be an officer in the British service. I observed that I could not dispose of myself in that way; I belonged to the Congress of the United States and I would abide the consequences.

She left me, and that was the last I heard of it. A guard was set at the door of my apartment.

In about four days I was sent down Lake Ontario to a place called Carleton Island, and from there down the St. Lawrence to Montreal, where I was placed in prison, and found forty or fifty of our American officers. Here we had the honor to look through the iron grates.

The Fourth of July was drawing near. Ten of us combined to celebrate the political birthday of our country. We found ways and means to have some brandy conveyed in to us unknown to the British guard, and we had a high day, after making a compromise with the guard.

But it was highly offensive to the British officers. We ten were taken out and sent to Quebec, and then down the St. Lawrence and put on the Isle of Orleans, where we remained until the last of September. A British fleet sailed about that time for New York and we were put on board. When we came to New York there was no exchange for us. General Carleton, who commanded the British army at New York, paroled us to return home.

In the month of March, 1783, I was exchanged, and had orders to take up arms again. I joined my company in March at Northumberland. About that time Captain Robinson received orders to march his company to Wyoming to keep garrison at Wilkes-Barre Fort. He sent myself and Ensign Chambers with the company to that station, where we stayed till November, 1783. Our army was then discharged, and our company likewise. Poor and penniless, we retired to the shades of private life.[6]

# That Is Your Great Captain

## DR. JOHN KNIGHT

I T IS with the greatest sorrow and concern," General George Washington wrote on July 27, 1782, "that I learned the melancholy tidings of Colonel Crawford's death. He was known to me as an officer of much care and prudence; brave, experienced, and active. The manner of his death was shocking to me." It was shocking, indeed, to everyone who learned the gruesome particulars—but to none more than Dr. John Knight, who was obliged by his Indian captors to watch Crawford's slow, painful death.

William Crawford, like his friend Washington, was born in Virginia. He had been an officer in the French and Indian War, in Pontiac's war, and in the Revolution, in which he commanded the Seventh Virginia Regiment. In 1781 he retired to private life. When Virginia and Pennsylvania decided to send a militia expedition to punish the Ohio Indians, who had been raiding the American settlements, this old soldier and frontier fighter seemed a natural choice to lead it.

For the militia, the expedition promised to be short and relatively painless. They planned a surprise attack—a quick victory, perhaps with plunder—and then back to their farms. But the citizen soldiers were poorly trained and undisciplined, and when the moment of their test came they fled in terror. The Wyandots (or Hurons) of San-

119

*dusky, four hundred strong, had been reinforced by four hundred Delawares and Shawnees. In addition, a company of Butler's Rangers, led by Captain Matthew Elliott, had come from the British stronghold of Detroit.*

*About seventy of the militia, including Colonel Crawford, never came home. Two who had been destined, like him, to die at the stake, made miraculous escapes: Dr. Knight and the scout John Slover. Hugh H. Brackenridge, a Pittsburgh lawyer and man of letters, interviewed them soon afterward and got their stories, Knight writing his own at Brackenridge's request. They were published in 1783 in Philadelphia under the title* Narratives of a Late Expedition Against the Indians.

*John Knight was a Virginian. Early in the Revolution he served as a private in Colonel Crawford's regiment. Later he was stationed at Fort Pitt, where he learned medicine as an apprentice to the surgeon of the regiment. He was serving there when Colonel Crawford asked him to accompany the expedition as surgeon. After his escape, Knight returned to his post at Fort Pitt and was discharged soon afterward. He married Crawford's niece and settled in Shelbyville, Kentucky, where he raised a large family. He died in 1838.*

About the end of March or the beginning of April, 1782, the western Indians began to raid the frontiers of Ohio, Washington, Youghogany and Westmoreland counties. This has been their constant practice ever since the war began between the United States and Great Britain.

As a result, the principal officers of these counties, Colonels Williamson and Marshall, tried every method in their power to organize an expedition against the Wyandot towns. They were able to succeed only by giving all possible encouragement to volunteers. The plan proposed was as follows: Every man furnishing himself with a horse, a gun, and one month's provisions should be exempted from two tours of militia duty. Likewise everyone who had been plundered by the Indians should have the plunder again if it could be found at their towns.

The time appointed for the rendezvous or general meeting of the volunteers was the twentieth of May, and the place the old Mingo town on the west side of the river Ohio, about forty miles below Fort Pitt.

Colonel Crawford was asked by these western counties and districts to command the expedition. He set out as a volunteer and came to Fort Pitt two days before the time appointed for the assembling of the men. As there was no surgeon appointed to go with the expedition, Colonel Crawford begged General Irvine to permit me to accompany him. (My consent had been previously asked.) The general agreed.

I left Fort Pitt on Tuesday, May 21, and arrived at the Mingo town the next day. On Friday, the twenty-fourth, the volunteers distributed themselves into eighteen companies, choosing their captains by vote. There were chosen also one colonel commandant, four field majors and one brigade-major. There were four hundred and sixty-five who voted.

We began our march on Saturday, May 25, heading almost due west. Tuesday, the twenty-eighth, in the evening, Major Brenton and Captain Bean went some distance from the camp to reconnoiter. Having gone about one-quarter of a mile, they saw two Indians, upon whom they fired, and then returned to camp. This was the first place in which we were discovered, as we understood afterwards.

On Tuesday, the fourth of June, we came to the spot where the Indian town of Sandusky had formerly stood, but found the inhabitants had moved away. Neither our guides nor any who were with us had known anything of their removal. We began to conjecture there were no Indian towns nearer than the lower Sandusky, at least forty miles away.

However, after refreshing our horses, we advanced in search of their settlements. We had scarcely gone three or four miles when a number of our men expressed their desire to return, some of them alleging that they had only five days' provisions. The field officers and captains held a council. They determined to proceed that afternoon and no longer.

Earlier, a small party of light cavalry had been sent forward to reconnoiter. Just as the council ended, a messenger returned from this party with word that they had seen a large body of Indians running towards them. In a short time the rest of the cavalry joined us. Having gone one mile further, we met a number of Indians who had partly got possession of a piece of woods before us. But our men alighted from their horses and, rushing into the woods, soon obliged them to abandon that place.

By this time the enemy had been reinforced. They flanked to the right. Part of them came up in our rear and quickly made the action more serious. The firing continued very warm on both sides from four o'clock until dusk. Each party held their ground.

Next morning, about six o'clock, some guns were discharged at two or three hundred yards. This continued till day, doing little or no execution on either side. The field officers assembled and agreed to retreat that night as the enemy were increasing every moment and we already had a number wounded. The whole body was to form into three lines, keeping the wounded in the center. We had four killed and twenty-three wounded, seven very dangerously, on which account as many biers were got ready to carry them. Most of the rest were slightly wounded, and none so bad but they could ride on horseback.

After dark the officers went to the outposts and brought in all the men there as expeditiously as they could. Just as the troops were about to form, several guns were fired by the enemy. Some of our men spoke out and said our intention was discovered by the Indians, who were firing alarm guns. Upon this, some in front hurried off and the rest immediately followed, leaving the seven men that were dangerously wounded. Some of these, however, got off on horseback with the help of good friends.

We had not got a quarter of a mile from the field of action when I heard Colonel Crawford calling for his son John Crawford, his son-in-law Major Harrison, Major Rose and William Crawford, his nephews. I came up and told him I believed they were in front.

He asked, "Is that the doctor?"

I told him it was.

"They are not in front," he replied, and begged me not to leave him.

I promised him I would not. We then waited and continued calling for these men till the troops had passed us.

The colonel told me his horse had almost given out, that he could not keep up with the troops, and wished some of his best friends to remain with him. He then exclaimed against the militia for riding off in such an irregular manner and leaving some of the wounded behind, contrary to his orders. Presently two men came riding after us, one of them an old man, the other a lad. We inquired if they had seen any of the above persons, and they answered they had not.

By this time there was very hot firing before us near where our main body must have been. We changed our course, then nearly southwest, and went north about two miles. The two men remained with us. Judging ourselves now out of the enemy's lines, we took a due east course, taking care to keep fifteen or twenty yards apart and directing ourselves by the North Star.

The old man often lagged behind and, when this was the case, never failed to call for us to halt for him. When we were near the Sandusky Creek he fell one hundred yards behind and bawled out as usual for us to halt. While we were preparing to reprimand him for making a noise, I heard an Indian halloo, as I thought, one hundred and fifty yards from the man and partly behind him. After this we did not hear the man call again, neither did he ever come up to us any more. It was now past midnight.

About daybreak Colonel Crawford's and the young man's horses gave out and they left them. We pursued our journey eastward, and about two o'clock fell in with Captain Biggs. He had brought Lieutenant Ashley, who had been dangerously wounded, from the field of action.

We went on for about an hour. A heavy rain came on. We decided it was best to encamp, since we had the wounded officer to look after. We stripped the bark off four or five trees, made a shelter and a fire, and remained there all night.

Next morning we continued our journey. After we had gone about three miles, we found a deer which had been killed recently. The meat was sliced from the bones and bundled up in the skin, with a tomahawk lying by it. We took all this with us and, about one mile further, saw the smoke of a fire. We gave the wounded officer into the charge of the young man and asked him to stay behind whilst the colonel, the captain, and myself walked up as cautiously as we could towards the fire.

When we came to it, we found no one. We decided, from several circumstances, that some of our people had encamped there the preceding night. Then we went about roasting the venison. When we were just about to march, we saw one of our men coming up on our tracks. At first he seemed very shy, but after we called to him he came up. He told us he was the person who had killed the deer, but when he heard us come up he was afraid we were Indians and he hid in a thicket and ran away. We gave him some bread and roasted venison and then we all proceeded on our journey.

About two o'clock we came to the road along which our expedition had come. Captain Biggs and myself did not think it safe to stay on it, but the colonel said the Indians would not follow the troops farther than the plains, which we were then considerably past. As the wounded officer was riding Captain Biggs' horse I lent the captain mine. The colonel and myself went about one hundred yards in front, the captain and the wounded officer in the center, and the two young men behind.

After we had traveled about one mile and a half, several Indians sprang up within fifteen or twenty steps of the colonel and me. At first we saw only three, and I immediately got behind a large black oak and made my gun ready. I was raising it to take sight when the colonel called to me twice not to fire. Then one of the Indians ran up to the colonel and took him by the hand.

Next, the colonel told me to put down my gun, which I did. At that instant one of the Indians whom I had seen very often in the past came up to me. He called me "Doctor," and took me by the hand. They were Delaware Indians.

Captain Biggs fired amongst them but missed. They told us to call our people and make them come there, or else they would go and kill them. The colonel obeyed, but our four comrades had escaped. The colonel and I were then taken to the Indian camp, which was about half a mile away.

On Sunday evening five Delawares who had posted themselves some distance further on the road brought back Captain Biggs' and Lieutenant Ashley's scalps, with an Indian scalp which Captain Biggs had taken in the field of action. They also brought in Biggs' horse and mine. They told us the two other men had gotten away from them.

Monday morning, the tenth of June, we were assembled to march to Sandusky, about thirty-three miles away. They had eleven of us, and four scalps; the Indians were seventeen in number.

Colonel Crawford was very desirous to see a certain Simon Girty,[1] who lived among the Indians. On this account he was permitted to go to town the same night, with two warriors to guard him. They had orders, at the same time, to pass by the place where the colonel had turned out his horse, so that they might find him if possible. The rest of us were taken as far as the old town, which was within eight miles of the new.

Tuesday morning, the eleventh, Colonel Crawford was brought to us to be marched in with the other prisoners. I asked the colonel if he had seen Mr. Girty. He told me he had, and Girty had promised to do everything in his power for him, but that the Indians, particularly Captain Pipe, one of the chiefs, were very much enraged against the prisoners. He likewise told me that Girty had informed him that his son-in-law, Colonel Harrison, and his nephew, William Crawford, were made prisoners by the Shawnees, but had been pardoned.

This Captain Pipe had come from the town about an hour before Colonel Crawford and painted all the prisoners' faces black. As he was painting me he told me I should go to the Shawnee towns and see my friends. When the colonel arrived he painted him black also, told him he was glad to see him and that he would have him shaved when he came to see his friends at the Wyandot town. When we marched, the colonel and I were kept back between Pipe and Wingenund, the two Delaware chiefs; the other nine prisoners were sent forward with another party of Indians.

As we went along we saw four of the prisoners lying by the path tomahawked and scalped, some of them half a mile from each other.

Finally we overtook the five prisoners that remained alive. The Indians had caused them to sit down on the ground. They made the colonel and me do so, too, at some distance from them. I was turned over to an Indian fellow, to be taken to the Shawnee towns.

In the place where we were now made to sit down there was a number of squaws and boys. They fell on the five prisoners and tomahawked them. There was a certain John McKinley amongst the prisoners, formerly an officer in the 13th Virginia Regiment. An old squaw cut off his head and the Indians kicked it about on the ground. The young Indian fellows often came where the colonel and I were and dashed the scalps in our faces.

We were being led away when Simon Girty met us, with several Indians on horseback. He spoke to the colonel, but as I was about one hundred and fifty yards behind I could not hear what passed between them. Almost every Indian we met struck us, either with sticks or their fists. Girty waited till I was brought up.

"Is that the doctor?" he asked.

I told him yes, and went toward him, reaching out my hand. But he bid me begone and called me a damned rascal. Upon this the fellow who had me in charge pulled me along. Girty rode up after me and told me I was to go to the Shawnee towns.

After we had marched about half a mile we came to a fire. The colonel was stripped naked and ordered to sit down by the fire. Then they beat him with sticks and their fists. I was treated in the same manner.

They tied a rope to the foot of a post about fifteen feet high, bound the colonel's hands behind his back and fastened the rope to the bond between his wrists. The rope was long enough either for him to sit down or walk round the post once or twice and return the same way.

The colonel called to Girty and asked if they intended to burn him. Girty answered yes. The colonel said he would take it all patiently.

Captain Pipe made a speech to the Indians, about thirty or forty men and sixty or seventy squaws and boys. When the speech was finished they all yelled a hideous and hearty assent to what had been said.

The Indian men took up their guns and shot powder into the colonel's body from his feet as far up as his neck. I think not less than seventy loads were discharged upon his naked body. They then crowded about him and, to the best of my observation, cut off his ears. When the throng had dispersed a little I saw the blood running from both sides of his head.

The fire, which was about six or seven yards from the post to which the colonel was tied, was made of small hickory poles. They were burnt quite through in the middle, each end of the poles remaining about six feet in length. Three or four Indians by turns would take up, individually, one of these burning pieces of wood and apply it to his naked body, already burned black with the powder. These tormentors presented themselves on every side of him, so that, whichever way he ran round the post, they met him with the burning faggots and poles. Some of the squaws took broad boards, put a quantity of burning coals and hot embers upon them, and threw this on him. In a short time he had nothing but coals of fire and hot ashes to walk upon.

In the midst of these extreme tortures he called to Simon Girty and begged him to shoot him. Girty made no answer. He called to him again. Girty, by way of derision, told the colonel he had no gun.

At the same time he turned about to an Indian who was behind him, laughed heartily, and by all his gestures seemed delighted at the horrid scene.

Girty then came up to me and bade me prepare for death. He said, however, I was not to die at that place but to be burnt at the Shawnee towns. He swore by G-d I need not expect to escape death, but should suffer it in all its extremities.

He then observed that some prisoners had given him to understand that if our people had him they would not hurt him. For his part, he said, he did not believe it, but desired to know my opinion of the matter. Being in great anguish because of the torments the colonel was suffering before my eyes, as well as the expectation of undergoing the same fate in two days, I made little or no answer. Colonel Crawford besought the Almighty to have mercy on his soul, spoke very low, and bore his torments with the most manly fortitude. He continued in all the extremities of pain for an hour and three-quarters or two hours longer, as near as I can judge. At last, being almost spent, he lay down on his belly. They then scalped him.

Repeatedly, they threw the scalp in my face. "That is your great captain," they told me.

An old squaw (whose appearance in every way answered the ideas people have of the Devil) got a board, took a parcel of coals and ashes and laid them on his back and head after he had been scalped. He raised himself upon his feet and began to walk around the post. They next put a burning stick to him as usual, but he seemed more insensible of pain than before.

The Indian fellow who had me in charge now took me away to Captain Pipe's house, about three-quarters of a mile from the place of the colonel's execution. I was bound all night, and thus prevented from seeing the last of the horrid spectacle.

Next morning, June 12, the Indian untied me, painted me black and we set off for the Shawnee town, which he told me was somewhat less than forty miles from that place. He was on horseback and drove me before him.

We soon came to the spot where the colonel had been burnt. I saw his bones, almost burnt to ashes, lying amongst the remains of the fire. I suppose after he was dead they had laid his body on the fire. The Indian told me that was my big captain and gave the scalp halloo. I pretended to this Indian I was ignorant of the death I was to die at the Shawnee town. Affecting as cheerful a countenance as possible, I asked him if we were not to live together as brothers, in one house, when we should get to the town. He seemed well pleased and said yes. He then asked me if I could make a wigwam. I told him I could. He then seemed more friendly.

We went that day, as near as I can judge, about twenty-five miles, the course partly southwest. The Indian told me we should next day come to the town. At night, when we went to rest, I attempted very often to untie myself, but the Indian was extremely vigilant and scarcely ever shut his eyes that night.

About daybreak he got up and untied me. He next began to mend up the fire. As the gnats were troublesome I asked him if I should make a smoke behind him. He said yes.

I took the end of a dogwood fork which had been burnt down to about eighteen inches long. It was the longest stick I could find, yet too small for the purpose I had in view. I picked up another smaller stick and, taking a coal of fire between them, went behind him. Then, turning suddenly about, I struck him on the head with all the force I was master of. This so stunned him that he fell forward with both his hands into the fire.

Seeing him recover and get up, I seized his gun. He ran off howling in a most fearful manner. I followed him with a determination to shoot him down, but, pulling back the cock of the gun with too great violence, I believe I broke the mainspring. I pursued him, however, about thirty yards, still endeavoring to fire the gun, but could not.

Going back to the fire, I took his blanket, a pair of new moccasins, his powder horn, and bullet bag (together with the gun) and marched off, directing my course toward the five o'clock mark. About half an hour before sunset I came to the plains, which I think are about sixteen miles wide. I lay down in a thicket till dark, and then by the assistance of the North Star made my way through them, and got into the woods before morning.

I proceeded on the next day, and about noon crossed the paths our troops had traveled. These paths were nearly east and west, but I went due north all that afternoon to avoid the enemy.

In the evening I began to be very faint, and no wonder: I had been six days a prisoner, the last two days of which I had eaten nothing, and but very little the first three or four. There were wild gooseberries in abundance in the woods, but they were unripe and required mastication, which I was not able to perform on account of a blow I had received on the jaw from the back of a tomahawk.

There was a weed that grew plentifully in that place, the juice of which I knew to be nourishing. I gathered a bundle of it, lay down under a large spreading beech tree and, having sucked plentifully of the juice, went to sleep.

Next day I traveled due east, a course which I generally kept the rest of my journey. I often imagined my gun was only wood-bound, and tried every method I could devise to unscrew the lock, but never succeeded, having no knife or anything adapted to the purpose. My jaw began to mend, and in four or five days I could chew any vegetable proper for nourishment. Finding my gun only a useless burden, I left it in the wilderness. I had no apparatus for making a fire to sleep by, so that I could get but little rest because of the gnats and mosquitoes. There are likewise a great many swamps in the beech ridge, and I very often had to lie in the wet.

I crossed the river Muskingum about three or four miles below Fort Laurens and aimed for the Ohio River. All this time my food was gooseberries, young nettles, the juice of herbs, a few serviceberries and some May apples; likewise two young blackbirds and a terrapin, which I devoured raw. When my food sat heavy on my stomach, I used to eat a little wild ginger, which put all things to rights.

I came upon the Ohio River about five miles below Fort McIntosh in the evening of the twenty-first day after I had made my escape. On the twenty-second, about seven o'clock in the morning of the fourth of July, I arrived safe, though very much fatigued, at the fort.

# To Eat Fire Tomorrow

## JOHN SLOVER

A FEW MILES *from Zanesfield, Ohio, is the site of Wapatomica, once an important Shawnee town, where the Indians used to gather to hold their ceremonies and celebrations. For one of these, in 1782, a special entertainment was provided: John Slover, an American soldier, was tied to a stake in the council house and piles of brushwood were lighted around him. It promised to be a gay, exciting day at Wapatomica.*

*Like Dr. John Knight, author of the preceding narrative, Slover accompanied Colonel William Crawford's ill-starred expedition against the Indians of the Sandusky River region. Slover was one of the expedition's scouts. He had spent his boyhood as a captive among the Indians. His father had died at their hands and his two little sisters had perished while being carried off, but he himself had fared rather well. Now, ten years later, he was meeting with very different treatment. . . .*

*Slover, although described as a sensible, intelligent man, had never learned to write. Hugh H. Brackenridge, the Pittsburgh lawyer who preserved Knight's narrative, took down Slover's account from his own lips. Brackenridge saw the scout eight or ten days after his return from the wilderness. He observed that Slover had a wound above his eyebrow, received from a tomahawk, and that his back and his body generally had been injured. To accompany Slover's story, Brackenridge obtained a statement from the scout's minister that he was "worthy of the highest credit."*

*Some time after Slover's escape a treaty was made with the Indians, and Brackenridge saw traders who had visited them at Sandusky. They reported that the Indians confirmed Slover's account in all details except one: the Indians insisted that Slover had not untied himself and escaped while they were sleeping, but that some squaws had helped him to get away. Apparently they were unwilling to admit that they had literally been "caught napping."*

*After the Revolution, John Slover settled on Canoe Creek in Henderson, Kentucky. It is said that he raised a large family and died at an advanced age.*

In the last war I was a prisoner among the Indians many years and so was well acquainted with the country west of the Ohio. I was employed as a guide in the expedition under Colonel William Crawford against the Indian towns on or near the river Sandusky.

On Tuesday, the fourth of June, we fought the enemy near Sandusky. The next day the Indians and our troops fired on each other at a distance of three hundred yards, doing little or no execution. In the evening Colonel Crawford proposed that we make an orderly withdrawal. We were just beginning our retreat when some Indians fired their guns and gave the alarm. Our men broke and rode off in confusion, treading down those who were on foot and leaving the wounded, who begged to be taken with them.

I was in the rear of our troops with some others, feeding our horses on the glade, when our men began to break. The main body of our people had left me far behind before I was ready to set out. I overtook them before they had crossed the glade, and came up close to the front.

The company of five or six men with which I had been connected had separated from me and tried to pass through a swamp. Coming up, I found their horses stuck fast in it. I did my best to get through, but mine also soon stuck fast. For a long time I tried to free my horse. Then I heard the enemy just behind me and on each side and I was obliged to leave him.

In a moment I was up to my middle in the ooze. It was with the greatest difficulty that I got across. After a while I came up with the six men, who had left their horses in the same manner I had. Two of them had lost their guns.

That night we traveled towards Detroit. We chose this route to avoid the enemy, who we believed were following the main body of our people. Just before day we got into a second deep swamp and had to remain there until it was light, so we could see our way through it.

The whole of this day we traveled toward the Shawnee towns, to get still further away from the area where the enemy would be searching.

About ten o'clock we sat down to eat a little. We had tasted nothing from Tuesday, the day of our engagement, until this time, which was on Thursday, and now the only thing we had to eat was a scrap of pork apiece.

Without suspecting it, we had sat down by a warriors' path. Suddenly eight or nine warriors appeared. We ran off hastily, leaving our baggage and provisions. But we were not discovered by the Indians and, after hiding in the grass and bushes for some time, we returned and recovered our baggage. The warriors had hallooed as they passed, and were answered by others on our flanks.

About twelve o'clock, as we were journeying through the glades, or wide dry meadows, we discovered a party of Indians in front of us. We skulked in the grass and bushes and they did not discover us. We were in great danger in these glades, as we could be seen at a considerable distance.

In the afternoon a heavy rain fell, the coldest I had ever felt. We halted till it stopped. Then, traveling on, we saw a party of the enemy about two hundred yards before us. We hid ourselves in the bushes and again had the good fortune not to be discovered.

That night we got out of the glades, crossing the paths by which we had traveled to Sandusky. It was our plan to leave all these paths on the right and return by the Tuscarawas. We should have made much greater progress, but two of my companions were lame—one had a burnt foot, the other a rheumatic swelling in his knee.

The next day, the second after our retreat began, the person with the rheumatic swelling was left some distance behind in a swamp. After waiting for him some time, we saw him coming within one hundred yards. I was sitting on the body of an old tree mending my moccasins, and I took my eye off him, and then I did not see him again. We whistled and hallooed for him, but in vain. He was fortunate in missing us, for he afterwards came into Wheeling safely.

We traveled along the waters of the Muskingum from the middle of this day. Having caught a fawn, we made a fire in the evening and had a meal. All this time we had eaten nothing but the small bit of pork I mentioned before.

At break of day we set off again. About nine o'clock we were attacked by a party of the enemy about twenty miles from the Tuscarawas, which is about 135 miles from Fort Pitt. They had come upon our tracks or had been on our flanks and discovered us. Getting in front, they waylaid us and fired before we even noticed them.

At the first volley, one of my companions fell in front of me and another just behind. These two had guns. There were six of us but only four guns—and two of these were useless, having got wet when we came through the swamp the first night.

When the Indians fired, I ran to a tree. An Indian showed himself fifteen yards in front of me and, holding his gun leveled at me, told me to surrender and I should not be hurt. My gun was in good order, but I was afraid the other Indians might shoot me down, so I did not risk firing. I had reason to regret this when I found what my fate was to be—and that the Indian who stood in front of me with his gun pointed at me had just fired it. Two of my companions also surrendered after the Indians had assured them they would not be hurt. But a third, James Paul, who had a gun in order, made his escape and has since come into Wheeling.

One of these Indians knew me—he was a member of the party by which I was taken in the last war. He came up and called me by my Indian name, Mannuchcothee, and upbraided me for coming to war against them. I will take a moment to relate some particulars of my first captivity and my life since.

I was taken from New River, Virginia, by the Miamis, a nation of Indians by us called the Picts. I lived among them six years. Afterwards I was sold to a Delaware, who put me into the hands of a trader. Then I was taken among the Shawnees, and stayed with them six years. My whole time among these nations was twelve years—from my eighth to my twentieth year.

In the fall of 1773 a treaty was made at Fort Pitt with the Indians. The Shawnees came in for it, bringing me with them. Here I met some of my relations and they urged me to give up the life of a savage. I did so with some reluctance—this manner of life had become natural to me, for I had scarcely known any other. I enlisted as a soldier in the Continental Army at the start of the present war and served fifteen months, when I was properly discharged. I have since married, have a family, and am in communion with the church.

To return: the party by whom we were made prisoners had taken some horses and left them at the glades we passed the day before. Going back to these glades, we found the horses and rode. We were taken to Wachatomakak, a town of the Mingoes and Shawnees.

I think it was on the third day we reached the town. When we were approaching it the Indians began to look sour, although they had been kind to us before and given us a little meat and flour to eat, which they had found or taken from some of our men on their retreat. This town is small, and we were told was about two miles distant from the main town, to which they meant to take us.

The inhabitants came out with clubs and tomahawks and struck, beat, and abused us greatly. They seized one of my two companions and, having stripped him naked, blacked him with coal and water. This was the sign that he was to be burnt.

The man seemed to surmise it and shed tears. He asked me the meaning of his being blacked, but I was forbidden by the enemy, in their own language, to tell him what was intended. In English, which they spoke easily, having often been at Fort Pitt, they assured him he was not to be hurt. I know of no reason for making him the first object of their cruelty, unless it was that he was the oldest.

A warrior had been sent to the greater town to acquaint them with our coming and prepare them for the frolic. On our coming to it, the inhabitants came out with guns, clubs and tomahawks. We were told that we had to run to the council house, about three hundred yards away.

The man that was blacked was about twenty yards before us in running the gauntlet. They made him their principal object. Men, women and children beat him. Those who had guns fired loads of powder on him, putting the muzzles of the guns to his body as he ran naked. They shouted, hallooed, and beat their drums in the meantime.

The unhappy man had reached the door of the council house, beaten and wounded in a manner shocking to the sight. Having arrived before him, we had it in our power to view the spectacle. It was indeed the most horrid that can be conceived. They had cut him with their tomahawks, shot his body black, burnt it into holes with loads of powder blown into him. A large wadding had made a wound in his shoulder, from which the blood gushed.

In keeping with the Indians' declaration when he first set out, he had reason to think himself safe when he reached the door of the council house. This seemed to be his hope, for, coming up with great struggling and endeavor, he laid hold of the door. But he was pulled back and drawn away by them. Finding they intended no mercy, he attempted to snatch or lay hold of some of their tomahawks, but was too weak to succeed. We saw him borne off, and they were a long time beating, wounding, pursuing and killing him.

That same evening I saw the dead body of this man close by the council house. It was mangled cruelly and the blood mingled with the powder was rendered black. The same evening I saw him after he had been cut into pieces and his limbs and his head put on poles about two hundred yards outside of the town.

That evening also I saw the bodies of three others in the same black and mangled condition. These, I was told, had been put to death the same way, just before we had reached the town. Their bodies were bloody and burnt with powder. Two of these were Harrison and young Crawford. I knew Colonel Harrison's face and I saw his clothing and that of young Crawford at the town. The Indians brought horses to me and asked if I knew them. I said they were Harrison's and Crawford's. They said they were.

I did not know the third of these men, but I believe he was Colonel McCleland, the third in command of the expedition.

The next day the bodies of these men were dragged outside the town. Their carcasses were given to the dogs and their limbs and heads stuck on poles.

Shortly after we reached the council house my surviving companion was sent to another town. I presume he was burnt or executed in the same manner.

In the evening the men assembled in the council house. This is a large building, about fifty yards in length, twenty-five yards wide, and sixteen feet in height, built of split poles covered with bark. Their first object was to question me. They could do this in their own language as I could speak Miami, Shawnee and Delaware, which I had learned during my captivity in the last war. I found I had not forgotten these languages, especially the first two; I was able to speak them as well as my native tongue.

They began by interrogating me concerning the situation of our country—what were our provisions, our numbers, the state of the war between us and Britain. I informed them Cornwallis had been taken. Next day, when Matthew Elliott and James Girty came, they affirmed this to be a lie,[1] and all the Indians seemed to give full credit to their declaration.

Hitherto I had been treated with some appearance of kindness, but now the enemy began to alter their behavior towards me.

Girty had informed them that when he asked me how I liked to live there, I had said that I intended to seize the first opportunity to take a scalp and run off. It was, to be sure, *very probable* that if I had such intentions I would communicate them to him. Another man came to me and told a story of having lived on the South Branch of the Potomac in Virginia and having three brothers there whom he pretended he wanted to assist in getting away. I was suspicious of him and said very little. Nevertheless, he reported that I had agreed to go off with him. In the meantime I was not tied and could have escaped, but I had nothing to put on my feet, so I waited some time longer to provide for this.

Every night I was invited to the war dances, which they usually continued until almost day. I could not accept their invitation, as I believed these things to be the service of the Devil.

The council lasted fifteen days. From fifty to one hundred warriors were usually present, and sometimes more. Every warrior is admitted to these councils, but only the chiefs or head warriors have the privilege of speaking. The head warriors hold this rank because of the number of scalps and prisoners they have taken.

On the third day, McKee [2] was in council, and afterwards was generally present. He spoke little and did not ask any questions or speak to me at all. He lives about two miles out of the town and has a house built of squared logs with a shingled roof; he was dressed in gold-laced clothes.

I think it was on the day before the end of the council that a speech came from Detroit brought by a warrior who had been conferring with the commanding officer at that place. The speech had been long expected, and was in answer to one sent from the town to Detroit. It was in a belt of wampum,[3] and began by addressing them as "My children," and inquiring why they continued to take prisoners.

"Provisions are scarce," it said. "When prisoners are brought in, we are obliged to maintain them, and still some of them run away and carry tidings of our affairs to the enemy. When any of our people fall into the hands of the Rebels, they show no mercy— why then should you take any prisoners? My children, take no more prisoners of any sort—man, woman, or child."

Two days after, a party was collected of every nation in the area and it was determined to take no more captives of any kind. They had held a large council, and the decision was that even if it were possible to find an American child only a span or three inches long, they would show it no mercy. At the end of the council it was agreed by all the tribes present—the Mingoes, Ottawas, Chippewas, the Wyandots, the Delawares, the Shawnees, the Munsees, and a part of the Cherokees—that should any of the nations who were not present take any prisoners, those present would rise against them, take away the prisoners and put them to death.

I understood perfectly what was said at these councils. They made plans to raid our settlements of Kentucky, the Falls, and towards Wheeling.

There was one council held at which I was not present. The warriors had sent for me as usual, but the squaw with whom I lived would not allow me to go, but hid me under a large quantity of skins. It may have been from an unwillingness to have me hear in council the decision that I was to be burnt.

About this time twelve men were brought in from Kentucky, three of whom were burnt on this day. The remainder were distributed to other towns, and all, the Indians informed me, were burnt. This was after the speech came from Detroit.

On this day also I saw an Indian who had just come into town, and who said that the prisoner he was bringing to be burnt, a doctor, had made his escape from him. I knew this must have been Dr. Knight, who went as surgeon of the expedition. In his head the Indian had a wound four inches long which the doctor had given him; he was cut to the skull.

This Indian's story was that he had untied the doctor, after the doctor had asked him to do so and promised that he would not run away. While the Indian was kindling a fire, the doctor snatched up the warrior's gun, came up behind and struck him. He then struck at the doctor with his knife. The doctor laid hold of it and his fingers were almost cut off when the knife was drawn through his hand. He gave the doctor two stabs, one in the belly, the other in the back. He said the doctor was a great big, tall, strong man.

Having been adopted into an Indian family and feeling some confidence for my safety, I took the liberty of contradicting this. I said that I knew the doctor, and he was a weak little man. The other warriors laughed immoderately and did not seem to believe him. At this time I was told that Colonel Crawford had been burnt, and they greatly exulted over it.

The morning after the council, about forty warriors, accompanied by George Girty, surrounded the house where I was. The squaw gave me up. I was sitting before the door of the house and they put a rope round my neck, tied my arms behind my back, stripped me naked, and blacked me in the usual manner. George Girty, as soon as I was tied, damned me and said that I now should get what I had deserved many years.

I was led off to a town about five miles away, to which a messenger had been despatched to ask them to prepare to receive me. Arriving at this town, I was beaten with clubs and the pipe ends [4] of their tomahawks, and was kept for some time tied to a tree before a house door. In the meanwhile the inhabitants set out to another town about two miles distant, where I was to be burnt. I arrived there about three o'clock in the afternoon.

Here there was also a council house, part of it covered and part without a roof. In the part of it where there was no cover, but only sides, there stood a post about sixteen feet in height. In the middle of the house, around the post, there were three piles of wood, about three feet high and four feet from the post.

I was brought to the post. My arms were tied behind me, and the thong or cord with which they were bound was fastened to the post. A rope also was put about my neck and tied to the post about four feet above my head. During the time they were tying me, piles of wood were kindled and began to flame.

Death by burning now appeared to be my fate. I had resolved to bear it with patience. The divine grace of God had made it less alarming to me.

On my way this day I had been greatly disturbed about my approaching end. I knew I had been a regular member of the church and had sought repentance for my sins, but though I had often heard of the assurance of faith I had known nothing of it. However, early this day, instantaneously, by a chance as sudden and perceivable as lightning, an assurance of my peace made with God had sprung up in my mind. The following words were the subject of my meditation: "In peace shalt thou see God." "Fear not those who can kill the body." "In peace shalt thou depart." I felt a deep peace of mind and was fully assured of my salvation. This being the case, I was willing, satisfied, and glad to die.

I was tied to the post, as I have already said, and the flame was kindled. The day was clear, not a cloud to be seen; if there were clouds low in the horizon, the sides of the house prevented me from seeing them, but I heard no thunder nor observed any sign of approaching rain.

Just as the fire of one pile began to blaze, the wind rose. From the time they began to kindle the fire and to tie me to the post, until the wind began to blow, was about fifteen minutes. The wind blew a hurricane, and rain followed in less than three minutes. The rain fell violently and the fire, though it had begun to blaze considerably, was instantly extinguished. The rain lasted about a quarter of an hour.

When it was over, the savages stood amazed. They were silent a long time.

At last one said: "We will let him alone till morning, and take a whole day's frolic in burning him." The sun at this time was about three hours high. It was agreed upon, and the rope about my neck was untied.

Making me sit down, they began to dance around me. They continued dancing in this manner until eleven o'clock at night, in the meantime beating, kicking and wounding me with their tomahawks and clubs.

At last one of the warriors, Half Moon, asked me if I was sleepy. I answered yes.

The head warrior then chose three men to take care of me. I was taken to a blockhouse. My arms were tied until the cord was hid in the flesh. They were tied in two places, round the wrists and above the elbows. A rope was fastened about my neck and tied to a beam of the house, but permitting me to lie down on a board.

The three warriors were constantly harassing and troubling me. "How will you like to eat fire tomorrow? You will kill no more Indians now," they said.

I kept waiting for them to go to sleep. At length, about an hour before daybreak, two lay down. The third smoked a pipe and talked to me, asking the same painful questions.

About half an hour later he also lay down. I heard him begin to snore.

I instantly went to work. As my arms were perfectly dead with the cord, I laid myself upon my right arm, which was behind my back. Keeping the cord fast with my fingers, which still had some life and strength, I slipped it from my left arm, over my elbow and my wrist.

One of the warriors got up and stirred the fire. I was apprehensive that I should be examined, and thought all was over with me. But he lay down again and my hopes revived.

I attempted to unloose the rope about my neck. I tried to gnaw it, but in vain. It was as thick as my thumb and as hard as iron, being made of buffalo hide. I worked with it a long time, then gave it up. There seemed to be no way out for me.

At this time I saw day break and heard the cock crow. I made a second attempt now, almost without hope, pulling the rope by putting my fingers between my neck and it. To my great surprise it easily came untied; it was a noose with two or three knots tied over it.

I stepped over the sleeping warriors. Having got out of the house, I looked back to see if there was any disturbance. Then I ran through the town into a cornfield. In my path I saw a squaw with four or five children lying asleep under a tree. Going into the field by a different way, I untied my right arm, which was greatly swollen and had turned black.

I observed a number of horses in the field and went to catch one. On my way I found a piece of an old rug or quilt hanging on a fence, and I took it with me. I caught the horse and rode off, using the rope with which I had been tied as a halter and the rug as a saddle.

The horse was strong and swift, the woods were open and the country was level. About ten o'clock I crossed the Scioto River about fifty miles from the town. I had ridden about twenty miles on this side of the Scioto by three o'clock in the afternoon when the horse began to fail and could no longer go at a trot. I instantly left him.

I ran about twenty miles farther that day, covering a total distance of nearly one hundred miles. In the evening I heard hallooing behind me, and for this reason did not halt until about ten o'clock at night. When I sat down, I was extremely sick and vomited. But when the moon rose, which might have been about two hours later, I went on and traveled until day.

During the night I had a path. But in the morning I judged it prudent to leave this path and travel in a line at right angles to my route. I did this for fifteen miles. To conceal my tracks from the enemy, as I went along I used a stick to put back the weeds I had bent. The next night I slept beside the waters of the Muskingum.

The nettles had been troublesome to me after I crossed the Scioto, as I was naked except for the piece of rug I had found. Now the briers and thorns were painful to me and prevented me from traveling at night until the moon appeared. In the meantime I was hindered from sleeping by the mosquitoes. Even by day I had to travel with a handful of bushes to brush them from my body.

The second night I reached Cushakim. The next day I came to Newcomerstown, where I got about seven raspberries—the first thing I ate from the morning the Indians had taken me to burn me, until about three o'clock the fourth day. I felt hunger very little, but was extremely weak.

I swam the Muskingum at Oldcomerstown, where the river was about two hundred yards wide. Reaching the bank, I sat down and looked back. I thought I had a good start on the Indians, if any were following.

That evening I traveled about five miles. Next day I came to Stillwater, a small river, where I caught two small crawfish and ate them. Next night I rested within five miles of Wheeling. I had not slept a wink during this whole time because of the mosquitoes, which I had to brush away constantly.

Next day I reached Wheeling and saw a man on the island in the Ohio opposite the fort. I called to him and asked after certain persons who had been on the expedition, and I told him I was Slover. Finally, with great difficulty, I persuaded him to come over and bring me across in his canoe.

# White Indian

## JOHN TANNER

**W**HITE INDIAN" was the name they gave John Tanner at Sault Sainte Marie, Michigan, where he spent the last, tempestuous years of his life. The name was a fitting one. For almost thirty years Tanner had lived among the Ottawas and the Ojibways, or Chippewas, in Canada and the Great Lakes region of the United States. He had taken two Indian wives and reared two families. In his bearing, thought, and habits he was more an Indian than a white. At the time of his return to civilization he had forgotten his native language and even his English name.

Tanner was born about 1780. In 1789 he was taken prisoner by Indian raiders in Kentucky, where his father had settled. After two years of bitter abuse by his captors, he was sold to Netnokwa, an aged Ottawa chieftainess, who adopted him and treated him as her own. For many years he lived the life of an Indian hunter and warrior. But blood called to blood, and in 1817 he came out of the wilderness and with the aid of Lewis Cass, governor of Michigan Territory, made his way to Kentucky, where he had a tearful reunion with brothers and sisters he had not seen for almost three decades.

Tanner had left his children behind him, and he soon returned to Canada to look after them. Later he made another trip to the States,

142

*this time with his children. Then he went north again and worked for the American Fur Company. In the late 1820's he was employed as an interpreter at Mackinac, and subsequently at Sault Sainte Marie, where he worked for Henry Rowe Schoolcraft, United States Indian agent, a leading pioneer in the study of the Indians.*

*The "white Indian" had lived through many remarkable experiences and he had extraordinary powers of recall. In Dr. Edwin James, explorer, botanist, and Army surgeon, Tanner found a fascinated listener—and a writer with the unique qualities needed to record the story of his life with sympathy and understanding. Dr. James relates that he set down that story as nearly as possible in Tanner's own words and in his own manner.*

*Tanner was about fifty in 1830 when the book James wrote,* A Narrative of the Captivity and Adventures of John Tanner, *was published. "His person," said Dr. James, "is erect and rather robust, indicating great hardiness, activity, and strength, which, however, his numerous exposures and sufferings have deeply impaired. His face, which was originally rather handsome, bears now numerous traces of thought and passion, as well as of age; his quick and piercing blue eyes bespeak the stern, the violent and unconquerable spirit which rendered him an object of fear to many of the Indians while he remained among them." The doctor noted that Tanner shared the Indians' notions of right and wrong and that, although he could be just and generous, he was profoundly vengeful when he felt he had been injured. Henry Schoolcraft reports that Tanner threatened to kill the doctor for writing things about him that led people to call him an "old liar." Whether this is true or not, Tanner did spend some time in jail because of his violent fits of bad temper.*

*Tanner married three times. He left his first wife, Red-Sky-of-the-Morning, in about 1810. His second wife was involved in an attempt to kill him in the 1820's and then disappeared. His third marriage, with a white woman of Detroit, was equally unsuccessful. She ran off with their child and later obtained a divorce from the legislature.*

*Tanner's end is veiled in mystery. In 1846 he disappeared without a trace. James L. Schoolcraft, brother of the Indian agent, had been shot to death, and suspicion had fallen on Tanner. Henry Schoolcraft, who in his* Personal Memoirs *describes Tanner as "suspicious" and "half-crazed," states flatly that Tanner murdered his brother and fled back to the Indians. This opinion was shared by many at the Sault.*

*The law attempted to find the vanished suspect, and soldiers and bloodhounds took part in the search, but with no result. Tanner was never seen again. A long time afterward a skeleton was found in a swamp near the Sault and was presumed to be Tanner's. It is reported that years after the event an ex-army lieutenant named Tilden confessed to the murder of James Schoolcraft. Tilden was supposed to have killed Tanner to cover up the crime.*

*The following episodes from the Tanner story cover the long span of years from 1789, when he was carried off by the Indians, to 1817, when he first returned to his relatives in the United States.*

### THERE WERE INDIANS LURKING ABOUT

The earliest event I distinctly remember is the death of my mother. This happened when I was two years old, and it made so deep an impression that it is still fresh in my memory. I cannot recollect the name of the settlement at which we lived, but I have since learned it was on the Kentucky River, at a considerable distance from the Ohio.

My father, whose name was John Tanner, was a farmer from Virginia, and had been a clergyman. Soon after my mother's death, we moved to a place called Elk Horn. This settlement was occasionally raided by hostile parties of Shawnee Indians, who killed some white people and sometimes killed or drove away cattle and horses. Once my uncle, my father's brother, went with a few men at night and fired upon a camp of these Indians. He killed one and brought home the scalp. All the rest jumped into the river and escaped.

While we were living at this place something happened which I blamed for many of the disasters of my later life. One morning my father had to leave for a distant village, and he gave strict orders to my sisters, Agatha and Lucy, to send me to school. But they neglected to do this until afternoon, and by then the weather had turned rainy and unpleasant and I insisted on remaining at home. When my father returned at night and found I had been at home all day, he sent me for a parcel of small canes and flogged me much more severely than I could suppose the offense merited. I was displeased with my sisters for placing all the blame on me when they had neglected even to tell me to go to school in the forenoon. From that time, my father's house was less like home to me and I often thought and said, "I wish I could go and live among the Indians."

I cannot tell how long we remained at Elk Horn. But while we lived there my father took a second wife and was blessed with a second family. I was about ten years old when we moved. We traveled two days with horses and wagons and came to the Ohio, where my father bought three flatboats. The sides of these boats had bullet holes in them, and there was blood on them, which I understood was that of people who had been killed by the Indians. In one of these boats we put the horses and cattle—in another, beds, furniture, and other property, and in the third were our Negroes. The cattle boat and the family boat were lashed together; the third, with the Negroes, followed behind. We descended the Ohio and in two or three days came to Cincinnati.

In one day we went from Cincinnati to the mouth of the Big Miami, opposite which we were to settle. There was some cleared land here, with one or two log cabins, deserted on account of the Indians. My father rebuilt the cabins and enclosed them with a strong wall. We were soon engaged in preparing a field to plant corn.

One morning, about ten days after our arrival, my father told us the horses were behaving very nervously and he thought there were Indians lurking about in the woods.

"John," he said to me, "you must not go out of the house today."

After giving strict orders to my stepmother to let none of the little children out, he went to the field with the Negroes and my elder brother to plant corn.

Three little children, besides myself, were left in the house with my stepmother. To prevent me from going out, she made me take care of my youngest brother, then a few months old. But I soon became restless and began to pinch him to make him cry. Finally my stepmother took him from me to give him suck. I watched my opportunity and escaped into the yard, and from there into the open field through a small door in the wall.

At some distance from the house there was a walnut tree where I had been in the habit of finding nuts. I had to use some precaution to reach this tree without being seen by the men in the field. I remember perfectly well seeing my father as I skulked towards the tree; he stood with his gun in his hand watching for Indians while the others were planting corn.

As I came near the tree I thought, "I wish I could see these Indians."

I had partly filled my hat with nuts when I heard a crackling noise behind me. I looked round and saw the Indians. Almost at the same instant I was seized by both hands and dragged off between two. One of them took my hat, emptied the nuts on the ground, and put it on my head.

The Indians who seized me were an old man and a young one— Manito-o-geezhik and his son Kishkauko. Later I learned that Manito-o-geezhik's youngest son had died recently. The old man's wife had complained that unless he "brought her son back" she could not go on living. This was a hint to bring her a captive whom she might adopt in his place. Manito-o-geezhik, with his son and two other men of his band, had left their home on Lake Huron and come east solely for this purpose. On the upper part of Lake Erie they had been joined by three other young men, relations of Manito-o-geezhik, and had proceeded to the settlements on the Ohio. They had arrived the night before my capture and concealed themselves within sight of my father's house.

After I was seized by the two Indians, I must have fainted. I can remember nothing that happened until they threw me over a large log a considerable distance from the house. I did not see the old man now; there were only Kishkauko and a very short, thick man, who must have been dragging me along between them. I had probably done something to irritate this man, for he took me to one side and, drawing his tomahawk, motioned to me to look up. From his expression I plainly understood this to be a direction for me to look up for the last time, as he was about to kill me. I did as he directed, but Kishkauko caught his hand as the tomahawk was descending and prevented him from burying it in my brains.

Loud talking followed between the two. Kishkauko raised a yell. The old man and the four others answered it by a similar yell and came running up. I have since understood that Kishkauko complained to his father that the short man had made an attempt to kill his little brother, as he called me. The old chief, after reproving the man, took me by one hand and Kishkauko took me by the other, and they dragged me between them. I could see they were afraid they were being pursued. Some of them were always keeping watch at our rear.

About one mile from my father's house they threw me into a canoe which was concealed under the bushes on the bank of the river. All seven of them jumped in after me, and we crossed the Ohio, landing at the mouth of the Big Miami. Here they abandoned their canoe and stuck their paddles in the ground so that they could be seen from the river.

At a little distance in the woods they had some blankets and provisions concealed. They offered me some dry venison and bear's grease, but I could not eat. My father's house was plainly to be seen from the place where we stood. They pointed at it, looked at me, and laughed.

After they had eaten, they began to travel along the bank of the Miami, dragging me between them as before. They took off my shoes, seeming to think I could run better without them. Although I was closely watched, all hope of escape did not immediately forsake me. As they hurried me along, I tried to take notice of such objects as would serve as landmarks on my way back. I tried, also, where I passed long grass or soft ground, to leave my tracks. I hoped to be able to escape after they fell asleep at night.

When night came they lay down, placing me between the old man and Kishkauko. We lay so close together that the same blanket covered all three of us. I was so fatigued that I fell asleep immediately and did not wake until sunrise, when the Indians were ready to proceed on their journey.

Thus we journeyed about four days, the Indians hurrying me on and I continuing to hope I might escape. My bare feet were often wounded, and finally they were very swollen. The old man, seeing that I was walking badly, examined my feet. He removed a great many thorns and splinters from them and gave me a pair of moccasins. Usually I traveled between the old man and Kishkauko, and they often made me run until my strength was quite exhausted. For several days I could eat little or nothing.

Four days after we left the Ohio we came to a considerable river. It was so deep I could not wade across it. The old man took me on his shoulders and carried me over. The water was nearly up to his armpits. As he carried me across, I thought I should never be able to pass this river alone, and gave up all hope of immediate escape.

When he put me down, I ran up the bank and into the woods. A turkey flew up before me. The nest she had left contained some eggs. I put these in the bosom of my shirt and returned towards the river. The Indians laughed when they saw me. But they took the eggs, kindled a fire, and put them in a small kettle to boil. I was very hungry and I sat watching the kettle.

Suddenly the old man came running from the ford where he had crossed. He immediately caught up the kettle and threw the eggs and water on the fire, saying something in a low, hurried tone to the young men. I understood we were being pursued—that some of my relatives and neighbors were probably on the opposite side of the river searching for me. The Indians hastily gathered up the eggs and scattered in the woods, two of them still making me run as fast as I could.

A day or two after this we met a party of twenty or thirty Indians on their way towards the settlements. Old Manito-o-geezhik had a good deal to say to them. Later I learned they were a war party of Shawnees and our party told them about the whites who were after us. The Shawnees went in pursuit of them and there was a severe skirmish in which numbers were killed on both sides.

Our journey through the woods was tedious and painful. About ten days after we met the war party we arrived at the Maumee River. As soon as we came near the river, the Indians scattered about the woods, examining the trees, yelling and answering each other. They soon selected a hickory tree, cut it down, and stripped off the bark to make a canoe. We all embarked in this canoe and went on till we came to a large Shawnee village.

As we were landing, large numbers of Indians gathered about us. A young woman came towards me crying and struck me on the head. Some of her friends had been killed by the whites. Many of these Shawnees showed a disposition to kill me. But Kishkauko and the old man stepped in and prevented them.

We remained at the Shawnee village two days and then continued our journey in the canoe. Not far from the village we came to a trading house where there were three or four men who could speak English. They wanted to purchase me from the Indians and let me go home to my family, but the old man would not consent. The traders told me I must go with the Indians and become the old man's son, but they promised that they would come to the village and release me in ten days. They treated me kindly while we stayed and gave me plenty to eat, which the Indians had neglected to do. When I had to leave with the Indians, I began to cry for the first time since my capture. Soon after leaving this trading house, we came to Lake Erie and three of our party left us.

I have little recollection of anything that happened from this time until we arrived at Detroit. We ran in near the shore and I saw a white woman, with whom the Indians held a little conversation. I also saw several white men on shore and heard them talk, but could not understand them; it is likely they spoke French. After talking a few minutes with the woman, the Indians pushed off.

About midday we landed in the woods. They found a large hollow log, open at one end, and they put their blankets, their kettle, and some other articles into it. Then they made me crawl in, too, and closed up the end. I heard them for a few minutes on the outside, then all was still.

I remained shut in here for many hours. Finally I heard them removing the logs with which they had fastened me in. I came out. Although it was night, I could see they had brought three horses. On one of these they placed me, on the others their baggage, and with sometimes one, sometimes another of the Indians riding, we traveled rapidly along.

In about three days we reached Saugenong, the village to which old Manito-o-geezhik belonged. This settlement consisted of several scattered houses. Two of the Indians left us soon after we entered it; now only Kishkauko and his father remained with me. They left their horses here and borrowed a canoe, and in it we at last arrived at the old man's house. This was a cabin built of logs, like some of those in Kentucky.

As soon as we landed, Manito-o-geezhik's old wife came down to the shore. He said a few words to her and she began crying. Then, hugging and kissing me, she led me to the house.

Next day they took me to the place where the old woman's son had been buried. The grave was enclosed with pickets, in the Indian manner, and there was a smooth, open place on each side of it. Here they all took their seats: the family and friends of Manito-o-geezhik on one side and strangers on the other. The friends had come with presents: *mukkuks* of sugar, sacks of corn, beads, tobacco and the like.

They had not been assembled long when my party began to dance, dragging me with them about the grave. Their dance was lively and cheerful, like the scalp dance. From time to time, as they danced, they presented me with one of the gifts they had brought, but as I came round in the dancing to the party on the opposite side of the grave, they snatched from me whatever had been given me. They continued this for a great part of the day, until the presents were exhausted.

It must have been early in the spring when we arrived at Saugenong, for I can remember that the leaves were small and the Indians were planting their corn. They made me help in their labors. After the planting they all left the village and went out to hunt meat and dry it, and they took me with them.

When they came to their hunting grounds, they chose a place where there were many deer. Here they built a long screen, like a fence, of green boughs and small trees. The Indians were to shoot the deer from one side of it, and they showed me how to remove the leaves and dry brush from that side. I sometimes had the help of the squaws and children in this work, but at other times I did it alone.

One day they left me alone at my labor. I was tired and thirsty; I lay down and I soon fell asleep. When I began to awake I thought I heard someone crying a great way off. I tried to raise my head but could not. Becoming more awake, I saw my Indian mother and sister standing by me and perceived that my face and head were wet. The old woman and her daughter were crying bitterly, but it was some time before I noticed that my head was badly cut and bruised.

It appears that after I had fallen asleep, Manito-o-geezhik had come along and seen me dozing. He tomahawked me and threw me into the bushes. When he got to his camp he said to his wife, "Old woman, the boy I brought you is good for nothing. I have killed him and you will find him in such-and-such a place." The old woman and her daughter had found me, discovered some signs of life, and stood over me a long time, crying and pouring cold water on my head, before I awoke.

In a few days I recovered somewhat from my injury and was again set to work at the screen, but I was more careful not to fall asleep. I tried to help them at their labors, but I was treated with great harshness, particularly by the old man and his two sons Shemung and Kwotashe.

When we returned from hunting I had to carry a large pack of dried meat all the way to the village. Although I was almost starved, I dared not touch a morsel of it. My Indian mother would sometimes steal a little food and hide it until the old man was gone, and then give it to me.

After we returned to the village my brothers were engaged in spearing fish and used to take me to steer the canoe. As I did not know how to do this very well, they often turned upon me, beat me, and knocked me down with the pole of the spear. I was beaten by one or the other of them almost every day. Other Indians, not of our family, would sometimes pity me and give me food when they could without being observed by the old man.

In the fall, after the corn was gathered and stored in the caches where they hide it for the winter, they went to hunt on the Saugenong River. I was very hungry here, as I had always been while among these Indians. I often saw my brothers eating something in the woods and tried to discover what it was, but they carefully concealed it from me. It was some time before I found some beechnuts and was tempted to taste them, though I did not know what they were. Finding them good, I showed them to the Indians. They laughed and let me know these were what they had been eating all along.

After the snow had fallen I was compelled to follow the hunters and often drag a whole deer home, though I did so with the greatest difficulty.

At night I always had to lie between the fire and the door of the lodge. When anyone passed out or came in, they commonly gave me a kick, and whenever they went to drink they threw some water on me.

The old man always treated me with great cruelty. One morning he caught me by the hair, dragged me out of the lodge, and rubbed my face in a mass of recent excrement for a long time, as one would the nose of a cat. Then he tossed me by the hair into a snow bank. After this I was afraid to go into the lodge, but finally my mother came out and gave me some water to wash. We were about to move our camp, and I was made to carry a large pack, as usual. I had not been able to wash my face clean, and when I came among the other Indians they noticed the smell and asked me about it. By signs and the few words I had learned I told them how I had been treated. Some of them helped me wash myself and gave me something to eat.

Often when the old man would begin to beat me, my mother would throw her arms about me and he would beat us both together.

Towards the end of winter we moved to the sugar grounds. At this time Kishkauko, who was about twenty years of age, joined with four other young men and went on a war party. The old man also, as soon as the sugar was finished, returned to the village, collected a few men, and made his preparations to start. As he left, he said to me, "Now I am going to kill your father and your brother and all your relations."

Kishkauko returned first. He said he and his party had been to the Ohio River. There they had fired upon a small boat and killed one man. The rest had jumped into the water. Kishkauko had wounded himself in his thigh with his own spear as he was pursuing them. The party brought home the scalp of the man they had killed.

Old Manito-o-geezhik returned a few days afterwards. With him he brought an old white hat which I knew, from a mark in the crown, to be my brother's. He said he had killed all my father's family, the Negroes, and the horses, and had brought me my brother's hat that I might see he spoke the truth. I now believed my relatives were all dead, and was less anxious to return. This was precisely the old man's purpose in telling me this story. Many years later I discovered that only a small part of it was true.

I lived with this family for two years and gradually came to have less and less hope of escape. The men were often drunk and, whenever they were, they tried to kill me. I learned to run and hide in the woods, and I dared not return before their drunken frolic was over. I constantly suffered from hunger.

The old woman—they called her "Otter Woman"—treated me with kindness, and so did her daughters and Kishkauko and Benaissa, the youngest son. Although Kishkauko was good to me, he, his father, and the two brothers, Kwotashe and Shemung, were bloodthirsty and cruel, and those who are left of them continue to be troublesome to the whites to this very day. This family named me Falcon, a name I kept all the time I lived with the Indians.

I had been at Saugenong about two years when a great council was called by the British agents at Mackinac. This council was attended by the Sioux, the Winnebagoes, the Menominees, and many remote tribes, as well as the Ojibways, Ottawas, etc. When old Manito-o-geezhik returned from this council, I learned he had met his kinswoman Netnokwa there. In spite of her sex, this woman was regarded as the principal chief of the Ottawas. She had lost a son of about my age and, having heard of me, wished to purchase me to take his place.

My old Indian mother, Otter Woman, protested vehemently. I heard her say, "My son has been dead once and has been restored to me—I cannot lose him again."

But these protests had little influence when Netnokwa arrived, bringing with her a ten-gallon keg of whiskey, blankets, tobacco and other articles of great value. Objections were made to the exchange until the keg had circulated for some time. An additional keg and a few more presents completed the bargain, and I was transferred to Netnokwa.

This woman was well on in years, but she was much nicer looking than my former mother. She took me by the hand and led me to her own lodge. Here I soon found I was to be treated more indulgently than I had been. She gave me plenty of food, put good clothes upon me, and told me to go and play with her sons.

We remained at Saugenong only a short time. Netnokwa would not stop with me at Mackinac, which we passed in the night, but traveled on to Point St. Ignace, where she hired some Indians to take care of me while she returned to Mackinac with one or two of her young men.

After finishing her business at Mackinac she returned, and we continued our journey. In a few days we arrived at Shabawywyagun. The corn was ripe when we reached there. We stayed a little while and then we went up the river. Finally we halted and set up our lodges for the winter.

Netnokwa's husband was an Ojibway of Red River called Tawgaweninne. He was seventeen years younger than Netnokwa. Tawgaweninne was always indulgent and kind to me, treating me like an equal. When speaking to me, he always called me his son.

Tawgaweninne himself was only of secondary importance in the family. Everything belonged to Netnokwa, and she had the direction in all affairs of any moment.

That first year, she gave me some tasks to do. She made me cut wood, bring home game, bring water, and perform other services not commonly required of boys my age, but she invariably treated me with so much kindness that I was far more happy than in Manito-o-geezhik's family. She sometimes whipped me, as she did her own children, but I was not beaten so severely and frequently as before.

Early in the spring Netnokwa and her husband took their family to Mackinac. They left me, as before, at Point St. Ignace, as they would not run the risk of losing me by letting me be seen by the British at Mackinac. On our return, we were detained by contrary winds on a point of land running out into the lake. We encamped here with some other Indians and a party of traders.

Pigeons were very numerous in the woods and the boys of my age and the traders were busy shooting them. I had never killed any game and, indeed, had never discharged a gun. Emboldened by Tawgaweninne's indulgent manner toward me, I asked permission to try to kill some pigeons with his pistol.

Netnokwa seconded my request. "It is time for our son to begin to learn to be a hunter," she said.

Tawgaweninne loaded the pistol and gave it to me. "Go, my son, and if you kill anything with this you shall immediately have a gun and learn to hunt."

I had not gone far before I met with pigeons. Some of them alighted very near me. I cocked my pistol and raised it to my face, bringing the breech almost in contact with my nose. Having brought the sight to bear upon the pigeons, I pulled the trigger. There was a humming noise, like that of a stone sent swiftly through the air.

I found the pistol some paces behind me and one of the pigeons under the tree on which he had been sitting. My face was bruised and covered with blood.

I ran home, carrying my pigeon in triumph. My face was speedily bound up and my pistol exchanged for a fowling piece; I was accoutered with a powder horn and furnished with shot, and allowed to go out after birds.

One of the young Indians went with me to observe my manner of shooting. I killed three more pigeons that afternoon and did not discharge my gun once without killing. Henceforth I began to be treated with more consideration and was allowed to hunt often.

A great part of the summer and autumn passed before we returned to Shabawywyagun. When we arrived we found the Indians suffering severely from the measles. We soon began to fall sick. Of ten persons belonging to our family, including two young wives of Tawgaweninne, only Netnokwa and myself escaped an attack of this complaint. Several were very sick, and the old woman and myself found it as much as we could do to take care of them. Numbers died in the village, but all of our family escaped. As the winter approached, they began to get better and we went to our wintering ground.

This winter was passed like the previous one, but as I became more and more expert in hunting and trapping I was no longer required to do the work of the women about the lodge.

The following spring Netnokwa went to Mackinac as usual. She always carried a British flag in her canoe, and I was told that whenever she came to Mackinac she was saluted by a gun from the fort. I was now thirteen years old. Before we left the village, I heard Netnokwa talk of going to Red River to her husband's relations. Many of the Ottawas determined to go with her—in all, six canoes.

This time, instead of leaving me at Point St. Ignace, they landed with me at night among the cedars, not far from the village of Mackinac. The old woman took me into the town, to the house of a French trader, and left me there. I was not allowed to go out at all, but otherwise I was well treated.

When we were ready to go on our journey, we were held up by head winds at the point where the missionaries now are. While we remained here the Indians began to drink heavily. My father, who was drunk but still able to walk about, spoke to two young men. Taking hold of the shirt sleeve of one of them, he tore it by accident. This young man—his name was Sugguttawgun—was irritated and gave my father a rough push. He fell on his back. Sugguttawgun then took up a large stone and threw it at him, hitting him in the forehead. I became alarmed for my own safety and ran off and hid in the woods.

The following day I became very hungry and returned and concealed myself in the low cedars near our lodge to see if it was safe to enter. After a while I discovered my mother calling me. I went up to her and she told me to go in and see my father.

When I went in, my father said, "I am dying." He made me sit down with the other children and talked much to us. He said, "Now my children, I have to leave you. I am sorry that I must leave you so poor."

He said nothing to us about killing the Indian who had struck him with the stone. He was too good a man to involve his family in the troubles such a course would have brought upon them. The young man who had wounded him remained with us, although Netnokwa told him it would not be safe for him to go to Red River, where her husband's relatives were numerous and powerful.

When we came to the Sault Sainte Marie, we found that the trader's vessel was about to sail to the upper end of Lake Superior. We were going in the same direction, so we put our baggage on board and then proceeded in our canoes. The winds were light, so that we were able to travel faster than the vessel, and we arrived ten days before it at the portage.

Finally the vessel came and anchored a little way out from shore. My father and his two sons, He-Who-Puts-on-Feathers and North Wind, went out in a canoe to get the baggage. North Wind jumped down into the hold of the vessel. His knee struck the knot of a rope tied around a bundle of goods and he received a painful injury.

That night North Wind's knee was badly swollen, and the next day he was not able to go out of the lodge. After eight or ten days we began crossing the Grand Portage. We carried him on a blanket fastened to two poles, but he was so sick that we had to stop often. We had left our canoes at the trading house, and when we reached the other side of the portage we had to make new canoes. When these were nearly finished, my father sent me and one of his wives back to the trading house to bring something which had been forgotten.

On our return trip we met two of our boys coming to tell me to hasten home, for my father was dying and wished to see me before he died. When I came into the lodge, he was not able to speak to me. In a few minutes he stopped breathing. Beside him lay the gun he had taken in his hand a few minutes before to shoot the young man who had wounded him.

In the morning, when I had left, he was apparently well. My mother told me it was not until afternoon he began to complain. He then came into the lodge and said, "I am dying. But since I have to go, this young man who killed me must go with me. I had hoped to live till I had raised you all to be men, but now I must die and leave you poor, without anyone to provide for you."

With the gun in his hand, he stepped out to shoot the young man, who was sitting by the door of his own lodge.

North Wind began to cry. "My father, if I was well I could help you kill this man, and could protect my young brothers from his relatives' vengeance after he is dead. But you see my situation, and that I am about to die. My brothers are young and weak, and we shall all be murdered if you kill this man."

My father had halted. "My son, I love you too well to refuse you anything you ask." He returned and laid down his gun. After saying a few words and asking them to send for me, he died.

The old woman procured a coffin from the traders and they brought my father's body in a wagon to the trading house on this side the Grand Portage, where they buried him in the burying ground of the whites. His two sons, as well as the young man who killed him, accompanied his body. This man was nearly killed by one of my brothers, but the other prevented him as he was about to strike.

It was but a very short time after my father died that we started on our journey to Red River. We carried my brother North Wind on a litter whenever it was necessary to take him out of the canoe. We had passed two carrying places when he said to us, "I must die here. I cannot go farther." So Netnokwa determined to stop here, and the remainder of the party went on. After they had started, there remained only the old woman, one of Tawgaweninne's younger wives, He-Who-Puts-on-Feathers, North Wind, and myself. It was about the middle of summer, for the small berries were ripe, when we stopped here on the borders of Moose Lake, which is cool and clear like Lake Superior.

At the approach of winter the old woman told us we could not remain there as the winter would be long and cold and there were no people, either whites or Indians, near us. North Wind was now so sick that in going back to the portage we were compelled to move slowly. When we arrived, the waters were beginning to freeze. He lived but a month or two after we arrived. It must have been in the early part of winter that he died. The old woman buried him by the side of her husband and hung up one of her flags at his grave.

### RED-SKY-OF-THE-MORNING

In the winter of my tenth year among the Indians one of the sons of the celebrated Ojibway chief Sweet of Leech Lake came to our lodge. This man was one of those who make themselves women, and are called women by the Indians. There are several of this sort among most Indian tribes, if not all. They are commonly called *agokwa*.

This creature, named Yellow Head, was nearly fifty years old and had lived with many husbands. I do not know whether she had seen me or only heard of me, but she let me know she had come a long distance to see me, with the hope of living with me. She often offered herself to me. Not being discouraged with one refusal, she repeated her disgusting advances until I was almost driven from the lodge.

Old Netnokwa was perfectly well acquainted with Yellow Head's character, and only laughed at the embarrassment I showed whenever she addressed me. She seemed to encourage Yellow Head to remain at our lodge. Yellow Head was very expert in the various employments of the women, and gave all her time to them.

Finally, despairing of success with me, or being pinched too much by hunger, which was often felt in our lodge, she disappeared. I began to hope I should not be troubled by her any more.

However, after three or four days she came back. She was loaded with dry meat. She said she had found the band of Chief He-That-Has-a-Bell, a relative of Netnokwa's, and he had sent an invitation for us to join him.

I was glad of this invitation, and we started immediately. At the first encampment, as I was doing something by the fire, I heard the *agokwa* whistling to me near by in the woods. Approaching, I found she had her eyes on a moose. I shot him twice, and he fell twice at the report of the gun, but I probably shot too high, for he escaped. The old woman reproved me severely, telling me she feared I should never be a good hunter.

Before the next night, we arrived at the lodge of He-That-Has-a-Bell, where we ate as much as we wished. Here, also, I found myself relieved from the persecutions of the *agokwa,* which had become intolerable. He-That-Has-a-Bell, who had two wives, married her. This introduction of a new inmate into his family caused some laughter and some ludicrous incidents—but it was attended with less uneasiness and quarreling than the bringing in of a new wife of the female sex.[1]

This band consisted of a large number of Indians. The country about them was hunted poor, so that few even of the best hunters were able to kill game often. It so happened that myself and another man, like me reputed a poor hunter, killed more frequently than others. I began to be dissatisfied at remaining here. I therefore made a road for myself and set my traps in a gang of beavers.

When I told He-That-Has-a-Bell that I intended to leave him he was afraid I should perish of hunger. He determined to accompany me to my traps to see the place I had selected and judge whether I should be able to support my family. When we arrived, he found I had caught one large beaver. He advised and encouraged me and, after telling me where I should find his camp in case we were pressed by hunger, he returned.

My family had now been increased by the addition of a poor old Ojibway woman and two children, who, being destitute of men, had been taken up by Netnokwa. Still, I thought it was best for us to live by ourselves.

I hunted with considerable success until the end of the season for making sugar, when Netnokwa determined to return to Menaukono-skeeg, while I should go to the trading house at Red River to purchase some necessary articles. I made a pack of beaver and started by my-self in a small buffalo-skin canoe, only large enough to carry me and my pack, and descended the Little Saskatchewan.

In a bend of that river, there is a beautiful landing place, with a little plain and a thick wood behind it, and a small hill rising abruptly in the rear. It looks like the kind of place the Indians would always choose to encamp at. But there is a story of fratricide connected with it—a crime so uncommon that the spot is regarded with terror and loathing. No Indian will land his canoe at "The Place of the Two Dead Men."

The Indians relate that many years ago, when they were encamped here, a quarrel arose between two brothers who had the rattlesnake for their totem. One drew his knife and slew the other. The band looked upon the crime as so horrid that they immediately killed the murderer and buried the two together.

As I approached this spot, I thought of the story of the two broth-ers, who bore the same totem as myself. I had heard that if any man encamped near their graves, they would come out of the ground and either re-enact the quarrel and the murder, or annoy their visitors so much in some other manner, that they could not sleep. I determined to discover the truth of these matters for myself. Part of my motive was curiosity, but I also wished to be able to tell the Indians I had not only stopped, but slept quietly at a place they shunned with so much fear.

The sun was going down as I arrived. I pushed my little canoe onto the shore, kindled a fire and, after eating my supper, lay down and slept.

Very soon, I saw the two dead men come and sit down by my fire. Their eyes were intently fixed upon me, but they neither smiled nor said anything. I got up and sat opposite them by the fire, and in this situation I awoke. The night was dark and gusty, but I saw no men, nor heard any other sound than that of the wind in the trees.

It is likely I fell asleep again, for I soon saw the same two men standing below the bank of the river, their heads just rising to the level of the ground I had made my fire on, and looking at me as before. After a few minutes they rose, one after the other, and sat down opposite me. But now they were laughing and pushing at me with sticks. I endeavored to speak to them, but my voice failed me. I tried to flee, but my feet refused.

Throughout the night I was in a state of agitation and alarm. Among other things, one of them told me to look at the top of the little hill which stood near. I did so and saw a horse fettered, looking at me.

"There, my brother," said the *jebi,* "is a horse which I give you to ride on your journey tomorrow. As you pass here on your way home, you can call and leave the horse, and spend another night with us."

At last the morning came. I was pleased to find that these terrifying visions had vanished with the darkness of the night. But my long residence among the Indians and the frequent instances in which I had seen dreams verified [2] made me think seriously of the horse the *jebi* had given me. I went to the top of the hill and I discovered tracks and other signs there. Following these a little distance, I found a horse which belonged to the trader I was going to see. I knew I could save several miles' travel by leaving my canoe and going overland from this point on the Little Saskatchewan to the Assiniboine. I caught the horse and put my load upon him, and then I led him towards the trading house.

In all my later journeys through this country I carefully shunned "The Place of the Two Dead," and the account I gave of what I had seen and suffered there confirmed the Indians in their dread of the spot.

In the fall, when I was something more than twenty-one years of age, I moved with He-Who-Puts-on-Feathers, our two families, and many other families of Indians to the Wild Rice. While we were collecting and preparing the grain, many were seized with a violent sickness. It began with cough and hoarseness, and sometimes bleeding from the mouth or nose. In a short time many died, and none were able to hunt. At first my attack appeared less violent than that of most others.

For several days there had been no meat in the camp. Some of the children had not been sick, and some of those who had been sick began to recover now and needed some food. There was only one man besides myself capable of exertion, and he, like myself, was recovering. We were wholly unable to walk, and could scarcely mount our horses when they were brought to us by the children.

In this emergency we rode into the plains and were fortunate enough to overtake and kill a bear. We could not eat a mouthful of the flesh of this animal, but we took it home and distributed an equal portion to every lodge.

I continued to get better, and was among the first to regain my health, as I supposed. In a few days I went out to hunt elk and killed two of them in two or three hours, but became somewhat excited and fatigued. I cut up the meat and took home a load on my back. When I arrived, I ate heartily of some which they cooked for me, then lay down and slept.

Before the middle of the night I was waked by a dreadful pain. It appeared to me that something was eating into my ears. I called He-Who-Puts-on-Feathers to look, but he could see nothing. The pain became more and more excruciating for two days, until I became insensible.

When my consciousness returned after two days, I found myself sitting outside the lodge. I saw the Indians on all sides of me drinking, some trader having come among them. Some were quarreling. Among them I distinguished He-Who-Puts-on-Feathers, and saw him stab a horse. Then I became insensible and remained so for some days, until the band were nearly ready to move.

My strength was not entirely gone, and when I came to my right mind I could walk about. I reflected much on all that had happened since I had been among the Indians. In the main I had been contented in Netnokwa's family, but I looked upon this sickness as the beginning of misfortune that would follow me through life.

Abscesses had formed and discharged in each ear, and I could now hear but very imperfectly. I sat down in the lodge and could see the faces of men and their lips moving, but did not know what they were saying. I took my gun and went to hunt, but the animals discovered me before I could see them. If by accident I saw a moose or an elk and tried to get near him, I found my cunning and my success had deserted me. I soon imagined the very animals knew I had become like an old and useless man.

Under the influence of these painful feelings I resolved to destroy myself, to escape the certain misery I saw before me.

When the Indians were ready to move, Netnokwa had my horse brought to the lodge and asked if I was able to get on and ride. I told her I was. I asked her to leave my gun with me and said I would follow the party at a little distance.

I took the rein of my horse's bridle in my hand and sat down and watched. Group after group of Indians passed me and disappeared. Finally the last old woman and her heavy load of mats had sunk behind the little swell of the prairie that bounded my horizon. I felt much relieved. I cast loose the reins and let my horse feed at large.

I cocked my gun. Resting the butt on the ground, I put the muzzle to my throat. With the ramrod, which I had drawn for the purpose, I proceeded to discharge the gun.

The piece had been well loaded a day or two before, but now I found the charge had been drawn. My powder horn and ball pouch had always contained ammunition, but now I found them empty. My knife, also, was gone.

Baffled in the attempt to take my life, I threw the gun from me and mounted my horse. I soon overtook the party, for He-Who-Puts-on-Feathers and Netnokwa had gone just far enough to conceal themselves from my view and then sat down to wait. Probably in my ravings I had talked of my intention to destroy myself, and so they had been careful to deprive me of the most direct means of carrying out my plan.

Suicide, incidentally, is not very infrequent among the Indians. They commit it in various ways—by shooting, hanging, drowning, poisoning, etc. The causes are just as various—misfortunes and losses of different kinds, sometimes the death of friends, and possibly disappointment in love.

After I recovered my health more perfectly, I began to feel ashamed of this attempt. My friends were so considerate as never to mention it to me. Though my health soon improved, I did not recover my hearing quickly. It was several months before I could hunt as well as I had been able to.

I was not among those who suffered most from this terrible sickness. Of the Indians who survived, some were permanently deaf, others injured in their intellects and some, in the fury caused by the disease, dashed themselves against the trees and rocks, breaking their arms or otherwise maiming themselves. This disease was entirely new to the Indians.

On going to Mouse River trading house, I heard some white people from the United States had been there to purchase articles for their party, then living at the Mandan village. I regretted I had missed the opportunity of seeing them. I have since been informed these men were some of the party of Governor Clark and Captain Lewis, then on their way to the Rocky Mountains and the Pacific Ocean.

Late in the fall we went to Kenukauneshewayboant. Game was plentiful here, and we determined to stay through the winter. One evening I was standing by our lodge when I saw a good-looking young woman walking about and smoking. She noticed me from time to time, and at last came up and asked me to smoke with her. I answered that I never smoked.

"You do not wish to touch my pipe—for that reason you will not smoke with me," she said.

I took her pipe and smoked a little, though I had not been in the habit of smoking. She remained some time and talked with me, and I began to be pleased with her. After this we saw each other often and I gradually became attached to her. Her name was Miskwabunokwa or Red-Sky-of-the-Morning.

Red-Sky-of-the-Morning and I grew more and more intimate. Though I said nothing to Netnokwa about it, I soon found she was not ignorant of what I was doing.

Once I spent a considerable part of the night with my mistress. It was the first time I had done so. I crept into the lodge at a late hour and went to sleep. A smart rapping on my naked feet waked me at the first appearance of dawn.

"Up," said the old woman. She stood by me with a stick in her hand. "Up, young man—you who are about to take yourself a wife— up, and start after game. It will raise you more in the estimation of your future wife to see you bring home a load of meat early in the morning than to see you dressed ever so gaily, standing about the village after the hunters are all gone out."

I could make no answer. I put on my moccasins, took my gun,

and went out. Before noon I returned with as heavy a load of fat moose meat as I could carry. I threw it down before Netnokwa.

"Here, old woman, is what you called for in the morning," I said harshly.

She praised me for my exertion. I, in turn, felt happy that she approved of my affair with Red-Sky-of-the-Morning. There are many Indians who neglect or cast out their old people, but I always felt the strongest regard for Netnokwa.

I redoubled my efforts in hunting, and often came home with meat early in the day. Then I used to dress myself as handsomely as I could and walk about the village, sometimes blowing the flute. For some time Red-Sky-of-the-Morning pretended she was not willing to marry me. It was not until she noticed some slackening of my ardor that she laid this affected coyness aside.

For my own part, my anxiety to take a wife was rapidly becoming less and less. I made several efforts to break off and not visit her any more, but a lingering inclination was too strong for me. When she noticed my growing indifference, she sometimes reproached me and tried to move me with her tears and pleading. But I said nothing to the old woman about bringing her home, and every day I became more unwilling to take her as my wife.

About this time I had to go to the trading house on Red River. I started with a half-breed who worked for that establishment and was mounted on a fleet horse. The distance we had to travel was seventy miles. We took turns riding and going on foot, and the one on foot kept hold of the horse's tail and ran. We traveled the whole distance in a single day. On the way back I was by myself and I did not have a horse. I made an effort to complete the same journey in one day, but darkness and fatigue forced me to stop about ten miles from home.

When I arrived at our lodge I saw Red-Sky-of-the-Morning sitting in my place. I stood by the door, hesitating to enter. She hung her head.

Netnokwa greeted me in a tone harsher than she generally used toward me.

"Will you turn away from the door and put this young woman to shame, who is better than you in every respect? This affair has been of your seeking, not of mine or hers. You used to follow her about the village—but now you want to turn from her and make it appear that she has thrust herself upon you."

I was aware that Netnokwa's reproaches were just, and I was also still fond of the girl. I went in and sat down by the side of Red-Sky-of-the-Morning, and thus we became man and wife.

While I was absent at Red River, old Netnokwa had made her bargain with the parents of the young woman and brought her home. She had done so without my knowledge or consent, rightly supposing it would not be difficult to reconcile me to the move.

### THE PROPHET

There was a man called Aiskawbawis in our band—a quiet, rather insignificant person and a poor hunter. His wife died and his children began to suffer of hunger even more than before. Aiskawbawis became melancholy and despondent.

After a while he called the chiefs together. With great solemnity he announced that he had been favored by a revelation from the Great Spirit.

He showed the Indians a round, smooth ball of earth. It was more than half as large as a man's head and was smeared with red paint.

"As I sat crying and praying and singing at my lodge," he declared, "suddenly the Great Spirit called to me. 'Aiskawbawis,' he said, 'I have heard your prayers. I have seen the mats in your lodge wet with your tears and I have listened to your request. I give you this ball. As you see, it is clean and new. I give it to you as your model, to make the whole earth like it. All old things must be destroyed. Everything must be made new. Into your hands, Aiskawbawis, I entrust this great work.' "

I was one of those he called in to listen. After he had sent us away I said to my companions: "It is good that we can be acquainted with the whole mind of the Great Spirit at so cheap a price. Now we have these divinely taught instructors springing up right in our own band —men who are fortunately worth nothing for any other purpose. Here is one too lazy and spiritless to feed his own family, yet he has been chosen by the Great Spirit—or so he would have us believe—to make the whole earth over."

I had never thought well of this man and I did not hesitate to ridicule his pretensions wherever I went. Although bad luck followed him constantly, he gained a powerful hold over the minds of the Indians. His incessant beating of his drum at night scared the game away from our neighborhood, and his insolent hypocrisy made him offensive to me, but he had found the way to control the minds of many of the people, and all my efforts against him were in vain.

Once, we had been suffering from hunger for some days. I went out to hunt and wounded a moose. On my return I said I believed the moose was so badly wounded that he must die. Early next morning Aiskawbawis came to my lodge. With the utmost seriousness, he said the Great Spirit had been down and told him about the moose I had wounded.

"He is dead now," he said, "and you will find him in such-and-such a place. Bring him here and cook him as a sacrifice. It is the will of the Great Spirit."

I thought it probable the moose was killed and went in search of him, but found he was not dead. This gave me another opportunity to ridicule Aiskawbawis's claims, but it did not shake the confidence of the Indians in him.

Shortly afterwards I again wounded a moose and went home without getting it.

"This," said Aiskawbawis, "is the moose which the Great Spirit showed me."

I went out and found that this time the moose was indeed dead. I brought him in. As many of the Indians were hungry, I made a feast. We were too few to eat all the meat, so we cut it off the bones, and these were heaped up before Aiskawbawis for a sacrifice. They were carried to a safe place and hung up out of the reach of the dogs or wolves, as no bone of an animal offered in this way must be broken.

The following day I killed another fat moose. Aiskawbawis made a long address to the Great Spirit and afterwards said to me, "You see, my son, how your goodness is rewarded. You gave the first you killed to the Spirit. He will take care you shall not want."

Next day I went out hunting with my brother-in-law and we each killed a moose. Aiskawbawis exulted greatly over the power of the sacrifice he had caused me to make, and his hold over the Indians was strengthened. Although he had obtained this high degree of favor by his cunning, this man had once eaten his own wife because of hunger and the Indians had wanted to kill him at the time as unworthy to live.

When the snow began to harden on top at the approach of spring the men of our band—Shegwawkoosink, Wauzhegawmaishkoon, Bapowash, Gishkauko, myself, and some others—went to make a hunting camp some distance from our lodges. Only Aiskawbawis was left at home with the women. We killed a good deal of game, as it is very easy to take moose and elk at that season. The crust on the snow will bear a man, but these animals sink through it and are almost helpless.

After a while Gishkauko went home to see his family. On his return he brought me a little tobacco from Aiskawbawis with this message: "Your life is in danger."

"My life," I said, "is in the hands of the Great Spirit, and when he sees fit to place it in danger or bring it to an end I shall have no cause to complain. But I cannot believe he has revealed his intentions to so worthless a man as Aiskawbawis."

The message from Aiskawbawis alarmed all the Indians with me, and they made their way to the place where he was encamped with the women. I took a longer route by myself to visit some of my traps and reached home some time after the others. I found all our lodges converted into one large one. Men, women, and children were shivering by a fire in the open air.

When I asked the meaning of this, they told me that Aiskawbawis was preparing to give an important communication from the Great Spirit. He had been preparing the lodge a long time and everyone had been kept out. He had arranged that Bapowash, who was to lead the dance, should enter at a signal. The others were to follow him and dance around the lodge four times and sit down.

I immediately entered the long lodge and seated myself by the fire. Aiskawbawis gave me one angry, malicious look, then closed his eyes and pretended to go on with a prayer that I had interrupted. After some time he began to drum and sing aloud. He stopped twice and then began again. At the third interval of silence, which was the signal agreed upon, Bapowash came dancing in, followed by the men, women, and children. After circling the lodge four times, they all sat down.

For a few moments all was silence. Aiskawbawis continued sitting with his eyes closed, in the middle of the lodge, next to a spot of smooth, soft ground which he had prepared. Then he began to call the men, one by one, to come and sit down by him. Last of all he called me. I went and sat down as he directed.

"Falcon, my son," he said, "I have very unpleasant information to give you. Lately the Great Spirit has been pleased to show me what is to happen to each of us in the future." He turned to the other Indians. "To you, my friends, who have been careful to obey the commands of the Great Spirit as communicated by me, he has given the gift of living to the full age of man. This long straight line shows the length of your lives. But, as for you, Falcon—you who have turned aside from the right path—this short crooked line represents your life. You are to reach only half the full age of man. This line turning off on the other side shows the life of the young wife of Bapowash."

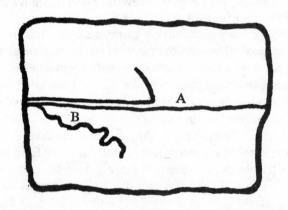

As he said this he showed us certain marks he had made on the ground. [*See illustration.*] The long straight line, A, represented the life of the Indians. The short crooked one, B, showed the brief and irregular course he foretold for my own. The one terminating abruptly on the other side represented the life of Bapowash's favorite wife.

It happened that Bapowash had dried the choice parts of a fat bear, intending to make a feast to his medicine [3] in the spring. A few days earlier, while we were at our hunting camp, Aiskawbawis had said to Bapowash's mother-in-law, "The Great Spirit has told me all things are not as they should be. See if the fat bear your son-in-law has hung up for a feast to his medicine is all where it was left." She had gone out and found the bear's feet were gone. (Aiskawbawis himself, who was a great glutton, had stolen them.)

This loss was now made known to Bapowash. He was greatly alarmed at the early death which threatened his wife and, to prevent it, he gave Aiskawbawis the rest of the bear and other valuable presents.

After this, we started for an island in the Lake of the Woods, where we intended to plant corn. On our way we stopped to make sugar and then we went to visit the traders. Again we left Aiskawbawis with our women.

The wife of Gishkauko, one of the Indians, had forgotten her kettle at the sugar camp, some distance from the place where the women were to wait for us. Some time after we had gone, Aiskawbawis sent for her. He lived by himself in a little lodge, pretending to be too holy to go into a common house, or to mingle with men in their ordinary pursuits. When she came, he said, "The Great Spirit is not pleased to see you lose your property. Go and get the kettle you left at the sugar camp."

The woman obeyed. Soon after she had left, he took his gun and went out in a different direction, pretending he was going hunting. But he was no sooner out of sight of the lodges than he turned and sought out her track.

Gishkauko's wife had been annoyed by his attentions before. Surmising his real object, she kept a lookout behind her. When she saw him come running after her, she began to run also.

Just at this time we were returning from the trading house. We saw this chase at a distance and were greatly alarmed—we thought the Sioux had come to our country and were murdering our women and children. But when we got a little nearer, the pretended prophet gave up his pursuit of the woman and came and sat down with us, to drink the rum we had brought from the trading house.

After the woman got home, she was compelled to give some account of the race. She said that Aiskawbawis had often looked for opportunities to be alone with her, but she was so afraid of him that she never dared to tell anyone or offer any other resistance than to try to escape. However, this discovery caused no disturbance and did not seem to diminish Aiskawbawis's influence in any way.

A large part of the rum we had brought was set apart for him. But when the chief of our band sent for him to call for it, he answered that he could not.

"Tell the chief," he said, "that if he has any business with me, he can come to my lodge."

The liquor was carried to him. Drinking seemed to make him more sociable, for about the middle of the night he came staggering into my lodge without the least covering on his body. He looked very ludicrous, and I enjoyed a good deal of irreverent merriment at his expense.

After this we went to the Lake of the Woods, where I hunted for about a month. Now I began to discover how unwise I had been to incur the ill will of Aiskawbawis. He prejudiced the Indians—particularly the relatives of my wife—against me, so that my situation became uncomfortable and I was compelled to return to Red River.

About this time a hundred or more Scots came to settle at Red River under the protection of the Hudson's Bay Company. These people were in desperate want of provisions, and soon after my arrival Mr. Hanie, the agent, hired me to hunt buffalo for them. In the four months that I hunted for the company I killed about one hundred. Mr. Hanie and the governor of the Hudson's Bay Company wanted to build me a house and engage me permanently. But I delayed accepting their offer, as I thought it doubtful that they would succeed in settling the country.

I was still at Red River when He-That-Has-a-Bell came and told me that several of the children of my wife's parents had died. He informed me that when the children were sick the parents called Aiskawbawis to do something for them. The prophet made an enclosure and then he said he had called me into it and made me confess I had shot bad medicine at the children—though I was then at Red River. He made my wife's parents and most of the Indians of the band believe it was my medicine which killed the children. He-That-Has-a-Bell warned me to be on my guard with these relatives as they were plotting my death.


### WHITE BIRD

Several seasons later I moved out into the prairie with a large band of Indians. We had been having little luck in hunting and there was often hunger in our camp. Some had starved to death, and others were close to dying.

One day I went out hunting with two young men. After walking about three hours we climbed a little hill and saw that the ground before us was black with buffaloes. We crawled up close to them and I immediately killed two fat cows. As I was cutting these up, I began to hear the guns of the men of our party—they had followed me and had now arrived among the buffaloes.

It was somewhat late when I got back to our camp. Most of the men were in before me. I had expected to hear the sounds of feasting and rejoicing, but all was silent and sad. I looked into one lodge after another. No one had anything to eat. Most of the men had come from a forest country and, never having hunted buffalo before, had all failed to make a kill.

At this time there was a man with us called White Bird, who seemed very jealous on account of my success in hunting. To avoid any unnecessary show and to keep from irritating this man, I decided not to make a feast in my own lodge, as would have been proper.

Nevertheless, one of the young men who had been with me made a feast. After setting aside enough food for my children, I sent the rest to the families around me. The young man who made the feast invited White Bird, among others. During the evening he did his best to prejudice the Indians against me, accusing me of pride, insolence, and of doing mischief among them. But I remained in my lodge and took no notice of this beyond contradicting his unfair statements.

Next morning, long before dawn, the women started after the remains of the two buffalo I had killed. I had shown some of the men which part of the buffalo to aim at; they went out again in pursuit of the herds, and several of them made kills. We soon had plenty of meat and all who had been sick or near death recovered.

The leader of this band was called Opoihgun. He and three lodges remained with me—the others scattered here and there in pursuit of the buffalo. Two of the men who remained with me were White Bird and his son-in-law. I killed great numbers of fat buffalo, and I had the choice parts of forty of them dried. We had suffered so much from hunger that I wished to protect my family against a return of it. I also planned to make my way to the States, and I knew I would have to leave them for some time without anyone to hunt for them. I made twenty large sacks of pemmican, filled ten kegs of ten gallons each with tallow, and preserved a considerable number of tongues, etc.

It was some time before I discovered why White Bird had decided to remain near my camp. His only purpose was to annoy me and molest me.

I had such large quantities of meat that when we moved I had to return four times with my dogs and carry one load after another forward to my camping place. One day White Bird contrived to meet me alone at the place where I was depositing my loads. I stopped. He thrust his hands violently into my long hair, which hung down on both sides of my head.

"This is the end of your road," he said. "Look down and see the place where the wolves and carrion birds will pick your bones."

I asked him why he was attacking me.

"You are a stranger," he said, "and have no right among us. But you set yourself up as the best hunter and want us to treat you as a great man. I have long been weary of your insolence. You shall not live another day."

He began to beat my head against a tree. I gave him a sudden push and threw him down, freeing my head at the expense of part of my hair.

A struggle followed. He caught three of the fingers of my right hand between his teeth and sank them quite to the bone, so that I could not draw my fingers out of his mouth. With my left hand I aimed a blow at one of his eyes. His jaws flew open and he leaped to his feet.

My tomahawk was lying near me. He caught it in his hand and aimed a powerful blow at my head. I eluded it and his own violence brought him to the ground. I jumped upon him, wrenched the tomahawk from his hand, and threw it as far as I could, while I continued to hold him fast to the ground.

I was enraged at his unprovoked attack. Still, I would not kill him. Seeing a piece of lodge pole there, I caught it in my hands and told him to get up. When he did, I began to beat him. He fled immediately. I followed and continued to beat him while he ran two or three hundred yards.

His son-in-law and two other young men belonging to his family had heard his cries. They came up.

"What have you done?" one of them cried angrily to me. The three immediately rushed upon me and threw me to the ground.

By this time White Bird had returned. Catching me by a black silk handkerchief I wore about my neck, he choked, kicked and beat me, and thrust my face down into the snow.

After a while I heard one of them say, "He is dead." I tried to encourage this opinion. They took their hands off me and stood at a little distance.

I sprang to my feet and seized a lodge pole. Whether through surprise or fear, they all fled. I pursued White Bird and gave him another severe beating with my pole.

For this time they left me. But later White Bird and his people went to my lodge. My wife had taken my dogs back there, and they were lying in front of the door, very tired. He drew his knife and stabbed one of them. My wife heard the noise and ran out, but he threatened to kill her also.

Next day, White Bird was bruised and sore, and his face was very badly swollen. I thought he would probably remain in his lodge. Since his dwelling was close to ours, I was afraid my wife might be in danger if I left her alone in my lodge. I sent her to carry the meat forward and remained at home myself. But I was worn out, and about midday I fell asleep. White Bird crept in slyly with his knife in his hand and was almost near enough to strike me when I awoke and sprang up. Seeing I was armed, he started back and fled, but I did not pursue him.

This was not the last of his persecutions. One day I had gone ahead of our party. As I was traveling a path which I knew the rest would follow, I went off it a little to place my camp, so I should not have to see White Bird. After a while he came to the fork of my path with his son, twelve years old. I heard him say to the lad, "Stop here while I go and kill this white man."

He threw down his load. Though his son begged him not to do anything, he came within fifty yards of me, drew his gun from its case, cocked it, and pointed it at me.

He held it in this position for some time. Then, seeing I was not frightened, he began to come closer, jumping from side to side and yelling the way warriors do when they approach each other in battle. He continued pointing his gun and threatening me so loudly that I became irritated and caught up my own gun.

The little boy ran up and, throwing his arms about me, begged me to spare his father, though he was a fool. I threw down my gun, seized the old man, and took his from him.

"I have put myself in your power so often," I said, "that by this time you ought to know you haven't the courage to kill me. You are not a man. You do not have the heart of a squaw or the courage of a dog. I am tired of your foolishness. If you trouble me any more, it will be at the risk of your life."

He left me and went on ahead with all the others, except my family. Next day I followed, drawing a loaded sled myself and driving my dogs with their loads before me. I was so glad to be free from his persecutions that I resolved to stop at Rush Lake and remain there. I thought White Bird and the other Indians intended to go on to the Lake of the Woods.

I selected a place to establish my camp for the rest of the winter. Here I left my children to take care of the lodge, and my wife and I returned to bring up loads of meat. When we came home at night, the children told us their grandmother had been to see them and left word for my wife and me to come and see her the following day. I readily agreed.

That night I dreamed. Several times before, when I had been hungry and in distress, I had fallen into a deep slumber and seen a beautiful young man who told me where I could find game. Now the same young man came down as usual through the hole in the top of my lodge and stood before me.

"You must not go tomorrow. If you disregard my warning, you shall take the consequences. Look there," he said.

He pointed in the opposite direction and I saw Shegwawkoosink, Mezhukkonaun, and some of my other friends coming. Then he pointed upwards and I saw a small hawk with a banded tail flying about over my head. He said no more, but turned and went out at the door.

I awoke deeply troubled and could not fall asleep again. In the morning I told my wife I could not go with her.

"What is the reason?" she asked.

I told her my dream, but she accused me of being afraid. She kept up her urging and finally I agreed to go.

In the morning I told my children that the Indians I had seen in my dream would come to the lodge that day. I said they must tell my friends that if I did not return by noon they would know I was dead. Then I started out with my wife.

I had not gone two hundred yards when I looked up and saw the same small hawk that had appeared in my dream. Again I told my wife I could not go. I turned back towards my lodge, but she again reproached me with being afraid.

I knew that my mother-in-law's family was strongly prejudiced against me. Refusing to visit her would only confirm that prejudice and make it stronger. Against my better judgment, I agreed to go on.

When I arrived at my mother-in-law's lodge I left my gun at the door and went in. I took a seat between two of my wife's sisters who were married to the same man. They had two children, and I was playing with them, with my head down, when I heard a sudden, loud noise and immediately lost my senses.

I saw no one and I remembered nothing till I began to revive. Then I found several women holding my hands and arms, and I saw terror in the faces of everyone about me. I knew nothing of what had happened until I heard a loud and insulting voice outside the lodge. It was White Bird's.

I began to feel something like warm water on my face. Putting my hand to my head, I laid my fingers on my naked skull.

I broke away from the women who were holding me and ran after White Bird. But I could not overtake him, because the Indians helped him to keep out of my way.

Towards night I returned to my lodge. I was very severely wounded and I believed the bones of my skull were broken. Very little blood had run down upon my face when I was wounded, and though I heard strange noises in my head I did not faint until I reached my own lodge. White Bird had taken my gun from the door of my mother-in-law's lodge and I had to return without it.

At my lodge I found Shegwawkoosink, Mezhukkonaun, and Otopunnebe, who was a relative of my Indian mother. The moment I took Shegwawkoosink by the hand the blood spouted in a stream from my head.

"What is the matter, my son?" he asked.

"I have been at play with another man and the game was rather rough." I wished to treat the matter lightly, but I immediately fainted away and they saw how serious my wound was.

When I had entered my mother-in-law's lodge I had neglected to pull off the hood of my thick moose-skin cloak, and it was this which prevented me from seeing White Bird come into the lodge. It is probable, also, that the blow would have killed me if my head had not

been covered. As it was, my skull was fractured and there is still a
large ridge upon it where the edge of the tomahawk struck. It was a
long time before I recovered fully from this wound.

The band that I was with had never hunted in the prairie before.
They now became afraid that the Sioux were near and would fall
upon them. They fled in terror, leaving their lodges and all their property behind. I was too weak to travel and I knew we were in no
danger from the Sioux. But my mother-in-law found much fault with
me because I did not go with the Indians.

I was convinced that my mother-in-law had helped White Bird in
his attempt on my life and I suspected that my wife had, too. I
therefore told them both to leave me if they wished. They went, and
took my children with them.

The only persons who did not desert me were Otopunnebe and
his cousin, a lad of fourteen. These two remained and nursed me,
while those who should have been my friends abandoned me to my
fate. After the fourth day I became much worse and was unable
to sit up until the tenth day.

Otopunnebe told me that he intended to punish White Bird for his
act of violence against me. We heard that my enemy had gone to
the village at Menawzhetaunaung, and after I had regained a little
strength we started out in that direction. It was arranged that I was
to stop at the trader's post and Otopunnebe was to go on to Menawzhetaunaung. We were to meet at an appointed place on the day
he said he would return from the village.

We met again at the time and place agreed. He told me that he
had gone to the village, entered the lodge of one of the chiefs, and
sat down. He had not been there long when White Bird came in and
sat down opposite him.

After they had looked at each other for some time, White Bird
said, "I know what has brought you so far to see us. You have no
brothers of your own—the Long Knives have killed all of them—
and now you are so foolish as to call the man I beat the other day
your brother."

"The Long Knives have not killed any brother of mine," Otopunnebe said. "But even if they had, I would not allow you to abuse and
injure my friend without provocation. It is true I call him my brother
—and I will avenge him as if he really were. But I won't spill blood
in the lodge of this chief, who has received me as a friend."

Seizing White Bird by the hand, he dragged him out. He was about to stab him when the chief caught his hand and took away the knife. Three or four men jumped on Otopunnebe and there was a scuffle. But he was a powerful man and he did not forget why he had come. He kept his grip upon White Bird until two of his ribs were broken.

I thought two broken ribs about equal to a broken head, and I was content. We feasted together on game I had killed, and then we returned to the deserted camp. About ten days later the people began to come back to look after their property and Otopunnebe returned to Red River, where he lived. Some time afterward this good man suffered the fate which overtakes so many of the Ojibways—he starved to death.

### HE CUT OFF MY LONG HAIR

By now I had a great store of meat laid aside—enough to supply my family's needs for a year or more. After setting my affairs in order, I took a canoe and started for Mackinac by myself. From there I intended to go to the States and find my relatives, if any were still alive.

At Mackinac, Major Puthuff, the United States Indian agent, gave me some provisions and a letter to Governor Cass at Detroit and put me on board a schooner. In five days we arrived at Detroit. I went on shore and, walking up into the street, I stood gazing around me. After a while I saw an Indian. I went up to him and asked who he was.

"An Ottawa of Saugenong," he answered.

"Do you know Kishkauko?"

"He is my father."

"And where," I asked, "is Manito-o-geezhik, his father and your grandfather?"

"He died last fall."

"It is well he is dead," I said, for I had not forgotten the many brutal things he had done to me. Then I asked the Indian to call his father to come and see me. He called him, but the old man would not come.

Next day, as I was standing in the street again, I saw an old Indian and ran after him. He turned about and looked anxiously at me for a few moments. Then he caught me in his arms. It was Kishkauko, but he looked very unlike the young man who had taken me prisoner so many years before.

"Is it true that your father killed all my relations?" I asked him.

He told me it was not. The year after I was captured, he said, Manito-o-geezhik had returned to the same field where he had found me, and had watched my father and his people planting corn. When they all went into the house except my brother, the Indians rushed upon him and caught him. Then they took him into the woods and crossed the Ohio. At night they left him securely bound to a tree. But he was able to free himself and ran away.

The Indians were roused by the noise he made and they pursued him into the woods but were not able to overtake him. His hat had been left at the camp, and they brought this back to make me believe they had killed him.

This was wonderful news, for till that time I had always supposed that most, if not all, of my father's family had been murdered by the Indians. I tried to persuade Kishkauko to take me to Governor Cass's house, but he was afraid to go. Some Indians told me in which house the governor lived and I went toward the gate. A soldier stopped me. I could not speak English well enough to be understood, but I saw the governor sitting on his porch and I held up Major Puthuff's letter. He told the soldier to let me pass in.

As soon as the governor had read the letter he gave me his hand and sent for an interpreter. He talked a long time with me. Kishkauko was sent for and confirmed my statement about my capture and two years' residence with the Ottawas of Saugenong.

The governor gave me clothing and sent me to his interpreter's house, where he told me I was to stay. He said he was going to assemble many Indians and white men to hold a council at St. Marys on the Miami, and from there he would send me to my relatives on the Ohio.

I waited two months or more. Then I became extremely impatient and left with Benaissa, Kishkauko's brother, and eight other men who were going to the council. I went without Governor Cass's knowledge and so I had no provisions. We suffered greatly from fatigue and hunger, particularly after we passed the rapids of the Miami, where we left our canoe. The Indians whom we encountered often refused to give us anything, though they had plenty.

Finally we reached St. Marys. Here I was taken sick with a fever and an ague which was extremely painful, though it did not confine me all the time.

About the time of the conclusion of the council, Governor Cass called me to dine with him. Many gentlemen asked me to drink wine with them and I was scarcely able to walk home. Afterwards the interpreter told me the governor had been curious to see whether I had acquired the Indians' fondness for liquor and would behave as they did when drunk. But I had not felt the influence of the wine so much as to forget myself, and had immediately gone to my lodge and lain down until I was sober.

The governor gave me goods valued at one hundred and twenty dollars. As I still had a considerable journey to make, I purchased a horse with part of the goods. At the council there were two men from Kentucky who knew some of my relatives, and I started out with them. My health was still very poor.

In a few days I became much worse. At last I was quite unable to move, and I stopped at the house of a poor man who seemed to pity me and did everything in his power to help me. One of the men with whom I had been traveling made me understand that he would go to the Ohio and either come back himself or send someone after me.

Finally a young man came for me, who said that he was my nephew and that he had been sent by my relatives in Kentucky. From him I heard that my father had died, and I also learned some particulars of my surviving relatives.

From this place we traveled to Cincinnati. The journey was very tedious and difficult. After resting a little, we went down the Ohio in a skiff. My fever continued to return daily. I was reduced to a skeleton, and did not have enough strength to walk or stand by myself. Finally we reached the place where my sister's children were living. Here I lay sick about a month.

A letter came for me now. They read it to me repeatedly, but I could not understand a single word. All the time since my arrival I had lain sick and no one had been with me for any considerable time, so I had not learned to understand English or make myself understood. After a while I recovered somewhat and was often able to walk about. Then a second letter came. From it I understood that my brother Edward, whose name I had never forgotten, had gone to Red River to search for me.

I was greatly concerned about Edward, and I immediately called for my horse, intending to return towards Red River and search for him. Twenty or thirty of the neighbors assembled around me and each gave me a little money: some one shilling, some two shillings, and others larger sums, and I got upon my horse and started out.

I had ridden about ten miles when fatigue and sickness overcame me and I was compelled to stop. I stayed for four days at the house of a man named Morgan. When I called for my horse again, the neighbors gathered round me as before. One gave me some bread in a bag, another tied a young pig behind my saddle, and among them all they furnished me with a good supply of provisions and some money.

As I was still very weak Mr. Morgan accompanied me to Cincinnati. I had found that it made me sick to sleep in a house and I refused to do so on this journey. Mr. Morgan would sleep in the houses where we stopped at night, but I chose a good place outside and lay down and slept there. Before long I had partly recovered my health. At Cincinnati Mr. Morgan left me and I traveled on alone.

A few days afterwards I stopped at a house where I saw a great quantity of corn lying in the yard. My horse was hungry. I got down and handed a dollar to the man who stood there, and then I counted ten ears of corn and laid them before my horse.

I could not make the people grasp that I was hungry myself—at least they seemed determined not to understand me. I went into the house and the woman looked displeased. Seeing part of a loaf of corn bread, I pointed first to it, next to my mouth. As she did not appear to understand, I took it in my hand and raised it to my mouth. She called to the man outside. He came in, took the bread from me, pushed me violently out of the house, then took the corn from my horse and motioned to me to be gone.

Next, I came to a large brick house and I determined to try here. As I was riding up, a very fat man came out and spoke to me in a loud, harsh tone. I could not understand his words, but I suppose he meant to forbid my entering the yard.

I was willing to go away, but this man ran up and caught my horse by the bridle. He said a good deal to me, but I understood very little of it. I thought he was cursing me because I was an Indian. Then he took hold of my gun and tried to wrench it out of my hand.

I was sick and hungry and irritable. When I found he wanted to take my gun from me, I became angry. I had a hickory stick about three or four feet long in my hand and I struck him over the head. He immediately relaxed his hold on my gun and I rode off.

One night I was taken very sick. In the morning I found that my horse had escaped. I was scarcely able to follow him, but I did. When I reached the forks of the Maumee River, opposite the trader's house, I saw the horse standing on the other side. I called to the trader and asked him to send or bring the horse over to me, as I was sick. He said no. I asked him to bring me a canoe, but he also refused this, and I was compelled to swim across. I finally got my horse and returned to my camp, but I was too sick to travel farther that day.

This journey was painful and unpleasant all the way. I traveled on from day to day, weak, dispirited, and alone, meeting with little sympathy and often suffering from hunger and sickness. I was willing to sleep in the woods and I constantly did, but it was not easy to kill any game, and the state of my health did not allow me to go far from the road to hunt.

I was two days' journey from Detroit when I saw a man in the road with a Sioux pipe in his hand. His strong resemblance to my father immediately caught my attention. I tried to make him stop, but he gave me a hasty look and passed on.

When I arrived at Detroit I learned that this man was my brother. But the governor would not allow me to go after him. He said that my brother would inquire at all the Indian traders' houses on the way and would very soon hear of me and return.

His opinion was well founded, for about three days afterwards my brother came back. He held me in his arms a long time. Because I hardly knew any English we were unable to speak, except through an interpreter. Later he cut off my long hair, on which I wore strings of brooches in the Indian manner.

We visited Governor Cass together, and he said he was very pleased that I had given up my Indian costume. But the dress of a white man was extremely uncomfortable to me, so that from time to time I was compelled to put on my old clothing.

My brother insisted that I should go to his house beyond the Mississippi, and we set off together. On the way we stopped at Fort Wayne and we received a good deal of friendly attention from the military commandant. Forty days brought us to the Mississippi, fifteen miles above New Madrid, where my brother's house was. Another of my brothers lived near by, and they both accompanied me to Jackson, fifteen miles from Cape Girardeau, where two of my sisters were living. From this place six or seven of us started out for Kentucky, where many of my relatives lived, not far from Salem and Princeton.

The night before my arrival my sister Lucy had dreamed she saw me coming through the cornfield surrounding her house. She had ten children. Relatives, friends, and neighbors crowded around to witness my meeting with my sisters. Though we could speak very little to each other, my sisters and most of those who gathered about us shed many tears.

# Three Came Back

## CHARLES JOHNSTON

L*ATE IN 1826, Charles Johnston, a Virginia lawyer, had an unusual visitor at Botetourt Springs, his estate in Roanoke County. It was a grizzled old Canadian trader, Francis Duchouquet, who was very much down on his luck. No one could have received a heartier welcome, and for very good reason. Many years before, in 1790, Johnston had been a prisoner in the hands of a party of Shawnees. One day the Indians decided that it would be easier for them to transport a scalp than their live prisoner. For Johnston it was fortunate that Duchouquet happened to be there that day, and that he had six hundred silver brooches on hand—about half the price of a good horse, but the full price of a young American.*

*The day of Johnston's redemption was his twenty-first birthday. It came only five weeks after the Indians had captured him. But those five weeks were the most harrowing ones he ever lived.*

*Young Johnston had been traveling down the Ohio with five others, bound for Kentucky. Their vessel was a flatboat or an "ark"—a large flat-bottomed boat without a keel and with high gunwales. He and his party had been told there were Indians lurking on the river bank and they had resolved not to set foot on land. But they were reckoning without an ancient and ingenious stratagem that the Indians used.*

*What the lure was, Johnston will soon tell you himself. Suffice it here to say that it had been employed many times before, and it wus to be used many times again. Simon Girty, the notorious "white renegade," is said to have helped the Indians practice it on occasion, no doubt for pleasure as well as profit.*

*Soon after he got back to Virginia, Johnston repaid the kindly trader who had advanced money for his ransom. In 1802 he saw Duchouquet again when the Canadian came to Washington as interpreter for a party of Indians negotiating with the government. Johnston gave a private dinner for Duchouquet and Tom Lewis, a Shawnee chief who had been one of his captors. When Duchouquet mentioned that he had redeemed other Americans besides Johnston, and five of them had been too poor to repay him, the grateful attorney drew up a petition to have him compensated and had it presented to Congress. Duchouquet was granted every cent he asked, interest as well as principal—$201.17 in all!*

*Like two others, James Smith and Alexander Henry, Johnston had a very busy life, and it was only in his later years that he found the leisure to retell these exciting events of his youth. He published his story,* A Narrative of the Incidents Attending the Capture, Detention, and Ransom of Charles Johnston, *in 1827, thirty-seven years after his liberation from captivity. He had lost the journal he kept while a prisoner of the Indians, and he had to rely on memory alone—but he did have old Duchouquet at his elbow to check a fact or two if it came into question. Johnston died in 1833.*

Mr. John May was a gentleman of wealth and respectability who lived at Bellevue, about five miles above Petersburg, Virginia. He was an early speculator in land in Kentucky, and his business was large and complicated. He needed an assistant, and in 1788 he made me such a good offer to come and work for him that I did not hesitate to accept.

The following year Mr. May's affairs took him to Kentucky, and I went with him. We were able to get only part of our business done, and in February, 1790, we set out again to complete it. On our first trip we had gone entirely by land, but this time Mr. May decided to travel on the Kanawha and Ohio Rivers part of the way.

We journeyed by land for several days. The weather was uncommonly cold; one night there was so heavy a fall of snow that in the morning we found it nine or ten inches thick on our blankets. Finally we arrived at Kelly's station, on the Great Kanawha. Here we contracted for one of those heavy, clumsy, slowly moving flatboats then used to carry travelers and their property to the western settlements. In a few days the boat was ready. We had been joined by a Mr. Jacob Skyles, who was going to Kentucky with a stock of dry goods, and all three of us went down the Great Kanawha to Point Pleasant together.

At Point Pleasant three persons joined us: William Flinn, Dolly Fleming and Peggy Fleming. Flinn was one of those hardy characters bred on the frontier and accustomed to its usual pursuits—hunting, and fighting with the Indians. The Miss Flemings were women of a humble station in life. They were sisters. One of them was the particular friend of Flinn and the other was her traveling companion. They were residents of Pittsburgh, bound for the country down the Ohio River.

We remained at Point Pleasant only a short time. We had heard a rumor that the savages had decoyed a boat to shore and killed everyone on board, and we decided that we would not set foot on land for any reason until we reached Limestone. The people we talked to at the point also warned us against going on shore—they had heard that parties of Indians were lurking along the banks of the Ohio. How well we held to our decision will soon be seen.

The river was high, which made it easy for us to move along. We had nothing more to do than to get to the middle of the stream and let our heavy, unwieldy boat float down. Our numbers were too few and our experience too limited to make the boat travel faster than the current. But there was perfect safety while we remained out of musket or rifle shot from the shore. And that was not difficult, as the part of the river down which we were to pass was about a mile wide.

We did not expect any danger from the savages while we were at a distance from land. It was not their habit to try to board a boat in midstream. Besides, the gunwales of our boat were so high that we could fight off a party much larger than our own, and Mr. May, Skyles, Flinn, and I had firearms. It is true they were nothing better than ordinary fowling pieces, except for Mr. Skyles', which was a small neat rifle. But they seemed good enough for our purposes.

Our boat was steered by an oar at the stern, and the male passengers took turns at it. We had gone down the river nearly to the point where it joins the Scioto when, about dawn on the twentieth of March, we were called by Flinn, who was standing at the steering oar. He directed our attention to some smoke hanging over the tree-tops on both sides of the river. We decided to find out on which bank the fire that produced this smoke was burning, and then to bear away from it.

After a short time we distinctly saw that the smoke was rising from a fire on the northwestern bank and we began to turn toward the opposite one. Then we noticed two white men on the side of the river where the fire was. They called to us and begged us to take them on board our boat. They declared the Indians had taken them prisoner a few weeks before at Kennedy's Bottom in Kentucky and they had been brought across the Ohio; then they had been lucky enough to make their escape. They said they were suffering severely from cold and hunger and were sure either to die or to fall into the hands of the Indians again unless we rescued them.

They continued to run along the bank of the river, keeping abreast of us and repeating their story with cries and wailings. After a while our suspicions began to weaken. They begged us with so much earnestness that our sympathy was aroused and we began to discuss going on shore.

When we first saw them we had asked them about the smoke rising from their side of the river, but they had denied there was any fire. This was clearly a falsehood—our own eyes disproved it—and it ought to have made us close our ears against everything they told us. However, we went on with the discussion.

Flinn and the two females, like most of the first settlers on our frontier, were used to thinking lightly of danger from Indians, and they urged us to land. Mr. May, Mr. Skyles, and I were against the idea. We reminded the others that the two white men had not told the truth about the fire, and therefore should not be trusted. But Flinn replied that they had had to make a fire on account of the cold—and then were unwilling to admit it because we might suspect there were Indians on the shore.

We were moving so much faster on the water than they were on land that by this time we had left the men far behind and were almost out of reach of their voices. Flinn now suggested a scheme by which he himself could bear all the danger of landing. He said we had gotten so far in front of the men that if there had been any Indians nearby we must be considerably ahead of them; we could touch the shore only long enough for him to leap on it, and immediately turn the boat back into the stream, where we would be safe. He argued that if there really were any Indians he could see them as soon as they saw him, and he could escape by outrunning them and rejoin us the next day at Limestone. However, if our fears proved groundless, we could put back to shore and take him and the two men on board.

This plan looked as if it could be carried out in safety, and we all agreed to try it. We began to steer toward the bank where the men were.

As we went across the current we stopped moving as rapidly as we had while traveling directly with it. The result was that it took us a long time to get to the bank. By the time we had reached it and put Flinn ashore, to our utter astonishment and dismay we saw a party of Indians rushing toward us armed to the teeth.

There were not many of them at first, since only the swiftest could get to the spot as soon as the boat reached it. We determined to resist, and Mr. Skyles and I took up our guns. We did not see the main group of the Indians, as they were running at some distance from the river and keeping in the background. However, in a few moments they began to come up. Mr. May saw their numbers increasing and he said we did not have a chance against them. He urged us to try to get back into the current.

Unfortunately, there was a large tree, with many strong branches, bending over the bank, and now we found our boat was caught in them. We worked desperately to free ourselves. Meanwhile the whole band of Indians—there were fifty-four of them—came up, firing a few scattered shots as they advanced. They took a position not over sixty feet from us. Filling the air with their horrible war whoops, they poured their whole fire into our boat.

Resistance was hopeless—to get away from the shore was impossible. To protect ourselves from their fire, we lay down on the bottom of the boat—but not before the Indians hit Dolly Fleming, who had taken shelter behind me. The ball had passed close over my left shoulder and struck her in the corner of her mouth, killing her instantly. Skyles was wounded in the shoulder by a rifle bullet.

Our enemies continued to fire into the boat until all our horses had been killed. The danger to which we were exposed was aggravated by these animals. They were so frightened by the smell of powder and the firing that it was extremely difficult to avoid being trampled by them. And after they were shot it was almost impossible to keep clear of them as they kicked and struggled in their dying agonies. After they had been killed the firing ceased and all was quiet on board.

Mr. May had not taken off his nightcap since he awoke in the morning. He got to his feet and held it up as a signal of surrender. Seeing him rise, I warned him to get down.

But it was too late. The moment I spoke, the firing started again and a ball went through his brain. I supposed that he had taken my advice and lain down of his own accord. I did not discover my mistake until a short time afterwards, when I looked at him and saw his face was covered with blood and there was a hole in his forehead. Once more the fire from the bank was discontinued.

By the time Flinn had reached the top of the bank he was their prisoner; Mr. May and Dolly Fleming were dead; Mr. Skyles was wounded; Peggy Fleming and I remained unhurt. About twenty of the savages plunged into the water and swam toward us with tomahawks in their hands. The rest stood with their rifles pointed towards us, ready to fire if we resisted the boarding party.

The Indians began to climb up the side of the boat. I rose and, reaching out my hand to the one nearest me, helped him get in. Then I went to the others and I helped as many of them on board as I could. When they entered, they shook hands with me.

"How de do! How de do!" they cried out in broken English.

I returned their greeting with a hearty squeeze of the hand, as if I was glad to see them. The truth was, I had expected that all of us would be put to the tomahawk. Finding our reception so different from what I had anticipated, the kind greetings I gave them were not altogether feigned.

After the momentary confusion produced by the capture was over, they pushed the boat to the shore. Then the rest of the party came aboard, their rifles in their hands. They, too, shook hands with us, and appeared highly delighted at the success of their enterprise. After the excitement of the moment had subsided a little, some of them began to examine the booty they had taken—principally dry goods belonging to Mr. Skyles—whilst others scalped and stripped the dead. After this operation, the bodies of Mr. May and Dolly Fleming were thrown into the river. Then the party all went on shore, taking us and the booty with them.

The first thing to be attended to was the kindling of a fire. Immediately afterwards we were stripped of the greater part of our clothes. The weather was uncommonly cold for March and I was wearing an overcoat and a broadcloth coat over a red vest. When the coats were unbuttoned, they discovered the red vest.

An Indian named Chickatommo, who had the chief command and could speak some English, exclaimed, "Oh! you cappatain?"

I answered in the negative.

He pointed to his breast. "Me cappatain," he said. Then he pointed to the other Indians. "All dese my sogers."

After taking my outer clothes, one of them repeated the word "Swap—swap," and demanded that I give him my shirt for his, a greasy, filthy garment that had not been washed during the whole winter. I was drawing it over my head when another Indian behind me, whose name I learned was Tom Lewis, pulled it back. He reproached the first Indian for his unkindliness, took the blanket from his own shoulders and threw it over mine.

After this, I sat down by the fire. I had some leisure for reflection now, and I began to consider the dreadful situation in which I found myself. No one who has not had a similar misfortune can imagine the terror I felt. I had been bred up with a horror of Indians and Indian cruelties, and now, suddenly, the thing I feared the most had happened. I felt I would never see my friends or the civilized world again. In my imagination I was already tied to the stake, and the flames were about to be kindled around me.

I had not been seated long when the scalps of Mr. May and Miss Fleming, which had been stretched upon sticks bent into a circular form, were set before me at the fire to dry. The sight of these scalps, so unfeelingly placed directly in my view—one of them torn from the head of a woman by our ferocious captors, the other from a man who had won my esteem and friendship—aroused feelings in me that are too painful to describe.

Now the two white men who had decoyed us on shore made their appearance. The name of one was Divine, the other Thomas. As soon as they came up, they began to apologize and protest that they were not at fault. They declared the Indians had compelled them to act the part which had brought us into their hands. They said they had really been taken from Kennedy's Bottom some weeks before, and that they were terribly sorry they were responsible for our capture.

We hesitated to believe them. Our doubts about Divine increased when a Negro arrived who had been captured by the Indians some time before. He told us that Thomas had been very much against the plot by which we were trapped—but that Divine alone had planned it and carried it out after the Indians promised they would set him free if he would get other white prisoners for them.

About the time of the Negro's arrival six squaws, most of them old women, with two white children, a girl about ten years of age and a boy a year or two older, joined us. The children had been taken prisoner in Kentucky.

Skyles' wound was painful and Flinn was permitted to examine it. He found that the ball had entered one shoulder, had ranged towards the other, and was lodged against it. Then he made an incision with a razor and extracted it. One of the squaws washed the wound. She caught the bloody water from it in a tin cup and made Skyles drink it, telling him it would hasten the cure.

By this time the fire had been extended considerably; it was at least fifty feet long. The Indians were all seated around it. Their rifles were arranged in a line at their rear, so near that each man could lay his hand on his own in an instant. The guns were supported by long poles, placed horizontally about three feet high on forks, and were neatly and regularly arranged.

Our captors consisted of Indians from various tribes. They were Shawnees, Delawares, Wyandots, and Cherokees. Much the largest number were Shawnees. An old chief of the tribe took a position at one end of the fire and harangued the party for ten or fifteen minutes. He frequently raised his eyes and pointed to the sun, sometimes to the earth, and then to me.

It was impossible for us to understand what they were up to. I was particularly alarmed because he pointed at me and at none of the other captives. This was soon explained when Chickatommo led me to an Indian seated on the ground and placed me at his side, telling me this man was "my friend." This Indian's name was Mes-shawa, and he belonged to the Shawnee tribe.

Chickatommo then addressed the party from the same spot where the old Shawnee chief had stood, and in very much the same manner.

He pointed at Skyles and, when he had finished his speech, delivered him to another Shawnee. The same ceremony was performed with Peggy Fleming and Flinn. She was allotted to the Cherokees and Flinn to the Shawnees.

None of us was given to the Delawares or Wyandots. Those tribes were at peace with the whites, and probably their members in the party were unwilling to risk involving their people in war by accepting any of the prisoners. Their presence on this occasion is not hard to account for. Young men of all the savage tribes frequently go out on raids without consulting their chiefs or nation.

After distributing the captives, the Indians made Divine, Thomas, and Flinn prepare four additional oars for our boat. They intended to use it to attack any other boat that might pass by while they were near the river.

We spent the first night of our captivity in the most painful anticipation. Next morning, at an early hour, our foes were busily occupied in painting their faces so they would look as terrifying as possible. Each individual had a small looking glass which he held in front of him while he put on the paint. The glass had a frame with a short handle and a string through a hole in the end of it for tying it to his pack. They always paint their faces this way when they expect to encounter an enemy.

About ten o'clock a canoe containing six men was observed coming up the river, near the opposite bank. All of us were compelled to go to the side of the water to induce the men in the canoe to cross over and come within range of the Indian rifles. I hoped it would be possible for me to signal and warn these unfortunate people of their danger.

Divine again seemed perfectly happy to help the savages in their plans. He made up a tale that we were traveling down the Ohio and our boat had suffered serious damage and we were unable to repair it because we did not have an axe. The unsuspecting canoemen turned towards us, but the current bore them down so far below us, I had no chance to put them on their guard. As they had done in our case, the Indians ran down the river at a distance from it, under cover of the woods. They were not discovered until the canoe was close to shore, when they fired into it and shot everyone on board. The men tumbled into the water and their little canoe turned over.

Two who were not yet dead kept themselves afloat, but were so severely wounded that they could not swim off. The Indians leaped into the river, dragged them to the shore, and tomahawked them. The bodies of the four who had been shot dead were also brought to land, and all six were scalped.[1] They were then thrown into the river.

Two or three hours afterwards, three boats came into view. The Indians waited until these boats were directly opposite them. Then they began firing with their rifles. The Ohio was so wide there that their bullets fell far short of their targets and the boats went past us.

The savages immediately made all the male captives get into the boat taken from Mr. May, which now was equipped with the additional oars made the day before. Every Indian jumped in, too.

Our captors were inexperienced in the use of the oar, so they assigned this work to us. They stood over us and compelled us to row as hard as we could, but we had as little experience as themselves. Unskilful as we were, we took care not to strike the water with all our oars at the same time. Still, the people we were pursuing had only one pair of oars in each boat and we had two pairs in ours. We shuddered to think of the outcome.

Good management on the part of the passengers in the three boats and intentional mismanagement on our part saved them. The middle boat waited for the one in the rear, took the people from it aboard, together with their oars, and then hastened forward to overtake the front boat. After some hard rowing they came alongside and everyone entered it. Now they had many hands to relieve each other in rowing, and six oars to our four. To our great joy, they shot rapidly ahead of us.

The Indians, seeing they could not overtake the boat, gave up the chase. Next, they turned their attention to the two boats which were adrift and found rich booty on board. It consisted mostly of dry goods and groceries intended for Lexington, Kentucky.

In the boats there were some very fine horses, too. Among them I recognized two remarkable animals, a mare and a stallion, belonging to Mr. Thomas Marshall, brother of the Chief Justice, with whom Mr. May and I had traveled through the wilderness on our return from the West the preceding year. That gentleman's hat was also among the abandoned articles. I recognized it at a glance. It was one of the cocked hats worn at that time, and a small piece had been cut or torn from the point, which was worn in front.

The boats were taken to the shore and their contents landed. The chiefs distributed the plunder among their followers. Flour, sugar and chocolate formed a part of it. They probably believed I understood the subject of making flour into bread better than they did, and that chore was assigned to me. They gave me the undressed skin of a deer, which was most disgustingly stained from having been used as a saddle on the sore back of a horse, and was now to serve as a tray.

I began by baking a number of loaves in the ashes. There was more dough than the fire would contain and I decided to make the remainder into small dumplings and boil them in a kettle of chocolate then on the fire. All savages are particularly fond of sweet things. To gratify this taste, they had mixed a large portion of sugar with the chocolate, and this made the dumplings quite sweet. The Indians were so delighted with this new delicious dish that they appeared to consider me a very clever fellow as a cook, and gave me that job as long as I was their prisoner.

They had found some whiskey on one of the boats, and they now began to drink very heavily. But they took a precaution which I believe they never neglect when there is a need for vigilance: a number of them refrained from tasting the liquor and guarded the captives.

The rest of the party drank to deep intoxication. Flinn went as far as any of them, and had a fight with one of the Indians, whom he easily beat. Some of the rest tried to help their brother. Then others intervened in Flinn's favor and protected him from attack. They said that the treatment he had received would only be tolerated by women and that, having acted like *a man,* they would not let him be abused.

Their habit is not to leave the bottle or cask while a drop of strong drink remains, and they kept pouring it down their throats until their stock was exhausted. This occurred the following night.

In the meantime our guard took us some distance from the Indians who were drunk. We lay down to sleep. Skyles and I had resolved to seize the earliest chance to make our escape. We flattered ourselves that the drunkenness of the main party, the darkness of the night, or a momentary relaxation of vigilance on the part of our guard might furnish the golden opportunity. Our scheme was to get into one of the boats lying along the bank of the river and to drop quietly down the stream. If we could get just a little distance from the shore, without being seen, there would be a good prospect of success.

We remained silent until we believed all our sentinels were asleep. Then we began to whisper. We presumed we would not be heard—or, if we were, that our guard would not understand us, as they did not know any English. But our keepers were always on the alert. When our whispers reached their ears, they put an end to our hopes by binding us tightly with cords.

Soon after this, one of the drunken Indians straggled from his companions and came to us, brandishing his scalping knife. He quickly worked himself up into a great rage and, throwing himself on Skyles, fastened on his hair. He seemed determined to take off Skyles' scalp, and it was with some difficulty that our guards stopped him.

During the night Divine and Thomas disappeared. So far as we could discover, the Indians made no effort to detain them.

The Indians seemed to think their booty was worth carrying to their towns, and we left the Ohio the following afternoon. Not all of them moved off together. Those who had Flinn remained at the river and we never saw them or him afterwards.

When we began our march a cow—she had been found in one of the boats the preceding day—was committed to my care. I was required to lead her by a rope tied to her horns.

This creature perplexed me greatly. I suppose she was not accustomed to travel this way, and she resisted my efforts to get her forward. She would leave the track on which we walked and frequently, when I went on one side of a tree, she would insist on taking the other. The Indians laughed very heartily at my troubles with this unmanageable animal.

Late in the evening we reached an encampment where our captors had left a number of horses stolen from the settlements of Kentucky, a quantity of dried bear meat, venison, pelts, and some of their people. It was a rich valley, with luxuriant tender grass below a covering of thick weeds, which protected it from the frost and cold. In this encampment there were shelters, made of skins stretched over poles. Here, to my great relief, they took the cow off my hands by slaughtering her.

After breakfast the next day, Chickatommo left the encampment, accompanied by a party belonging to his tribe and by the Cherokees with Peggy Fleming. The horses (all of which he took with him) were packed with the meat and furs. The rest of the party followed soon afterward. We traveled through a trackless wilderness. It abounded in game, and the Indians depended on this entirely for food during the journey. Their plan was to carry the dried meat home for the summer use of their families.

On the first or second day the Indians observed a tree, the bark of which was marked by the claws of a bear. They immediately went to work with axes they had found in the captured boats and they soon felled the tree. Two very small cubs were found in its hollow trunk. Their dam, attracted by the noise, came up when the tree fell and was shot.

We regaled ourselves upon the flesh of the cubs. To me it was excellent eating, although the manner of dressing would hardly suit a delicate taste. The entrails were taken out and, after the hair was thoroughly singed from the carcasses, they were roasted whole.

The Indians now seemed inclined to loiter and waste time. By contrast, I was impatient to move on as rapidly as possible. I had conceived the hope that when we reached their towns I might meet some trader who would ransom me and bring my sufferings and dangers to an end.

An accident, in other respects unimportant, subjected me to a night's torture. The savages had left a few of their party in the rear to watch and give them warning if the whites should attempt to pursue them and take their prisoners or plunder from them. My protector, Messhawa, belonged to the men left in the rear.

In his absence I was committed to the custody of another Shawnee altogether unlike him in temper. When he was about to secure my arms at night by lashing a rope around them, I foolishly complained that he was drawing it too tight.

"Damn you soul!" he exclaimed and tightened the rope with all the vigor he could, so that by morning it was buried in the flesh of one of my arms.

I could get no rest that night. When Messhawa came up with us the next day my arm was exceedingly swollen and throbbed with agony. The moment he saw this he loosened the rope and harshly rebuked the other man for his severity towards me.

The Indians still continued their habit of daily lounging. If a bear was killed or if they got any other food and they swallowed an abundant meal, immediately afterward they lay down to sleep. When they awoke, if there was still enough food they would again eat plentifully and go to sleep.

Some packs of cards were found among their plunder. They amused themselves daily with these by playing a game whose Indian name was translated into English as "Nosey." Only two hands were dealt out, and the object of each player was to keep part of his own cards and get all of his opponent's. The winner had a right to a number of fillips at the nose of the loser equal to the number of cards in the winner's hand.

When the winner was about to begin, the loser would place himself firmly in his seat, assume a solemn look, and not permit the slightest change in any muscle of his face. At every fillip the bystanders would burst into a peal of laughter, while the loser was not even allowed to smile. The penalty was doubled if he violated this rule. It is astonishing how greatly they were delighted with this childish diversion. The game often continued hour after hour.

While the Indians were busy with their cards, I tried to begin a journal of my travels. A copy of the Debates of the Convention of Virginia, assembled to decide on the adoption or rejection of the Federal Constitution, had been found in one of the boats taken on the Ohio. I had brought it from the river to read and pass the time, and now I determined to write my notes on the margins of its pages. With a scalping knife I made a pen of the quill of a wild turkey. I made ink by mixing water and coal dust, and began my journal.

This attracted the attention of the Indians. Tom Lewis, the man who gave me the blanket when another Indian was about to strip me of my shirt, took my journal from my hands, carried it to the others who were sitting around the fire, and showed it to them all. They seemed surprised and gratified. Although they could not understand it, they appeared to think it indicated something extraordinary about me.

When the party had satisfied themselves with "Nosey," we resumed our march and arrived at a large branch of the Scioto. My shoes had been taken from me, and one of the squaws had made me a pair of moccasins from the leather of a greasy pair of old leggings. I was in front when we came to the edge of the water. The stream was rapid. I was unacquainted with its depth, could not swim, and hesitated to enter.

An old woman, who was behind me, took the lead. In her hand she carried a staff, and she supported herself with this against the force of the current. If a man had gone in before me I should still have hesitated. But being confident I could wade safely wherever the old woman could go, I followed her.

The bed of the creek was formed entirely of round smooth stones. My greasy moccasins kept slipping so incessantly that at every moment I was in extreme danger of losing my footing, and I had the greatest difficulty reaching the opposite bank.

The Shawnee chief Chickatommo and his party had waited for us and in two or three days we caught up with them. I found that the Cherokees and their prisoner, Peggy Fleming, had taken a different route from the one we were following. This girl's behavior, by the way, had astonished me greatly. I had expected that the death of her sister before her very eyes, her own captivity and probably dreadful fate would have plunged her into grief and despair. But from the day of our capture, up to the time she was led away by the Cherokees, she seemed perfectly indifferent to the horrors of her situation. She enjoyed high spirits and appeared contented and happy.

At about this time we came to a line of trees which had been marked by surveyors. The savages feel the deepest hatred for these men. They consider them the agents who take their lands from them, because they are invariably the forerunners of settlement by the whites. The sight of the trees with the chops of the axe in their bark irritated our party so greatly that we feared for our safety. They cursed us with bitterness and fury, and they did not become calm again until we had gone some distance beyond the marked line.

Every night, before we went to sleep, our captors took the most rigorous measures to make sure we did not escape. Our arms were pinioned by a strong rope of buffalo hide, which was stretched in a straight line and each end secured to a tree. Our keepers lay down near us on these ropes, three or four of them on each side—but they were free to change their positions, while we could only lie on our backs.

We were generally placed on different sides, sometimes on the same side of the fire. No covering was allowed me except a child's blanket, for the one Tom Lewis had thrown over my shoulders on the first day of my captivity had been given back to him. Skyles' blanket was much larger than mine, but we were not permitted to keep each other warm by lying together.

Usually, about the time the fire burnt down we would awake, fatigued from our position and numb with cold. The rest of the night was nothing more than a series of severe pains. When morning arrived I was frequently incapable of standing, until the warmth of the fire restored my strength. A deerskin under us formed our sole protection from the cold and dampness of the earth.

Skyles and I repeatedly talked about a plan of escape. The weather had been dry for some time. A vast multitude of leaves covered the ground, and it was impossible to pass over them without producing a loud noise, which was certain to betray our flight to the Indians. We hoped it would rain before many days passed, and were determined to try to regain our liberty as soon as the leaves were moist and we could walk among them unheard.

Skyles had carefully concealed a knife in the pocket of his breeches. He intended to use it to cut the cords that tied us at night and then we planned to run off into the woods.

But one morning, when Skyles rose from the spot on which he had slept, I saw the knife lying on his deerskin. I thought the Indians were not watching and I pointed it out to him. However, they saw it as quickly as he did. They instantly stripped our breeches from both of us. To take their place, the Indians gave us the same kind of covering they wore themselves.

The incident of the knife made the Indians treat us more sternly than they had before. When we lay down to sleep at night, each of us had one end of a cord tied around his neck and the other end fastened to a tree or stake five or six feet from his head. A small bell was suspended from this cord and it rattled when we made the slightest motion, telling the whole party that we were stirring.

During the day the cords around our necks were bound up at the ends into a sort of club, which hung down our backs. The club on Skyles' neck reached to his wound and irritated it severely. All the same, the Indians loaded him with a very heavy pack. He did not dare to complain, because he knew that his cruel master would double his burden. As for myself, I had been carrying a large pack of booty on my back ever since we left the Ohio River, and they had also given me an uncommonly heavy rifle to bear. This burden gave me great trouble.

Soon after Skyles and I were captured, the Indians invented names for us. I was called Ketesselo. I never found out whether this word was intended to express any particular idea. Their name for my fellow-prisoner was "Stinking white man." It was applied to my unfortunate friend because his wound had become offensive to the smell, although I washed it for him regularly every day.

After traveling ten or twelve days we reached the eastern bank of the Scioto. The water was too deep for fording, and everyone was soon busy preparing a raft. They selected dead timber and felled it, and then it was carried on the shoulders of the men to the waterside.

One of the logs was so large and heavy that even two persons could not carry it. Some of the Indians helped a couple of their people get the smaller end of this log on their shoulders, while I was made to carry the larger end by myself. They helped me pick it up, but I quickly saw the burden was too much for me. After staggering with it a short distance, I had no alternative but to drop it.

I could not speak their language, so I called to the men who were in front of me with the smaller end and told them in English what I was about to do. They probably did not understand me, and when I let my end fall to the ground the whole weight of the log was thrown violently upon them. The sudden jolt brought them to the earth with the log on top.

This mishap aroused the two Indians to such a pitch of rage that for a few moments I was afraid my life was in danger. However, the injury they had received was so severe that they were unable to get up for a while. The other Indians roared with laughter, while my fellow-laborers kept crying, "Damn Ketesselo! Damn Ketesselo!" Only two of the Indians could speak our language, but there was not one of them who did not know how to curse in English, and all of them had picked up the common greeting, "How d'ye do?"

The adventure of the log had a fortunate result for me: They no longer made me help them carry the trunks of trees to the river. They completed the raft by tying the logs together with grapevines, and men, women, prisoners, and baggage were carried over in several trips. The horses swam across.

Not long after crossing the Scioto we met a hunting party, who encamped close to us. Some of our Indians took me to their encampment. They boasted how they had captured us and how they had chased the boats on the Ohio, and they exulted in their success. I did not understand their language, but their signs, their gestures, and their faces told me everything.

About this time we came to a creek. A log lay over it, five or six feet above the surface, connecting one bank with the other. We began to walk across this. The greasy moccasins I wore were so slippery that I tumbled into the stream. Luckily, it was no deeper than my waist and I had no difficulty getting to the other side. The savages are so well known for their sternness that we are ready to suppose they are entire strangers to mirth. But any happening like this never failed to draw loud, repeated bursts of merriment from them.

I had never experienced trials and hardships such as those I was now undergoing. Still, my health was not injured by wading creeks, falling into the water, sleeping in the open air in all kinds of weather, or by any of the other inconveniences I encountered on this long, painful march, the first of its kind I had ever made.

Mr. Skyles and I soon found we had fallen into very different hands. The contrast in character between his keeper and mine was striking. Messhawa, my master, was humane and generous; Skyles' keeper was ferocious and brutal. Messhawa was very watchful and alert to make certain I should not escape; still, he always showed a regard for my feelings and a desire to relieve my suffering. The conduct of Skyles' keeper, however, was calculated to hurt his feelings and aggravate his pain in every way.

At our meals Messhawa would share his food with me down to the last morsel. The other Indian was very different. He gave his prisoner just enough to keep him alive and nothing more.

Once, after a fatiguing day's march, Skyles was eating some boiled raccoon out of a kettle. He had taken just a few morsels when his keeper snatched the kettle from him and in an angry tone told him he had eaten enough. Messhawa had given me more than plenty and I wanted to share it with Skyles. But I could do this only by stealth. If his brutal keeper had caught me, he would have made us both feel his anger.

These two Indians were as different physically as they were in the qualities of their hearts. Messhawa was tall, straight, and muscular. His complexion was very dark and he did not have the harsh, ferocious look that savages usually do; his face expressed mildness and humanity. He was distinguished as a swift runner. The other man was old, under middle height, and lame. His face looked mean and bitter.

Skyles and I had observed that our captors watched every move we made. We resolved to say very little to each other; we were afraid the Indians might think we were planning an escape and put an end to all communication between us. We kept this resolution for some time, until a delightful April day so lifted our spirits that we talked much more than we meant to.

We were immediately punished for our carelessness. A party of eight or ten Indians took Skyles and left for the villages on the Maumee River. The others headed for the towns on the Sandusky with me and the two white children.

My heart sank when I saw them preparing to take Skyles away. But his misery was far greater than mine. His wound demanded attention, and I had been in the habit of washing it daily; no one else had touched it for a long time. Now he was entirely in the hands of his unfeeling keeper, who took a savage delight in mistreating him, and there was no one around him who spoke English.

Mr. Skyles and I had become close friends in the weeks we had spent together. We shook each other warmly by the hand and we embraced. Our faces were wet with tears. We took leave of each other without a ray of hope to brighten our prospects.

Soon after we parted, the people to whom I belonged halted, about midday, to rest. An Indian well on in years lay down and fell asleep. A young man who had kept his eyes on him waited until he was slumbering soundly. Then he crept cautiously to where the other man was lying quietly, raised and dropped his tomahawk several times over his body, and at last struck its blade into his back with all his strength.

The wounded man sprang to his feet and ran off as fast as his legs could carry him. But he was not pursued, nor did he rejoin us afterwards. I was never able to obtain a clue to this murder attempt. Incidents of this kind go far to show the character of this strange and savage people.

A number of days passed. The party sometimes traveled, often halted for the purpose of eating, sleeping, and playing their favorite game, "Nosey." They also occasionally amused themselves by dancing, invariably accompanied with a song composed of the words

"*Kon-nu-kah—he-ka-kah—we-sa-too—hos-ses-kah*"—repeated in a tone which did not strike the ear with a very musical effect.

When they became tired of this, they sometimes compelled me to imitate them in both the dance and the song. Once when the blaze of the fire was very high, they made me leap through it, and I only escaped injury by performing the act as quickly as possible.

They carried two or three tobacco pipes, which every man smoked when he chose, often to great excess. A circle was frequently formed and the pipe passed round from one to the other until all were satisfied. While enjoying the fumes of their tobacco they rarely spoke. Sometimes, a short, dry observation would escape one of those within the circle, and the others would express their assent by a grunt. They are much in the habit of conveying their ideas by a gesture, always made with striking emphasis.

We were now deep in the interior of a wild, uninhabited country. I was compelled to abandon anything like an effort or a hope to escape from my captors. Even if I had succeeded in eluding their vigilance, I should have been unable to procure food of any kind or find my way through the woods for I did not know how many miles. I would surely have died of hunger or fallen into the hands of other parties of Indians, who were wandering about in every direction. I therefore resigned myself to staying with them until we should arrive at their towns, where I hoped some kind-hearted trader might ransom me.

During the whole march we lived on bear's meat, venison, turkeys, and raccoons. The country through which we passed had an abundance of every kind of game, but it diminished as we approached their villages.

I had been on this journey nearly four weeks when we found a Negro in the woods, under a tent. It contained a quantity of whiskey and pelts belonging to his master, an Indian of the Wyandot tribe, then at peace with the United States. This Negro was a runaway from Kentucky, and he had fled across the Ohio to the country of the savages. I was told it was a law among the Indians that the first one who laid hands on a runaway had a right to keep him, and the Negro had been acquired by his Wyandot master in this way. The Wyandot himself was off on a hunt when we met this Negro.

The poor Negro, whom I should have kept at a distance under other circumstances, now became my companion and friend, and I felt quite at home. He treated me with great kindness and hospitality and offered me whatever food and drink he had. It was good to taste bread and salt again—I had not had either since we left the Ohio River.

As soon as my captors found the Negro had whiskey for sale, they bartered part of their booty for it. A disgusting revelry began which lasted for three days. As usual, enough of them remained sober to guard the prisoners—the two children and myself.

On the first night we were taken some distance from the spot where the drunken Indians were. The two children had never been tied, but I was bound as usual, and Indians lay down on each side of me. I slept until about midnight, when I was awakened by the falling of rain.

Soon after, the Negro came to our camp. He kindly invited me to go to his tent with him and sleep under it, protected from the rain. I pointed out that I could not accept his invitation without the consent of my guards, who were lying on each side of me on the rope I was tied with.

These men heard the Negro and myself talking. They did not understand what we said, but they suspected he was helping me plan an escape. They immediately sprang up, seized the Negro, and set up a tremendous yell. This was answered by the party of drunken Indians and soon most of them came running towards us, their tomahawks in their hands.

The Negro could speak their language, and they took him a short distance off and asked him what he was doing there. After this I was questioned separately by one who spoke English. Our answers corresponded and the Indians did not doubt their truth. They allowed me to accept the invitation of my new friend.

I soon reached his tent. Nearly all the Indians went with us. They appeared much sobered by the incident. I lay down in the tent, near the entrance. There was a fire in front of it.

Sheltered from the rain and free of my ropes, I soon fell into a deep sleep. I should probably have enjoyed it till morning if my slumbers had not been interrupted by a sensation like a nightmare— but which was, in fact, produced by the weight of a large Indian sitting composedly on my breast, smoking his pipe before the fire. I turned over and dropped him on the ground, where he continued to sit as if nothing had happened, indulging in his favorite amusement of smoking.

In the morning, a frightful scene presented itself: the Indians were preparing for the war dance. A pole had been cut. After stripping the bark from it, they painted it black, with streaks of red winding around it like snakes. The lower end was sharpened, and at the top they hung the scalps of my late companions, with others which they had obtained during their expedition.

Each Indian had dressed himself for the occasion. Some had painted their faces black, with red around the eyes. Others, reversing it, had painted their faces red, with black around the eyes. All had feathers stuck in their heads and all looked like so many demons.

When they had finished decorating themselves, the pole was stuck into the ground. They formed a circle around it and then the dance began. It started with the fierce war whoop, which had not ceased to ring in my ears since the fatal morning of our capture. They danced around the pole, writhing their bodies and distorting their faces in a most hideous manner.

On these occasions it is their practice to repeat the injuries inflicted on them by their enemies the whites: to tell how their lands were taken from them—their villages burnt—their cornfields laid waste—their fathers and brothers killed—their women and children carried into captivity. In this instance, by constantly repeating their wrongs and sufferings, they had worked themselves up to a pitch of the greatest fury.

The dance lasted about half an hour. I had seated myself on a log to witness it. When it ended, Chickatommo, with eyes flashing fire, advanced towards me and struck me a violent blow on the head. I immediately left my seat, seized him over the arms, and demanded why he had struck me.

"Sit down! Sit down!" he replied.

I loosened my grasp and resumed my seat on the log.

At that moment, seeing the two prisoner children nearby, he snatched up a tomahawk and went towards them with a quick step and determined look. They were alarmed at the menacing way he approached them and they ran away. He went after them. Messhawa saw they were in danger and bounded off like a deer to help them.

Chickatommo overtook the girl first. He raised the tomahawk to strike her dead. Just at that moment, Messhawa reached the spot. Coming up behind Chickatommo, he seized him around the arms and flung him violently back.

Messhawa darted towards the frightened child, snatched her up in his arms, and went after the boy. Not understanding Messhawa's good intentions, the boy tried twice as hard to escape, and they ran a considerable distance before he was overtaken. When Messhawa came up with him, the boy thought all was over and gave a bitter shriek. His sister, in the arms of Messhawa, answered it with one still more bitter.

They both soon learned they had nothing to fear. Although Messhawa spoke to them in an unknown tongue, his manner could not be misunderstood. In a few moments they came back to our camp. The children were walking by the side of Messhawa, who held them by the hand and spoke soothingly to them.

The next day two Mingo Indians arrived. They immediately joined in the drunken debauchery of our camp. One of these men told my captors that he had killed a Wyandot the summer before. This had plunged the Mingo into a desperate situation, as I shall explain.

All the savage tribes have the custom of adopting prisoners of war to fill the place of Indians who have been killed in battle or otherwise. If one man takes the life of another, he is obliged to make amends to the dead man's family, either by payment or by furnishing a substitute for him. This substitute occupies the dead man's position in the community and assumes all his responsibilities—he becomes the husband of his widow and the father of his children. If the murderer does not make reparation within a limited period he may be killed with impunity by the dead man's relatives or any other member of his tribe.

According to the Mingo, he was so poor that he could not pay the price for the Wyandot he had slain, and therefore he would have to forfeit his own life—unless he could fulfill the other condition.

My captors had drunk a good deal of liquor and their mood, for the moment, was warm-hearted. They yielded to the Mingo's pleas— and I was turned over to him to be substituted for the Wyandot he had murdered.

When I saw my captors prepare to continue their journey and

leave me in the hands of the Mingo, I was utterly astonished. I could not imagine what had happened, or why they were going off without me. I questioned the Negro. He knew as little as I did, and he asked the Indians for an explanation. From them we learned what I have already related: that I was to take the place of the dead Wyandot, who, incidentally, had been a husband and a father.

The prospect of leading an Indian squaw to the altar was not very rapturous, especially since she was already the mother of several children. Still, I began to hope that this marriage might increase my chance of escaping from the savages—and there was something extremely consoling in that thought.

Immediately after they surrendered me to the Mingo, my old masters took up their packs. Each of them made it a point to shake me by the hand and say good-bye. Several showed feelings of kindness—even of regret—at parting. My friend Messhawa had formed a real attachment to me, and he showed more of this feeling than any of them.

After they left, I had leisure to think about my new situation. The marriage which had been arranged for me without my consent occupied my mind. I felt a strong curiosity about my bride-to-be. Was she old or young? Ugly or handsome? Deformed or beautiful? These were questions not without their interest for me.

I asked the Mingo about them through my interpreter, the Negro. But he had never seen her, and could give me no information except that she was the mother of three or four children. Still, no matter what she might be like, my course was clear. After the marriage the Indians would stop watching every move I made—and I would seize the first favorable opportunity to escape and return to civilization. With hopes like these, I became impatient to reach the home of my intended bride.

At almost every idle moment I thought about my marriage, my Indian family, and my escape. However, these reveries were soon to be brought to an end.

After two or three days the Mingo began to move on with me towards the town where the bridal ceremony was to be performed. Before he had met the party from the Ohio, they had been traveling along the warpath leading to the Indian towns on the Sandusky and Miami. They had continued on this path when they left the Mingo and myself. As he was taking me along the same route, in their rear, we were bound to overtake them if they halted for a few days.

The fact was, my first owners had begun to regret their liberality. After the generous feeling produced by the whiskey had worn off, they determined to reclaim me. And so they stopped and waited for us to come up with them.

We were greeted with smiles and they all shook us by the hand. But this mood did not last long. A bitter argument began, which soon developed into a fierce quarrel. I felt quite uneasy when I saw them pointing at me from time to time and realized that I was the subject of their argument. The danger was that one party might slay me rather than give me up to the other.

The dispute was brought to an end by Messhawa. He caught two horses that were browsing in the neighborhood, mounted one of them, and had me get on the other. Then, with his rifle on his shoulder, he led me off toward the Indian town at Upper Sandusky. He did this on orders from Chickatommo.

After riding about five miles we reached the town. There were no streets in it—the bark-covered lodges were arranged without regard to order or distance from each other. Soon afterward the rest of our party followed us in and encamped in the center of the town.

At the place where the party had waited for the Mingo and me, we had met Mr. Francis Duchouquet, a Canadian trader who had lived among the Indians in this town for some years. He had assured me he would make an attempt to ransom me when we got to Upper Sandusky. Soon after we encamped there, he visited us. I instantly asked him to talk to the Indians about purchasing my freedom, and he did so. But the Indians said they did not intend to let me go.

When Mr. Duchouquet told me he had failed, I began to tremble. In my imagination, I saw myself being tortured to death slowly and ingeniously by the savages. I was filled with despair.

Next morning the Mingo Indian appeared at our encampment. I was afraid he might cause more trouble for me and I tried to avoid him. My fears vanished, however, when he drew a book from his bosom and presented it to me with a smiling face. It was my copy of the Debates of the Virginia Convention, which I had forgotten at the place where the Indians had quarreled.

Soon afterwards several Wyandots arrived from Muskingum with a quantity of whiskey in kegs, each of which contained about ten gallons. My captors immediately began to barter with the new arrivals for this article. The Wyandots turned their whiskey to good account. Five gallons were enough for the purchase of a horse worth two hundred dollars—a finely formed, handsome animal. Horses worth less were exchanged at a comparable price, and drunkenness soon spread through our encampment. A few of the Indians stayed sober to guard me.

I had observed, when the savages gave me to the Mingo, how generous they were under the influence of drink. I urged Mr. Duchouquet to talk to them again about my ransom at this moment. But they rejected his propositions a second time.

Next I begged him to ask the Indians where they planned to take me and what my fate was to be. They answered that they intended to take me to their towns on the Miami River, and that they did not know what final disposal they would make of me.

I had been told in unmistakable terms that captives taken to the Miami towns were certain to die a dreadful death, and that the savages always conceal their purposes from the prisoners they mean to sacrifice. Therefore, when Mr. Duchouquet reported that they had refused his offers my alarm was greater than ever before. My case seemed hopeless.

The Indians kept drinking until their funds ran out. Four or five days of unbounded riot and intoxication had passed when they suddenly found themselves reduced from wealth to their usual poverty. They were ashamed of their wasteful expenditures and unwilling to return home empty handed, so they decided to go back to the Ohio and try to capture some more white men and their property. They told this to Mr. Duchouquet and added that they had decided to put me to death, since a scalp was easier to take along than a living man. However, they said that if he wanted to ransom me, now was the time.

Without informing me, they began to discuss terms. It was agreed that Mr. Duchouquet should pay one hundred dollars' worth of goods for my freedom. The price was paid in six hundred silver brooches—the brooch serves all the purposes of money with them—and I was immediately surrendered to the trader. By a striking coincidence, this took place on the twenty-eighth of April, 1790, the day I reached the age of twenty-one. I regarded it as a second birth. It is impossible for me to describe the joy I felt.

After the Indians had disposed of me, they separated into two parties. A small number of the Shawnees, the Mingo, the women, and the two captive children set out for the Miami towns. Chickatommo and the other Shawnees began their journey back to the Ohio River. Their departure seemed to ensure my safety.

My worries were not over, however. Among the Wyandots at Upper Sandusky there was a white man who had been carried into captivity when he was very young, and had been reared in their tribe. This man knew the savages and their treacherous habits very well, and he advised me not to take my liberation for granted. He told me that he suspected Chickatommo and his party intended to get me back. Since they had already reclaimed me once, his words had an ominous sound.

The following day the Shawnee chief and his followers actually reappeared at Upper Sandusky. I was terror stricken. I thought of the miseries I had been through and the gruesome end that I could expect if I fell into their hands a third time. It seemed far better to resist them and die on the spot rather than let them become my masters again.

I provided myself with a tomahawk. Then I calmly sat down on a log and chopped away with an air of indifference. I knew what I had to do if they approached. However, they did not come near me, but withdrew and made an encampment on the river near the town.

Mr. Duchouquet agreed that their conduct was highly suspicious. They had disappeared the preceding day, after receiving my ransom and declaring they planned to return to the Ohio. Now they had suddenly come back without any apparent reason. Moreover, they had encamped at a different place than before—one that was out of our sight and better suited for a surprise attack on us by night.

We determined to prepare for them. Mr. Duchouquet and a laborer of his kept watch with me all night. We locked and barred our door. We had an axe, several guns, and tomahawks.

But we did not need to use them. The Indians left us undisturbed and departed the next day. Their whole party, with their packs on their backs, came through the town. They shook hands with Mr. Duchouquet and myself, said they had decided to visit the British post at Detroit, and went away.

I still feared they might be lurking in the neighborhood, watching for a favorable opportunity to return and bear me off. But after several days of anxiety we were informed by a party of Indians from Lower Sandusky that they had met Chickatommo and his followers far from our village, steadily continuing their journey towards Detroit.[2]

I immediately began to think about returning home to Virginia. I was alone, and utterly ignorant of the country through which I would have to pass. There were two routes I could take. One lay through the wilderness—this was the route I had just traveled with the Indians, and it was far too dangerous for me. The other, by way of Detroit, was more roundabout but safer. Mr. Duchouquet told me he intended to go to Detroit in about five weeks with the furs he had purchased at the Indian villages. I had no choice but to remain at Upper Sandusky until that time, and then go to Detroit with him. From there I would have to travel down the lakes into the state of New York. After that the road to my native state would be perfectly easy and safe.

I spent the time between my liberation and my homeward journey helping Mr. Duchouquet sell his merchandise to the Indians and attending to his books and accounts. Now and then I also went on some excursions. On one of these I visited the spot where Colonel Crawford had been tortured and burnt to death some years before by the Delawares. [See page 127.] The sapling to which it was said he had been bound was still alive and was pointed out to me by my guide—the white captive who had been adopted by the Wyandots.

About this time a Shawnee Indian arrived at Upper Sandusky and brought the heart-chilling news that my late fellow-prisoner, William Flinn, had been burnt at the stake and devoured by the savages at one of the Miami towns. This monster declared that he had been present when the miserable man was sacrificed and had partaken of the horrid banquet. He said Flinn's flesh was sweeter than any bear's meat!—a food in highest repute with the Indians.

The small band of Cherokees, three in number, to whom Peggy Fleming had been allotted on the Ohio, brought her to Upper Sandusky while I was there. She was no longer the cheerful, lively creature she had been when she was taken away from us. Her spirits were sunk, her gayety had fled—she looked utterly melancholy and wretched. I tried to learn the cause of this extraordinary change, but she answered my questions only with her tears, leaving me to form my own conclusions. Her stay with us was only for a few hours, during which I could not extract a word from her except an occasional yes and no. We both cried when the Indians took her away.

Every year, about the middle of autumn, all the traders in the fur business were in the habit of going to the Indian towns scattered through the Northwest. With them they carried ammunition, blankets, calico for shirts, coarse cloths for leggings, trinkets, vermilion, tomahawks, scalping knives, and whatever else suited their tawny customers. The traders sold the Indians the goods they wanted for winter use on credit. In the spring the Indians brought in the furs they had collected on their winter expeditions in the woods and paid for their fall purchases and the articles they would need through the summer.

In general, the Indians paid their debts punctually, but there were some who forgot or disregarded their promises, like many of our white people. The traders at the Indian towns generally completed their collections by the first of June and then brought all their furs to Detroit; from here they were sent down the Great Lakes and the St. Lawrence to Montreal and Quebec. The quantities of fur produced by this trade were immense and of very great value.

Mr. Duchouquet made his living in this trade at Upper Sandusky. Finally the time came for him to transport his furs to Detroit, and with a light heart I set out with his party. The Sandusky River is not navigable from the upper town, and Mr. Duchouquet's furs were carried on pack horses to the town of Lower Sandusky, from where there is good navigation to Detroit.

When we reached Lower Sandusky, the traders in the town were in a state of great alarm. We learned that on the previous day the three Cherokees who owned Peggy Fleming had brought her there and encamped a quarter of a mile outside the town. The traders in the town heard about the white female captive and instantly decided to visit the Cherokees' camp and see her.

Among the traders there was a man named Whitaker, who had been carried into captivity by the Wyandots in his early life. He had acquired so much influence with his tribe that they had made him a chief. His business had frequently led him to Pittsburgh, where Peggy Fleming's father kept a tavern, and Whitaker had often stayed there.

As soon as Whitaker appeared at the camp of the Cherokees, the daughter of his old landlord recognized him. She called him by name and begged him to help her regain her freedom. Without hesitation he agreed.

Whitaker did not speak to the Cherokees about her. Instead, he returned to the town and informed the principal chief, King Crane, that the white female captive was his sister. The king readily promised to obtain her release.

Crane immediately went to the Cherokees. He told them that their prisoner was the sister of a friend of his, and asked them, as a favor, to make a present of Peggy Fleming to him. They rejected his request. Next, he offered to buy her. They refused this, too, telling him bitterly that he was "no better than the white people" and that he was "as mean as the *dirt*"—terms of the grossest reproach among them.

At this insult, Crane became exasperated. He went back to the town, told Whitaker about his reception, and said he intended to take Peggy Fleming by force. However, he was afraid such an act might start a war between his nation and theirs and he urged Whitaker to raise the sum that would be needed to ransom her. With the help of the other traders Whitaker immediately got together a sufficient number of silver brooches.

Early next morning, King Crane and eight or ten young warriors marched out to the camp of the Cherokees. He found them asleep. Their captive was completely naked and was tied to a stake. Her body was painted black, a sign that she was condemned to death. Crane cut her bonds and gave her back her clothes.

Next he awakened the Cherokees. He told them the captive was his and he had brought her ransom. Then he threw down the silver brooches and bore the terrified girl away to his town. He delivered her to Whitaker, who disguised her as a squaw and after a few days sent her to Pittsburgh under the care of two trusty Wyandots.[3]

The Cherokees were furious and cried for revenge. They painted themselves for war and entered the Wyandot town of Lower Sandusky. Then they stalked about the town in great anger, declaring they were going to take the life of some white person. This was why the traders were so alarmed at the time we arrived. We shared their concern, for we had to stay in this town several days to unpack Mr. Duchouquet's pelts from the horses and transfer them to bateaux for the rest of the journey to Detroit. We provided ourselves with weapons and we all stayed in the same house that night. In the morning we were happy to find that the Cherokees had disappeared. I never heard of them afterwards.

My stay at Lower Sandusky was memorable to me for still another reason. It was the home of the Indian widow I would have had to marry if the Mingo had been permitted to dispose of me. I felt an irresistible curiosity to have a view of this female, and I determined to find her dwelling and see her there.

I had been making inquiries about her for some time when she was at last pointed out to me as she walked about the village. I could not help chuckling at my escape from the fate which had been intended for me. She was old, ugly, and disgusting.

Finally the bateaux were loaded with the furs and we embarked for Detroit, arriving there in a few days. The population of the town then consisted of about one thousand persons and it was occupied by a British garrison. I was told that my friend and brother in misfortune, Mr. Jacob Skyles, had spent several days here hiding from a band of Indians who had pursued him to Detroit after he escaped from captivity. I had not heard anything about him since we had parted and I was delighted to learn that he was safe and on his way back to the United States.

I stayed in Detroit nine or ten days, until the sloop *Felicity* left to go down Lake Erie and the commandant kindly obtained passage for me on her. I was destitute of cash for my expenses on the long journey home, but the people of the town kindly furnished me with enough money for my purposes.

After a voyage of five or six days I arrived at Fort Erie, and then traveled to Fort Schlosser and Fort Niagara. All of these posts were in the hands of the British, who generally tried to make my brief stay pleasant. Next I went to Schenectady and Albany. Finally, several weeks after leaving Detroit, I arrived in New York City. The first Congress was in session there and I was warmly greeted by members of the Virginia delegation as well as other sons of the "Ancient Dominion."

Adventures like the ones I had just lived through were rarely brought to the attention of the people of the northern cities, and mine excited some interest and much conversation in New York. They came to the ears of General Washington, then President of the United States. His private secretary, Mr. Thomas Nelson of Virginia, visited me at my lodgings with a message from the President that he wished to see me. I was conducted by Mr. Nelson to his house and introduced to him. General Washington congratulated me heartily on my fortunate release from the Indians and asked many questions about the strength of the tribes in the country through which I had traveled while a captive. After I had answered his questions as well as I could, he asked me about the forces of the British garrisons at the military posts I had passed and the state of their fortifications. On these last points I could not tell him anything helpful. As an American citizen I would have been liable to suspicion and even danger if I had looked into such subjects while I was at the British fortifications. Besides, military affairs were outside the range of my experience and observation.

President Washington's inquiries led me to believe that the government of the United States planned to punish the Indians for the many depredations they had committed on the Ohio lately—and also to seize the military posts the British occupied within our territory in violation of the treaty of 1783. The disastrous expedition of General St. Clair [4] soon showed that my first inference was correct, and I have little doubt the second would also have proved accurate but for the peaceful solution arranged by Mr. Jay's treaty.[5]

There was nothing to keep me from going home any longer and I began the trip to Virginia in the stagecoaches traveling the mail route to Richmond. There I borrowed a gig and horse from a friend and went out to a small plantation I owned in upper Hanover. When I got to my estate I found some good friends and my eldest brother, who had come to look into the state of my affairs during my absence. This unexpected meeting produced an effect on him which, he has always said, he never experienced before or since; he shed tears plentifully, but they were tears of joy.

From here I traveled to my mother's neighborhood, in the county of Prince Edward. My mother was old and my long absence had caused her grave concern; I feared what might happen to her if I rushed in without preparing her first. Therefore, in the evening, I rode to the house of a friend, Mr. Miller Woodson, three miles away, and he kindly wrote my mother that I would reach home the next day.

When I arrived at my mother's house, tears of joy flowed from every eye. Even the sturdy slaves ran hastily from the field of labor. Some of them caught me in their arms and wept, whilst others fell upon their knees and returned thanks to Heaven for my deliverance.

# The Headhunters of Nootka

## JOHN RODGERS JEWITT

CAPTAIN JOHN SALTER of the brig Boston *thought he knew his Indians. When he anchored near the village of the Nootka tribe on Vancouver Island, British Columbia, in 1803, he gave the natives gifts and treated them to rum, molasses, and biscuits. And, before he allowed the Nootkans to come aboard, he searched every one of them carefully for concealed weapons.*

*But then Captain Salter committed a fatal blunder. He lost his temper at the genial Chief Maquina and failed to see he had made the chief lose face before his tribe. A few days later, at Maquina's suggestion, the unsuspecting skipper sent a third of his men ashore to fish, leaving the rest heavily outnumbered by the Indians visiting on board. The Indians entertained the crew with tricks, singing, and dancing—they were the perfect picture of innocence and friendliness —while they waited for Maquina to give the war cry.*

*The destruction of the* Boston *was the most famous act of piracy committed by the western Indians. Only two members of the crew survived. One was a bad-tempered, illiterate sailmaker named Thompson. The other was a lighthearted young English blacksmith or armorer, John Rodgers Jewitt. Jewitt's spectacular story of the massacre, his two and one-half years of bondage, and his dramatic escape was one of the bestsellers of the last century.*

*Jewitt kept a diary which he published in Boston after he was liberated from the Nootkans. Then he married and settled in Middletown, Connecticut. Later he made the acquaintance of Richard Alsop, a native of Middletown, who was a wealthy merchant and a man of letters. From Jewitt's diary and interviews he had with him, Alsop reconstructed the story of the* Boston *and her two survivors in a book called* The Adventures and Sufferings of John Rodgers Jewitt, *which was published in 1815. It met with immediate success and Jewitt became a celebrity of sorts. Two years later the story was adapted as a drama in Philadelphia. Jewitt himself played the leading role—the same one he had played in real life—and supervised the staging of the Indian dances. He capped his performance by singing a Nootka war song and reciting a ballad especially written for him, called* The Poor Armorer Boy.

*For a number of years Jewitt traveled along the northeastern coast with a horse and wagon, selling his book. He was a memorable figure, for he still bore on his forehead the scar of the wound made by the Indian's axe on the day the* Boston *was captured. He died in Hartford in 1821.*

I was born in Boston, a large town in Lincolnshire, Great Britain, on the 21st of May, 1783. My father, Edward Jewitt, was a blacksmith, and esteemed among the first in his line of business in that place.

It was my father's intention that I should enter one of the learned professions, and he saw to it that I received a superior education. When I was fourteen he decided to apprentice me to an eminent surgeon. However, I much preferred his own trade and begged him to give up this plan. At length he consented. He took me into his shop and I soon became uncommonly expert at the work to which I was set.

About a year later my family moved to Hull, an event that greatly influenced my future destiny. Hull was one of the best ports in England and my father had full employment for his numerous workmen there, particularly in vessel work. This naturally led me to an acquaintance with the sailors on some of the ships. The many remarkable stories they told me of their voyages and adventures excited a strong wish in me to visit foreign countries, which was increased by my reading the voyages of Captain Cook and other celebrated navigators.

Among our principal customers at Hull were the Americans who frequented that port. From their conversation my father and I formed the most favorable opinion of that country as affording excellent prospects for the establishment of a young man in life.

In the summer of 1802, the ship *Boston*, belonging to Boston in Massachusetts, and commanded by Captain John Salter, arrived at Hull. She came to take on board a cargo of goods to trade for furs with the Indians on the northwest coast of America, after which she was to proceed to China and then home to America. The ship needed many repairs and alterations for so long a voyage and the captain applied to my father to do the smith's work. Being of a social turn, the captain spent many of his evenings at my father's house with his chief and second mates.

In the evenings he passed at my father's, Captain Salter used to speak of his voyages, and observed me listening with much attention. One day, when I had brought him some work, he said to me in rather a joking manner, "John, how should you like to go with me?"

I answered that it would give me great pleasure, that I had for a long time wished to visit foreign countries, and that if my father would give his consent and the captain was willing to take me with him, I would go.

"I shall be very glad to do it," said he. "I want an expert smith as an armorer, and I have no doubt that you will answer my purpose well. On my return to America I shall probably be able to do something good for you in Boston. I will take the first opportunity of speaking to your father about it."

The next evening that he called at our house, Captain Salter introduced the subject. My father at first would not listen to the proposal, for he could not bear to think of parting with me. But Captain Salter told him that it was a pity to keep a promising young fellow like myself confined to a small shop in England, when I might do so much better in America, where wages were much higher and living cheaper. At length he gave up his objections and consented that I should ship on board the *Boston* as an armorer, at the rate of thirty dollars per month. It was agreed that the amount due me, together with a certain sum of money which my father gave Captain Salter, would be laid out by him on the northwest coast in the purchase of furs for my account, to be disposed of in China for such goods as would yield a profit on the return of the ship. My father wanted to give me every advantage in establishing myself in my trade in Boston or some other maritime town of America.

The ship, having undergone thorough repair and been well coppered, took on her cargo, which consisted of English cloths, Dutch blankets, looking glasses, beads, knives, razors, sugar and molasses, about twenty hogsheads of rum, ammunition, cutlasses, pistols, and three thousand muskets and fowling pieces. When she was ready for sea, I took an affectionate leave of my father, whose feelings would hardly permit him to speak, and my brother, sister, and stepmother. Then I went on board the ship.

I found myself well accommodated on board for my work. An iron forge had been erected on deck, while a corner of the steerage was set aside for my vise-bench, so that in bad weather I could work below.

On the third day of September, 1802, we sailed with a fair wind, in company with twenty-four other American vessels. I was seasick for a few days, but on my recovery I found myself in uncommonly fine health and went zealously to work at my forge, putting in order some of the muskets and making daggers, knives, and small hatchets for the Indian trade. In wet and stormy weather I was occupied below in filing and polishing them.

We had a pleasant passage of twenty-nine days to the Island of St. Catherine, on the coast of Brazil, where we stopped to take on wood, and water, and fresh provisions. Then we put to sea, and on the twenty-fifth of December passed Cape Horn. We had made the cape no less than thirty-six days before, but were repeatedly forced back by contrary winds, experiencing very rough weather in doubling it.

Captain Salter, who had been for many years in the East India trade, was an excellent seaman. He preserved the strictest discipline on board his ship, though he was a man of mild temper. We had on board a fine band of music with which on Sunday nights, when the weather was pleasant, we were accustomed to be regaled. This to me was most delightful, especially during the serene evenings we experienced in traversing the Southern Ocean.

With a fair wind and easy weather, we pursued our voyage to the northward until the 12th of March, 1803, when we made Woody Point in Nootka Sound,[1] on the northwest coast of America. We immediately sailed up the sound for the village of Nootka, where Captain Salter had determined to stop, to supply the ship with wood and water before proceeding up the coast to trade. To avoid any molestation from the Indians, he proceeded about five miles north of the village, which is situated on Friendly Cove. The ship came to anchor so near the shore that we secured her by a hawser to the trees.

The next day several of the natives came on board in a canoe from the village of Nootka, with their king, called Maquina. He appeared pleased to see us, and with great seeming cordiality welcomed Captain Salter and his officers to his country.

The king was a man of dignified aspect, about six feet in height and extremely straight and well proportioned. His features were good, and he had a large Roman nose, a very uncommon form of feature among these people. His complexion was a dark copper, though his face, legs, and arms were so covered with red paint that their natural color could scarcely be perceived. His eyebrows were painted black in two broad stripes like a new moon, and his long black hair, which shone with oil, was fastened in a bunch on the top of his head and strewn with white down, which gave him a most curious appearance. He was dressed in a large mantle of black sea-otter skin which reached to his knees and was fastened around his middle by a broad belt of cloth painted with figures in several colors. This apparel was by no means unbecoming, but had an air of savage magnificence.

His men were dressed in kutsacks or mantles of the cloth of the country, which is made from the bark of a tree, and has some resemblance to straw matting; these mantles are nearly square, and have two holes in the upper part large enough to admit the arms; they reach as low as the knees, and are fastened round their bodies with a broad belt of the same cloth.

Having frequently visited the English and American ships that traded along the coast, Maquina had learned a number of English words, and could make himself pretty well understood in our language. He remained on board for some time, during which the captain took him into the cabin and treated him with a glass of rum and some biscuit and molasses, which these people prefer to any kind of food we can offer them.

We immediately set about getting our water casks in readiness. Part of the crew were sent on shore to cut timber and assist the carpenter in making it into yards and spars, while those on board refitted the rigging, repaired the sails, etc. During this time I kept myself busily employed in repairing the muskets, making knives, tomahawks, etc., and doing ironwork for the ship.

Meantime, the natives came on board daily, bringing with them fresh salmon and receiving in return some trifling articles. Captain Salter was always very particular, before admitting these people on board, to see that they had no arms about them, obliging them to throw off their garments, so that he felt perfectly secure from attack.

On the 15th the king came on board with several of his chiefs. Captain Salter invited them to dine with him, and it was curious to see how these people seat themselves upon our chairs with their feet crossed under them, like Turks. They cannot endure the taste of salt, and the only thing they would eat with us was the ship's bread, dipped in molasses; they had also a great liking for tea and coffee when well sweetened.

As iron weapons and tools are in much request among them, whenever they came on board they were very attentive to me, crowding around the forge to see how I did my work. In this way they became well acquainted with me—a circumstance, as will be seen in the end, of great importance to me.

The salmon they brought us furnished a delicious treat to men who for a long time had lived almost wholly on salt provisions. We feasted most luxuriously, and flattered ourselves that we should not want for plenty of fresh provisions, little imagining that this dainty food was to prove the unfortunate lure to our destruction!

On the 19th the king came on board again and was invited by the captain to dine with him. He had much conversation with Captain Salter, and informed him there were plenty of wild ducks and geese near Friendly Cove. At this, the captain made him a present of a double-barreled fowling piece with which he appeared greatly pleased.

On the 20th we were nearly ready for our departure, having taken in what wood and water we were in want of.

The next day Maquina came on board with nine pair of wild ducks as a present. He brought the gun, one of the locks of which he had broken, and told the captain it was *peshak*—bad. Captain Salter was very much offended, considering it a mark of contempt for his present.

He called the king a liar, adding other scornful terms and, taking the gun from him, tossed it indignantly into the cabin.

"John," he called to me, "this fellow has broken this beautiful fowling piece. See if you can mend it."

On examining it, I told him that it could be done.

As I have already observed, Maquina knew a number of English words, and unfortunately understood but too well the meaning of the reproachful terms the captain addressed to him. He said not a word in reply, but his face expressed the rage he felt. I observed him, while the captain was speaking, repeatedly put his hand to his throat and rub it upon his bosom. This, he afterwards told me, was to keep down his heart, which was rising into his throat and choking him. He soon went on shore with his men, evidently much upset.

On the morning of the 22nd the natives came as usual with salmon and remained on board. About noon, Maquina came alongside with a considerable number of his chiefs and men in their canoes. After going through the customary examination, they were admitted into the ship. He had a whistle in his hand and over his face a very ugly mask of wood, representing the head of some wild beast. He appeared remarkably good-humored and gay, and whilst his people sang and capered about the deck, entertaining us with comic tricks and gestures, he blew his whistle to a kind of tune which seemed to regulate their motions.

As Captain Salter was walking on the quarter-deck, amusing himself with their dancing, the king inquired when he intended to go to sea.

"Tomorrow," the captain answered.

Maquina then said, "You love salmon—much in Friendly Cove. Why not go there and catch some?"

The captain thought that it would be very desirable to have a good supply of these fish for the voyage. Maquina and his chiefs stayed and dined on board, and after dinner the chief mate went ashore with nine men in the jolly boat and yawl to fish at Friendly Cove.

Shortly after the departure of the boats, I went down to my vise-bench in the steerage, where I was employed in cleaning muskets. I had not been there more than an hour when I heard the men hoisting in the longboat and, a few minutes after, a great bustle and confusion on deck. I immediately ran up the steerage stairs.

Scarcely was my head above deck when I was caught by the hair by one of the savages and lifted from my feet. Fortunately for me, my hair was short and the ribbon with which it was tied slipped, so that I fell from his hold into the steerage. As I was falling he struck at me with an axe. It cut a deep gash in my forehead and penetrated the skull, but because he lost his hold I escaped the full force of the blow, which otherwise would have cleft my head in two. I fell, stunned and senseless, upon the floor.

How long I continued in this situation I know not. On recovering my senses, I tried to get up, but I was so weak from loss of blood that I fainted and fell. I was, however, soon recalled to my recollection by three loud yells from the savages, which convinced me they had got possession of the ship.

It is impossible for me to describe my feelings at this terrific sound. Some faint idea may be formed of them by those who have known what it is to half-awaken from a hideous dream and still think it real. When I heard the song of triumph that followed these infernal yells, my blood ran cold in my veins.

Having sufficiently recovered my senses to look around me, after wiping the blood from my eyes, I saw that the hatch of the steerage was shut. This was done, I afterwards discovered, by order of Maquina. The king, seeing the savage strike at me with the axe, told him not to hurt me, as I was the armorer and would be useful to them in repairing their arms; at the same time, to prevent his men from injuring me, he had the hatch closed. But to me this circumstance wore a very different appearance, for I thought these barbarians had only prolonged my life in order to deprive me of it by the most cruel tortures.

I remained in this horrid state of suspense for a very long time. Then the hatch was opened and Maquina ordered me to come up. I groped my way up as well as I was able, almost blinded with the blood that flowed from my wound, and so weak I could hardly walk.

The king, perceiving my situation, ordered one of his men to bring a pot of water. When the blood was washed from my face I was able to see with one of my eyes, but the other was so swollen from my wound that it was closed.

But what a terrific spectacle met my sight! Six naked savages stood in a circle around me, covered with the blood of my murdered comrades, with their daggers uplifted in their hands, prepared to strike. I thought my last moment had come.

The king entered the circle and, placing himself before me, addressed me.

"John—I speak—you no say no. You say no—daggers come!"

He then asked me if I would be his slave, fight for him in his battles, repair his muskets and make daggers and knives for him—with several other questions, to all of which I was careful to answer yes.

He then told me that he would spare my life and ordered me to kiss his hands and feet to show my submission to him, which I did. His people were very clamorous to have me put to death, so there should be no one left to tell our story to our countrymen and prevent them from coming to trade with them. But the king opposed their wishes in the most determined manner.

I was without my coat, and what with the coldness of the weather, my feebleness from loss of blood, the pain of my wound, and the extreme terror that I felt, I shook like a leaf. Observing this, the king went into the cabin and, bringing up a greatcoat, threw it over my shoulders, telling me to drink some rum from a bottle which he handed me. I took a draught. Then, taking me by the hand, he led me to the quarter-deck.

There the most horrid sight presented itself that ever my eyes witnessed. The heads of our unfortunate captain and his crew, to the number of twenty-five, were all arranged in a line. Maquina ordered one of his people to bring a head and asked me whose it was. I answered, the captain's. In like manner the others were shown me and I told him the names, excepting a few that were so horribly mangled I was not able to recognize them.[2]

I now discovered that all our unfortunate crew had been massacred and learned that, after getting possession of the ship, the savages had broken open the arms chest and magazine and, supplying themselves with ammunition and arms, sent a party on shore to attack our men, who had gone there to fish. These Indians were joined by numbers from the village, and overpowered and murdered our men without difficulty. Cutting off their heads, they brought them on board, after throwing their bodies into the sea.

Looking upon the deck, I saw it was covered with the blood of my poor comrades. Their throats had been cut with their own jack knives, the savages having seized the opportunity, while the sailors were busy hoisting in the boat, to grapple with them and overpower them by their numbers. In the scuffle the captain was thrown overboard and killed by those in the canoes, who immediately cut off his head. What I felt on this occasion may be more readily conceived than expressed.

Maquina then ordered me to get the ship under way for Friendly Cove. I cut the cables and sent some of the natives aloft to loose the sails, which they performed in a very bungling manner. But they succeeded so far in loosing the jib and topsails that, with a fair wind, I succeeded in getting the ship into the cove. There, by order of the king, I ran her ashore at eight o'clock at night.

We were received by the men, women, and children of the village with loud shouts of joy and a horrible drumming with sticks upon the roofs and sides of their houses, in which they had stuck a great number of lighted pine torches to welcome their king's return.

Maquina took me to his house, which was very large and filled with people. I was received with much kindness by the women, particularly those belonging to the king. He had no less than nine wives. All of them came around me and expressed much sympathy for my misfortune, gently stroking and patting my head in a soothing manner.

In the meantime all the warriors of the tribe, to the number of five hundred, had assembled at the king's house. They exulted greatly at having taken our ship, and each one boasted of his own particular exploits in killing our men. But they were much dissatisfied that I had been allowed to live and urged Maquina to deliver me to them, to be put to death. This he obstinately refused to do, telling them that he had promised me my life and would not break his word.

The king then seated me by him and ordered his women to bring him something to eat. They set before him some dried clams and whale oil. He ate very heartily and encouraged me to follow his example, telling me to eat much and take a great deal of oil, which would make me strong and fat. Despite his praise of this food, I could not eat it; both the smell and taste were loathsome to me. Besides, I felt such pain and terror that I had very little inclination for eating.

The people again became clamorous that Maquina should consent to my being killed. They finally became so boisterous that he caught up a large club in a passion and drove them all out of the house.

During this scene a son of the king, about eleven years old, came up to me. I caressed him; he returned my attentions with much pleasure. This looked like a fortunate opportunity to gain the good will of the father, and I took the child on my knee. Cutting the metal buttons off the coat I had on, I tied them around his neck. He was highly delighted and became so attached to me that he would not leave me.

The king appeared much pleased with my attention to his son. Telling me that it was time to go to sleep, he directed me to lie with his son next to him, as he was afraid some of his people would come while he was asleep and kill me. I lay down as he ordered me, but neither the state of my mind nor the pain I felt would allow me to sleep.

About midnight I was greatly alarmed by the approach of one of the natives. He informed the king that one of the white men was still alive, and had knocked him down as he went on board the ship at night. Maquina communicated this to me, giving me to understand that as soon as the sun rose he should kill the sailor. I tried to persuade him to spare his life, but he bade me be silent and go to sleep. I said nothing more, but lay revolving in my mind what method I could devise to save the life of this man.

While I was thinking of some plan for his preservation, it all at once came into my mind that this man was probably the sailmaker of the ship, named Thompson, since I had not seen his head among those on deck. As Thompson was nearly forty years of age and had an old look, I conceived it would be easy to make him pass for my father, and by this means prevail on Maquina to spare his life.

Towards morning I fell into a doze, but was awakened with the first beams of the sun by the king. He told me he was going to kill the man on the ship, and ordered me to accompany him. I rose and followed him, leading the young prince, his son.

Coming to the beach, I found all the men of the tribe assembled. The king told them a white man had been found alive on the ship and asked whether he should spare his life or put him to death. They were unanimously for death. Having arranged my plan, I pointed to the boy, whom I still held by the hand, and asked the king if he loved his son. He answered that he did. I then asked the child if he loved his father and, on his replying in the affirmative, I said, "And I also love mine." I threw myself on my knees at Maquina's feet and implored him to spare my father's life, if the man on board should prove to be him. I told the king that if he killed my father, it was my wish that he should kill me too or I would kill myself—and that he would thus lose my services.

Maquina appeared moved, and promised not to put the man to

death if he should be my father. He then explained to his people what I had said and ordered me to go on board and tell the man to come on shore.

To my unspeakable joy, on going into the hold I found that my conjecture was true. Thompson was there. He had escaped without any injury, except a slight nose wound. Finding the savages in possession of the ship, he had secreted himself in the hold, hoping for some chance to escape.

I informed him that all our men had been killed, that the king had preserved my life, and had consented to spare his on the supposition that he was my father. After giving him his cue, I went on shore with him and presented him to Maquina. The king immediately knew him to be the sailmaker and was much pleased, observing that he could make sails for his canoe. He then took us to his house and ordered something for us to eat.

On the 24th and 25th, the natives were busily employed taking the cargo out of the ship, stripping her of her sails and rigging, cutting away the spars and masts and, in short, rendering her as complete a wreck as possible. The muskets, ammunition, cloth, and all the principal articles taken from her were deposited in the king's house.

While they were thus occupied, my companion and myself were obliged to aid them. I took possession of the captain's writing desk, which contained some paper and implements for writing. I also had the good fortune to find a blank account book, in which I resolved to write an account of our capture and the most remarkable occurrences that I should meet with among these people, hoping it would not be long before some vessel would arrive to release us. I likewise found in the cabin a volume of sermons, a Bible, and a Common Prayer book of the Church of England. As these people set no value upon things of this kind, I found no difficulty in appropriating them by putting them in my chest. In this I also put some small tools belonging to the ship and several other articles.

On the 26th, two ships were seen heading for Friendly Cove. At their first appearance the inhabitants were thrown into great confusion. Collecting a number of muskets and blunderbusses, they ran to the shore and kept up a brisk fire at them. The ships fired a few rounds of grapeshot, which did no harm to anyone, and then stood out to sea. They were scarcely out of sight when Maquina expressed regret that he had permitted his people to fire at them. He feared they would inform others how they had been received, and prevent them from coming to trade with him.

A few days after hearing of the capture of the ship, there arrived at Nootka a great number of canoes filled with savages from no less than twenty tribes to the north and south, among them the Aitizzarts, Aytcharts, and Wickinninish.[3] Maquina, who was very proud of his new acquisitions, was desirous of welcoming these visitors in the European manner. He ordered his men, as the canoes approached, to assemble on the beach with loaded muskets and blunderbusses, and placed Thompson at the cannon, which had been brought from the ship. Then, taking a speaking trumpet in his hand, he ascended the roof of his house with me and began drumming violently upon the boards with a stick.

Nothing could be more ludicrous than the appearance of this motley group of savages on the shore, dressed with their ill-gotten finery in the most fantastic manner—some in women's smocks taken from our cargo, others in cloaks of blue, red, or yellow broadcloth, with stockings drawn over their heads, and their necks hung round with powder horns, shot bags, and cartridge boxes. Some of them had no less than ten muskets apiece on their shoulders, and five or six daggers in their girdles. It was diverting to see them squatting upon the beach, holding their muskets perpendicularly with the butts pressed upon the sand, instead of against their shoulders, awaiting the order to fire.

Maquina at last called to them with his trumpet to fire. They did this in the most awkward and timid manner, with their muskets pressed upon the ground. At the same moment the cannon was fired by Thompson. They immediately threw themselves back and began to roll and tumble over the sand as if shot. Then, suddenly springing up, they began a song of triumph. Running backward and forward upon the shore, with the wildest gesticulations, they boasted of their exploits and exhibited their trophies. I could not avoid laughing at their awkward movements and the singular contrast of their dress and arms.

When the ceremony was concluded, Maquina invited the strangers to a feast at his house. It consisted of whale blubber, smoked herring spawn, and dried fish and whale oil, of which they ate most plentifully. The feast being over, the trays out of which they ate and other things were removed to make room for the dance, which was to close the entertainment.

Three of the principal chiefs, dressed in their otter-skin mantles, with their heads covered with white down and their faces highly painted, came forward into the middle of the room. Each was furnished with a bag filled with white down, which they scattered around to represent a fall of snow. The chiefs were followed by Maquina's son, Satsatsoksis, whom I have already spoken of. He was dressed in a long piece of yellow cloth, with a cap on his head to which was fastened a curious mask like a wolf's head. The rear was brought up by the king himself in his robe of sea-otter skin, with a small whistle in his mouth and a rattle in his hand, with which he kept time to a tune on his whistle. After passing very rapidly around the house, each of them seated himself, except the prince. He immediately began the dance, springing up into the air in a squat posture and constantly turning around on his heels with great swiftness in a narrow circle.

This dance, with a few intervals of rest, continued about two hours. The chiefs kept up a constant drumming with sticks on a long hollow plank and accompanied this with songs. The women applauded each feat of the dancer with the words *"Wocash! Wocash, Tyee!"*—"Good! very good, Prince!"

As soon as the dance was finished, Maquina gave presents to the strangers. These were pieces of European cloth, muskets, powder, shot, etc. Whenever he gave them anything, they snatched it from him with a very stern, surly look, repeating *"Wocash, Tyee."* This I understood to be their custom, and was considered a compliment. Maquina gave away no less than one hundred muskets, the same number of looking glasses, four hundred yards of cloth, and twenty casks of powder, besides other things.

After receiving these presents, the strangers retired on board their canoes. They were so numerous that Maquina would not allow any but the chiefs to sleep in the houses. To prevent the property from being pillaged by them, he ordered Thompson and myself to keep guard during the night, armed with cutlasses and pistols.

In this manner tribes of savages from various parts of the coast continued coming for several days, bringing with them blubber, oil, herring spawn, dried fish, and clams, for which they received presents of cloth, etc., after which they returned home.

Early on the morning of the 19th the ship was discovered to be on fire. One of the savages had gone on board with a firebrand at night for the purpose of plunder and some sparks had fallen into the hold. The whole vessel was soon enveloped in flames. The natives regretted her loss, as a great part of her cargo still remained on board. To my companion and myself it was a most melancholy sight, for with her disappeared every trace of civilization. I had luckily saved all my tools, but most of our stock of provisions was lost.

About two days later, examining their booty, the savages found a cask of rum. This was towards evening and Maquina, having assembled all the men at his house, gave a feast. They drank so freely of the rum that in a short time they became extremely wild. Thompson and myself, apprehensive for our safety, retired to the woods, where we stayed till past midnight.

On our return we found the men all lay stretched out on the floor in a state of complete intoxication. The burning of our ship, which we had lamented so much, now appeared to us in a different light. Had the savages got possession of the rum, of which there were nearly twenty casks on board, we must inevitably have fallen a sacrifice to their fury in some of their moments of intoxication. To prevent a similar danger, I bored a hole in the bottom of the cask with a gimlet, which completely emptied it.

By this time the wound in my head began to be much better. I found myself sufficiently well to go to work at my trade, and made the king and his wives bracelets and other small ornaments of copper or steel, and repaired his weapons. This was very gratifying to Maquina and his women and secured me their good will.

The Nootkans are great hunters of the whale and at this time of the year are dependent on this animal for their food. Maquina met with little success in his whaling this season, but great numbers of people from the other tribes kept flocking to Nootka, bringing with them, in exchange for the ship's plunder, such quantities of provision that the natives seldom experienced any want of food during the summer. As to myself and Thompson, we fared as they did, never wanting for such provision as they had, though we were obliged to eat it cooked in their manner, with whale oil as a sauce.

Poor Thompson, who was no favorite with the natives, would have suffered from hunger much oftener had it not been for my furnishing him with provision. Maquina allowed me the privilege, when not employed for him, to work for myself in making bracelets and other ornaments of copper, fish hooks, daggers, etc., either to sell to the tribes who visited us or for our own chiefs. They supplied me with as much as I wished to eat, and enough for Thompson, and almost always made me a present of a European garment or small bundles of penknives, razors, scissors, etc.

Thompson presently became very insistent that I begin my journal. As I had no ink, he proposed to cut his finger to supply me with blood for the purpose whenever I should want it. On the 1st of June I began a regular diary. I had no need to accept his offer, for I obtained a very tolerable ink by boiling the juice of the blackberry with finely powdered charcoal and filtering it through a cloth. As for quills, I found no difficulty in procuring them whenever I wanted from the crows and ravens with which the beach was almost always covered.

The extreme concern of Thompson that I should begin my journal might be considered odd in a man who knew neither how to read nor write. However, he had been many years at sea and thus considered the keeping of a journal indispensable. This man was born in Philadelphia, and at eight years old ran away and served as a cabin boy on a ship bound to London. On his arrival there, he was engaged as an apprentice to the captain of a collier. Then he was impressed on board an English man-of-war, and continued in the British naval service about twenty-seven years. He was a very powerful man, an expert boxer, and perfectly fearless. So little was his dread of danger that, when irritated, he was wholly regardless of his life, as the following incidents will show.

One evening about the middle of April, as I was at the house of one of the chiefs, word was brought me that Maquina was going to kill Thompson. I immediately hurried home. I found the king in the act of pointing a loaded musket at Thompson, who was standing before him with his breast bared, calling on him to fire. Maquina was foaming with rage. I begged him for my sake not to kill my father, and at length succeeded in taking the musket from him.

I learned that while Thompson was lighting the lamps in the king's room, some boys—the young prince was among the most forward of them—had begun to run around him and pull him by the trousers. This caused Thompson to spill the oil, which threw him into a passion. He struck the prince a violent blow, knocking him down. The

king saw his son's face covered with blood. He seized a musket and
began to load it, determined to take instant revenge. If I had arrived
a few minutes later, my companion would certainly have paid with
his life for his rash conduct. I found the utmost difficulty in pacifying
Maquina. He did not forgive Thompson for a long time.

Even this narrow escape produced little effect on Thompson. Not
many weeks later he was guilty of a similar indiscretion. He struck
the eldest son of a chief, who had provoked him by calling him a
white slave. This affair caused a great commotion, and the tribe
clamored for his death. But Maquina would not consent, again
wholly out of regard for me.

I frequently used to beg Thompson to control his temper better
and do nothing to exasperate the savages. But he declared he had
much rather be killed than be obliged to live as a slave among such
a poor, ignorant, despicable set of beings. As for myself, I thought
very differently. I sought to gain their good will by always trying to
look cheerful, appearing pleased with their sports and buffoon tricks,
and making little ornaments for the wives and children of their chiefs.
As a result I became quite a favorite with them.

In order to win their favor still more, I decided to learn their
language, and in a few months was able to make myself well understood. I tried to persuade Thompson to learn it, but he refused. He
said he hated both them and their cursed lingo and would have nothing to do with it.

The village of Nootka consists of about twenty houses on a small
hill, which rises gently from the shore. The houses are of different
sizes, according to the rank of the *Tyee* or chief who lives in them.
Each house has one. These dwellings are usually about forty feet wide,
but of very different lengths. The king's house is much the longest—
about one hundred and fifty feet. The smallest contain only two families and do not exceed forty feet in length. There is only one entrance.

Through the middle of the building, from one end to the other,
runs a passage about eight or nine feet broad. On each side live the
several families that occupy the house. Each family has their own
fireplace, but no kind of wall to mark the limits of their dwelling
area. The chief has his apartment at the upper end, and the next in
rank is opposite, on the other side. They have no other floor than

the ground. Whenever a fire is made, the plank over it is thrust aside by means of a pole.

The furniture of these people is very simple. It consists only of boxes, in which they put their clothes, furs and such things as they hold valuable; tubs for their provisions of spawn and blubber; trays from which they eat; baskets for their dried fish and other purposes, and bags made of bark matting. Of this they also make their beds. They use no other bed covering than their garments.

Their mode of living is very simple. Their food consists almost wholly of fish, or fish spawn fresh or dried, the blubber of the whale, seal, or sea cow, mussels, clams and berries. All of these are eaten with whale oil for sauce. The whale is considered the king's fish. When he is present, no other person is permitted to touch it until the royal harpoon has drawn its blood.

Their slaves form their most valuable property. These are either captives taken in war or purchased from the neighboring tribes. They reside in the same house and are usually kindly treated. They are compelled, however, at times to labor severely and the females are prostituted by their masters whenever they think proper, for the purpose of gain. None but the king and chiefs have slaves. Maquina had nearly fifty, male and female, in his house, a number about one half of its inhabitants.

The Klahars, a small tribe, has been conquered and incorporated into that of Nootka. They are not permitted to have any chiefs, and live by themselves in a cluster of small houses near the village. The Nootka tribe, which consists of about five hundred warriors, is not only more numerous than almost any of the neighboring tribes, but far exceeds them in the strength and martial spirit of its people.

But to return to our unhappy situation. Though my comrade and I were faring better than we could have expected, our fears that no ship would come to our release were a source of constant pain to us. Our principal consolation was to go on Sundays to the borders of a pond about a mile from the village. Here, after bathing and putting on clean clothes, we would seat ourselves under a beautiful pine. Then I would read the Bible and some prayers, ending with a plea to the Almighty to rescue us from the hands of the savages.

I explained to Maquina as well as was in my power why we withdrew at this time, and far from objecting, he readily consented to it.

In July we thought our hope of escape was on the point of being gratified. A ship appeared in the offing; but alas! instead of making for the shore, she passed to the northward and soon disappeared.

As the summer drew near its close, we began to suffer from want of food. Maquina and the chiefs were out whaling, but he would not permit Thompson and myself to take part, lest we make our escape to some of the neighboring tribes. At these times the women seldom cook, and we were often hungry.

In the meantime, we frequently received accounts from the tribes who came to Nootka that there were vessels on the coast. We were advised by their chiefs to make our escape, and they also promised to put us on board. I afterwards learned these stories were almost all invented by these people to get us into their power, in order to make slaves of us.

On the 3rd of September the whole tribe left Nootka to pass the autumn and winter at Tashees and Cooptee, the latter lying about thirty miles up the Sound, in a deep bay. They took everything with them, even the planks of their houses, in order to cover their winter dwellings, the frames of which are left standing. To a European such a removal exhibits a scene quite novel and strange—canoes piled up with boards and boxes, and filled with men, women, and children, making the air resound with their cries and songs.

The longboat of our ship had been repaired and furnished with a sail by Thompson, and Maquina gave us the direction of it. After loading her as deep as she could swim, we proceeded in company with them. We left Nootka with heavy hearts, as no ships ever came to the part of the coast for which we were bound. Passing Cooptee, which is on the southern bank, just within the mouth of a small river, we proceeded about fifteen miles up this stream to Tashees, between a range of lofty forest-covered hills. On our arrival, all went to work covering the house frames with the planks we had brought. In a very short time we were established in our new residence.

Tashees is pleasantly situated, in a secure position from winter storms, in a small hollow at the foot of a mountain. These people come to Tashees to obtain their winter stock of provisions—salmon, salmon spawn, herrings and sprats. The salmon are taken at Tashees principally in pots or weirs made of twigs. The weirs are placed at the foot of a rapid, where the water is not very deep, and the fish, driven from above with long poles, are caught in the weirs and taken into the canoes. In this manner I have seen more than seven hundred salmon caught in fifteen minutes.

I frequently used to go out with Maquina upon these fishing parties, and was always sure to receive a handsome present of salmon. I was also permitted to go out with a gun, and was several times very successful in shooting wild ducks and teal.

One day Maquina observed me writing in my journal and inquired what I was doing. I told him I was keeping an account of the weather. He said it was not so, that I was speaking bad about him—telling how he had taken our ship and killed the crew, so as to inform my countrymen. He added that if he ever saw me writing in it again, he would throw it into the fire. I was happy that he did no more than threaten, and became very cautious afterwards not to let him see me write.

Not long after, I finished some daggers for him which I polished highly. These pleased him much, and he gave me directions to make a cheetolth, or war club of whalebone. I succeeded so well that he gave me a present of cloth sufficient to make a complete suit, besides other things. Thompson also became rather more of a favorite since he had made a fine sail for Maquina's canoe, and some garments for him out of European cloth.

Maquina knew that the chiefs of the tribes who came to visit us had endeavored to persuade me to escape, and he frequently cautioned me not to listen to them. He said that, should he catch me trying to get away, he would certainly put me to death. While here, he gave me a book in which I found the names of seven persons belonging to the ship *Manchester* of Philadelphia. These men, Maquina informed me, ran away from the ship and came to him, but soon afterward went off in the night, intending to go to the Wickinninish. They were recaptured and put to death. Four men held each prisoner on the ground and forced open his mouth, while they choked him by ramming stones down his throat.

The king was delighted to find that I wanted to learn their language and took great pleasure in talking to me. On one of these occasions he explained his reasons for killing our crew. He said that he bore my countrymen no ill will, but that he had been treated very badly by them several times.

The first injury he complained about was done him by a Captain

Tawnington, who commanded a schooner which passed a winter at Friendly Cove. One day, when Maquina was away, this man entered his house. Only the women were there, and he searched the chests and took away all the skins Maquina had. About the same time, four of their chiefs were barbarously killed by a Captain Martinez, a Spaniard.

Soon after, he said, Captain Hanna of the *Sea Otter* came to Nootka. One of the natives stole a chisel from the ship's carpenter. Hanna fired upon their canoes, which were alongside, and killed upwards of twenty of the natives. Maquina himself was on board the vessel, and had to leap from the quarter-deck and swim under water a long way in order to escape.

These injuries had given Maquina a strong desire for revenge. Although many years had passed he had not forgotten his wrongs, and only lack of opportunity prevented him from avenging them. Unfortunately for us, the long-wished-for opportunity had finally presented itself with our ship. Maquina had found it was not guarded with the usual vigilance of the northwest traders. When Captain Salter insulted him, his desire for revenge was rekindled and he had formed a plan of attack. His chiefs had readily agreed to his proposal.

Here I cannot help but mention a thought that has frequently occurred to me about the way our people behave toward the natives. I have no doubt that many disasters have happened mainly because of the imprudent conduct of some of the captains and crews of the trading ships, who insult, plunder, and even kill the Indians on slight grounds. Nothing is more sacred to a savage than revenge—and they will wreak their vengeance upon the first vessel they see. All too often they make the innocent suffer for the wrongs of the guilty, as few of them can tell the difference between persons of the same general appearance, especially when they speak the same language. This, I believe, is the cause of the bloodthirsty disposition with which these people are reproached. Maquina repeatedly told me that it was not his wish to hurt a white man, and that he never would have done it if they had not injured him.

On the morning of the 13th of December, there began what appeared to us a singular farce. Maquina discharged a pistol close to his son's ear, who fell down as if killed. All the women of the house set up a lamentable cry, tearing handfuls of hair from their heads and exclaiming that the prince was dead. At the same time a great number of the inhabitants rushed in armed with daggers, muskets, etc., inquiring the cause of the outcry. These were followed by two others dressed in wolf skins, with wolf masks over their faces. They came in on their hands and feet like beasts and carried the prince off upon their backs. We saw nothing more of the ceremony, as Maquina came to us and, giving us some dried provision, ordered us to leave the house and not return for seven days. He said that if we appeared within that period, he should kill us.

Taking our provisions, a bundle of clothes, and our axes, we withdrew into the woods, where we built ourselves a cabin with the branches of trees. Here we passed our exile with more content than much of the time while with the Nootkans.

When we got back, we learned this performance was a celebration held by them annually in honor of their god, Quahootze. It terminated with a most extraordinary exhibition on the day after our return. Three men, each of whom had two bayonets run through his sides, between the ribs, apparently regardless of the pain, traversed the room backwards and forwards, singing war songs and exulting in this display of firmness.

On the 25th, we could not but call to mind that this was Christmas. With the king's permission we withdrew into the woods. We read the service appointed for the day, sang the hymn of the Nativity, and prayed that Heaven would permit us to celebrate the next festival of this kind in some Christian land.

On our return we were desirous of having a better supper than usual, as is the custom of our country. With this view, we bought from one of the natives some dried clams and oil, and a root called kletsup, which we cooked by steaming, and found it very palatable.

On the 31st the tribe left Tashees for Cooptee, where they go to pass the remainder of the winter and complete their fishing. They took everything with them in the same manner as at Nootka. We arrived at Cooptee in a few hours. This place stands in a very narrow valley at the foot of a high mountain and is nearly as secure as Tashees from the winter storms. Immediately we set about covering the houses.

The natives now began to take herring and sprat in immense quantities, with some salmon, and there was nothing but feasting from morning till night. About the beginning of February, Maquina gave a great feast, at which not only his whole tribe were present, but one hundred persons from the Aitizzart and a number from the Wickinninish. It is customary with them to give an annual entertainment of this kind, and they always eat to the greatest excess. At this feast I saw upwards of a hundred salmon cooked in one tub.

On the 25th of February we returned to Nootka. A few days before we left Cooptee, some men from a neighboring tribe had brought Maquina information that there were twenty ships to the north preparing to come against him and destroy his whole tribe for seizing the *Boston*. This news threw him into great alarm. He treated us with much harshness and kept a very suspicious eye upon us. Afterwards we discovered that these people had invented the story to disquiet Maquina.

The whaling season began now, and Maquina was out almost every day in his canoe. For a considerable time he had no success. One day he broke the staff of his harpoon. Another day the shell point of the weapon broke after it had been inside a whale for a long time, and it came out. He had several similar accidents, due to the imperfection of the instrument.

At these times he always returned very morose and out of temper and upbraided his men for violating their obligation to continence before whaling. In this state of ill humor he would give us very little to eat.

After a number of these accidents I told Maquina I could make him a harpoon of steel, which would be less liable to fail him. The idea pleased him, and in a short time I completed one. He was delighted with it and the very next day went out to try it.

He succeeded in taking a whale with it. There was great joy throughout the village as soon as this was reported by a person stationed at the headland. All the canoes were immediately launched. Furnished with harpoons and sealskin floats, they hastened to assist in buoying the whale up and towing it in. As the canoes appeared at the mouth of the cove, all who were on shore—men, women, and children—mounted the roofs of their houses to congratulate the king, drumming furiously on the planks and exclaiming, *"Wocash—wocash, Tyee!"*

The whale, on being drawn on shore, was immediately cut up. A great feast of the blubber was given at Maquina's house, to which all the village were invited. I was highly praised for the goodness of my harpoon and a quantity of blubber given me. I boiled it in salt water with some young nettles and other greens for Thompson and myself, and we found it tolerable food.

Several of the chiefs, among whom were Maquina's brothers, were very eager to have me make steel harpoons for them, but Maquina would not permit this. He reserved this improved weapon for himself.

At about this time, a brother-in-law of Maquina's died under unusual circumstances. This man, Tootoosch by name, had killed two of our poor comrades when our ship was taken. While enjoying good health, he was suddenly seized with a fit of delirium in which he fancied that he saw the ghosts of the two dead men. He said they were constantly standing by him and threatening him, and he would take no food, except what was forced into his mouth. Insanity was most uncommon among the inhabitants and all were greatly disturbed to see him raging and wasting away. Many considered Thompson and myself responsible for his condition and accused us of witchcraft.

The death of Tootoosch increased still more the uneasiness which his delirium had excited among the savages. The chiefs who had killed our men became alarmed lest they should be seized with the same disorder and die like him; more particularly as I had told Maquina that I believed Tootoosch's insanity was a punishment inflicted on him by the god Quahootze for his cruelty in murdering two innocent men.

Our situation had now become unpleasant in the extreme. The summer was far advanced, and we nearly despaired of a ship arriving to rescue us. We were treated, too, with less indulgence than before. Both Thompson and myself were obliged, in addition to our other employments, to cut and collect fuel, which we had to bring on our shoulders from nearly three miles' distance.

To add to this, we suffered much abuse from the common people. When Maquina or some of the chiefs were not present, they would insult us, calling us wretched slaves. They asked us where our *Tyee* or captain was, and made gestures signifying that his head had been cut off and they would do the like to us. However, at such times they generally took good care to keep well out of Thompson's reach, as they had more than once experienced the strength of his fist.

We were also brought to great distress for want of provisions. Often we were reduced to collecting a scanty supply of mussels and limpets from the rocks, and compelled to part with some of our most necessary articles of clothing to purchase food. This was, however, chiefly because the inhabitants themselves were experiencing great scarcity. Very few salmon were caught at Friendly Cove this season. The natives said the fish had been driven away by the blood of our men who had been thrown into the sea. With true savage inconsistency, they blamed the scarcity on Maquina, who had proposed attacking our ship.

Nor were the king and chiefs much more fortunate in their whaling, even after I had furnished Maquina with the improved weapon. Only four whales were taken during the season. These afforded but a short supply to a population of fifteen hundred persons. They were so improvident that they would feast gluttonously whenever a whale was caught and then be reduced to eating once a day for a week at a time, collecting cockles and mussels from the rocks.

After the cod and halibut fishing began in June, they met with tolerable success. But such was the savage caprice of Maquina that he would often give us little to eat. Finally he ordered us to buy a canoe and fishing implements and go out ourselves and fish, or we should have nothing. To do this we were compelled to part with our greatcoats, which were not only important to us as garments, but of which we made our beds. From our want of skill, however, we met with no success and Maquina ordered us to remain at home.

We were nevertheless, treated at times with much kindness by Maquina, who would give us the best he had to eat and occasionally some small present of cloth for a garment. He promised me that if any ship should arrive within a hundred miles of Nootka, he would send a canoe with a letter from me to the captain, so that he might come to our release. He showed us these marks of attention, however, when he thought himself in danger from a mutiny in the tribe, or when he was fearful of an attack from some of the other tribes who were irritated with him for seizing the *Boston,* as it had prevented ships from coming to trade with them. At such times he made us keep guard over him night and day, armed with cutlasses and pistols. He was apparently afraid to trust any of his own men.

In July Maquina informed me that he was going to war with the Aytcharts, a tribe about fifty miles to the south, and that I must make daggers for his men and cheetolths for his chiefs.

When these people have determined on war, for three or four weeks prior to the expedition they go into the water five or six times a day and wash and scrub themselves with brushes mixed with briers, so that their bodies and faces will often be entirely covered with blood. During this self-torture they continually exclaim: "Great God, let me live—not be sick—find the enemy—not fear him—find him asleep, and kill a great many of them." During this period they have no intercourse with their women or any kind of merriment.

Maquina informed Thompson and myself that he would take us with him. He wanted us to scrub ourselves in the same way, telling me that it would harden our skins, so enemy weapons would not pierce them. But as we felt no great inclination to amuse ourselves in this manner, we declined it.

The expedition consisted of forty canoes, carrying ten to twenty men each. Thompson and myself armed ourselves with cutlasses and pistols, but the natives took only daggers and cheetolths, with a few bows and arrows. The arrows were about a yard in length, and pointed with copper, mussel shell, or bone; the bows were four feet and a half long, with strings of whale sinew.

After traveling about thirty miles up a river, at midnight we came in sight of the Aytchart village, which was on a steep hill. The attack was deferred until dawn, as Maquina said that was when men slept the soundest.

When all was ready for the attack, we landed with the greatest silence. Going around so as to come upon the foe in the rear, we clambered up the hill. While the Nootkans entered the huts creeping on all fours, my comrade and myself stationed ourselves outside to cut off those who should escape or come to the aid of their friends. I wished, if possible, not to stain my hands in the blood of any fellow-creature, and Thompson was too brave to think of attacking a sleeping enemy.

Maquina uttered the war whoop as he seized the head of the chief and gave him the fatal blow. At once all began the work of death. The Aytcharts, taken by surprise, were unable to resist. Except for a few who escaped, all were killed or taken prisoner. I had the good fortune to take four captives. Maquina, as a favor, permitted me to consider them as mine, and occasionally employ them in fishing for me. Thompson, who thirsted for revenge, succeeded in killing seven stout fellows, an act which won him the admiration of Maquina and the chiefs.

After putting to death all the old and infirm of either sex and destroying the buildings, we re-embarked for Nootka with our booty.

We were received with great joy by the women and children, accompanying our war song with a most furious drumming on the houses. The next day a great feast was given by Maquina in celebration of his victory, which ended as usual with a dance by Satsatsoksis.

No ship appeared off Nootka this season. With heavy hearts my companion and myself accompanied the tribe on their move in September to Tashees, giving up for six months even the remotest chance of release.

Soon after we reached Tashees, Maquina informed me that he and his chiefs had determined I must marry one of their women. He said the sooner I adopted their customs the better, and that a wife and family would make me more contented with their mode of living. I objected strongly, but he told me that, should I refuse, both Thompson and myself would be put to death. He added, however, that if none of the women of his tribe pleased me, he would go with me to some of the other tribes, where he would purchase for me any woman I should select. With death on the one side and matrimony on the other, I thought proper to choose the lesser of the two evils. As I did not fancy any of the Nootka women, I asked to be permitted to make choice of one from some other tribe.

The next morning Maquina, with about fifty men in two canoes, set out with me for Aitizzart, taking a quantity of cloth, muskets, sea-otter skins, etc., for the purchase of my bride. With the aid of our paddles and sails we arrived at the village before sunset. Our arrival excited a general alarm; the men hastened to the shore, armed with weapons, and made many warlike gestures. We remained quietly in our canoes. Finally the messenger of the chief came to invite us on shore. We followed him to the chief's house, where we were ushered in with much ceremony. My seat was next to Maquina by his request.

After a feast of herring spawn and oil, Maquina asked me if I saw any that I liked among the women there. I immediately pointed out a girl of about seventeen, the daughter of Upquesta, the chief. Maquina sent two of his men to bring the boxes of presents from the canoes and, taking me by the hand, walked into the middle of the room. In the meantime Maquina's master of ceremonies, Kinneclimmets, made himself ready for the part he was to act, by powdering his hair with white down. When the chests were brought in, specimens of the articles were shown by our men, one holding up a musket, another a skin, a third a piece of cloth, etc.

On this, Kinneclimmets stepped forward and informed the chief that all these belonged to me, and that they were offered to him for the purchase of his daughter Eustochee-exqua, as a wife for me. As he said this, the men who held up the various articles walked up to the chief and with a very stern, morose look—the complimentary one on these occasions—threw them at his feet. Immediately all the tribe set up a cry of *"Klack-ko-Tyee"* ("Thank you, chief").

After this ceremony Maquina made a speech of more than half an hour, saying much in my praise to the Aitizzart chief. While he was speaking, his master of ceremonies skipped about, making the most extravagant gestures and exclaiming, *"Wocash!"*

When Maquina had ceased, the Aitizzart chief arose and began to set forth the many good qualities of his daughter, saying he could not think of parting with her. He spoke in this manner for some time, but finally consented to the marriage, requesting that she might be kindly treated by her husband. At the close of the speech, Kinneclimmets again called out as loud as he could, *"Wocash!"* cutting a thousand capers and spinning himself around on his heel like a top.

Upquesta directed his people to carry back the presents to me, and gave me two young male slaves to assist me in fishing. Then we were invited by one of the chiefs to a feast of dried herring at his house. Kinneclimmets amused the company very highly with his tricks, and the entertainment was closed with war songs from our men and the Aitizzarts, accompanied with expressive gestures and wielding of their weapons.

After this our company returned to lodge at Upquesta's. In the morning the chief gave me his daughter, with an earnest request that I would use her well, which I promised him. She accompanied me with apparent satisfaction on board the canoe.

When we reached Tashees all the inhabitants were collected on the shore and welcomed us with loud shouts. The women conducted my bride to Maquina's house and kept her with them for ten days. It was the custom that no intercourse should take place between the newly married pair during that period. At night Maquina gave a great feast, followed by a dance in which all the women joined, and thus ended the festivities of my marriage.

Maquina assigned me as an apartment the space in the upper

part of his house between him and his elder brother. Here I established myself with my family—myself and wife, Thompson and little Satsatsoksis, who had always been strongly attached to me.

I determined to live in a more comfortable, cleanly manner than the others. For this purpose I erected a partition with planks about three feet high between the adjoining rooms and mine, and made three bedsteads of planks, which I covered with boards. This was much more comfortable than sleeping on the floor amidst the dirt.

I found my Indian princess both amiable and intelligent. She was very attentive to keeping her garments and person neat and clean, and appeared eager to please me. She was, I have said, about seventeen. Her person was small but well formed, as were her features. Her complexion was fairer than any of the women, with considerable color in her cheeks, her hair long, black, and much softer than is usual with them, and her teeth small, even, and of a dazzling whiteness. Her expression indicated sweetness of temper and modesty. She would indeed have been considered very pretty in any country.

With a partner possessing so many attractions, many may conclude that I must have found myself comparatively happy. But a compulsory marriage, even with the most beautiful and accomplished person in the world, can never prove a source of real happiness. I could not but view my marriage as a chain that was to bind me down to this savage land. In a few days Maquina informed me there had been a meeting of his chiefs and it had been determined that, as I had married one of their women, I must be considered one of them and conform to their customs. In future, neither myself nor Thompson was to wear our European clothes, but dress in kutsaks or mantles like themselves. This order was most painful to me.

Their religious celebration this year began on the 15th of November and continued fourteen days. As I was now considered one of them, Maquina directed Thompson and myself to remain and pray with them to Quahootze to be good to them, and thank him for what he had done. All the men and women in the village assembled at Maquina's house in their plainest dresses and sang mournful songs. The king beat time on his hollow plank, accompanied by one of his chiefs with the great rattle. The natives ate little and went to bed late, rising at dawn. They even interrupted this short period of repose by getting up at midnight and singing.

The ceremony ended with a cruel exhibition. A boy of twelve, with six bayonets run into his flesh, one through each arm and thigh, and through each side close to the ribs, was carried around the room suspended upon them, without showing any symptoms of pain. Maquina informed me that it was an ancient custom to sacrifice a man at the close of this ceremony, in honor of their god, but his father had substituted this in its place. The whole closed on the evening of the 29th with a great feast of salmon spawn and oil.

A few days later I was sent for by my neighbor Yealthlower, the king's elder brother, to file his teeth. After this operation, he informed me that a new wife whom he had purchased had refused to sleep with him and it was his intention to bite off her nose. I endeavored to dissuade him, but he was determined. He performed his savage threat that very night, saying that since she would not be his wife, she should not be that of any other, and in the morning sent her back to her father.

This inhuman act did not proceed from any innate cruelty. He was far from being of a barbarous temper. But such is the despotism of these savages over their women that he no doubt considered it a just punishment for her offense.

In December we left Tashees for Cooptee. As usual, we found the herring in great plenty. The same scene of riotous feasting that I had witnessed last year was repeated by our natives.

In some respects my situation was more comfortable after my marriage. I lived in a more cleanly manner and had my food better and more neatly cooked. I always had plenty, my slaves generally furnishing it to me, and Upquesta never failed to send me an ample supply from Aitizzart. Still, from being obliged at this season of the year to dress like the natives, with only a piece of cloth about two yards long thrown loosely around me, I suffered more than I can express from the cold, especially as I was compelled to cut and bring firewood for Maquina.

On the 20th of February, we returned to our summer quarters at Nootka. By now I almost despaired that any vessel would ever come to release us, or that we would be permitted to depart if one should.

Soon after our return Maquina ordered me to make a good number of harpoons for himself and his chiefs. I had completed several, with some lances, when I was taken very ill. I suppose I fell sick because I had suffered so much from the cold, in going without proper clothing. For a number of hours I was in great pain and expected to die.

When the fever left me, I was so weak as scarcely to be able to stand. I had nothing comforting to take, nor anything to drink but cold water.

My Indian wife, as far as she knew how, did everything for me she could. But the feebleness in which my disorder had left me, the dejection I felt at the almost hopelessness of my situation and the want of warm clothing and civilized nursing still kept me very much indisposed. Maquina perceived this. He finally told me that if I did not like living with my wife, and that was the cause of my being so sad, I might part with her. I readily accepted this proposal and the next day Maquina sent her back to her father.

On parting with me she showed much emotion. She begged me to allow her to remain till I had recovered, as there was no one who would take such good care of me as herself. But I told her she must go, as I honestly did not think I should ever get well. She took an affectionate leave, and left her two slaves to take care of me.

I was greatly affected with the simple expressions of her regard for me, and could not but feel strongly concerned for this poor girl. Had it not been that I considered her a serious obstacle to my being permitted to leave the country, I should have felt a real sense of loss. After her departure, I requested Maquina to permit me to wear warmer clothing or I should certainly die from the cold. He consented, and I was once more comfortably clad. In a short time the change of clothing restored me to health, and I again went to work making harpoons for Maquina.

It was now past midsummer, and our hopes of release were daily becoming fainter. Though we heard of no less than seven vessels on the coast, none appeared inclined to venture to Nootka.

The destruction of the *Boston*—the largest, strongest, and best-equipped ship ever fitted for the northwest trade—had inspired the commanders of others with a dread of coming to Nootka. Since our capture, I had written sixteen letters and entrusted them to friendly natives belonging to other tribes, for delivery to any ship that might visit along the coast. In my letters I stated the cause of the *Boston*'s capture, and there was not the least danger in coming to Nootka, provided they would follow the directions I laid down. Still, I felt very little hope that any of these letters would fall into the right hands.

On the morning of the 19th of July I was employed with Thompson in forging daggers for the king. Suddenly we heard the sound of three cannon and the cries of the inhabitants exclaiming, *"Weena, weena—Mamethlee!"* ("Strangers—White men!").

Soon after, several people came running into the house to inform me a vessel under full sail was coming into the harbor. Though my heart bounded with joy, I repressed my feelings. I told Thompson to be on his guard and not betray any joy. Our release, and perhaps our lives, depended on our conducting ourselves so as to make the natives suppose we were not anxious to leave them. We continued our work as if nothing had happened.

In a few minutes Maquina came in. Seeing us at work, he appeared much surprised. He asked me if I did not know a vessel had come.

I answered in a careless manner that it was nothing to me.

"How, John," said he, "you no glad go board?"

I replied that I cared very little about it, as I had become reconciled to their manner of living. He then told me that he had called a council of his people respecting us, and we must be present at it.

The men having assembled at Maquina's house, he asked them what should be done with Thompson and myself now that a vessel had arrived, and whether he had not better go on board himself to make a trade and procure such articles as were wanted.

Each one of the tribe who wished gave his opinion. Some were for putting us to death and pretending to the strangers that a different nation had destroyed the *Boston*. Others were for sending us fifteen or twenty miles back into the country until the departure of the vessel. Several of the chiefs were for immediately releasing us. But this by no means appeared to be Maquina's wish.

With regard to Maquina's going on board the vessel, which he showed a strong inclination to do, there was but one opinion. All opposed it, telling him the captain would kill him or keep him prisoner, because he had destroyed our ship. Maquina told them that he was not afraid, but he would be guided by John, whom he had always found true. He then asked me if I thought there would be any danger in his going on board.

I reminded him that he had almost always experienced good treatment from the white men, nor had he any reason to fear the contrary now. I told him that they never harmed those who did not injure them, and he might go on board with security.

After reflecting a few moments, he said, with much apparent satisfaction, that he would go if I would write a letter telling the captain that he had treated Thompson and myself kindly and to use him well.

It may easily be supposed that I felt much joy at this decision. But I was careful not to show it. I treated his going or staying as a matter perfectly indifferent to me. I then proceeded to write the letter. As the reader can imagine, it was somewhat different from the one Maquina had asked for.

The letter I wrote was nearly in the following terms:

*Nootka, July 19, 1805*

SIR:—The bearer of this letter is the Indian king Maquina. He was the instigator of the capture of the ship *Boston*, John Salter, captain, and of the murder of twenty-five of her crew, the two only survivors being now on shore. Therefore I hope you will take care to confine him according to his merits, keeping so good a watch over him that he cannot escape from you. By so doing, we shall be able to obtain our release in the course of a few hours.

JOHN R. JEWITT, *Armorer of the*
Boston, *for himself, and*
JOHN THOMPSON, *Sailmaker*
*of the said ship*

When I gave the letter to Maquina, he asked me to explain it to him. I did this line by line, as he pointed them out with his finger— but in a sense very different from the real one. I gave him to understand I had written that, as Maquina had been kind to me since I had been taken by him, it was my wish the captain should treat him accordingly, and give him what molasses, biscuit, and rum he wanted.

When I had finished, he placed his finger in a significant manner on my name at the bottom. Eyeing me with a look that seemed to read my inmost thoughts, he said, "John you no lie?"

Never did I undergo such a scrutiny, or experience greater fear than I felt at that moment. My destiny was suspended on the slightest thread. The least mark of embarrassment on my part or suspicion of treachery on his would probably have cost my life.

Fortunately I was able to preserve my composure—and my being painted in the Indian manner prevented any change in my expression from being noticed. I replied with considerable promptness, looking at him with all the confidence I could muster—

"Why do you ask me such a question, *Tyee?* Have you ever known me to lie?"

"No."

"Then how can you suppose I should tell you a lie now, since I have never done it?"

As I was speaking, he still continued looking at me with the same piercing eye. But, observing nothing to excite his suspicion, he told me that he believed me and gave orders to get his canoe ready.

His chiefs again attempted to dissuade him. His wives crowded around him, begging him on their knees not to trust himself with the white men. Fortunately, so strong was his wish to go on board the vessel that he was deaf to their pleas.

"John no lie," he said, and left the house, taking four prime skins with him as a present to the captain.

Scarcely had the canoe put off than he ordered his men to stop paddling. Calling to me, he asked if I did not want to go on board with him. Suspecting this question was intended to ensnare me, I replied that I had no wish to do it.

On going on board the brig, Maquina gave his present of skins and my letter to the captain. He read it and asked Maquina into the cabin, where he gave him some biscuit and rum. At the same time he privately directed his mate to go forward and return with five or six armed men. When they appeared, the captain told Maquina he was his prisoner and should continue so until we were released. At the same time the captain ordered him put in irons.

Maquina was terrified at this reception. He made no attempt to resist, but requested the captain to permit one of his men to come and see him. One was called, and Maquina said something to him which the captain supposed to be an order to release us. The man returned to the canoe and it was paddled off to the shore.

As the canoe approached, the inhabitants showed some uneasiness at not seeing their king on board. On its arrival, they were told the captain had made him a prisoner, and John had spoken badly about him in the letter. They all set up a loud howl, and ran backwards and forwards upon the shore like so many lunatics, scratching their faces and tearing their hair in handfuls from their heads.

After some time, the men ran to their huts for their weapons. Maquina's wives and the rest of the women came around me and begged me to spare his life. Satsatsoksis, who kept constantly with me, took me by the hand, wept bitterly, and joined his entreaties to theirs. I told them not to worry—that Maquina's life was in no danger.

The men, however, were extremely exasperated with me. The common people came running furiously towards me, brandishing their weapons and threatening to cut me in pieces. Others declared they would burn me alive over a slow fire, suspended by my heels. All this fury caused me little alarm. I felt they would not dare to harm me while the king was on the brig.

The chiefs took no part in this violent conduct, but asked if the captain intended to kill Maquina. I told them the captain had confined Maquina only to make them release Thompson and myself. If they would do that, their king would receive no injury; otherwise he would be kept a prisoner.

Many of them did not appear satisfied with this, and began to repeat their murderous threats.

"Kill me," I said to them, "if it is your wish. But unless you want to see your king hanging by his neck to that pole"—I pointed to the yardarm of the brig—"and the sailors firing at him, you will not do it."

"Oh, no!" was the general cry. "That must never be. But what must we do?"

I told them their best plan would be to send Thompson on board, to ask the captain to treat Maquina well till I was released, which would be soon. They were perfectly willing to do this, and I directed Thompson to go on board. But he objected, saying he would not leave me alone with the savages.

I told him not to be under any fear for me—if I could get him off, I could manage well enough for myself. I advised him, immediately on getting on board the brig, to request the captain to keep Maquina confined till I was released, as I was in no danger while he had him safe.

When I saw Thompson off, I asked the natives what they intended to do with me. They said I must talk to the captain in another letter and tell him to let his boat come on shore with Maquina, and that I should be ready to jump into the boat at the same time Maquina should jump on shore. I told them the captain knew they had killed my shipmates and would never trust his men so near the shore; but if they would select three of their number to go with me in a canoe, when we came within hail I would ask the captain to send his boat with Maquina, to receive me in exchange for him.

This appeared to please them. After some whispering among the chiefs, they selected three of their stoutest men to go with me. Fortunately, being accustomed to see me armed, they paid no attention to the pistols I had about me.

As I was going into the canoe, little Satsatsoksis, who could not bear to part with me, asked me if the white men would let his father come on shore, and not kill him. I told him no one should injure his father. Taking an affectionate leave of me, he ran to comfort his mother with the assurance I had given him.

I seated myself in the prow of the canoe, facing the three men. I had determined, if it was practicable, to get on board the vessel before Maquina was released, hoping by that means to obtain the restoration of any property belonging to the *Boston* that still remained in the possession of the savages. I was confident now that nothing could thwart my escape or prevent the execution of the plan I had formed, as the men were armed with nothing but their paddles.

When we came within hail of the brig, they ceased paddling. I pointed my pistols at them and ordered them to go on instantly, or I would shoot them. Greatly frightened, they resumed their paddling. In a few moments I found myself alongside the ship. All the crew crowded to the side to see me.

I immediately climbed on board, where I was welcomed by the captain, Samuel Hill, of the brig *Lydia* of Boston, who congratulated me on my escape. He informed me that he had received my letter from the chief of a neighboring tribe, and had at once sailed to Nootka to aid me.

I thanked him in the best manner I could, though I was so excited that I hardly knew what I said. I have no doubt that, what with my strange dress—I was painted with red and black from head to foot, had a bearskin wrapped around me, and my long hair was fastened on top of my head in a large bunch, with a sprig of green spruce—I must have appeared more like a lunatic than a rational creature.

The captain asked me into the cabin, where I found Maquina in irons with a guard over him. He looked very melancholy, but on seeing me his face brightened.

"*Wocash,* John," he said.

Taking him by the hand, I asked the captain's permission to take off his irons. The captain consented. Maquina smiled at this mark of attention from me.

When I had freed the king from his irons, Captain Hill wished to learn the particulars of our capture. He said an account of the destruction of the ship and her crew had been received at Boston but nothing more was known, except that two of the men were living, for whose rescue the owners had offered a liberal reward. He had been able to get nothing out of old Maquina, whom the sailors had supplied too plentifully with grog.

I gave him a correct statement of the whole proceeding, together with the manner in which my life and that of my comrade had been preserved. He was greatly irritated against Maquina and said he ought to be killed. I observed that, however he had acted in taking our ship, it might be wrong to judge a savage with the same severity as a civilized person. That Maquina's conduct arose from an insult he thought he had received from Captain Salter, and from the unjustifiable conduct of some masters of vessels who had robbed him and killed a number of his people. Besides, revenge of an injury is held sacred by these people, and they would not fail to retaliate on the first vessel that should give them an opportunity, should we kill their king.

The captain said he would leave it wholly with me whether to spare or kill Maquina. I replied that I most certainly should never take the life of a man who had preserved mine. As some of the *Boston*'s property still remained on shore, I told the captain we ought to keep Maquina on board till it was given up. The captain agreed.

During this conversation Maquina was in great anxiety, as he understood the subject of our deliberation. He constantly interrupted me to inquire what we had determined to do with him, and if I did not think that Thompson would kill him. I pacified him as well as I was able by telling him that he had nothing to fear. But I found it extremely difficult to convince him of this, as it agreed so little with the ideas of revenge entertained by his people. I told him, however, that he must restore all the property still in his possession, belonging to the ship. He was perfectly ready to do this, happy to escape on such terms.

But it was now past five, and too late for the articles to be collected and brought off. I told him that he must remain on board with me that night, and in the morning he should be set on shore as soon

as the things were delivered. To this he agreed, on condition that I
would remain with him in the cabin. I then went up on deck. The
canoe that brought me had been sent back. I hailed the inhabitants
and told them their king had agreed to stay on board till the next day
and that no canoes must attempt to come near the vessel during the
night.

"*Woho, woho,*" they answered. "Very well, very well."

I returned to Maquina. So great were his terrors that he would
not allow me to sleep. He constantly disturbed me with his questions,
repeating, "John, you know, when you were alone, and more than
five hundred men were your enemies, I was your friend and prevented
them from putting you and Thompson to death. Now that I am in
the power of your friends, you ought to do the same by me." I
assured him that as soon as the property was released he would be
set at liberty.

At daybreak I hailed the natives and told them it was Maquina's
order that they should bring off the cannon and anchors, and whatever remained of the cargo of the ship. They set about doing this with
the utmost speed, transporting the cannon and anchors by lashing
together two of their largest canoes and covering them with planks.
In two hours they delivered on board everything that I could recollect.

When everything belonging to the ship had been restored, Maquina
was permitted to return in his canoe, which had been sent for him
with a present of sixty skins for the captain, in acknowledgment of
his having spared the king's life.

Such was Maquina's joy when Captain Hill told him that he was at
liberty to go, that he threw off his mantle and gave it to the captain.
In return, the captain presented him with a new greatcoat and hat,
with which he appeared much delighted. The captain then desired
me to inform him that he should return to that part of the coast in
November, and he wished him to keep what skins he should get,
which he would buy of him.

Maquina promised to do this.

"John," he said to me, "you know I shall be at Tashees then, but
when you come, make pow" (which means, fire a gun) "to let
me know, and I will come down."

When he came to the side of the brig, he told me that he hoped
I would come to see him again and bring plenty of blankets, biscuit,
molasses and rum. He said he would never again take a letter of

recommendation from anyone, or trust himself on a vessel unless I was there. Then, grasping both my hands, while the tears trickled down his cheeks, he bade me farewell, and stepped into the canoe.

As soon as Maquina left us, we proceeded to the north, touching at various places for the purpose of trading. After nearly four months we sailed for Nootka, where we arrived in November. The tribe was absent and the agreed signal was given by firing a cannon. In a few hours a canoe appeared. It landed at the village and, putting the king on shore, came off to the brig. Kinneclimmets, who was one of the men in the canoe, asked if John was there. I went forward and invited them on board. They told me that Maquina had a number of skins with him, but he would not come on board unless I would go on shore for him. I agreed to, provided they would remain in the brig. They consented, and I went on shore in the canoe, in spite of the objections of Thompson and the captain.

As I landed, Maquina came up and welcomed me with much joy. He inquired after his men. I told him they were to remain till my return.

"Ah, John," said he, "I see you are afraid to trust me. If they had come with you, I should not have hurt you, though I should have taken good care not to let you go on board another vessel."

He then took his chest of skins and stepped into the canoe. I paddled him alongside the brig, where he was received with the greatest cordiality by Captain Hill, who bought his skins. He was much pleased with his reception, inquiring how many moons it would be before I should come back again to see him and his son. He said that he would keep all his furs for me. He also told me that my Indian wife had borne me a son, and that he would send for him and take care of him as his own.

As soon as Maquina had left, we got under way. We continued on the coast until August, 1806, when, having completed our trade, we sailed for China.

We had a prosperous passage, arriving at Macao in December, and then went on to Canton. There I had the good fortune to meet an old acquaintance, the mate of an English East Indiaman, whose father was a next-door neighbor to mine. This young man supplied me with clothes and a small sum of money. I gave him a letter for my father, in which I mentioned my wonderful preservation and escape through the humanity of Captain Hill, with whom I should return to Boston.

We left China in February, 1807, and after a pleasant voyage of one hundred and fourteen days arrived at Boston. In the post office I found a letter from my mother expressing the great joy of my family that I was alive and well, as they had for a long time given me up for dead. While in Boston I was treated with much kindness and hospitality by the owners of the ship *Boston,* Messrs. Francis and Thomas Amory, to whom I feel under great obligations for their goodness to me and the assistance they so readily afforded a stranger in distress.

# Remember the River Raisin!

## ELIAS DARNELL

$E$ARLY IN 1813—*the War of 1812 was in its seventh month—a force of British and Indians occupied a village called Frenchtown (modern Monroe) on the River Raisin, in southeastern Michigan. General James Winchester sent a detachment of his Kentucky riflemen to take the town. On January 18, the Americans came in sight of the neat frame houses of the French, who had built the town and given it its name.*

*An old Indian was smoking by the fireside of a Frenchman in the village when word came of the Americans' approach.*

*"Ho, de Mericans come," the Indian exclaimed. "I suppose Ohio men come. We give them another chase."*

*Still smoking, he walked unconcernedly to the door and watched the Americans till they formed their battle line and rushed at the enemy with a blood-curdling shout.*

*"Kentuck, by God!" the Indian cried and, picking up his gun, he scurried for the woods like a frightened beast.*

*They were a proud, valorous group of fighting men, those Kentuckians who charged against the expectant foe. If valor could have won the battle on the River Raisin, victory would have been theirs. But the odds were heavily against them. When their general, Win-*

256

*chester, came up with more men and encamped for the night, he neglected to fortify the right wing of his troops. Meanwhile the British commander, Colonel Henry Procter, came on from nearby Amherstburg, in Canada, with a larger force; his men outnumbered the Kentuckians two to one. And reinforcements that had been promised (or so Winchester claimed later) never arrived.*

*Most of Winchester's army was killed or surrendered. In this account Elias Darnell, a Kentucky private, describes the battle and the surrender with considerable drama, and the aftermath as well— an aftermath so terrible that "Remember the River Raisin!" became one of the great rallying cries of the War of 1812.*

*General Winchester spent a year in Canada as a prisoner of war. Later he was accused of gross negligence and military incapacity, not altogether a novel experience for him. He left the army and went into business, becoming one of the founders of Memphis, Tennessee.*

*Elias Darnell managed to escape from the Indians and find safety in the custody of the British at Amherstburg. During the next two weeks he and some other American prisoners marched hundreds of miles through snow and bitter cold, finally arriving at Fort George on the New York border, where they were paroled on February 10, 1813. From here they made their way back to Kentucky.*

*Darnell published his journal soon after he got home, giving a complete story of the Kentuckians' expedition from the day they left Kentucky with hearts high and banners flying, after being addressed by the Honorable Henry Clay, until they were cut to pieces on the River Raisin. With his journal Darnell included two short narratives, written at his request by other former Indian captives. One of them, Timothy Mallary, said that he had found the infamous renegade James Girty stationed at Amherstburg, still plying his barbarous trade. "His business," wrote Mallary, "was to receive scalps from the Indians; his pay for this service was three dollars per week. I saw here about half a bushel of scalps in a kettle. The number I cannot guess at."*

**January 17th**  A Frenchman came from the River Raisin yesterday. He said two companies of British had just arrived from Canada, and the Indians were collecting and intended to burn Frenchtown in a few days. After receiving many pleas from the French and taking counsel with his field officers, General Winchester ordered a detachment of five hundred and seventy men to march to the River Raisin.

The detachment started early. After traveling twenty miles we drew close to Presqu'Isle, a French village on the south side of the Maumee River. The sight of this village filled us with joy, for we had been in the wilderness nearly five months, exposed to every inconvenience.

When the inhabitants of the village saw us, they met us with a white flag and expressed warm feelings of friendship for us. They said the British and Indians had left Frenchtown a few days ago. About three hours after dark, a reinforcement of one hundred and ten men overtook us, commanded by Colonel Allen.

Late that night a courier came from the River Raisin and informed Colonel Lewis there were four hundred Indians and two companies of British there, and that Colonel Elliott was to start the next morning from Malden with a reinforcement for them.

*18th* We started early, in order to get there before Colonel Elliott. After traveling fifteen miles, mostly on the ice, we received information that the enemy were there waiting for us. We were then within three miles of Frenchtown. We went on with no other view than *to conquer or die.*

When we advanced in sight of the town and were about a quarter of a mile from it, the British saluted us by the firing of a cannon. They fired it three times, but no injury was sustained.

During this time we formed the line of battle and, raising a shout, advanced on them briskly. They began firing their small arms, but this did not deter us from a charge. We advanced close and let loose on them. They gave way, and we soon had possession of the village without the loss of a man! Three were slightly wounded. Twelve of their warriors were slain and scalped, and one prisoner taken before they got to the woods.

In retreating, the Indians kept up some firing. We pursued them half a mile to the woods, which were very brushy and suited to their mode of fighting. As we advanced they were fixing themselves behind logs, trees, etc., to the best advantage. Our troops rushed on them resolutely and gave them Indian play—took advantage of trees, etc.—and kept them retreating a mile and a half in the woods. During this time a heavy fire was kept up on both sides. At length, after a battle of three hours and five minutes, we were obliged to stop the pursuit on account of the approach of night, and retire to the village, leaving our dead on the ground.

In this action the Kentuckians displayed great bravery, although they were very weary from marching on the ice. Each man was anxious to excel his fellow-soldiers; only those who were most fatigued went to the rear. Our loss in this action was eleven killed and fifty wounded. (It would have been better for us if we had been contented with the village, without pursuing them into the woods!) Although the enemy had the advantage of the village in the first attack, and of the woods in the second, their loss, by the best information, far exceeded ours. A Frenchman stated they had fifty-four killed and a hundred and forty wounded, part of whom were carried to his house on Sand Creek, a few miles from the village.

*19th* A party was sent out to the battleground to bring in the dead, which were found scalped and stripped, except one. In going over the battleground, great signs were seen (by the blood and where they had been dragged through the snow) of a considerable loss on the part of the enemy. The British left a considerable quantity of provisions and some store goods, which were very valuable to us. Our wounded could have been as well accommodated here with every necessity as in any part of Kentucky. Apples, cider, sugar, butter and whiskey appeared to be plentiful.

The River Raisin runs an east course through a level country, interspersed with well-improved farms, and is seventy or eighty yards wide; the banks are low. Frenchtown is on the north side of this river, not more than three miles from the place it empties into Lake Erie. There is a row of dwelling houses, about twenty in number, principally frame, near the bank, surrounded with a fence made in the form of picketing, with split timber, four to five feet high. This was not designed as a fortification, but to protect their yards and gardens.

*21st* A reinforcement of two hundred and thirty men arrived in the afternoon; also General Winchester, Colonel Wells, Major M'Clanahan, Captain Hart, Surgeons Irvin and Montgomery and some other gentlemen, who came to eat apples and drink cider, having been deprived of every kind of spirits nearly two months. The officers viewed and laid out a piece of ground for a camp and breastworks, but decided that it was too late to move there and erect fortifications that evening. Since they planned to move early next day, it was not thought worth while to fortify the right wing, though materials were at hand; it therefore encamped in the open field. For this lack of precaution we were soon to pay a terrible price.

A Frenchman arrived here late in the evening from Malden, and stated that a large number of Indians and British were coming on the ice with artillery to attack us; he judged their number to be three thousand. He was not believed by some of our leading men, who were regaling themselves with whiskey and loaf sugar. But most of the troops put great confidence in the Frenchman's report. They expected some fatal disaster to befall us because General Winchester had taken up his headquarters nearly half a mile from the encampment and the right wing was exposed.

Just at daybreak the reveille began to beat, as usual. This gave joy to the troops, who had passed the night under the apprehension they would be attacked before day. The reveille had not been beating more than two minutes before the sentinels fired three guns in quick succession. This alarmed our troops, who quickly formed and were ready for the enemy before they were near enough to do execution.

The British immediately discharged their artillery, loaded with balls, bombs, and grapeshot, which did little injury. They then attempted to make a charge on those in the pickets, but were repulsed with great loss.

The men on the right were vulnerable, being in an unfortified position. They were overpowered by a superior force and were ordered to retreat to a more advantageous piece of ground. They got in disorder and could not be formed. The Indians pursued them from all quarters and surrounded, killed, and took most of them.

The enemy again charged on the left with redoubled vigor, but were again forced to retire. Our men lay close behind the picketing, through which they had portholes, and everyone having a rest took sight, that his ammunition might not be spent in vain.

After a long and bloody contest the enemy found they could not, either by stratagem or force, drive us from our fortification. They retired to the woods, leaving their dead on the ground, except a party that kept two cannon in play on our right. A sleigh was seen going towards the right, three or four hundred yards from our lines, and we supposed it was laden with ammunition to supply the cannon. Four or five men rose up and fired at once, and killed the driver and wounded the horse. Some Indians who were hid behind houses continued to annoy us with scattering balls.

At this time bread from the commissary's house was handed round among our troops, and we sat composedly eating and watching the enemy. After we had refreshed ourselves, we discovered a white flag advancing toward us. It was generally supposed to be for a truce, that our enemies might carry off their dead, which were numerous, although they had been bearing away both dead and wounded during the action. But how surprised and crushed we were when we heard that General Winchester and Colonel Lewis had been taken prisoner by the Indians in attempting to rally the right wing, and that General Winchester had surrendered us to Colonel Procter!

Major Madison, then the highest in command, did not agree to this until Colonel Procter had promised that the prisoners should be protected from the Indians, the wounded taken care of, the dead collected and buried and private property respected. Then, with extreme reluctance, our troops accepted this proposition. There was scarcely a person that could refrain from shedding tears. Some pleaded with the officers not to surrender, saying they would rather die on the field.

We had only five killed and twenty-five or thirty wounded inside of the pickets. When the British came in, they asked what we had done with our dead, as they saw but few on the ground. A barn had been set on fire to drive the Indians from behind it and they concluded that we had thrown our dead into these flames to conceal the number.

In this battle, officers and privates had exhibited the utmost firmness and bravery. Whilst the men were at their posts firing on the enemy, the officers were passing along the lines, supplying them with cartridges. Major Graves, in passing around the line, was wounded in the knee. He sat down in a tent, bound up his wound, and cried: "Boys, I am wounded. Never mind me, but fight on!"

The British collected their troops and marched in front of the village. We marched out and grounded our arms, in heat and bitterness of spirit. The British and Indians took possession of them.

All the prisoners, except those that were badly wounded and Dr. Todd, Dr. Bowers, and a few attendants, were marched towards Malden. The British said that they had a great many of their own wounded to take to Malden that evening and it would be out of their power to take ours before morning, but they would leave a sufficient guard, so that they should not be disturbed by the Indians. You will presently see what harm resulted from their failure to keep this promise.

My brother, Allen Darnell, had been badly wounded in the right shoulder on the eighteenth and I was appointed to attend the wounded, so I stayed with them.

Before the British and prisoners marched off, the Indians ransacked the camp and got all the plunder that remained—tents, kettles, buckets, pans, etc. Then, coming amongst the wounded, they insulted them greatly and took some of their belongings.

After they went out, I bolted the door. They came again and broke it open with their tomahawks. I immediately applied to a British officer, and told him the Indians were disturbing the wounded. He turned round and called to another officer to send the guard.

The Indians at that time had plundered the commissary's house (which was near the houses in which the wounded were) of everything they wanted and piled rails against it and set them on fire. With the assistance of two British officers, I put it out.

One of the British officers (Major Rundels) inquired where the ammunition was. I told him if there was any, it was above stairs. We went up, but could find none. There was a large quantity of wheat in the loft. He said it was a pity it was there, for the Indians would burn the house. I apprehended by that, the town was to be burned, and began to lament our wretched condition. After we went downstairs, Rundels asked me how many we had killed and wounded on the eighteenth. I told him, but he very haughtily disputed it. I had the return in my pocket. He read it, but made no reply.

Those of us that remained were hungry and I applied to one of the British in the evening for some flour, as there were a good many barrels in the commissary's house, which I considered to belong to them. He told me to take as much as I wanted.

I asked him if there was a guard left. He said there was no necessity for any, for the Indians were going to their camp, and there were interpreters who would walk from house to house and see that we should not be disturbed. He told me I had better keep in the house, for the Indians would as soon shoot me as not—although he had just told me we should not be disturbed!

As they did not leave the promised guard I lost all confidence in them, and expected we would all be massacred before morning. Since

I was the only person in this house not wounded, with the assistance of some of the wounded I prepared something for about thirty to eat.

The Indians kept searching about town till after dark. One who could talk English came in the house and said he had commanded a company that went after the retreating party, and that most of the party were slain. He said the men gave up their guns, pleaded for quarter, and offered them money if they would not kill them—but his boys, as he called them, tomahawked them without distinction. He said the plan that was fixed on by the Indians and British, before the battle commenced, was that the British were to attack in front to induce us to charge them. Five hundred Indians were placed on the right hand and five hundred on the left, to flank round and take possession of the town. But he said we were too cunning for them—we would not move out of the pickets.

We passed this night under the most serious apprehensions of being massacred by the tomahawk or consumed in the flames. I frequently went out during the night to see if the house had been set on fire.

At length the long-wished-for morn arrived and filled us with hope of being delivered from the cruelty of the savages. We were making every preparation to be ready for the promised sleighs—but, alas! instead of the sleighs, about an hour after sunrise a great number of savages, painted with various colors, came yelling in the most hideous manner! They rushed into the houses where the wounded lay and insolently stripped them of their blankets and all their best clothes, and ordered them out of the houses.

I ran out of the house to inform the interpreters what the Indians were doing. At the door an Indian took my hat and put it on his own head. I then discovered the Indians had been at the other house first, and had treated the wounded the same way.

As I turned to go back into the house an Indian took hold of me and made signs for me to stand by the corner of the house. I made signs to him I wanted to go in and get my hat, for I desired to see what they had done with the wounded. The Indians sent in a boy who brought out a hat and threw it down to me and I could not get in the house. Three Indians came up to me and pulled off my coat.

My feeble powers cannot describe the dismal scenes that followed. I saw my fellow soldiers, naked and wounded, crawling out of the houses to avoid being consumed in the flames. Some that had not been able to turn themselves on their beds for four days, through fear of being burned to death, arose and walked out and about through the yard. Some cried for help, but there were none to help them. "Ah!" some exclaimed in the anguish of their spirit, "what shall we do?" A number, unable to get out, perished in the flames kindled by the savages. The savages rushed on the wounded and, in their barbarous manner, shot and tomahawked and scalped them, and cruelly mangled their naked bodies while they lay agonizing and weltering in their blood.

A number were taken towards Malden, but, being unable to march with speed, were massacred. On the twenty-second, the road was strewn for miles with the mangled bodies left for the birds and beasts to tear to pieces and devour.

The Indians plundered the town of everything valuable and set the best houses on fire. The Indian who claimed me gave me a coat, and when he had got as much plunder as he could carry he ordered me, by signs, to march, which I did with extreme reluctance, in company with three of the wounded and six or seven Indians.

After traveling about a quarter of a mile, two of the wounded lagged behind about twenty yards. The Indians, turning round, shot one and scalped him. They shot at the other and missed him. Running up to them, he begged that they would not shoot him. He said he would keep up, and give them money. But these murderers were not moved with his pitiful cries. They shot him down and, rushing on him in a crowd, scalped him.

My brother Allen perished the same way. He marched with difficulty about two or three hundred yards behind the wounded and was barbarously murdered. My feelings at the sight and recollection of these inhuman butcheries cannot be described.

Every moment I expected that the same kind of cruelty and death would be my portion. The Indians that guarded me and one of the wounded observed our consternation. One that could talk English said, "We will not shoot you." This revived our hopes a little.

After traveling two miles we came to a house where there were two British officers. The Indian made a halt and I asked one of the officers what the Indian was going to do with me. He said he was going to take me to Amherstburg.

A few miles farther we came to the Indian encampment, where there were a great many hallooing and yelling in a hideous manner. I thought this my place of destiny. The Indian took off my pack, broiled a piece of meat and gave me part; I ate this merely in obedience to him. Then we started and arrived at Amherstburg, eighteen miles from Frenchtown. Amherstburg, or Malden, is on the east side of Detroit River, near its junction with Lake Erie, and contains about one hundred houses, mostly frame.

The other prisoners had just arrived. The British were firing their salute. The Indian took me into a house not far from the fort. It was probably their council house—it would have held five hundred. It was inhabited by a large number of squaws, children and dogs. They welcomed me by giving me some bread, meat and hominy to eat.

After this an Indian asked me if I had a squaw.

"No," I told him.

He immediately turned round and talked to the squaws in Indian, while I sat in a pensive mood, observing their motions. By their tittering and grinning, I discovered the squaws were pleased. One, I observed, had a great desire to express her joy by showing her teeth, but the length of time she had lived in this world had put it out of her power. I suspected, from their maneuvers, I would have to undergo a disagreeable adoption (as other prisoners had) and, what was still more unpleasant, be united in marriage to one of these swarthy animals.

The Indian asked me a few questions—where we had come from—how far it was—when we started—and if there were any more coming. My replies to these questions gave him little satisfaction.

After this they spread blankets down and made signs for me to go to bed. I did, and soon fell asleep, as I was much fatigued and had not slept much for four nights past.

Early next morning the Indian collected his family and all his property and started; he gave me a knapsack and gun to carry. I did not know where he was going and I despaired of getting with the other prisoners, unless I could desert from the Indians. I expected I would be taken to an Indian town and undergo a disagreeable adoption or be burned to death with firebrands.

As he led me near Fort Malden, I took as good a view of it as I could while I passed it. It stands about thirty yards from the river bank. I judged it to be seventy or eighty yards square; the wall appeared to be built of timber and clay. The side from the river was not walled, but had double pickets, and was entrenched round about four feet deep; the second row of pickets was in the entrenchment.

As we went on through the edge of town [Amherstburg] I asked an Englishman where the other prisoners were. He said they were in town, in a wood yard; the Indian hurried me along and would not let me talk to the Englishman. The Indian had a little horse, packed with his plunder, which I resolved to take if possible and ride into town that night.

He took me to his place of residence, about three miles from Malden. I was anxious for the approach of night, so that I might make my escape. While I was consoling myself with the anticipation of seeing my fellow sufferers at Malden, night made its approach. Some time after dark the Indian spread blankets down and made signs for me to lie down, and he put my coat, shoes, and socks under his own head. I wanted him to leave my socks on, for my feet would get cold; he made signs to warm them by the fire. Thus I was sadly disappointed.

Next day he examined all his plunder. He had a very good suit of clothes, besides several other coats, socks, shoes, etc. Among these were Wesley's Sermons and a great many papers, which he gave me to read. I found several old letters, but nothing of value. He discovered I wanted to shave, and got his razor, shaving box and a piece of glass, and made signs for me to shave. After this I lay down on some blankets and fell asleep. He came and awoke me and gave me a twist of tobacco, which I received as a token of friendship.

A short time after, he started for Malden, and made signs for me to stay there till he would come back. He returned in the evening with a blanket, tied full of loaves of bread just out of the oven, besides some meat. The Indians always gave me plenty to eat and served me before any of the family, with more politeness than I expected to find amongst them.

The third night at length arrived. The Indian made my bed as usual and took my coat and shoes, but accidentally left my socks on. I lay down with the determination to leave him before morning.

I slept very well for a while. When I awoke, the house was dark. I thought this as good an opportunity of deserting as I could get. With considerable timidity, I made the attempt.

I crawled to the door very slowly and raised the blanket that hung up at the door. Just as I was going out he coughed. I stopped until

I thought he was asleep. Then, without shoes or coat, I started for Amherstburg.

When I got there I examined several yards and gardens to see if there was any fire. After going through many streets, I turned towards the river and accidentally came to the house where the prisoners were. The sentinel, who was standing at the door, let me in without much ceremony.

Providence had smiled on my attempt to extricate myself from the Indians. Thus, through mercy, I escaped from the savages, and was delivered from the danger of being sacrificed in some barbarous manner to gratify their bloodthirsty souls.

I got in between two of my comrades who were lying next to the door. My feet were almost frozen before morning.[1]

# Ambush

## RANSOM CLARK

IN 1832, *fifteen Seminole chiefs signed a treaty agreeing that their people would give up their last remaining lands in Florida and move to a place beyond the Mississippi in three years. When their time was up, many of the Indians refused to go. Hiding their women and children in the swamps, they began a campaign of harassment against the white soldiers who came to evict them.*

*The Seminoles started their war in earnest in December, 1835. They fired the opening shots at Major Francis L. Dade and about one hundred soldiers who were making the long march from Fort Brooke (Tampa) to Fort King (Ocala). In command of the attack were Chief Jumper and Chief Micanope, but their guiding spirit was a valiant part-white Indian patriot named Osceola. Only three Americans survived the attack, and two of them died soon afterward. This is the story of the third, Private Ransom Clark.*

*The war with the Seminoles lasted almost eight years. It is said to have been the most expensive war the United States ever fought against the Indians: it cost twenty million dollars and the lives of fifteen hundred soldiers, many of them killed not by Indians but by disease. In the end most of the Seminoles were transported to Okla-*

*homa. Some bands held out, and two small tribes still remain in Florida—the Muscogee and the Micosukee.*

*Dade City and Dade County were named to commemorate the sacrifice of Major Dade and his men, and there is a state park on the site of the massacre. The crude log breastwork which the soldiers threw up and behind which Ransom Clark crouched and fired as long as he could has been reproduced in concrete there.*

*Clark gave his story to the editor of the* Morning Post *of Boston while on a visit to that city in the summer of 1837. He was a resident of Livingston County, New York.*

Our detachment, consisting of one hundred and seventeen men, under command of Major Dade, started from Fort Brooke, Tampa Bay, on the twenty-third of December, and arrived at the scene of action about eight o'clock on the morning of the twenty-eighth. It was on the edge of a pond, three miles from the spot where we had bivouacked on the night previous. The pond was surrounded by tall grass, brush and small trees.

A moment before we were surprised, Major Dade said to us, "We have now got through all danger. Keep up good heart, and when we get to Fort King I'll give you three days for Christmas."

At this time we were in a path or trail on the border of the pond, and the first notice that we received of the presence of the enemy was the discharge of a rifle by their chief, as a signal to commence the attack.

The pond was on our right and the Indians were scattered round, in a semicircle, reaching to the edge of the pond; they had left an opening for us to enter the trap and a similar opening up ahead for our advance guard, which was permitted to pass through without being fired on, and was unconscious of the ambuscade through which they had marched. At the time of the attack this guard was a quarter of a mile in advance, the main body following in column two abreast.

The chief's rifle was followed by a general discharge from his men. Major Dade, Captain Frazier and Lieutenant Mudge, together with several noncommissioned officers and privates, were brought down by the first volley. Our rear guard had a six-pounder, which, as soon as possible, was hauled up and brought to bear upon the ground occupied by the unseen enemy, secreted among the grass, brush, and trees.

The discharge of the cannon checked them and made them fall back for about half an hour.

About twelve of us advanced and brought in our dead. Among the wounded was Lieutenant Mudge, who was speechless. We set him up against a tree. He was found there two months after, when General Gaines sent a detachment to bury the bodies of our soldiers.

All hands commenced throwing up a small triangular breastwork of logs. Just as we had raised it about two feet, the Indians returned and renewed the engagement. A part of our troops fought within the breastwork, and a part outside. I remained outside till I received a ball in my right arm and another near my right temple, which came out at the top of my head. I next received a shot in my thigh, which brought me down on my side, and I then got into the breastwork.

We gave them forty-nine discharges from the cannon. While loading for the fiftieth—and the last shot we had—our match went out. The Indians chiefly aimed at the men who worked the cannon. In the meantime the main body of our troops kept up a general fire with musketry.

The loss of the enemy must have been very great, because we never fired until we fixed on our men; the cannon was necessarily fired at random, as only two or three Indians appeared together. When the firing commenced, our vanguard wheeled and, in returning to the main body, were entirely cut up.

The battle lasted till about four in the afternoon, and I was about the last man who handled a gun, while lying on my side. At the close I received a shot in my right shoulder which passed into my lungs. The blood gushed out of my mouth in a stream and, dropping my musket, I rolled over on my face.

The Indians entered the breastwork, but found not one man standing to defend it. They secured the arms, ammunition, and the cannon, and finished such of our fallen soldiers as they supposed still to be alive. Their Negroes [1] then came in to strip the dead. By this time I had revived somewhat. A Negro, observing that I was not dead, took up a musket and shot me in the top of the shoulder, and the ball came out at my back. After firing, he said, "Dere, d—n you, take dat." He stripped me of everything but my shirt.

The enemy then disappeared to the left of the pond. I was so weak and frightened, I remained still till about nine o'clock at night. I then began crawling on my knees and left hand. As I was crawling over the dead, I put my hand on one man who felt different from the rest; he was warm and limber. I roused him up and found it was De Courcy, an Englishman and the son of a British officer, resident in Canada. I told him that it was best for us to attempt to travel, as the danger appeared to be over and we might find somebody to help us.

As he was only wounded in the side and arm, he could walk a little. We got along as well as we could that night, and continued on till next noon, when, on a rising ground, we observed an Indian ahead, on horseback, loading his rifle. We agreed that De Courcy should go on one side of the road and I on the other. The Indian took after De Courcy, and I heard the discharge of his rifle. This gave me time to crawl into a hammock, or dense growth of trees and shrubs, and hide away.

The Indian soon returned with his arms and legs covered with blood, having, no doubt, according to custom, cut De Courcy to pieces after bringing him down with his rifle. The Indian came riding through the brush in pursuit of me and approached within ten feet, but gave up the search. I then resumed my route back to Fort Brooke, crawled and limped through the nights and forenoons, and slept in the brush during the middle of the day, with no other nourishment than cold water.

I got to Fort Brooke on the evening of the fifth day, and five months afterwards was discharged as a pensioner, at eight dollars per month. The doctor attributes my not dying of my wounds to the circumstance that I bled a good deal, and did not partake of any solid food during the five first days.

Two other soldiers, by the names of Thomas and Sprague, also came in afterwards. Although badly wounded, they ascended a tree and thus escaped the enemy on the evening of the battle. They joined another expedition, two months after, but before their wounds were healed, and they soon died of them.

# The Attack on the Lighthouse

## JOHN W. B. THOMPSON

**T**RADITIONALLY *a lighthousekeeper's lot is a quiet one, made up of lonely days or weeks or months spent tending a beacon in some remote and inaccessible spot. For John Thompson, however, it proved very different that day in July, 1836, at the Cape Florida lighthouse. Suddenly he found himself surrounded by uninvited guests—over forty of them—nor was it any fault of theirs that he was not roasted alive.*

*Cape Florida lighthouse stood on Key Biscayne, a small island off the site of present-day Miami. The brick tower, completed in 1825, rose sixty-five feet. At the base its walls were five feet thick, but these gradually tapered to two feet at the top. For ten years its beacon lighted the way for vessels past the treacherous Florida Reef. Then, late in 1835, the Seminole Indians began their war of resistance against the Americans. Swooping out of the Everglades, they ravaged plantations and killed and scalped the settlers. Across the water, on Key Biscayne, it was just a question of time till the Indians would come.*

*Keeper Thompson's story is a short one and a strong one. He related it in a letter to the editor of the Charleston* Courier, *soon after he was brought to South Carolina to recuperate from his injuries. The*

272

*light he had tended on Cape Florida stayed dark a long time. Money was appropriated in 1837 to rebuild the burned-out tower, but there were still hostile Indians in the area. It was not until 1846 that the beacon flashed across the Florida waters again. It was discontinued permanently in 1878.*

On the twenty-third of July last, about 4 P.M., as I was going from the kitchen to the dwelling house, I discovered a large body of Indians within twenty yards of me, back of the kitchen. I ran for the lighthouse and called out to the old Negro man that was with me to run, for the Indians were near. At that moment they discharged a volley of rifle balls, which cut my clothes and hat and perforated the door in many places.

We got in, and as I was turning the key the savages had hold of the door. I stationed the Negro at the door, with orders to let me know if they attempted to break in. Then I took my three muskets, which were loaded with ball and buckshot, and went to the second window. Seeing a large body of them opposite the dwelling house, I discharged my muskets in succession among them, which put them in some confusion.

For the second time they began their horrid yells, and in a minute no sash or glass was left at the window, for they vented their rage at that spot. I fired at them from some of the other windows and from the top of the lighthouse; in fact, I fired whenever I could get an Indian for a mark. I kept them from the lighthouse until dark.

They then poured in a heavy fire at all the windows and lantern. That was the time they set fire to the door and window even with the ground. The window was boarded up with plank and filled up with stone inside, but the flames spread fast, being fed with yellow pine wood. Their balls had perforated the tin tanks of oil, consisting of two hundred and twenty-five gallons; my bedding, clothing, and in fact, everything I had was soaked in oil. I stopped at the door until driven away by the flames.

I took a keg of gunpowder, my balls, and one musket to the top of the house, then went below and began to cut away the stairs about halfway up from the bottom. I had difficulty in getting the old Negro up the space I had already cut; but the flames now drove me from my labor, and I retreated to the top of the house. I covered over the scuttle or opening that leads to the lantern, which kept the fire from me for some time.

At last the awful moment arrived: the crackling flames burnt around me. The savages at the same time began their hellish yells. My poor old Negro looked to me with tears in his eyes, but could not speak. We went out of the lantern and lay down on the edge of the platform, two feet wide.

The lantern now was full of flame and the lamps and glasses were bursting and flying in all directions. My clothes were on fire, but to move from the place where I was would be instant death from their rifles. My flesh was roasting.

To put an end to my horrible suffering, I got up and threw the keg of gunpowder down the scuttle. It exploded instantly and shook the tower from the top to the bottom.

It did not have the desired effect of blowing me into eternity, but it threw down the stairs and all the wooden work near the top of the house. It damped the fire for a moment, but it soon blazed as fiercely as ever. The Negro man said he was wounded, which was the last word he spoke.

By this time I had received some wounds myself. Finding no chance for my life, for I was roasting alive, I took the determination to jump off. I got up, went outside the iron railing, recommending my soul to God, and was on the point of going head foremost on the rocks below when something dictated to me to return and lie down again. I did so, and in two minutes the fire fell to the bottom of the house. It is a remarkable circumstance that not one ball struck me when I stood up outside the railing, although they were flying all around me like hailstones. I found the old Negro man dead, being shot in several places and literally roasted.

A few minutes after the fire fell, a stiff breeze sprang up from the southward, which was a great blessing to me. I had to lie where I was, for I could not walk, having received six rifle balls, three in each foot.

The Indians, thinking me dead, left the lighthouse and set fire to the dwelling house, kitchen and other outhouses, and began to carry their plunder to the beach. They took all the empty barrels, the drawers of the bureaus, and in fact everything that would act as a vessel to hold anything. My provisions were in the lighthouse, except a barrel of flour, which they took off.

The next morning they hauled out of the lighthouse, by means of a pole, the tin that composed the oil tanks, no doubt to make grates to manufacture the coonty root [1] into what we call arrowroot. After loading my little sloop, about ten or twelve went into her; the rest took to the beach to meet at the other end of the island. This happened, as I judge, about 10 A.M. My eyes being much affected, prevented me from knowing their actual force, but I judge there were from forty to fifty, perhaps more.

I was now almost as bad off as before—a burning fever on me, my feet shot to pieces, no clothes to cover me, nothing to eat or drink, a hot sun overhead, a dead man by my side, no friend near or any to expect, and placed between seventy and eighty feet from the earth, and no chance of getting down. My situation was truly horrible.

About twelve o'clock, I thought I could perceive a vessel not far off. I took a piece of the old Negro's trousers that had escaped the flames by being wet with blood, and made a signal.

Some time in the afternoon I saw two boats with my sloop in tow coming to the landing. I had no doubt but they were Indians who had seen my signal and returned to finish their murderous design.

But it proved to be boats of the United States schooner *Motto,* Captain Armstrong, with a detachment of seamen and marines under the command of Lieutenant Lloyd, of the sloop-of-war *Concord.* They had retaken my sloop after the Indians had stripped her of her sails and rigging and everything of consequence belonging to her. They informed me they heard my explosion twelve miles off and ran down to my assistance, but did not expect to find me alive. Those gentlemen did all in their power to relieve me, but, night coming on, they returned on board the *Motto,* after assuring me of their assistance in the morning.

Next morning, Monday, July 25, three boats landed, among them Captain Cole, of the schooner *Pee Dee,* from New York. They had made a kite during the night to get a line to me, but without effect. They then fired twine from their muskets, made fast to a ramrod, which I received, and hauled up a tail block [2] and made it fast round an iron stanchion. I passed the twine through the block, and they below, by that means, passed a two-inch rope through and hoisted up two men, who soon landed me on terra firma. I must state here that the Indians had made a ladder by lashing pieces of wood across the lightning rod, near forty feet from the ground, as if to have my scalp at any cost. This happened on the twenty-fourth.

After I got on board the *Motto* every man, from the captain to the cook, tried to alleviate my sufferings. On the twenty-seventh I was received in the military hospital, through the politeness of Lieutenant Alvord, of the fourth regiment of United States Infantry. He has done everything to make my situation as comfortable as possible.

I must not omit here to return my thanks to the citizens of Key West, generally, for their sympathy and kind offers of anything I would wish that it was in their power to bestow. Before I left Key West two balls were extracted, and one remains in my right leg; but, since I am under the care of Dr. Ramsey, who has paid every attention to me, he will know best whether to extract it or not.

These lines are written to let my friends know that I am still in the land of the living and am now in Charleston, S.C., where every attention is paid me. Although a cripple, I can eat my allowance and walk about without the use of a cane.

Respectfully yours,

JOHN W. B. THOMPSON

# Three Years
# Among the Comanches

## NELSON LEE

$\mathbf{F}$OR *fifty-six days Nelson Lee wandered through an unknown wilderness somewhere in western Mexico or the southwestern United States. He inched his way up the steep fronts of great cliffs where snakes hissed in his face when he lifted himself to a resting place. He plunged through dark ravines where the underbrush was almost impenetrable, and wolves and bears were never far away. He starved, he thirsted. He had abandoned his exhausted horse, he was hopelessly lost, but he could not stop going for long. He had tomahawked a Comanche chief, and he was sure the vengeful braves were on his trail. When finally a Mexican trader found him, he was more dead than alive.*

*In a few months, Lee was back in his native New York. He had a story to tell such as few had told before—a story of a terrible massacre, of torture, of a miracle that saved his life, of three years as a slave and medicine man among the Comanches, and of a daring escape. People believed this bearded, prematurely aged man, who bore the scars of his remarkable adventures. Urged on by a desire to repair his ruined fortunes and bring to the attention of his countrymen the des-*

*perate plight of other white captives, many of them women, he told his story to a writer. It was rushed into print early in 1859, buttressed with testimonials of prominent citizens of upper New York, among them Eli Perry, mayor of Albany.*

*Nelson Lee's life is the tale of a country boy turned adventurer. He was born in 1807 at Brownsville, near Watertown, New York, the son of a farmer. He tells us that as a youngster he was "remarkable for nothing save a hardy constitution and an athletic frame and an intense longing to move out into the world."*

*Lee satisfied that longing more fully than most men do. Reaching manhood, he became a boatman on the St. Lawrence River. Like his contemporary, Abraham Lincoln, he enlisted in the Black Hawk War, but too late to see action. Roaming south to New Orleans and up to Washington, D. C., he joined the naval service as a master's mate. For seven years he sailed on sloops of war, chasing pirates and protecting American fishermen. Then he left one American navy to join another. Reports of troublous times lured him to Texas, where he signed up in the navy of the new Lone Star Republic and fought against the Mexicans off Yucatan. After a short tour of duty he settled in southern Texas.*

*In those days Indians, Mexican guerrillas, and bandits were constantly raiding the border settlements. The Texas Rangers, organized in 1835 to help Texas win her freedom, were kept busy protecting the frontier. In 1840, Lee enlisted in the Rangers. With Colt, rifle, and bowie knife he gave an excellent account of himself in many a bloody foray on both sides of the Rio Grande. He was in Mexico with the Rangers and General Winfield Scott in 1847 when the destiny of Texas was decided once and for all.*

*After the Mexican War, as he had in intervals of peace before it, Lee captured wild horses, broke them to saddle and harness, and traded in livestock. Profits were good, and he was eager to see them better. It is at this moment in his restless history that we meet Nelson Lee, Texas Ranger, horse wrangler and trader, in old Corpus Christi.*

In the year 1855 I became acquainted with a man named William Aikens, who had lately arrived from California through the Indian country. An energetic, enterprising person, Aikens had conceived the notion of purchasing a drove of mules and horses for the California market. He was confident they could be driven through in safety and it would prove a profitable speculation. Not having enough money of his own, he wanted to form a joint company and, as I had much experience in stock buying, he urged me to unite with him and others in the undertaking. I agreed and the company was soon formed, with a capital of seven thousand dollars.

We made our headquarters at first at San Patricio, thirty miles above Corpus Christi. Aikens and myself visited New Orleans, where we purchased arms, ammunition, blankets, saddles, tents—in short, an outfit sufficient to furnish twenty-seven men.

While picking up these supplies, I discovered a large silver watch of such unusual and extraordinary dimensions as to attract attention. My curiosity excited, I requested of the shopkeeper the privilege of examining it.

I found it to be an alarm watch—one that would make a far louder and longer racket than any I had ever before seen. It could be regulated so as to go off at any required moment, and so powerful was its machinery, it would move across a table whilst ringing the alarm. It occurred to me that such an article would be of signal service on our trip, and I purchased it at an expense of forty-five dollars. I mention these details for the reason that this watch has been closely connected with my destiny, and to it I am indebted for life and liberty this day.

Returned to San Patricio, we hired nineteen assistants. With this company, well-mounted, and fourteen pack mules, we left San Patricio and set out directly for the city of Matamoros. Our plan was to start northward from this point, collecting our drove as we advanced. This was in March, when vegetation is rank near the mouth of the Rio Grande, and it was our intention to proceed leisurely, keeping within the latitude of its healthy growth; in other words, "to follow the grass."

From the adjacent ranches, as we moved along, we collected such animals as we deemed advisable to purchase. On our arrival at San Fernando, a frontier town forty miles west of Fort Duncan, our means were exhausted and our drove had increased to the number of 395.

From San Fernando we moved forward, leaving civilization behind us at the settlement of San Augusta. We pushed on diligently in the direction of Paso del Norte, aiming to penetrate the gorges of the mountains until we should strike the California trail. We traveled slowly, at the average rate of fifteen miles a day, it depending entirely upon the distance between watering and feeding places.

After leaving the settlements, it was our custom to sound the bugle at half-past three in the morning. All hands then arose. Some went to round up the drove, some packed the mules, and others prepared breakfast, which consisted of the broiled flesh of deer, bear, or buffalo, with coffee and hard biscuit.

Breakfast over, we moved forward briskly at the word of command, a squad of five or six riding a considerable distance in advance to look out for Indians and prevent a stampede.

A stampede was especially dreaded. Over the prairies of the Southwest thousands of mustangs, or wild horses, are roaming constantly. If they happen to come upon and mingle with a drove of their own kind, the latter, however gentle, seem instantly to change to an untamed state and run off with their wild companions. Such, in the language of the prairie, is a stampede.

Behind the advance party some half a dozen mares were led, having bells suspended from their necks. Behind these came the drove, with horsemen riding in single file on each side. The remainder of the party, with the pack mules, brought up the rear. We generally halted about noon, resting until the next morning. While resting, especially during the night, the men acted alternately as sentinels, riding constantly round the camp.

In this manner, day after day, we moved on. We crossed wide valleys and wound through ravines and mountain passes. Sometimes we followed the course of streams, at others we toiled directly over precipitous heights. At last we buried ourselves far within the depths of that wild and mountainous district 350 miles northwest of Eagle Pass.

When we came to a river, our manner of proceeding was as follows: The animals carrying the bells were taken over, and the men who led them would commence shaking the bells violently. The drove grazing on the other shore would immediately erect their ears, look intently in the direction of the sound, move to the water's edge, and, if the bank was high, run up and down the stream in an agitated mood. Finally they would plunge in, however deep or rapid the water might be, and swim to the other side.

On the last day of March we entered an enchanting valley. This spot afforded such an abundance of grass, wood and water, we determined to remain six weeks, or rather until the foaling season was passed.

The second of April was remarkably fine. From early morning I had been in the saddle, riding up and down the valley, ascertaining its capabilities of furnishing forage, and whether there were wild horses in the neighborhood. In the evening we gathered around the camp fire, each broiling his buffalo steak or frying brook trout taken from the adjacent stream, while the boys amused each other with narrations of many a frolicsome adventure. The whole party was in excellent spirits, lying down to rest on their buffalo skins when the meal was over, laughing and joking and singing snatches of familiar songs.

It was my watch that night until twelve o'clock. I rode about the camp, chatting with the other sentinels, and at midnight came in with them when the relief sentinels appeared. Taking off my coat, I laid it down on the buffalo robe to serve as a pillow, set my watch so the alarm would strike at half-past three, the usual hour of rising, and placed it under the coat. Then I lay down outside the tent, near the fire. All my companions had sunk into profound slumber. About one o'clock I, too, dropped asleep.

Was it a dream? Was it a real shriek that rang out? The first moment of awakened consciousness assured me it was indeed reality. Springing to my feet, I discovered the camp was full of painted, yelling savages. Seizing the rifle which lay by my side, I drew it to my shoulder, knowing well there was no hope of safety but in desperate resistance.

At almost the instant I arose, a lasso was thrown over my head, jerking me violently to the ground. Half a dozen Indians sprang upon me, some holding down my arms, others my legs, another astride my body with his hand upon my throat. They tied my feet together, and bound my hands behind my back with stout thongs of buffalo hide, drawing them so close as to cause me severest pain.

All this occurred within the space of five minutes. Of course, I was greatly confused—not so much, however, as to be unable to comprehend the dreadful situation I was in. My knowledge of Indian character and customs taught me that three or four of us might be spared to figure in the accursed rites of their triumphant war dance. Whether I was to be reserved for such a purpose or slaughtered on the spot was a matter of terrible conjecture.

I soon became aware that the only members of the party who

escaped the massacre were Thomas Martin, John Stewart, Aikens, and myself. The first two had been secured much in the same manner I was, but Aikens, who was sleeping in a tent, had succeeded in escaping a short distance, and had engaged in a hot scuffle, during which he fired upon his assailants before he was overpowered.

The first step taken by the savages, after the confusion had subsided, was to strip us of every particle of apparel, and clothe us in their own fashion of dress. It consisted simply of buckskin leggings, with a hunting shirt of the same material.

While they were stripping and dressing me, one of them picked up my coat and discovered the watch. He seized it with avidity and turned it over and over, looking immensely pleased with the singular and pretty bauble.

While he regarded it, the minute hand ticked round to half-past three and the alarm went off.

The utter astonishment of the Indian was beyond description. He held the watch out at extreme arm's length, his head thrown back and staring wildly, too surprised, as it roared and rattled for two minutes, to decide whether it was safest to let it fall or retain it in his grasp.

By the time it ceased, a dozen had gathered round him, looking into each other's faces in silent wonder. The one who held it presently pointed to me, then at the watch, then at the spot where he had found it, speaking at the same time fast and earnestly. Approaching and holding it out to me, they made signs that I should cause it to repeat the alarm.

The idea at once flashed upon my mind that I might make it serve a useful purpose. They untied my hands and I accepted the watch with an air of reverence and adoration. I wound it up solemnly, and so regulated it that in a few minutes off it went again. Again the dusky crowd was struck with wonder and astonishment.

This was repeated frequently, the savages meantime holding the watch to their ears to hear it tick as they had seen me do. Then the chief wrapped it carefully and tenderly in his deerskin pouch and placed it in his bosom. I comprehended from their gestures, such as pointing upwards, then at the watch, then at myself, that they regarded it as something supernatural which connected me with the Great Spirit.

Their next step was to collect the plunder. Not only did they gather up all our buffalo skins, blankets, rifles and revolvers, culinary utensils, and the like, but the dead were stripped to the last shred, and everything was tied on the backs of their mules. Nothing was left behind.

By this time the morning light began to break on the eastern mountains, and preparations were made to depart. Before starting, the Indians unbound our feet and conducted us through the camp, pointing out the stark corpses of our butchered comrades, who had lain down to sleep with such light and happy hearts.

The scene was awful and heart-rending. They had cut and hacked the poor, cold bodies in the most brutal manner; some had their arms and hands chopped off, others were disemboweled, and still others had their tongues drawn out and sharp sticks thrust through them. All the dead were scalped, and the scalps, still fresh, were dangling from the savages' belts.

The Indians then led us out some three or four hundred yards from the camp and pointed out the dead bodies of the sentinels. The bodies were lying close together at the south side of a thicket. The night had been chilly and, instead of riding round the camp at proper distances from each other, they had undoubtedly huddled together under the thicket, to protect themselves from the cold wind that swept down the valley. In this position the Indians had crept up unperceived and dispatched them so suddenly there was no opportunity to make an outcry. Beyond question we had been watched from the mountains ever since our arrival in the valley.

During all the time they were exhibiting the result of their savage work, the Indians resorted to every hideous device to inspire us with terror. They would rush toward us with uplifted tomahawks, stained with blood, as if determined to strike, or grasp us by the hair, flourishing their knives around our heads as though intending to take our scalps. So far as I could understand their infernal shouts and pantomime, they sought to tell us that the fate which had overtaken our unfortunate companions not only awaited us, but likewise the whole race of the hated white man.

Now dressed deerskins were thrown over our heads, drawn down over the face, and tied with a string, closely about the neck. We were thus completely blindfolded, and would soon have suffocated, had not a small hole been cut through the skin in front of the mouth. We were then each mounted on a mule over an Indian saddle without stirrups, our hands tied behind us at the wrists, our feet brought as near together as possible under the body of the animal and firmly lashed. It was possible for us to roll off sidewise, but it was impossible to extricate ourselves from the beasts.

Our position, bound as we were, was not comfortable. We were utterly powerless to guide the animals. Like the wind, my mount wandered where he wished, sometimes pushing and crowding in among the pack mules, sometimes suddenly stopping to take a bite of grass, throwing me forward on the pommel of the saddle with the impression I was going over his head—the next moment starting suddenly on a sharp trot, throwing me as far backward.

But these were only the light afflictions of the prairie. When our journey came to lead us through strips of timberland the measure of our tribulation was full, indeed. The first time the thoughtless brute ran under a limb, striking me in the face and knocking me off, or rather turning me round so that my head reversed positions with my feet, the sensation was horrible. My frequent repetitions of this performance rendered me an adept in this sort of somersault. There was one consolation: the moment I went over, the mule would invariably stop and an Indian as invariably run and right me up again.

My somersaults afforded the Indians most excellent sport, and every performance was treated with "tremendous applause." Indeed, I could tell sometimes from the laughter that would begin to arise that danger was near and, lying close on the mule's neck, escape it.

At dark the Indians stopped for the night. When permitted to dismount, and the blindfold had been taken from my eyes, I discovered we were in a narrow ravine. The cords were here unloosed from my wrists; nevertheless, I was pinioned back from the shoulders so that I could just raise my hands to my mouth. The drove properly herded, one or two horses were shot, and the meat brought in for supper.

A fire was kindled, and the warriors gathered round it, the prisoners in the center. Martin was silent and dejected, apparently absorbed in his own reflections and little disposed to converse. Stewart was nervous and frightened, bewailing his hard fate in tears. But Aikens maintained a cheerful spirit, advising us to keep up our courage and look the matter coolly in the face until the last.

While we conversed, the Indians boiled and ate their meat. Having satisfied themselves, they now seemed to take into consideration the appetites of their captives. They resolved to make their disgusting horseflesh serve the double purpose of supplying us food for the body and themselves food for mirth.

In our Indian dresses, which consisted of leggings rising only to the knee, and a short hunting coat, the portion of the leg above the legging was necessarily bare. As we sat upon the ground together, our feet tied, it was likewise necessarily exposed. When the meat designed for us had boiled until the fat began to sputter, they would throw it with such marvelous dexterity from the end of their roasting sticks that it would fall on our naked limbs hissing hot.

If the laziest reader of this book will try a similar experiment on himself, he will find it admirably calculated to arouse his activity. I venture to affirm he will squirm more energetically and turn over quicker than he ever did before in his life. It had the same effect on us, and the muscular demonstrations we made "brought down the house." It resulted in my declining supper altogether, having a prejudice against the waiters in attendance, and raised broad blisters on my person, the scars of which I will carry to the grave.

At the conclusion of these exercises, the warriors threw themselves on the ground to sleep. They lay near each other, forming a large circle. Our sleeping apartment was in this space, and we were "put to bed" in the following original fashion: First, we were made to lie down upon our backs, with arms and feet extended. Four stakes were then driven firmly through the sward, to which our hands and feet were fastened as wide apart as possible. Then two other stakes were driven close on either side of the neck, and a strong strip of buffalo hide tied from one to the other, so that it passed under the chin, across the throat. Thus we lay upon our backs, unable to move head, hand, or foot.

During the entire trip I was subjected to the same annoyances of being run under the trees, burned with hot horseflesh, and staked down at night. I was so overwrought I did not sleep a wink.

Early in the afternoon of the fourth day the warriors raised the war whoop, and afar off was heard another war whoop in reply. As we advanced, the answering voices grew more and more distinct, until finally the approaching parties met. I was taken from the mule and, when allowed the liberty of my eyes, found myself and companions standing in the midst of a great number of tents, and surrounded by five or six hundred men, all pushing forward to catch a glimpse of us.

Some little time elapsed, when the crowd gave way, forming a passage. Through it advanced the leader of the war party, accompanied by an aged chief and a squaw. Having reached us, the watch was produced and handed to me, with signs indicating they wished me to exhibit its marvelous qualities.

I now put forth all my powers as an actor, and feigned emotions far different from the real ones struggling in my bosom. My object was to take advantage of their superstition to establish among them the notion that it was a thing of life—a spiritual medium having powers of speech—through which their chiefs, prophets, and great warriors who had gone to the land of spirits could converse in a language perfectly intelligible to me, but utterly incomprehensible to them; to indoctrinate them into the solemn belief that my old "turnip" was the brother of the sun, and could foretell through me the precise moment he would reach any given point in the heavens. Finally, and most especially, I wanted to persuade them that any mishap that should befall either the watch or myself would disarrange the machinery of nature and send us "all to smash."

Accordingly, I received the watch in an attitude of great humility, and gazed upon it with an air of reverence. Winding it up, I held it to my ear and listened to the tick, tick, tick with a solemnity intended to convey the same idea as if I had said to them in their own language: "Gentlemen Indians, I am now receiving important telegraphic dispatches from the other side of Jordan!"

Presently, it sounded the alarm. It would have been a curious and interesting picture for an artist, could he have watched the expressions of astonishment, awe and wonder that overspread their features during the whir and whirl and whiz of the cunning mechanism. Ejaculating their impressive "ugh, ugh," they looked seriously and inquiringly into each other's faces as much as to say, "Well, I never; did you ever!"

Finally, the watch was taken by the old chief and formally presented to the squaw, his favorite wife. I was conducted to the chief's tent and regaled with a late dinner, horseflesh being the only dish mentioned on the bill of fare.

Seated at the entrance of the wigwam, I had a brief opportunity of taking a view of the Indian village. It stood in a valley, and consisted of four hundred tents, covering a space of six or seven acres. In the center was a capacious square, perhaps one acre, and in the center of the square stood a lodge, the largest in the town, the business tent of the chief. Around the square the wigwams were arranged with great particularity. Leading into it on the four sides were regularly laid-out streets, the tents standing in line on both sides. Those of the principal men were the largest, and fronted the square; those of their inferiors, according to their rank, diminishing in size and extending backwards.

I had remained in the chief's tent but a short time when I was conducted to the square. There I found Aikens, Martin, and Stewart. It was soon revealed we were to "cut a conspicuous figure" in a war dance.

The Indians came forth bedizened in their traps and feathers, their tomahawks and scalping knives in their uplifted hands, great daubs of red paint above and below their eyes. They circled round and round us on a spasmodic trot, uttering their hoarse guttural songs, which seemed to flow up through their savage throats over sharp rifts of phlegm. As they proceeded, their pace accelerated, and their songs grew loud and louder, rising gradually from a monotonous grunt into a hideous howl. Very often, one of them, deserting his place, would dart towards us with his drawn hatchet, threatening to brain us, while another would seize us by the hair and go through the pantomime of scalping.

For two hours they continued to sing and dance, and whoop and yell, flourishing their tomahawks and knives over us, until at last they were compelled to stop from exhaustion. The captives were then separated, myself being led back to the chief's tent, where I was tied down to stakes again. Four days had now passed without repose, and I sank into a troubled sleep.

In the morning I was released from the uncomfortable position I had occupied during the night. I soon comprehended the number and character of the household in which necessity had forced me to take up lodging. It consisted of the chief, a tall, stout, elderly Indian named Osolo, which signifies "Big Wolf," and his four wives. None of these exceeded twenty-three or twenty-four years. The youngest, Moko, was by far the most comely and graceful, and the favorite. Each wife had her separate small tent adjoining the husband's. Mine host of the wigwam had tied a deerskin cord to the corner of each of his wives' buffalo mattresses, the other end extending into his own tent, thus rendering only a slight twitch necessary to indicate their presence was required. It was their duty to attend him, come at his call and go at his bidding. There were four children, who lived in their mothers' lodges.

The wives of Big Wolf served him a breakfast of roast meat and boiled corn. An hour or two later a party of fifty Indians collected and held a council, Big Wolf presiding. It was evident that I was being spoken of in connection with the watch. Moko was called and presented it to me, signifying I should make it go. I resolved to risk the result of a refusal. Pointing to the heavens, I uttered a rigmarole of words and tried to impress them that operating the alarm, just at that time, would be attended with the wreck of the world. Instead of manifesting any ill humor, they quietly submitted to the disappointment, and continued their consultation.

Immediately after the council had adjourned, I discovered the warriors assembling outside the village at a point distant a quarter of a mile. At length, I was taken by a strong guard and escorted into their midst. I found my fellow captives had preceded me. There were Aikens, Martin, and Stewart, stripped entirely naked, and bound as follows: High posts had been driven in the ground about three feet apart. Standing between them, their arms had been drawn up as far as they could reach, the right hand tied to the stake on the right side and the left hand to the stake opposite. Their feet, likewise, were tied to the posts near the ground.

Martin and Stewart were strung up side by side. Directly in front of them, and within ten feet, was Aikens, in the same situation. A short time sufficed to divest me of my scanty Indian apparel and place me by the side of the latter. Thus we stood, or rather hung, Aikens and myself facing Stewart and Martin.

Big Wolf and a number of his old men stationed themselves near us. Then a long line of warriors, of whom there were probably two hundred, moved forward slowly, silently, and in single file, with the leader of the war party at their head. Their pace was half walk, half shuffle, a spasmodic, nervous motion, like the artificial motion of figures in a puppet show. Each carried in one hand his knife or tomahawk, in the other a flint stone, three inches or more in length and fashioned into the shape of a sharp pointed arrow.

The head of the procession, as it circled a long way round, first approached Stewart and Martin. As it passed them, two of the youngest warriors broke from the line, seized them by the hair, and scalped them, then resumed their places and moved on. This operation consists of cutting off only a portion of the skin which covers the skull, of the dimensions of a silver dollar, and does not necessarily destroy life. Blood flowed from them in profusion, running down over the face and trickling from their long beards.

The warriors passed Aikens and myself without harming us, marching round again in the same order as before. Up to this time there had been entire silence, except a yell from the two young men when in the act of scalping, but now the whole party halted a half-minute and, slapping their hands upon their mouths, united in an energetic war whoop. Then in silence the circuitous march was continued.

When they reached Stewart and Martin the second time, the sharp flint arrowheads were brought into use. Each man, as he passed, with a wild screech, would brandish his tomahawk in their faces an instant, and then draw the sharp point of the stone across their bodies. By the time the line had passed, our poor suffering companions presented an awful spectacle.

Still they left Aikens and myself unharmed; nevertheless, we regarded it as certain that very soon we should be subjected to similar tortures. We would have been devoutly thankful at that terrible hour could we have been permitted to choose our own mode of being put to death.

How many times they circled round, halting to sound the war whoop, and going through the same demoniac exercise, I cannot tell. They persisted in the hellish work until every inch of the bodies of the unhappy men was hacked and covered with clotted blood.

In the progress of their torture there occurred an intermission of some quarter of an hour. During this period, some threw themselves on the ground and lighted their pipes, others collected in little groups. All, however, laughed and shouted, pointing their fingers at the prisoners in derision, as if taunting them as cowards. The prisoners bore themselves differently. Stewart uttered not a word, but his sobs and groans were such as only the most intense pain and agony can wring from the human heart. The pitiful cries and prayers of Martin were unceasing. Constantly he was exclaiming: "Oh! God have mercy on me!" "Oh, Father in heaven, pity me!" "Oh! Lord Jesus, come and put me out of pain!"

I hung down my head and closed my eyes to shut out the heart-sickening scene before me. But this poor comfort was not vouchsafed me. They would grasp myself as well as Aikens by the hair, drawing our heads back violently, compelling us, however unwillingly, to stare directly at the agonized and writhing sufferers.

At the end of two hours the warriors halted and formed a half-circle. Two of them moved out from the center, striking into the war dance, raising the war song, advancing, receding, now moving to the right, now to the left, occupying ten minutes in proceeding as many paces. Finally, they reached the victims, danced before them for some time, then drew their hatchets suddenly and sent the bright blades crashing through their skulls. The bodies were taken down and rudely thrown aside upon the ground.

Aikens and myself now anticipated we would be compelled to suffer the same fate. To our astonishment, however, we were unbound, taken by separate guards, dressed in our hunting shirts and leggings, and started towards the camp.

As we moved off, I turned my head to take a last lingering look at my dead companions. The Indian dogs had already gathered round the corpses and were lapping the blood from their innumerable wounds.

Returned to the same tent and again tied hand and foot, I had abundant food for reflection. Fully believing the novelty of the watch would presently pass away and that I must also suffer at the stake, I pondered how I might reach death, yet avoid torture.

The more I mused on the atrocities I had seen—the more the bleeding, ghastly forms of Stewart and Martin rose before me, as they did constantly—the more bitter became my feelings towards their murderers. My bosom scorched and burned with the desire of vengeance. I luxuriated in daydreams—at one time fancying myself with an invading army come to sweep the savages from the face of the earth—at another, with my old companions in arms, the Texas Rangers, dashing upon them, slaughtering and slaying until they whined for mercy, like their own vile curs.

Indulging such moods as these, I was one day unbound and ordered to perform some simple labor. Previously, however, I had determined to kill at least one or more of them the first opportunity that offered. I hoped that, prompted by sudden wrath, they would slay me at once and save me from a lingering death at the stake.

When, therefore, I stood erect with free limbs, I seized the first thing within my reach, a wooden pothook, and hurled it at an Indian with all my strength. It missed its aim. Instantly I was surrounded and borne down. But, instead of producing the effect intended, the unexpected assault convulsed them with laughter.

The next day, and the next, and every few days thereafter, I was unloosed and directed to skin a deer or bring wood or water, they taking special care to keep all dangerous weapons out of my reach. But I refused, absolutely and defiantly. Also, when the watch was brought out, I would not touch it. The life I was leading had become so irksome that I became utterly reckless, longing only to shake off the heavy nightmare of existence.

I had not seen Aikens since the day we separated at "the place of torment." It was consequently with much surprise that I saw him one day led into my tent, surrounded by a formidable guard. He was permitted to sit down beside me for an hour and converse.

I learned he had been kept a close prisoner and had experienced severer treatment than I. He was now about to be carried to some distant tribe, and this interview was allowed that we might bid each other farewell. There remained not a doubt in his mind but that he was doomed to die by torture. But, as for me, he was confident that through the watch I might eventually be enabled to escape. He had witnessed its effect on the chiefs and warriors on our first arrival. He said they believed it was a living spirit in a silver body.

Aikens advised me to submit in all things, and to deceive them into the belief that I preferred to dwell with them rather than with my own people. By pursuing this course, he said, the time would come when their vigilance would relax and an opportunity of escaping from them would occur.

We conversed of many things, losing not a moment of the precious hour. At its close, he was ordered to leave. I have never seen or heard of him since.

Soon after this, early one morning, I discovered the squaws busily engaged taking down the tents. One after another the dingy white cones came down. Every canvas, buffalo mattress, and blanket was rolled up, the cooking kettles and the tent poles collected, and all packed on the backs of a crowd of mules. While the women toiled and strained and lifted, the men moped around, smoking their pipes, or lolled upon the ground.

Everything in readiness, I was once more blindfolded, mounted, and tied. Then the entire town, not only its men, women, and children, but its furniture, its tents, its public and private buildings, all moved off on the backs of mules and horses.

After three days we reached the end of the journey. Here I found myself in a small village, of not more than twenty or thirty tents, inhabited by a portion of Big Wolf's tribe, on the bank of a considerable river in a large valley. On our arrival, the squaws unpacked the mules, and immediately erected the tents. In a few days, though a hundred miles distant, we were to all appearances occupying the same village, having the same square and the same streets.

In time I came to understand that this was the usual summer residence of the tribe, where their corn and beans and tobacco were cultivated. It was their main camping ground and the other valley was only resorted to for hunting, during those moons when the hair on the buffalo is thick and long.

The confidence I had in the judgment of Aikens inspired me with hope, and I resolved to follow his advice to the letter. My fame, evidently, had spread abroad through the new community. It was not long before Moko came with a group of the new faces and presented me the watch.

My obstinacy was now abandoned, and I fell again, very deep, into the mysterious mood. Winding the watch up and setting the alarm a minute or two ahead, I bowed my face before it—clasped it affectionately to my bosom—held it out at arm's length before me in my two hands, regarding it with that intensity of expression with which a tragedian on the stage regards a love letter just received—turning up my eyes adoringly towards the heavens—and let it whiz!

The effect was solemn and satisfactory. I felt that I had made "a hit"—that the sharp eyes which could detect a trail had failed to penetrate the thin veil which covered the deception. Up to this time, and never afterwards, did they attempt to open it or manage it themselves; nor did any other than Moko ever have it in charge.

When untied, I obeyed every order given me. I ran to the waterside and filled Big Wolf's buffalo horn when he was thirsty, pounded his corn, spread his mattress, lighted his pipe, and made myself generally useful. As Aikens had predicted, their vigilance did relax to such a degree that I was permitted to wander through the village, but not beyond it—to have a knife—to sleep without being bound—and so far gained their confidence that they christened me *Chemakacho*— "the good white man."

This was not done, however, until I had entered into a solemn covenant with the chief. A stick of wood about ten inches long and two inches square was produced. On its sides were carved numerous figures representing skeletons, scalps, tomahawks and other like devices.

Receiving the stick from Big Wolf, I opened a vein on the back of my hand and carefully painted the carved characters with blood. This agreement, as it was understood by the party of one part, was that I would remain in the quiet and peaceable possession of said Big Wolf, his heirs and assigns, without any attempt, effort, or intention of running away, while he, the aforesaid Big Wolf, on his part, promised and agreed, in case I did, to make a skeleton of me in the shortest possible space of time, according to the Indian statutes in such case made and provided.

As week after week passed wearily away, I had opportunities of observing their customs and peculiarities, and to become thoroughly conversant with life in a Comanche camp.

The sole business of the male portion of the tribe was war and hunting. While in camp the Indian is idle, sleeping the greater part of the day and all night. He is slovenly in his dress, except when he meets in council or goes on the warpath, when he decorates himself with the scalps he has taken, which at other times hang in his tent. His prowess as a warrior is estimated in proportion to the number he possesses.

To supply the necessaries of life, more or less of the warriors must daily go out upon the hunt. In this, their only labor, they rarely range more than four or five miles from the town. Their weapons, on these excursions, are the bow and arrow and the lance, which they use with great skill, especially on horseback. In horsemanship I doubt whether there is a race on earth that equals the Comanches. They will lie along the the sides of their horses, while under full speed, directing their course at the same time and discharging arrows from under their horses' necks with deadly effect, in a manner astonishing to witness.

If a deer is captured, the Indian brings it in on his horse and throws it to the women, whose business it is to dress and cook it. If he kills a mustang or a buffalo, he rides into the village and informs his squaw where the carcass may be found. She straightway mounts and goes in search of it, skins it, cuts the flesh into strips, and returns.

The women are remarkable for their industry. Besides attending to the menial duties of the camp and working in the fields during the planting and harvesting seasons, they perform extraordinary labors in preparing buffalo hides and making them soft and pliable. To do this properly requires about three weeks.

When the hide is first brought in green, it is placed upon a log so hewed that it presents a flat surface, perhaps a foot in width. With an instrument similar to a common adze, the squaws cut away all the flesh and part of the bulkiest portions of the hide, until it presents a uniform thickness. This is a long and tedious operation. The hide is then stretched upon a frame and rubbed with a kind of pumice stone until the surface becomes furzy. If it should dry in this state, however, it would be hard and stiff. To avoid this, they use a preparation composed of basswood bark pounded very fine and mixed with the brains of the deer or buffalo. They apply this day after day, until the skin is thoroughly saturated, when it is soft and flexible.

The buffalo robe is, as far as I know, their only article of commerce. At a certain season of every year the robes are transported to Mexico, and sold to Mexican traders who meet them there. They receive in compensation hatchets, knives, and other implements, together with cheap calicoes, mescal and trinkets.

In their personal habits they are supremely dirty. Occasionally, in warm weather, they bathe in the river, but daily washing is not thought of, so that they are constantly covered with dirt and vermin.

It is a custom among them to paint their faces daily. I was compelled, every morning, to pursue this practice—to anoint my features with a preparation composed chiefly of a kind of clay—so that it would be difficult for a stranger to distinguish me from one of their own number.

They have many traditions but no records. Still, they have certain hieroglyphics by which they can communicate as accurately as if they knew how to write letters.

For instance, if one party goes out before another has returned and wishes to let them know where they have gone and why, they will seek some point where it is probable their trail will be discovered. Then they provide themselves with a thin piece of birch bark, which can be folded without breaking. On this they make figures and emblems to represent the idea they wish to express.

If they are on the warpath, the character will be a tomahawk and a scalp; if on a visit to a friendly tribe, it will be a pipe; if on a buffalo or deer hunt, there will be no characters, but the folded bark will simply enclose some of the hair of the animal they are after. If they intend to be absent a month, the emblem will be the full moon; if two weeks, a half-moon, if only a few days, the new moon. Then they strike a hatchet deep into the trunk of a tree and withdraw it. They place the end of the bark letter in the cut, with the outer end pointing in the direction they have gone.

They measure time by the changes of the moon. In the new, they give themselves up to contemplation and worship, thanking the Great Spirit for permitting another moon to take the old one's place. For every change, there is some peculiar ceremony. For example, when the moon is full the festival of the roasted dog occurs. Except for the refreshments it is very much like a modern picnic. The squaws go out to a spring in some pleasant and shady spot, taking with them a number of curs which have been fattened for the occasion. Kindling a fire, they butcher and roast them. Now the warriors come and sit down in the grass with the squaws. They speedily strip the canine bones amidst much fun and laughter.

As I became more and more acquainted with those who inhabited the village, I observed four girls, the youngest twelve and the oldest eighteen, whose appearance attracted my attention. They were copper-colored but they possessed the Anglo-Saxon face and they had fine light hair, inclined to auburn. They knew no other than the language of the Comanches, and conformed to their manners and customs. It was evident they had been captured in early childhood and remembered no other life than that they were leading.

We were frequently visited by the chiefs and warriors of the surrounding tribes. They were cordially welcomed and entertained. Then there was a pipe dance, which is the dance of friendship. They were invited to repose on the largest buffalo skins, and given to eat the flesh of a roasted dog, a great luxury. Many were attracted to our camp through curiosity to see and hear the wonderful watch.

There was one visitor, in particular, a stout, surly chief named Spotted Leopard, who visited our camp many times. He appeared fascinated with the watch, never growing weary of listening to the alarm. After Moko had finally placed it affectionately in her bosom, he would have long, earnest interviews with Big Wolf about the mysterious timepiece.

Lounging about the camp, I now led a monotonous life until November, or at least until the season of buffalo hunting had arrived, when I was ordered, unexpectedly, one morning, to mount a mule and ride forth, accompanied by Big Wolf and half a dozen of his warriors.

After a two-days' journey we came in sight of a large town at the foot of a mountain. A mile outside we were met by a party of eight or ten, who escorted us in. When we had reached the square, the same surly chief who had so often visited Big Wolf to listen to the watch bade us welcome. Then I knew we were in the camp of Spotted Leopard.

A short half-hour only had passed when the horn sounded the war dance. I was conducted to the center somewhat nervous and apprehensive, the apparitions of Martin and Stewart flitting before my mental vision. Nevertheless, there remained an inward confidence I would not be put to death, because I had kept the covenant. While I was in this state of perplexity, the warriors were issuing from their tents, whither they had gone when the horn sounded, to gird on their belts and decorate themselves with their scalps. They assembled round me, the signal was given, and the dance began. It was brief—unusually so—and terminated without any damage, very much to my relief.

In the morning a large number of mules and horses were collected in the square. Piles of buffalo, deer, and beaver skins, also, were brought and packed on mules. Big Wolf produced the bloody stick and delivered it to Spotted Leopard, at the same time informing me I had been sold. I had to reopen the vein on the back of my hand and again stain the carved figures with blood. Then Big Wolf and his warriors departed, taking with them the proceeds of the sale. In this business transaction I had the satisfaction of learning how much, in Indian estimation, I was worth, to wit: 120 animals of the horse kind, and as many skins as three pack mules could carry.

From the first I entertained a deep dislike of Spotted Leopard. He was morose, reserved, unsocial, and there was a malignant expression about his mouth and eyes that told me he could delight in cruelty.

At the end of four days Big Wolf again made his appearance, attended by his wives and a number of warriors. Their arrival was celebrated by a pipe dance. This ceremony was conducted as follows. The wives of the two chiefs, myself, and several old men were stationed in the center of a ring. At its side stood Spotted Leopard, with a lighted pipe of red sandstone. As the warriors danced around, each, as he came opposite the chief, received the pipe at his hands, took a whiff or two, and handed it back. This ceremony was accompanied by one of their wild and peculiar songs. When it was concluded, Moko came forward with the watch, kissed it, presented it to me and, turning about, broke through the circle of warriors, crying, and disappeared in a neighboring tent.

I caused it to sound the alarm, probably a dozen times. Then Spotted Leopard approached me with one of his wives, Kianceta, by his side. Into her possession the weird, mysterious thing, through which the Great Spirit spoke in a strange voice, was delivered.

Next morning the tribe assembled and they indulged in a long, jolly feast. Moko and the three other wives of Big Wolf kissed me again and again, and then, bestriding their mules, rode away towards their own valley, weeping as they went.

Among the wives of Spotted Leopard there was one who treated me with all the kindness I had previously received at the hands of Moko, and she was Kianceta, the Weasel. Kianceta was tall and slim, and erect as the young cedar. She had an easy, elastic gait, as if shod with velvet springs, and in her movements there was a nameless grace and dignity which drew all eyes after her. She was dressed in buckskin moccasins and leggings colored red—a blue broadcloth skirt, tastefully embroidered with beads, and over this a bright calico short gown. Her long hair, blacker than the feathers of the crow, fell halfway to the ground, and around her forehead was a tin band, scalloped on the upper edge, after the fashion of a crown.

Kianceta was indeed comely to look upon, but her soul was far more lovely than her form. Though she was an untutored woman of the prairie, I have reason to remember her with respect and gratitude. She sympathized with me, poor captive, when others laughed at my calamities—sat down by my side and looked sorrowfully into my face when the young savages in the village beat me with stones and sticks until I sought shelter in the tent. A hundred times she stood between me and those who threatened harm—gave me corn when others had it not—attended me when sick, casting red-hot stones into a trough of water to make me a steam bath, and wrapping me in thick buffalo skins until my cold was broken up and my health restored.

My time was now passed either in attending upon Spotted Leopard or sauntering idly through the village, continually thinking of escape. This subject was never out of my mind.

Finally my plan was perfected—which was to steal away in the night, trusting to travel many miles before the chief would awake.

About twelve o'clock one night, when the chief was lost in slumber and the camp was silent, I crawled softly from the tent. I was about to make my way from the village and fly across the plain when I was startled by the growl of a big dog that confronted me, showing his white teeth. He was joined by another, and another, until I found myself surrounded. Their growls awakened all the other curs, and instantly snarling and barking was heard from one end to the other of the camp. The disturbed women and warriors shouted to them, in a half-sleeping, half-waking state, to be still and lie down.

Further advance was useless. I made my way back into the tent stealthily, having avoided observation.

Though disappointed beyond measure, I was by no means discouraged. My orders were not to go beyond the village. However, as the Indians' watchfulness over me became less strict, I so far disregarded them, occasionally, as to wander a short way down the creek, or out to a little grove some rods from the village. This practice I kept up until finally it became almost unnoticed.

Emboldened by their increasing indifference just at dusk, one evening, I started off at a slow, careless pace towards the mouth of a ravine that lay beyond the village. I had proceeded about six hundred yards and was about to make a trial of my speed when I saw three warriors in advance, approaching me directly.

Taking me by the arm, they led me back into camp and called the chief to one side and had a long interview with him. At its close the chief pointed me into his tent, where I was tied down to stakes, on my back. This, I supposed, was the extent of the penalty I was to suffer, but a short time taught me I was sorely mistaken.

Spotted Leopard, drawing down my legging, with the coolness of the most practiced surgeon, drew the edge of his knife across the tendon just below my right knee. The muscle was not entirely severed, as was evidently his intention. The object of this surgical operation was to cripple me so as to make escape impossible. For two weeks

I was kept tied down, the chief frequently bending the leg back and forth, each time breaking open the wound afresh. Eventually I was unbound and the wound permitted to heal. It left a formidable scar, and rendered the limb extremely stiff, not so much, however, as it was his purpose to make it.

In the winter following, some 250 of the warriors set out on their annual grand buffalo hunt. They were mounted on their choice horses, while I, who accompanied the chief as his servant, rode, unarmed, a dilapidated mule. The party moved west, threading their winding way over the mountains and across numerous streams and valleys.

In the afternoon of the third day we struck a wide, rolling prairie. In the center was a high, smooth ridge. As we approached this ridge, our scattered cavalcade extended, perhaps, a quarter of a mile, moving forward carelessly. I was at the rear, by the side of Spotted Leopard, and surrounded by the pack mules.

As the foremost horsemen reached the height, they halted suddenly, making hurried signs. Two or three of the braves galloped back down the slope, riding eagerly to and fro among their brethren, as if urging them to push forward without delay. The whole band, thereupon, dashed up the hill, except Spotted Leopard and myself, who remained with the mules in the rear. Reaching the summit, the braves formed a line. I heard the cry "the Apaches, the Apaches," and knew at once there was hot work at hand.

Two or three minutes after, the air was rent with the noise of the war whoop, and up the opposite ascent, at full speed came the Apaches, in a solid body, like a black cloud. A shower of arrows were discharged from both lines, and they rushed upon each other in a hand-to-hand encounter.

The battle was fierce and terrible. Horses reared and plunged and fell upon each other. Their riders dealt blow for blow and thrust for thrust, some falling from their saddles to the ground and others trampling madly over them.

The Comanches outnumbered the enemy; nevertheless, they were forced to retreat, falling back down the hill almost to my position. But still they were not pursued, the Apaches appearing to be content to hold possession of the ground.

Soon the tribe of Spotted Leopard rallied and dashed once more to the attack. Again the fierce blow was given and returned, again horses and men intermingled in the melee—stumbled, fell, and rolled upon the ground, while the wide heavens resounded with their hideous shrieks and cries. My blood thrilled through my veins as I looked upon the scene.

I hoped devoutly during the engagement that the Comanches would be beaten, believing that if I should fall into the enemies' hands my chances of escape would be increased, for I had often heard that the Apaches were more merciful to prisoners than others of their race. But in this I was disappointed. The Apaches at length gave way, disappearing beyond the ridge. Instead of pursuing their advantage, however the Comanches hastily gathered up their dead and retreated. As soon as they had left, the Apaches again appeared upon the height and bore away their dead also. It was a drawn battle.

This encounter was unexpected on both sides. The Apaches, as I learned, were gathered around a spring, cooking their meat, when our party came upon them. At that time a deadly strife existed between the tribes, and it would have been a scandalous violation of an Indian's idea of manhood to have separated without a bloody tilt at arms.

The Comanches lost in this battle seventeen warriors, the Apaches probably as many more. The close of this eventful day was occupied in burying the slain. The Comanches seemed to chant the death song with more energy and feeling than on ordinary occasions. When a warrior dies on the field of battle, their joy knows no bounds, for their religion assures them his departed spirit is at once caught up by the Great Spirit and borne to the Happy Hunting Grounds.

We saw no more of the Apaches, and the following day crossed the mountains into a wide prairie. Here we remained two months. Thousands and thousands of buffalo, in immense droves, were roving over the plain. It was an easy task to obtain as many hides as the mules could carry home.

On the return, we fell in with a party of two or three hundred, a friendly tribe, who accompanied us back to the camp. Their chief was Kansaleumko, Rolling Thunder. He was agreeable, though sedate —a compound of benign dignity and solemnity.

Rolling Thunder and his tribe remained with us a week, and it was indeed a week of carnival and merriment. During these entertainments the good Kianceta and myself played a conspicuous part in the exhibition of the watch. As on all former occasions, it captivated the simple children of nature, and particularly Rolling Thunder.

Soon after the departure of Rolling Thunder and his people, another large party came and pitched their hunting tents outside the town. The day following, I observed our warriors, belted and decorated with trinkets and scalps, moving toward their encampment. Something unusual, I felt confident, was about to take place. A quarter of a mile away, I could distinctly hear the sound of their voices singing their savage song.

Presently, mingling with the loud, shrill war whoop a shriek of mortal agony came thrilling through the air. Again and again it was repeated, growing fainter and fainter, until finally it ceased.

At length, a party of six or seven came after me. While passing through the strange encampment, I discovered pieces of soldier's clothing, which I recognized as the United States uniform. Moving on beyond the camp into a grove, a spectacle presented itself that froze my blood. A white man had been subjected to the torture. A sharp stick had been thrust through his heel cords, by which he was suspended from a limb, with his head downward, as a butcher suspends a carcass.

He, also, had been sacrificed with the accursed flints, his ears cut off and tongue drawn out. A slight convulsive shrug of the shoulders indicated that life was not wholly extinct. I gazed upon him in silence and terror and was relieved when they led me away.

Rolling Thunder was a frequent visitor at our camp. He exhibited a regard for me, and would often fall into a profound revery when I had caused the watch to deliver its message from the Great Spirit in the usual, rattling offhand manner in which it was accustomed to converse. His interviews with Spotted Leopard became so long that I had no doubt I was to be subjected to another sale.

My surmises proved to be entirely correct. Just previous to the annual buffalo hunt, Spotted Leopard and some of his distinguished warriors, Kianceta, and his other wives, with myself and a considerable drove of pack mules, set off over the mountains. After a journey of several days, we entered a town of perhaps two hundred tents, in a narrow, luxuriant valley, over which Rolling Thunder presided.

On our arrival, the customary dances were performed—the bloody covenant of the square stick was solemnly renewed—and the purchase money, consisting of skins and animals, was delivered. The price paid for me, so far as I could judge, exceeded even the price paid on the former sale. Kianceta braided into my long hair an incredible number of beads as a parting token of friendship.

Rolling Thunder had four wives. The youngest, Semawnaw, the Wise, took charge of the watch, preserving it with care and tenderness. She had a cheerful and lively disposition, always frolicsome as the young antelope of the prairie.

Rolling Thunder possessed a remarkably inquisitive mind and was extremely sociable. Hour after hour he would converse with me in his tent about the customs of the whites. I endeavored to illustrate their superiority and power. With a piece of charcoal, I would sketch on a sheet of birch bark the figure of a ship, telling him that its masts were taller than the tallest cedar on the mountains, and that it was capable of carrying more than a thousand pack mules could bear; that in this great canoe the white man would sail away to a vast continent, distant more than a hundred days' journey to the east.

He had never seen the ocean, nevertheless he comprehended its vastness through the traditions of his fathers, who once dwelt upon its shore; but no logic could convince him that the mighty land beyond it was a part of this globe. His reasoning led him irresistibly to the conclusion that it must belong to another planet.

When I told him the earth was round, and on the opposite side were extensive countries and millions of people—that if we could bore a hole through it beneath our feet, we would emerge into those countries —he laughed me to scorn. He argued that the inhabitants would have to walk with their heads downward, and must fall off; besides, the premise was false, as the earth was not round, but flat, a fact obvious to the naked eye.

I described a train of cars, wooden tents placed above wheels, filled with a crowd of people outnumbering all his tribe. I described the immensity of the towns of the whites, the number of their warriors. Usually, when I had concluded, the old man would remain silent a long time, absorbed in deep study, from which he would, at length, arouse and exclaim: "Wonderful! Wonderful are the works of the white man, but the Great Spirit will destroy them all!"

Rolling Thunder evidently entertained a favorable opinion of me. This was shown soon after my arrival by his insisting I should take a wife. I endeavored to decide what effect it might have on my chances of escape. My conclusion was that the effect would be favorable, and I signified that "Barkis was willin'."

The next step was to make a selection from the dusky daughters of the tribe. The chief sent for some half-dozen. Some were hideous or fat and flabby, having a fiery red new moon painted over each eye, and the full moon in the center of the forehead. These were rejected without ceremony.

At length one was brought that was entirely satisfactory. She was small and slender, very young and very agile. There was the grace of nature in her carriage and, besides, she was not quite as filthy as her companions. She was arrayed in the latest Indian fashion—prettily embroidered moccasins, colored leggings, calico short gown of many colors, with a great diversity of beads braided in her hair. She was distinguished as the most expert swimmer and deepest diver in the tribe, wherefore they had bestowed upon her the name of Sleek Otter. Altogether, she was rather a dirty but very comely maiden, much fairer than the great majority of her race.

With her I entered into the holy estate of matrimony. The squaws generously assisted her in building a tent, bringing in presents of buffalo skins to construct it, and when it was finished we moved in. Sleek Otter made me a faithful, affectionate wife, skinned the deer, cooked the venison, pounded the corn, and mended my moccasins, in all respects performing her duties with cheerfulness and promptness.

After the marriage my privileges were very much enlarged, it being considered improbable I would tear myself away from the partner of my bosom. I was no longer made the center post at their war dances, but permitted to wear gaily colored feathers in my hair and to join in dances with the warriors. But I was by no means at liberty. I was not allowed to leave the village alone, nor to carry arms.

My duties were those of an attendant upon the chief. He kept me near him always, whether on buffalo hunts or visits to neighboring tribes. He frequently made these visits, when they required but one day's ride, with no one accompanying him but myself. We never passed the night together alone on these excursions. In a thousand little ways it was made evident he did not regard it exactly safe to place himself within my power.

My soul still longed to reach the abodes of civilized man. Though greatly discouraged, I never entirely despaired of sooner or later effecting an escape.

At this time I had no apprehensions whatever in regard to my safety so long as I remained an obedient captive. A detected attempt at escape, however, I was aware, would be followed by the severest penalties. I had so long, and so intensely, contemplated the subject that there was no aspect of it that had not received my careful scrutiny. Of one thing I had become convinced: if I had been successful in escaping from the tribe of Spotted Leopard without the means of killing game or making a fire, I should most assuredly have perished from starvation among the mountains surrounding his town.

It became necessary, therefore, to devise some plan to provide myself with these indispensable conveniences. It is probable I could, on many occasions, have reached the mountains unperceived after my marriage. But it was utterly impossible to do so, providing myself at the same time with arms—the watchfulness over me in respect to them being strict and constant.

It was while indulging in these never-ending speculations that Rolling Thunder ordered me to saddle my mule and accompany him on a long journey.

His destination was a village three days' journey to the north. At this place a convention had been called of all the chiefs of tribes inhabiting the country between northern Mexico and the regions of perpetual snow. The object of the convention was to induce the Indian nations to bury the hatchet among themselves and unite in a universal bond of brotherhood to prevent the whites from passing through their territories to the Pacific Coast.

Rolling Thunder, before taking his departure, arrayed himself with extraordinary care. A dozen scalps were attached to his war shirt, silver trinkets representing the moon in all its phases were fastened on his breast; his feet were clad in new, cunningly embroidered moccasins, and on his head rested a crown of feathers dyed by his wives in all the colors of the rainbow. Of all the horses that grazed round his camp, he was mounted upon the most fleet and spirited. His weapons of war were a knife thrust through his belt, a hatchet suspended from the pommel of his saddle, and a Mexican rifle upon which he prided himself exceedingly.

I bestrode the same old mule that had so often borne me on her back, with nothing hanging from my saddle bow but a huge buffalo horn to furnish my master with cool draughts from the streams as we journeyed. Saluting Sleek Otter, who little thought it was the last nod she would ever receive from her long-haired spouse (I had not seen a razor for three years), we trotted away from the village, myself in advance.

Neither of us was destined ever to return.

From early morning, we traveled steadily. At sunset we entered a valley where a small tribe resided. The usual hospitalities were extended.

An Indian's dignity, whether chief or subject, never rises to that elevated degree which prevents his getting drunk every opportunity that offers. The sedate old chief became beastly intoxicated—forgot his customary decorum—vainly attempted to be funny—danced out of place—and whooped when there was no occasion for it—in fact, was as boisterous and silly as about half a gallon of bad Mexican whiskey could make him.

However, bright and early in the morning, the chief was again on his legs, ready to set forward on the journey. Very soon we passed out of the valley and entered the mountains. The last night's debauch had set the old chief on fire, and before the sun had halfway ascended to the zenith his throat was parched and he was mad with thirst.

But there was no water to be found. On and on we went, threading our way through thick bushes, around the sharp points of overhanging cliffs, across rough and rugged ravines, but nowhere did a spring or running stream greet his longing eyes.

We continued to press forward until about one o'clock in the afternoon, when, reaching the bottom of a deep hollow, we discovered water oozing from the base of a precipice and trickling down a little muddy channel through the grass.

Rolling Thunder called impetuously upon me to fill the horn at once. Though I attempted to obey his order with all possible speed, the rills was so extremely shallow that, with every dip I made, the contents of the horn would come up in the proportion of three parts mud to one of water.

Perceiving the difficulty, he leaped from his horse, directing me to hold him by the bridle. He threw his rifle on the ground and, lying down upon it in the grass, thrust his scorched lips into the little stream.

Standing by the horse's side, I observed the hatchet hanging from the pommel of the saddle.

The thought flashed through my mind quick as the fierce lightning that the hour of my deliverance had come at last.

Snatching the hatchet, in that instant, from its place, I leaped towards the chief and buried the dull edge a broad hand's breadth in his brain. A moment sufficed to draw the rifle from beneath him and jerk the long knife from his girdle.

Then, mounting his horse, I dashed wildly away over an unknown path towards the land of freedom.

I remembered that, some two miles back, I had seen a narrow ravine stretching to the west. I turned about and retraced the path we had followed. Coming to the ravine, I plunged into it and spurred on at a breakneck pace over piles of broken stones and through barricades of tangled thorns and brushwood. All the while the mule followed closely at the horse's heels. At the end of six miles I found my way blocked by a tall bluff extending entirely across the western end of the ravine.

Wheeling northward, I moved along the base of the bluff. Finally I reached an opening—a narrow crevice half filled with sharp-angled fragments of rock. With great difficulty, I, the horse, and mule managed to clamber up this until we gained a comparatively level spot. It was a kind of terrace, some twenty feet wide, about halfway to the summit. We followed this terrace as it wound around the precipice. The path became more and more narrow as we advanced, until, to my unutterable horror, it was less than two feet wide. Just in front of me it circled around a sharp point which hid the view beyond, but to all appearances the path ended there.

On one side were great, loose overhanging rocks impossible to ascend and threatening to fall. On the other, there was an almost sheer drop of at least a hundred feet. As if conscious of the danger, the horse hesitated to proceed. Between the wall of rock on the right and the precipice on the left there was not sufficient room for either horse or mule to turn around, and their bodies filled the path so completely that I could not turn back without pushing the poor brutes over the edge.

I turned my eyes away from the dizzy depth below. Then, closely hugging the upper side, I crawled carefully to the sharp point before me. I peered around it. To my enormous relief, it expanded into a broad, smooth road. With much urging and coaxing, I finally succeeded in inducing the horse to pass the point of danger. The mule followed cautiously.

I gazed around. Never had I observed a wilder or more dreary scene. On all sides, mountain was piled upon mountain as far as the eye could reach. Here and there, among the ravines, I discovered strips of timber, but the summits, in the distance, were bare and rocky, their bald peaks stretching to the clouds.

A narrow opening to the southwest attracted my attention, and I headed for it. It proved to be another ravine, over which cedar trees and clusters of thick bushes were scattered. By the time I reached the southwestern end of this little solitary valley, the sun had set. I pushed into the center of a dense thicket, the loneliest spot around, and halted for the night.

Securing the horse to a limb by the bridle, and removing the buffalo-skin saddle, I sat down upon it and tried to figure out what it was best to do. My safety depended much upon circumstances. If the body of the chief should be discovered immediately, my escape was doubtful. The moment it was found, a party would start upon my trail. At the same time messengers would be sent to all the tribes far and near, calling on them to keep a sharp lookout for me. I had as much to fear in front as in the rear.

I had the dead chief's rifle and ammunition, and consequently the means of kindling a fire and killing game. But doing either, at least for some days, would be a dangerous experiment, as the noise of the rifle or the light of the fire might expose me. Hunger, however, would force me to risk both. I was famished, not having eaten since early in the morning.

It was impossible at that hour to capture game. My thoughts turned to the mule. She had followed me unexpectedly and could be of no possible use. In all probability, she would prove an annoyance. Necessity suggested how I could turn her to account. Walking up to the unsuspicious beast, I pulled out the chief's long knife and drew it across her throat.

When the mule was dead, I cut long thin slips of flesh from her hams. Then I decided to run the risk of kindling a fire, trusting that the body of Rolling Thunder was still undiscovered. I gathered a pile of sticks and, withdrawing the charge from the rifle, ignited them with a priming of powder. I soon had a ruddy blaze going. After the mule meat was broiled and my appetite satisfied with a portion of it, I laid the rest carefully aside for future use. It occurred to me that I might suffer from lack of water on those thirsty mountains. I cut the bladder from the mule, blew it up, and dried it by the fire. Next I filled it from a sluggish pool and tied the mouth with a strong buffalo string. Now I had a serviceable canteen.

With the reloaded rifle in my hands, I sat down on the buffalo skin at the foot of a cedar tree and leaned against its trunk. Here a new terror awaited me.

The mule's blood had been scented by wolves and panthers. The panthers began to scream. The most terrifying sound that has ever fallen on my ears is the cry of these animals, it is so like the plaintive, agonized shriek of a human being. Nearer and nearer the beasts approached, until the horse snuffed and snorted. I could hear their teeth snap and the dry sticks crackle beneath their feet. A dozen times I was on the point of climbing the tree, expecting to be attacked at any moment. With such a crash would they break through the thicket that many times I bounded to my feet, thinking the Indians were upon me.

The fortunate resolution I had taken to build a fire undoubtedly kept the animals off. But it was a fearful night. It taught me an unforgettable lesson—never to encamp where I had killed my game.

In the morning, very early, I proceeded on my journey. In half an hour I again found my way blocked by a mountain. It was high noon when I reached the summit. During the afternoon I kept my course along the ridge of the highlands. The route was so rugged, that I probably had not traveled ten miles in a direct line from the place of departure in the morning when night again overtook me.

I passed the night under a ledge, in a little nook where a portion of the rock had fallen out. In such an exposed position as this it would have been madness to light a fire—nothing less than a signal to any in pursuit to come up and take me. The tough mule meat and the yet unemptied bladder furnished me with a repast. My poor horse, however, was not so well supplied, there being neither water nor grass here and few bushes on which to browse.

Wrapping the buffalo skin around me, I tried to sleep. But my slumbers were broken and troubled, full of fearful dreams in which I was clambering over rocks or pursued by Indians, yelling close on my trail, and yet I was unable to flee, having lost the power to move. I arose with the first faint glimpse of the rising sun, sore and un-refreshed.

For several days I wandered over these mountains, going from ridge to ridge until I attained and passed the summits. In the evening of the sixth day I descended into a dark, cavernous gorge, where I found a spring of water and many deer browsing around it. The mule meat was now nearly gone. Here, for the first time, I discharged the rifle, bringing down a plump doe. Leaving most of the animal for the wolves, I carried the skin and hindquarters four or five miles and halted for the night. Under an overhanging cliff I found a secluded spot hidden behind thick brushwood, and here I kindled a fire and prepared a meal of venison.

The seventh day found me toiling over a succession of mountains smoother and less steep than any I had yet crossed. My course here led southwest; I had conceived the idea (which proved very mistaken) that it would conduct me to the Mexican state of Chihuahua. At length I reached a point where I found a wide prairie unexpectedly spread out before me, over which numerous Indian horsemen were riding. At my feet stood an Indian town of at least three hundred tents.

I was anxious to escape at once from so dangerous a vicinity. In order to do so, however, I had to retrace my steps many rough and weary miles. Late in the evening of the next day I rounded the point of the prairie and encamped in a snug fastness of the mountains on its western side. Until I had passed far beyond this Indian settlement, I exercised the same caution as if I knew they had received news of Rolling Thunder's death and were on the watch for me.

For nearly two weeks now I was lost in a vast range of mountains. Sometimes I went forward, at others I was compelled to turn back. I often suffered from hunger and thirst. During the day I directed my course by the sun, always keeping in view, as far as I could, some prominent peak in the distance. At night I was guided by the North Star. However, there were many cloudy days and nights, during which I was unable to proceed with certainty and lost much time.

I encountered many hardships and dangers on this lonesome journey. For instance, I was frightfully annoyed by snakes. There was a flat-headed adder I frequently discovered on wet ground, and rattlesnakes were everywhere. But more terrifying than any of these was another species, a kind I had never seen before. It was brown, rather slim, and often over nine feet in length. It inhabited the clefts of the rocks, and stretched itself out on the ledges in the sun. One of its peculiar characteristics was to blow, when disturbed, emitting a loud disagreeable noise, half hiss, half bellow. Frequently, I would draw myself up a steep slope by grasping twigs that had sprung up in the crevices of the rocks; as my head emerged above the surface I was striving to reach, one of these monsters would raise itself to a height of three feet and blow directly in my face. It made my hair stand on end. Bears were numerous and occasionally I saw a panther stealing noiselessly through the underwood.

On the twentieth day, I discovered Indians again. I had reached another valley and was studying the terrain from a secure point when I saw a hundred horsemen, followed by a train of pack mules, moving towards the west. There was no village to be seen and the buffalo-hunting season was past, so I supposed they were a party on a visit to some neighboring tribe. I watched until the last one had disappeared. Then I hurried over the narrow valley and began to labor up the mountain on the other side.

By this time the horse had suffered so much from thirst and want of forage that he had become terribly emaciated. His hoofs, likewise, were broken, and he was lame and spiritless. My feet also were covered with bruises, and my whole body was sore and stiff. In this condition, one day we reached a deep basin among the hills. It was ten or fifteen acres in extent, covered with patches of grass and thickets of brush, and wholly shut in by tall mountains. A clear spring gushed from the base of the mountain on one side, and a number of deer were feeding at different points. I remained here twelve days.

Though I had no mirror with me to make a detailed examination, I expect my personal appearance was not especially attractive. Three years had elapsed since my beard or the hair on my head had known a comb, brush, or razor. My moccasins were worn out and my leggings and hunting shirt in shreds. I still retained the deerskin band which bound my head and fastened on the forehead with a clasp, preventing the hair from falling over my eyes. But the little painted feathers with which Sleek Otter had adorned it were long since blown to the winds of heaven.

Each day of my stay in this solitary place I toiled up the neighboring peaks to see if an enemy was approaching. In the center of the densest thicket I erected a fireplace of stone, my object being to kindle a fire where the thick shrubbery would conceal the light. Here I set to work to prepare provisions and replenish my wardrobe. I shot four or five deer, dried as much of the flesh as I planned to carry, and made the skins into clothing. The only tool I possessed was a knife.

The moccasins were made of the hide while in its green state, applied to the foot with the hair inside. I inserted stout thongs of the same material through holes made with the point of the knife, tied them, and left the moccasins to dry. I was familiar with the Indian mode of dressing buckskin with the brains of the deer itself, and had no difficulty in preparing new leggings and a hunting coat. I delayed several days after this on account of the horse. But although he had plenty of pasture and water, he did not improve. He seemed completely broken down.

I set out again at the end of twelve days, dressed in my new clothes and with a bundle of dried venison hanging at the saddle bow. I wildly imagined myself in the neighborhood of Santa Fe. My course now led over a mountainous region, if possible more difficult and barren than any I had traveled before. Water was scarce, and in many parts there was not sufficient grass on a thousand acres to supply the horse with one night's forage. He became more and more tender-footed and lame. I was compelled to lead him, stopping frequently for him to lie down. At length the supply of water I had brought with me from the last spring was exhausted, and I was obliged to leave him.

Rolling up the buffalo skin enclosing my drinking horn and other articles and tying it into the form of a knapsack with the bridle reins, I threw it upon my back. Then I shouldered the rifle and, bidding the poor horse a sorrowful farewell, started on alone.

Now for the first time my heart died within me. For all I could discover, civilization was as far off as when I started the journey. I began to doubt myself, to fear that I had become crazed. Instead of pursuing a southwesterly course, I imagined I was only wandering around and around over the same everlasting solitudes. Moreover, since parting from the horse, who had been a companion to me— whose presence during the silent hours of the night, stamping and feeding around me, seemed like a protection—I was lonesome and desolate indeed. And I was sick in body as well as soul. My limbs had become swollen and the wounds and bruises that covered me were inflamed and painful.

Day by day I grew weaker as I advanced. Often I prayed God that when I fell asleep I might never wake again.

The fifty-sixth day brought me to a wide rolling prairie dotted with many small groves of timber. Into one of these I made my way to avoid the hot sun. I was lying in the shade, in a drowsy, half-sleeping state, when I was startled by the sharp crack of a rifle close at hand.

My first thought was: Is it possible they have chased me so far?

Bounding to my feet, I held the rifle in my hands, resolving, weak as I was, to defend myself.

In ten minutes, instead of being rushed by a band of Indians, I saw a mounted Mexican, wearing a wide-brimmed sombrero, come riding leisurely along. Thrown over his horse's back, behind the saddle, lay a deer which had received its death wound from the discharge that had so astounded me.

"How do you do?" he exclaimed in Spanish, looking greatly astonished.

I walked up to him and replied in his own language, with which I am familiar:

"Sick and dying. Will you help me, my friend?"

"How did you get here?" he inquired.

Not knowing the character of the company into which I had fallen, I decided to conceal my true story for the present.

"I have been lost among the mountains," I answered, "and have been trying to make my way to the settlements."

He informed me he was one of a party of three who had been on a trading expedition to the Apaches, and were now about to return to their home in San Fernandez, near the Rio Grande. He said his companions were not far off and invited me to accompany him to their camp. Seeing how difficult it was for me to go on foot, he dismounted and helped me into the saddle. He walked by the side of the horse, conversing kindly, and evidently much interested in my behalf.

His companions were cooking when we arrived, and were greatly astonished to behold me. They gave me a hospitable and generous welcome. Their kindness won my confidence at once, and I told them the whole story of my adventures. They were deeply moved and spared no pains to make me comfortable. The packs were rearranged to free one of the mules for me to ride and we started off.

The third day we crossed the Rio Grande on a raft, swimming the mules and horses. We passed through a number of frontier settlements, at all of which my misfortunes were related by the traders and I received the kindest treatment. On the seventh day we entered the town of San Fernandez.

I remained six weeks at San Fernandez under the care of a physician. At the end of this time one of the traders accompanied me to Matamoros. From here I proceeded to Brazos Santiago and shipped for Havana, where I obtained passage on the schooner *Elizabeth Jones,* and on November 10, 1858, reached the United States. I was home at last, and my adventures with the Indians were at an end forever, although I would never forget the awful scenes of agony and torture I had witnessed among them.

# Revolt of the Sioux

## LAVINA EASTLICK

*AVINA EASTLICK'S story is one episode in the history of the bloodiest massacre of the West. It began on August 17, 1862, with an unprovoked murder of some white settlers by four young Indians at Acton, Minnesota. It ended a little over a month later with the rout of the Indians by troops under Colonel H. H. Sibley. But, in between, the rampaging Sioux had shot and hacked to death a large but unverifiable number of whites. President Lincoln estimated that at least eight hundred lost their lives. Thirty thousand persons fled from their homes in eighteen counties, and many did not return for more than a year, if ever.*

*In 1862 the Sioux, or Dakotas, in southwestern Minnesota had been living on a reservation for eight years. The hope of the Government had been that the Indians would settle down and become farmers, like the immigrants (Lavina Eastlick and her husband among them) who were establishing homesteads everywhere in the region. But changes in age-old ways come slowly. Only one Indian in ten cut his hair, put on trousers, and tilled the soil. The other nine—the traditional "blanket Indians"—looked down their noses at the "cut-hair" and went on hunting. But so much of their best land had been ceded to the whites that game was hard to find.*

*Things grew worse instead of better as the Civil War moved along
in its second year. The Indians complained (with justification) that
they were robbed or cheated by the traders on the reservation. They
were paid annuities—a small annual sum for each Indian, in compensation for the millions of acres they had surrendered to the whites—
and now, because of the war, payment of their money was held up.
In the bargain, the traders refused them credit. The Sioux were hungry
and angry. The situation was inflammable—and the hostile act of the
four young Indians on August 17 provided the spark.*

*Lake Shetek, where Lavina Eastlick lived, was about fifty miles
from the reservation. It was not until August 20 that the trouble
reached Shetek and the eleven white families who dwelled around it.
They sought shelter in the log house of John Wright, for it was larger
and stronger than their shanties. There were some Sioux living on
Wright's property, but the settlers looked upon them, and particularly
their leader, Pawn, as friends and allies. This, they were to discover,
was a grave error.*

*Lavina Eastlick was born in 1833 in Colesville, New York. She
was married to John Eastlick when she was seventeen. They had five
sons, ranging in age from Merton, eleven, to the baby, Johnny, fifteen
months. The other boys were Fred, Frank, and Giles. The family had
already made several moves, each one bringing them further west.
When they settled at Lake Shetek in 1861 they had hoped that this
would be their final move.*

*And, for four of them, it was.*

Early in the morning of August 20, 1862, Charles Hatch came to
our house and greatly alarmed us by information that the Sioux
Indians were close upon us. He informed us that the Indians had
killed Mr. Voight and that they were then at Mr. Koch's. We had
heard quite enough and stayed no longer to listen to details. My
husband caught up his two rifles and the baby and hastily left for Mr.
Smith's house.

The child had nothing on but a night dress. I asked my husband
if I should take my clothes. He said, "No." I wanted to get my shoes.
He said, "You have no time to spare." So I started barefooted, with
quite a load of powder, shot, and lead. I was so frightened that I
could hardly run.

We finally came in sight of Mr. Smith's house, which gave me great courage. When I got to the house and found no one there I thought I must sink to the ground helpless. I then happened to think of my boy that was at Mr. Wright's and hurried on with greater speed than ever.

We soon overtook Mr. Smith and his wife. They were going to Mr. Wright's, which Mr. Smith thought would be the best place of defense.

There were six Indians living in tepees at Mr. Wright's. As soon as they discovered us they waved their hands and told us to come on.

We soon reached the house, and found everything in confusion. Indians were running here and there, loading their guns, throwing off their clothes, pounding out balls, hiding their packs, and having quite a time. They told the men that they would fight for them and pretended to be very sorry for the whites.

People kept arriving. Soon there were over thirty of us there— men, women, and children. I saw Mrs. Koch come in. Her clothes were wet to the waist. She said she had waded through the lake (Shetek) and through the swamps to give information to the folks at the lower end of the lake. She said the Indians had come to her house, taken Mr. Koch's gun, and gone out and shot him with it.

Mrs. Koch felt very bad. I tried to get her quiet. I told her that my husband might be killed before night and then I should be worse off than she was, for I should be left with five children and she had none.

She said she could not stand it, for her husband was lying in the barnyard with his face in the mud. She told Pawn and he said that was very bad, and if two white men would go with him he would bring Mr. Koch down there. But no one would go with him.

The men said they could not see anything of the Indians yet. They then took the horses into the back part of the house, knocked out some chinking on every side of the house, got clubs and axes, and put them upstairs with the women. They were determined to fight the Indians, should they come into the house.

The women would all have fought well, for we were determined to sell our lives as dearly as possible. My husband brought me my knife, and told me to use it, if it became necessary. It was not a small knife by any means. Had we stayed in the house, I certainly should have used it, had the Indians come in.

Some Indians came to Mr. Smith's house. We saw them taking

clothes out of the house, shaking them, and folding them up. Some of the Indians rode out into the field as fast as their horses could run, fired their guns, and then rode back and cut a good many such capers. Pawn told the men that if they would fire their guns it would scare the Indians. They all fired their guns, Mrs. Wright with the rest.

Two or three of the Indians in the house with us did not fire. I thought there was something wrong going on. I told Mr. Smith and my husband that, should they fire again, to let the Indians fire first. I feared that they wished the men to fire and then would turn and shoot them before they could reload.

The Indians soon came in sight, and Pawn and two more Indians went and met them and talked awhile with them. These new Indians were on horseback. They rode away. Then Pawn came to us and said there were a great many Indians near and that they would burn the house. He acted as though he was badly frightened. He started off and wanted us all to go to the timber.

The men hardly knew what to do. Some wished to stay and some desired to go. Some started and some remained behind. I ran upstairs and caught my baby, then asleep, left my bonnet and my butcher knife on the bed, and was soon hurrying over the prairie with the others.

Two of the men went with the horses to Mr. Everett's to get a wagon to carry the women and children. They soon overtook us, and the women and children all got in but myself and Mrs. Wright. We walked about a mile and then we got in also, Mrs. Duley and some of the children getting out.

I saw ten Indians leave the house and come after us as swiftly as they could ride. We urged the horses on, but did not get them off of a walk. The Indians soon came so close that the men thought we had better leave the wagon. We did so and hurried along as fast as we could, the men keeping along with us.

Mr. Smith and Mr. Rhodes ran on and left us. Some of the men called to them, while others commanded them to stop and come back. My husband told Mr. Rhodes to come back and bring his rifle, as he had the best one among them. But nothing would stop them. There were two or three Indians that were trying to head them off or drive them back.

The Indians behind us came up to the wagon and began to strip the harness off the horses. Several of the men turned and fired upon them. The Indians soon mounted the horses and came on, keeping up a dreadful fire. The men told us to go to a swamp not far off. Meanwhile the Indians were trying to surround us.

While we were running for the swamp I was shot in the heel but did not stop. William Duley's oldest son and daughter were both shot through the shoulder. Mrs. Ireland's youngest child was shot through the leg.

We all soon got to the tall grass and hid ourselves as well as we could—the men standing round the edge, trying to get a shot at the Indians, who were skulking behind the hills. The Indians had got the advantage, and too well they knew it. My husband snapped four caps at an Indian. He then took a pin and pricked some powder into the tube (he had loaded his gun while running), fired at an Indian and shot him, but did not know whether he killed him or not.

The Indians had now surrounded us entirely. I soon heard someone groaning.

"Who was shot?" somebody asked.

"Me." It was Charlie Hatch's voice.

Mrs. Everett wished to go to him. He told her not to come. She then wished him to come to her, but he said they had both better keep still. Mrs. Ireland's next-to-youngest child was shot through the bowels.

The ball and shot, at this time, were falling around us like hail. I was struck with a ball, which passed through my clothes and just grazed my side. It was not long until a small shot struck my head, and I told John, my husband, that I was shot and thought I would die. I told him not to come to me, but if he had any chance of shooting an Indian, to stay and shoot him, for he could not do me any good.

Mr. Everett was shot and Mrs. Everett wanted to go to him. But he said she had better keep still, for the Indians might see her.

"Oh, Billy! *do* let me come," she replied.

"No, Mirie. Stay where you are."

She was soon shot in the neck and bled very freely. I heard her say to Mr. Everett, "We will both have to die." She then asked him if they should not pray.

"Yes," he replied.

I heard Mrs. Everett praying. Next I heard a ball strike someone. I could tell when a ball struck anyone.

I heard someone groan twice. I asked my husband if he was shot. He made no answer. I asked him again.

"He's dead," Mrs. Koch said.

I thought I would go to him, but Mrs. Koch told me it would do no good. She said she was sure he was dead and that I had better stay where I was with my children.

Now my children clung so close to me that I could scarcely move. They asked me over and over again if their father was dead.

"You must keep still," I replied, "or you will be killed."

It was now very warm in the tall grass. The sun was hot, and not a breath of air was stirring. Several times I tried to crawl away from the children to give the Indians less of a target. But as soon as I moved away they came after me. Frank and Fred seemed to think that Mother could save them.

Now the Indians were not shooting quite so often. I think quite a number of them had been killed. They came so close that we could hear them talking quite plainly. They fired two or three times and shot Mrs. Smith through the hip. She screamed several times and the Indians laughed about it.

They called to us to come out. I asked Mr. Everett if he had not better talk with them. He called to Pawn, and requested him to come to him.

"You come to me," Pawn answered.

"I can't. I am almost dead."

"You are lying," Pawn said.

Two of them shot at Everett but did not hit him. He told his wife that he would say no more, and wanted her to tell Pawn that he was killed.

Mrs. Everett got up and told Pawn, in the most pitiful tone, that her husband was dead. Pawn wanted her to come to him. He said he would not kill her; he wanted her and Mrs. Wright for his wives.

Mr. Everett told his wife perhaps she had better go. She said she would go if I would go with her. I told her someone had better go that could talk with them, and at the same time asked Mrs. Wright if she would not go. She said she would. She and Mrs. Everett took their children and went out to the Indians.

I saw Pawn take some of the children in his arms. Mrs. Wright told us that the Indians said they would not kill any of the women and children.

I got up and went to my husband. He lay on his left side, with his right hand on his face. I kissed him two or three times. I felt his face and hands. They were cold. I could not shed a tear, although I knew it was the last time I should ever see him.

I started for the Indians, but found I could walk only with great difficulty. My two oldest children came and helped me along. Mrs. Wright, seeing what trouble I had to walk, came and helped me, too. One by one the women came from the swamp, with their children. Most of us sat down. The Indians were standing around. Some were leaning on their guns and one or two got on their horses. One Indian took a shawl and a bag of shot from Rosa Ireland.

It began to rain. Now the Indians seemed to be in a great hurry. One Indian took Mrs. Koch and started off. Some more of them took Mr. Ireland's two oldest girls. The largest, blackest Indian took Mrs. Duley and myself by the hand and started off, neither of us making any resistance.

I looked back to see if the children were coming. Freddy started, but an old squaw ran and struck him over the head with something, I did not know what, and pounded him on the back. Then she let him get up and come on after me. His face was all streaming with blood. Not satisfied with her fiendish cruelty, she ran after him and knocked him down again, pounded him some more, took him up in her hands, raised him up as high as she could, and threw him down on the ground.

Pawn told me to go on. I went a few steps, looked back, and saw Frank on his knees, with both hands raised.

"Mother! Mother!" he called. The blood was running out of his mouth in a stream.

Mrs. Smith and Mrs. Ireland were both shot on the spot. Again old Pawn told me to go on. The Indian that was leading me went on and left me. I started again and asked Pawn if he was going to kill me. He said he was not.

Mrs. Duley had one child in her arms and one at her side, holding on to her dress. She was pleading for their lives. The Indians told her the same as the rest—that they would not kill them. She had not gone fifteen yards when they shot her eldest son.

I saw Mrs. Everett running toward her husband, and an Indian just ready to take hold of her. Some Indian shot, and she fell. Pawn stopped and loaded his gun.

I trudged on, thinking how brutally my children had been murdered and I could not help them. As I was hurrying along to overtake Mrs. Wright, Pawn shot me. The ball entered my back and came out at my side, just above my hip, passing through my right arm.

I had given Merton my baby, about fifteen months old, and told him to carry him as long as he could. He passed by where I fell, and supposed I was dead. When I fell, I thought my back was broken. Now I began to think that there were some ponies behind and they might step on me. I tried to move and found I could crawl. I had gone a few yards out of the trail when a young Indian came along and pounded me over the head and shoulders with a rifle. I expected every moment he would take my scalp, but he did not. He threw the rifle down by my side and went on.

I remained perfectly still for two hours or more, thinking there might be more Indians about. Then I tried to move. To my astonishment, I found I could get up, but with great difficulty. When I raised up, I found I had been bleeding very badly. It was now raining hard, but not hard enough to wash away the blood.

I sat up until dark. I heard William Duley call "Mother! Mother!" and then "Mrs. Smith! Mrs. Smith!" This frightened me very much, for I had supposed he was dead. I got up and started back to where the women and children had been killed. I passed by William Duley, but did not speak to him, as I thought the boy would feel very bad if I went away and left him; so I thought I would not let him know that I was there. He lay on his face as he had fallen.

Next I found Mrs. Smith. I felt her face. She was quite dead. I thought I would take her apron off and put it around me, as it was still raining very hard and I was quite wet and cold.

I hunted around for my children that had been murdered. I found Mrs. Ireland lying on her back, dead. I took two pins out of her waist. Her child, about two years old, was sleeping with its head upon her breast. It had been shot through the leg slightly.

I found one of my children dead, with his limbs straightened out and his arms lying by his side. It seemed he had died without a struggle. I felt him and all the rest of them. I then found Freddy, the one the squaw had beaten. He was quite warm. He rattled very badly in his throat. I called him and rubbed his limbs, but he did not answer.

I found Mr. Everett's children near. The eldest, a boy, was dead. The youngest boy and the oldest girl were living. Charley was lying on his back, sobbing in his sleep, like a child that had worried itself out crying. Lilly lay with her head and knee drawn under her, as though she was cold. I spoke to her.

She raised her head. "Mrs. Eastlick!" she said.

I answered her.

"I wish you would take care of Charley," she begged.

I said, "I cannot, Lilly, for I must go and find Johnny." I knew that he and Merton were alive somewhere.

She asked for a drink. I told her that I could not get her any. She then asked if there was water in heaven.

I said, "Yes, Lilly. When you get to heaven, you will have all you want." I thought it would be a comfort to her to tell her so. I was very sorry to leave them, but was obliged to, for I had hard work to get along myself. I could not find Frank around there.

It was now quite light and I went into a bunch of weeds and lay down, and lay there until night. This was Thursday, the 21st of August. A little more than one day had passed since we were all at our homes, but seemingly an age had passed since that time.

I could not find my children. I imagined they had gone to sleep somewhere among the dead and wounded. About nine or ten o'clock the Indians came back to where they had fought our folks. I heard them shooting.

During the day I heard the children crying most of the time; sometimes I heard them screaming and crying. I could not see them, for I had gone over the ridge a little.

No one can imagine my feelings. I wished I could die. I thought then, and think now, that they were torturing the children. It was a great punishment to me to hear the children crying and moaning under the cruel tortures of the Indians. I thought they were my children that I heard. I wanted to die, and yet I feared to die by the hands of the Indians. Had I not feared this horrible mode of death, I should have run away out of hearing of these innocent sufferers.

About four o'clock in the afternoon I heard three guns fired. The children then ceased crying. Poor, innocent ones!—they were now at rest. I kept still until dark and then started for the timber. I could see a great way off.

Toward midnight I lay down, my clothes being wet about a foot or more high. The dew was very heavy, and I was very thirsty. I had neither had a drop of water nor a bite to eat for two days. I tried to dip up some dew with my hands, but could no more than wet them. I took up the skirt of my dress and drank the water out of it. It tasted very good.

While I was lying in the grass I heard something stepping along. It stopped close by my side and I heard it smelling around. I supposed it was a fox.

After resting awhile, I started on again. I soon got into a swamp, where I found water. I stooped down and dipped some up with my hand and drank it. I now got out where the water was so deep that I could drink without sitting down. The grass was so heavy that I could hardly get along. I had to stamp the grass down with my left foot, as I could not raise my right three inches from the ground.

I cannot tell how long I was going through this swamp. It must have been a large one, for the moon arose while I was in it, and when I got out the moon was at least an hour high. I was tired enough to lie down and sleep. I took a good nap, then got up and looked around. I saw, about half a mile off, what I supposed to be Buffalo Lake.

As I was eager to get away I walked on as fast as I could. Think of my surprise when I heard chickens crowing and saw houses in different directions. I then knew that I was at *Lake Shetek,* from which I had fled on the morning of the 20th of August!

I looked around for a place to lie down. I was almost discouraged, but hid myself in the grass until about noon, when I again got up and thought I would go to the house to look after something to eat. I had a narrow swamp to cross, in which the water was very deep.

It was with the greatest difficulty and pain that I succeeded in getting through it. Then I had a hill, not very high, but steep, to climb up. I went a few yards up the hill and lay down among the bushes, entirely discouraged. I thought I would die then.

But, after lying there a long time, I found I could not die when I pleased. I took a cloth and wrapped it around my feet, for they were very sore; the flesh was almost all worn off my toes, which gave me great pain. Then I crawled to the top of the hill and lay down again, rested a few moments, and went on again. Seeing a cornfield a little way off, I went to it and pulled an ear of corn and ate a little. The corn made me sick. I lay down on the damp ground and pretty soon began to feel better.

I got up and went to the house. Everything was torn to pieces. A dead dog lay in the corner of the house and several dead pigs lay around outside, and also the head and horns of a steer. There were five different places where they had built their campfires. I found a small tin can, went to the well and got a drink.

I hid in some brush close by and stayed there until sundown. Then I went to the hen house, caught a chicken, tore off its breast, and put it into some brine that was left in a barrel, to salt it. I put it into a tin pail, with three ears of corn. I was now fixing to start away. I looked around and found an old coat and put it on. Then I started for Buffalo Lake the second time. I knew I must travel east to find the road.

It was a beautiful night. The moon shone very bright, and the North Star was my guide. I was so weak that I could not walk more than a quarter of a mile without resting. Still, I got along very comfortably. I could sleep quite warm—the old coat was a great help to me. I traveled all night and made the distance of two miles and a half.

When I reached the wood, I lay down and slept a long time. When I arose I found I was quite a distance from Buffalo Lake. I went on very slowly. I found, after resting, that I was very lame, but I managed to get to the lake finally.

Now I had an outlet of the lake to cross. In this outlet I fell, and got wet to my waist. I got out the best way I could, took off my skirt, wrung out the water, and hung it on the bushes to dry. Then I lay down and slept for some time.

When I was about ready to start again I saw some ducks fly out of the swamp. I thought there might be Indians coming. Looking back, I could just see a horse. I supposed it was an Indian and got back in the brush as quick as I could.

I soon found that I was mistaken: it was the mail carrier. I stepped out in sight and called to him. He stopped and seemed much surprised. He talked to me in the Indian tongue, but I could not understand what he said.

I knew he was a Frenchman, so I talked to him in the same tongue. I told him the people were all killed at Lake Shetek.

"You are pretty white for a squaw," he said.

I could not blame him for thinking I was an Indian, for I had on an old ragged coat and an apron over my head. I told him I was no squaw, but a white woman who was wounded and wanted to get away. He said he could take me as far as Dutch Charley's, a Dutchman, who lived about eleven miles from there. I rode with him in his sulky.

We got there about four o'clock and found Mr. Ireland there alone. I was greatly surprised to see him, for I thought he was dead. He was so discouraged before we got there that he could not get himself a drink. He looked more like a ghost than anything else. He was very pale, his eyes sunk in his head, and his voice was very weak. He had been wounded eight times.

The mail carrier fed his horse and then looked around for something to eat for himself. He soon found some cheese and we all ate what we wanted and rested awhile and then started again, taking some of the cheese with us. Mr. Ireland was so much encouraged that he walked several miles that night.

At the end of seven miles we stopped for the night, taking care to get far enough from the road so as not to be seen or heard. I did not sleep much. Mr. Ireland had told me, when I first saw him, that Merton had started with Johnny to try and get to some settlement. I thought I heard Johnny cry a great many times through the night.

We started at daylight the next morning. The wind was blowing very hard and the air was quite cold. The Frenchman tried to make me as comfortable as he could. He put his blanket around me, but I was very cold. He was very kind and did all he could for Mr. Ireland and myself.

At ten o'clock, just as we reached the top of the hill, I saw three objects which I took for white men. I told the men what I saw. They watched them a few moments and came to the conclusion that they were Indians. The Frenchman then turned the horse around and drove around under the hill for near a mile. He then crept to the top of the hill and watched them until they went out of sight. He said he was certain they were Indians.

He did not know what to do. He soon came to the conclusion that he would go on at all events. When we came near the place where we last saw them, the Frenchman went on before and crawled to the top of a high hill, where they had gone. He saw nothing of them. I drove on and when we got to the top of a high ridge I saw the same objects and was satisfied that one was a woman and that the others were children.

We hurried along as fast as we could. I waved my hand and the woman stopped and sat down. One of the children went on out of sight. We soon came up and found it was Mrs. Hurd. She was very much overcome with joy. She said she had taken care of my baby and that Merton and Johnny were on ahead with her two children and were the objects I saw. Johnny was my youngest and Merton my oldest child.

When I came in sight of the children I could hardly wait for the horse to get to them.

Merton stood by the side of the road, with Johnny sleeping in his arms. Oh, how I wanted to press him to my bosom! He had carried his little brother, fifteen months old, a distance of fifty miles! I did not think he could carry him so far.

Merton was very poor; more so than the baby. Johnny was very sick. I laid him down in the bottom of the sulky. He did not seem to notice much of anything. His face was covered with a scab. He had pulled the hair all out of the back part of his head. He did not look much like *my* Johnny.

We were then about two miles from the house of Mr. Brown, where we expected to get help. But when we reached the house we found the folks had all fled, taking most of their goods with them. We found some bread on the table, and that was all we found cooked. There was plenty of pork and potatoes, and vegetables of all kinds, and plenty of fat chickens.

The mail carrier left us all at this place, saying he would go on about seven miles to another house, where there lived a man he could get, he thought, to come for us that same night. But no one came.

We waited until Wednesday. On that day the mail carrier came back in the afternoon. The Frenchman told us that New Ulm was burned. He had seen soldiers or Indians there; he did not know which. He came quite close to two Indians and they both fired their guns at him. He had run into a swamp and made his escape.

We tried to persuade him to go to Mankato, but he would not. He said he would go back to Sioux Falls and send the soldiers from there to take us away.

We were so frightened when we heard the Indians had made a general outbreak that we could not stay in the house any longer. I finally persuaded the Frenchman to carry me on his horse about half a mile from the house, into the brush on the bank of the Cottonwood and leave me there. Mrs. Hurd cooked enough victuals to last us two days and brought bedclothes and pillows to our retreat in the woods. Here we stayed two nights and one day.

In this retreat we suffered more than ever. The mosquitoes nearly ate us up. We were a short distance (about halfway) between the top of the bank and the water in the river, and the brush was so thick that not a breath of air could get to us.

Before the mail carrier started back for Sioux Falls he kissed us all and bade us good-bye. We had cooked some chickens for him and prepared him a small quantity of parched corn. I now felt that our last hope was gone. There was no one left to report our circumstances or procure us any aid. I believed we would soon be discovered by some band of Indians and be brutally murdered.

The next morning Mr. Ireland determined to go to the house, where he could rest. He started and had hardly time to get out of the bushes when we heard the barking of two dogs, which we took to be the dogs of the Indians and expected every moment to hear the report of their guns. We were much frightened.

We heard something coming through the brush toward us. I held my breath, and could hear my own heart beat. Soon the dogs came within a few yards of us and stood and looked at us. I feared they would bark and thus reveal our hiding place, but they went off. Mrs. Hurd was so frightened that she became quite ill.

The dogs came back a second time. The largest one approached me and lay down, and looked very wistfully at me. I snapped my fingers toward him. He got up, wagged his tail, and went slowly away. I told Mrs. Hurd if they came back again I would try and make friends with them.

Sometime in the afternoon they came back. We began to take more courage, concluding the dogs belonged to some white man. I called them to me and gave them some meat, which they ate. Soon after, Mr. Ireland came back and told us that he thought the dogs belonged to Mr. Brown, as they seemed perfectly at home at the house. We remained another night at our place in the brush, and such a night as we spent there can hardly be imagined. The next morning Mr. Ireland came and begged us to go to the house. I decided to go if I could get there. I could not walk without help and Mr. Ireland's assistance was hardly sufficient—wounded as he was—to render me much aid. I got down on my hands and knees and crawled to the house.

I was so weak from loss of blood that I could not stand when I got there. I could not raise my head from my pillow without fainting.

About noon I recovered strength to sit up long enough to have my foot dressed. I could not leave the house and had no disposition to try. Mr. Ireland said to us, for our comfort, that if he kept on gaining as he now did, he would be able to start for New Ulm the next Monday. I was truly glad to see him doing so well.

Monday came and he started out, saying he would succeed or die in the attempt. Now I felt more lonely than ever. There we were, with our children, all alone. Oh, what long days were the Monday and Tuesday that followed! We lay down at night, still hoping that Mr. Ireland had been so fortunate as to reach New Ulm.

About midnight we were awakened by the dogs barking most furiously. I could not get out of bed to see what was the matter. I hoped the soldiers had come for us, but the dogs were so fierce, I decided that Indians were about the house.

Mrs. Hurd went to the window and listened. I asked her several times what she heard or saw. She made no reply. I thought our time had come. I could see my little ones tortured in the most cruel manner. It seemed to me that I could hear the hatchet cleave their skulls. I prayed the Lord to give me strength to die without a groan. I had forgotten everything, only that myself and my children must die.

Imagine how I started when I heard Mrs. Hurd exclaim, "My God! Koch, is that you?" I jumped off the bed, but could not walk. Mr. Koch and Mr. Wright, two of our neighbors, and fifteen soldiers came into the house. Mrs. Hurd and myself wept for joy, and there were few dry eyes among the soldiers.

A guard was set around the house by order of the lieutenant in charge, and Messrs. Koch and Wright were ordered to get supper for the soldiers. Chickens were soon dressed and cooked, and the soldiers on guard were called in to partake of the joyous midnight meal. We were requested to eat, but could not, so great was our joy at the idea of soon getting away.

By the time the repast was fairly over, it was nearly daylight, and we all left the house of Mr. Brown for New Ulm. After we had gone about five miles, Mr. Brown's family and three men and three women not of his family were found murdered. Mrs. Brown's head was split open with a hatchet, and some of the men were scalped. Their wagon was left standing in the road, and among the goods left by the Indians were two feather beds and a large quantity of books. The soldiers carried the beds away with them. Within a few miles of New Ulm, three more wagons, all plundered, were found in the road and one man, lying dead, had been scalped.

About noon we reached New Ulm. The people of the town had all left. Captain Dane, with a company of soldiers, was guarding the place. We were taken to Captain Dane's headquarters. I was taken out of the wagon, carried up two flights of stairs, and put upon a bed. Here I was well cared for and my wounds dressed, some of them for the first time. This was the fifteenth day since I had been wounded and left for dead at Lake Shetek.

We remained at New Ulm two days and on the third were all sent to the hospital at Mankato, thirty miles from New Ulm. Captain Dane accompanied us in person one-half the way, taking with him a guard of twenty men. I had no other clothes than those I had on when driven from my home, and a part of these I had lost. Captain Dane found some clothes in the street at New Ulm which he gave to Mrs. Hurd and myself, and Lieutenant Roberts gave each of us a dollar.

At Mankato I was taken to the hospital for treatment. My wounds soon healed, except the one in my foot. I wished to go to my friends in Ohio as early as possible, but I did not have the means to do so. I applied to Judge Charles E. Flandrau, who gave me a pass to St. Paul and advised me to go to General Pope for further assistance. General Pope directed me to Governor Ramsey.

I called on Governor Ramsey with a sad heart, thinking that he would do nothing for me and mine. But I was disappointed. I found him to be a kind-hearted, sympathizing man. He gave me fifteen dollars and paid my fare to Winona. With the fifteen dollars and the help of many kind-hearted strangers I reached my friends, who were very glad to see me and my children.[1]

# Ho for Idaho!

## FANNY KELLY

**O**N DECEMBER 12, 1864, *escorted by eight chiefs and a band of more than a thousand Sioux warriors, Fanny Kelly rode up to the gates of Fort Sully, a small army outpost in the frozen wilderness of South Dakota. The Indians' pretext for coming was that they were restoring the young white captive to her own people. But their true design was to use her to gain entrance to the fort and then massacre the garrison of two hundred.*

*No sooner had Fanny and the Indian chiefs entered the fort than the gates swung shut, locking out the horde of braves. Fanny had contrived to forewarn the soldiers of the Indians' plot, using as her messenger a Blackfoot warrior eager to win her favor.*

*For two weeks the Indians camped around the fort, fretting and fuming under the noses of its well-placed cannon. They tried to persuade Fanny to visit them in their lodges, but she was not so trusting. Finally they departed, leaving presents for her. On her long journey to safety, Fanny had been severely frozen, and she was under medical treatment at the fort for two months.*

*One day the mail coach stopped at Fort Sully and from it stepped a familiar, well-loved figure—Josiah Kelly, Fanny's husband. She had not seen him since that day in July when the Sioux had descended on the Kellys' Idaho-bound wagon train, scattering and killing their party and carrying Fanny off to captivity. For months Josiah had been scouring the region in vain attempts to find and rescue Fanny.*

*Their dream of finding their fortune in the Far West gone, Fanny and Josiah returned to their former home in Geneva, Kansas. Then they went on to the frontier town of Ellsworth, Kansas, and opened a hotel. In 1867, Josiah died of cholera.*

*In 1870 Fanny appeared in Washington, to ask compensation of the government for her losses at the hands of the Indians. President Grant extended his warmest sympathies to her, and Congress awarded her five thousand dollars in recognition of her services in saving Fort Sully and Captain Fisk's wagon train, about which she tells here.*

*Fanny Kelly married a second time, in 1880. She died in Washington, D.C., in 1904. Little is known of her life beyond what she reveals in this account, published in 1871. It is a harrowing, adventurous story of pioneer days and dangers, memorable for its pictures of the way the Sioux lived and battled. From its pages Fanny emerges unabashedly as a heroine—a quick-witted, courageous girl of nineteen, who must have possessed more than ordinary beauty to cause Indian chiefs to fight over her, and Jumping Bear, the Blackfoot brave, to betray his people in the hope of winning her love.*

I was born in Orillia, Canada, in 1845. Our home was on the lake shore, and there, amid pleasant surroundings, I passed the happy days of early childhood.

The years 1852 to 1856 witnessed, probably, the heaviest immigration the West has ever known in an equal length of time. Those who had gone before sent back to their friends such marvelous accounts of the fertility of the soil, the rapid development of the country, and the ease with which fortunes were made, that the "Western fever" became almost epidemic. Whole towns in the Eastern States were almost depopulated.

In 1856 my father, James Wiggins, joined a colony bound for Kansas. They were favorably impressed with the country and its people, and founded the town of Geneva. Then my father returned for his family.

We had reached the Missouri River, on our way to our new home, when my father was attacked with cholera and died. In obedience to his dying instructions, my mother, with her little family, continued onward to the prairie home he had prepared for us. Here, some eight years later, I was married to Josiah S. Kelly.

My husband's health was poor, and he decided upon a change of climate. On the 17th of May, 1864, a small train of covered wagons set out from Geneva. The party consisted of six persons—Mr. Gardner Wakefield, my husband, myself, our adopted daughter, Mary (my sister's child), and two colored servants, Frank and Andy. We had high hopes of a romantic and delightful journey across the plains and of future prosperity among the golden hills of Idaho.

Several days after beginning our journey we were joined by Mr. Sharp, a Methodist clergyman, and then by a Mr. Taylor. A few weeks later we overtook a large wagon train of emigrants, among whom were a family we were acquainted with—Mr. Larimer and his wife and child, a boy eight years old. Preferring to travel with our small train, they became members of our party. The addition of one of my own sex to our little company was cause of much rejoicing to me, and helped relieve the dullness of the long journey.

The hours of noon and evening rest we spent in preparing our frugal meals, gathering flowers with our children, picking berries, hunting curiosities, or gazing in wonder at the beauties of the strange, bewildering country through which we passed.

We kept each Sabbath as a day of thought and rest. We had divine service performed, observing the ceremonies of prayer, preaching, and singing, which we appreciated all the more because we were far from home.

The 12th of July was a warm and oppressive day. The burning sun poured forth its hottest rays upon the great Black Hills and the vast plains of Montana.

We looked anxiously forward to the approach of evening. Our journey had been pleasant but toilsome, for we had been long weeks on the road.

Slowly our wagons wound through the timber that skirted the Little Box Elder and, crossing the stream, we ascended the opposite bank.

We had no thought of danger or misgivings on the subject of savages.

At the outposts and ranches we had been told repeatedly that the Indians would not molest us. At Fort Laramie, where information that should have been reliable was given us, we had renewed assurances of the safety of the road and friendliness of the Indians. Being persuaded that fears were groundless, our small company preferred to travel alone on account of the greater progress we made that way.

The beauty of the sunset and the scenery around us filled our hearts with joy. Mr. Wakefield's voice was loud and strong as he sang, "Ho for Idaho!" Little Mary's low sweet voice, too, joined in the chorus. She was happy that day, as she always was. She was the star and joy of our whole party.

Without a sound of preparation or a word of warning, the bluffs before us were covered with a party of about two hundred and fifty Indians, painted and equipped for war, who uttered their wild war whoop and fired a signal volley of guns and revolvers into the air.

We had no time to think before the main body halted and sent out a part of their force, which circled round us at regular intervals, some distance from our wagons.

Recovering from the shock our men instantly decided to resist and corralled the wagons. My husband was looked upon as leader, as he was principal owner of the train. We were just a handful, but he was ready to stand his ground.

With all the power I could command, I begged him not to fight but to attempt to make peace with the Indians. "They seem to outnumber us ten to one," I said. "If you fire one shot, they will massacre all of us."

Love for the trembling little girl at my side, my husband, and friends made me strong to protest against anything that would lessen our chance to escape with our lives. Poor little Mary! From the first she had entertained an ungovernable dread of the Indians. In our dealings with friendly savages, I had tried to show how unfounded it was, and persuade her they were harmless, but all in vain. Mr. Kelly bought her beads and many little presents from them which she much admired, but she would always add, "They look so cross at me, and they have knives and tomahawks, and I fear they will kill me."

My husband advanced to meet the chief and demand his intentions. The savage leader immediately came toward him, riding forward and uttering the words "How! how!"

His name was Ottawa, and he was a war chief of the Ogallala band of the Sioux nation.[1] He struck himself on his breast, saying, "Good Indian, me." He pointed to those around him. "Heap good Indian, hunt buffalo and deer."

He assured us of his utmost friendship for the white people. Then he shook hands and his band followed his example, crowding around our wagons, shaking us all by the hand over and over again until our arms ached. They grinned and nodded with every demonstration of good will.

Our only safety seemed to be in delay, in hope of assistance approaching. To gain time, we allowed them to do whatever they fancied.

First, they said they would like to change one of their horses for the one Mr. Kelly was riding, a favorite race horse. Very much against his will, he gave in to their request.

My husband came to me with words of cheer and hope, but oh! what a marked look of despair was upon his face—a look such as I had never seen before.

The Indians asked for flour, and we gave them what they wanted. The flour they emptied upon the ground, saving only the sack. They talked to us partly by signs and partly in broken English. As we were anxious to suit ourselves to their whims and keep things friendly as long as possible, we allowed them to take whatever they desired, and offered them many presents besides.

It was, I have said, extremely warm weather, but the Indians remarked that the cold made it necessary for them to look for clothing, and begged for some from our stock. We gave it to them without the slightest objection. I, in a careless-like manner, said they must give me some moccasins for some articles of clothing that I had just handed them. Very pleasantly a young Indian gave me a nice pair, richly embroidered with different-colored beads.

Our anxiety to stay on good terms with them increased every instant. The hope of help arriving from some quarter grew stronger as the moments passed. Unfortunately, it was our only one.

The Indians grew bolder and more insolent in their advances. One of them laid hold of my husband's gun. Repulsed, he gave up.

The chief at last told us to proceed on our way, promising that we should not be molested. We obeyed, without trusting them.

Soon the wagon train was again in motion. The Indians insisted on driving our herd and grew ominously familiar. My husband called a halt. He saw that we were approaching a rocky glen, in whose gloomy depths he anticipated a murderous attack. Our enemies urged us forward, but we resolutely refused to stir. Finally they asked us to prepare supper. They said they would share it with us and then go to the hills to sleep. The men of our party concluded it would be best to give them a feast.

Each man was soon busy preparing the supper. Mr. Larimer and Frank were making the fire. Mr. Wakefield was getting provisions out of the wagon. Mr. Taylor was attending to his team, Mr. Kelly and Andy were out some distance gathering wood, and Mr. Sharp was distributing sugar among the Indians. Then, suddenly, our terrible enemies threw off their masks and displayed their true natures.

There was a simultaneous discharge of arms. When the cloud of smoke cleared away, I could see the retreating form of Mr. Larimer and the slow motion of poor Mr. Wakefield, for he was mortally wounded.

Mr. Sharp was killed within a few feet of me. Mr. Taylor—I can never forget his face as I saw him shot through the forehead with a rifle ball. He looked at me as he fell backward to the ground. I was the last object that met his dying gaze. Our poor faithful Frank fell at my feet pierced by many arrows. I recall the scene with a sickening horror. I could not see my husband anywhere and did not know his fate. Actually, he and Andy made a miraculous escape but I did not learn this until long afterward.

I had but little time for thought, for the Indians quickly sprang into our wagons, tearing off covers, crushing, and smashing everything that stood between them and their plunder. They broke open locks, trunks, and boxes, and distributed or destroyed our goods with great rapidity, using their tomahawks to pry open boxes, which they split up in savage recklessness.

They filled the air with fearful war whoops and hideous shouts. I knew that an indiscreet act on my part might jeopardize our lives. I felt certain that we two women would share death by their hands, but, with as much of an air of indifference as I could command, I kept still, hoping to prolong our lives even if only a few minutes.

I was not allowed this quiet but a moment. With tomahawks in their hands, two of the most savage-looking of the party rushed up into my wagon and seized me. They pulled me violently to the ground, almost breaking my arms and legs. My little Mary, with outstretched hands, was standing in the wagon. I took her in my arms and helped her to the ground.

I turned to the chief, put my hand upon his arm, and implored his protection for my fellow-prisoner and our children. At first he seemed utterly indifferent. Partly in words and partly by signs, he ordered me to remain quiet, placing his hand upon the revolver in his belt as an argument to enforce obedience.

A short distance in the rear of our train a wagon was in sight. The chief immediately dispatched a detachment of his band to capture or to cut it off from us. They rode furiously in pursuit of the small party, which consisted only of one family and a man who rode in advance of the single wagon.

The horseman was almost instantly surrounded and killed by a volley of arrows. The man in the wagon quickly turned his team around and, starting them at full speed, gave the whip and lines to the woman, who held a young child close in her arms. He then went to the back end of his wagon and threw out boxes, trunks, everything that he possessed. His wife meantime gave all her mind and strength to urging the horses forward.

The Indians had by this time come very near. They riddled the wagon cover with bullets and arrows. But the man kept them at bay with his revolver, and finally they left him and rode furiously back to our wagon train.

I was led a short distance from the wagon with Mary and told to remain quiet. I tried to obey. A terrible yearning sprang up in my heart to escape, as I hoped my husband had done. But many watchful eyes were upon me. I realized that any effort then at escape would result in failure, and probably cause the death of all the prisoners.

Mrs. Larimer, with her boy, came to us, trembling with fear. "The men have all escaped and left us to the mercy of the savages."

"I do hope they have. What benefit would it be to us to have them here? They would be killed, and then all hope of rescue for us would be at an end."

Her agitation was extreme. Her grief seemed to reach its climax when she saw the Indians destroying her property. It consisted principally of articles belonging to the art of daguerreotype photography. She had indulged in high hopes of fortune from practicing this art among the mining towns of Idaho. As she saw her chemicals, picture cases, and other property being destroyed, she uttered a wild, despairing cry. It brought the chief of the band to us. With gleaming knife, he threatened to end all her further troubles in this world.

My own agony was no less than hers. But the loss of my worldly possessions—a large herd of cattle, groceries, and goods of particular value in the mining regions—I gave no thought to. The possible fate of my husband and the dark, fearful future that loomed before myself and little Mary were the only thoughts that flashed through my mind.

But my poor companion was in great danger. I went to the side of the chief. Assuming a cheerfulness I was very far from feeling, I pleaded successfully for her life, but received no evidences of kindness or relenting that I could then understand. He did present me, however, with a wreath of gay feathers from his own head. I afterward learned it was a token of his favor and protection. He then left us, to secure his own share of plunder.

We were surrounded by a special guard of armed men. Giving up all struggle, we sat down upon the ground in despair. Night came upon us while we sat there.

It was pitiable to see the terrified looks of our children, who clung to us for the protection we could not give. Mrs. Larimer was unconscious of the death of any of our party. I did not tell her what my eyes had seen. I was afraid she could not endure it, and her excitement would anger our captors. So I tried to encourage and enliven her.

We both feared that when the Indians made their arrangements for departure we would be quickly disposed of by the scalping knife. Then a young Indian whose name was Wechela gave me a few articles of clothing. From among the confused mass of material of all kinds scattered about he also brought me a pair of shoes and a pair of little Mary's. He looked kindly as he laid these articles before me, saying by his gestures that our lives were to be spared and that we should have need of these objects and other clothing.

This same young Indian also brought me some books and letters, all of which I thankfully received. I quickly formed a plan to make good use of them and hid as many as I could about my clothing.

I said to Mrs. Larimer: "If I can keep these papers and letters, and we are forced to travel with the Indians into their country, I shall drop them at intervals along the way as a guide that our friends may find and follow. Or, if we have an opportunity to escape, these papers will help us retrace our steps."

The property the Indians could not carry with them they gathered into a pile and lighted. The light of the flames showed us the forms of our captors busily loading their horses and ours with plunder, and preparing to depart. When their arrangements were completed, they led horses up to us and motioned for us to mount. The horse assigned to me was one that had belonged to Mr. Larimer, and was crippled in the back. I tried to make them understand this but failed.

Mrs. Larimer had climbed into her saddle. Her boy was placed behind her and she started off, accompanied by a party of Indians. I also climbed into my saddle, but was no sooner there than the horse fell to the ground with me under him. I was in great pain. This accident detained me some time in the rear. A dread of being separated from the only white woman in that awful wilderness filled me with horror.

Soon they had another horse saddled for me and assisted me to mount him. I looked around for my little Mary. There she stood, a poor, helpless lamb, in the midst of bloodthirsty savages. I stretched out my arms to her imploringly. For a moment the Indians hesitated. Then, to my unspeakable joy, they yielded and gave me my child. Soon they started off, leading my horse. They also gave me a rope that was fastened around the horse's underjaw.

The air was cool and the sky was bright with the glitter of starlight. Straining my eyes, I sought to penetrate the shadows of the woods where our fugitive friends might be hidden. The smoldering ruins of our property fell into ashes and the smoke faded away. Night covered the traces of confusion and struggle. All seemed quiet and unbroken peace.

I turned for a last look and even the smoke was gone. With my child clinging to me, I rode on helpless, without guide or support save my trust in God.

The Indians traveled northward, chanting their monotonous war songs. After a ride of two miles through tall weeds and bushes we left the bottom lands and ascended some bluffs, and soon after came to a creek, which we easily forded. The hills beyond began to be more difficult to ascend, and the gorges seemed fearfully deep as we looked into the black shadows.

In the darkness of our ride, I conceived a plan for the escape of little Mary.

"Mary," I whispered, "we are only a few miles from our camp, and you can easily wade through the stream we have crossed. I have dropped letters on the way, you know, to guide our friends in the direction we have taken. These papers will guide you back again. Drop gently down and lie on the ground for a little while to avoid being seen. Then retrace your steps. If I can, I will follow you."

The child, whose judgment was remarkable for her age, readily agreed to this plan.

Watching for an opportunity, I dropped her gently to the ground and she lay there. The Indians pursued their way, unconscious of their loss.

I was firmly convinced that my course was wise—that I had given my child the only chance of escape within my power. Yet the terrible uncertainty of what her fate might be was almost unbearable.

I continued to think of it so deeply that at last I grew desperate. I felt I must follow her at every risk. I, too, slipped to the ground under the cover of night. My horse went on without its rider.

My plan was not successful. My flight was soon discovered, and the Indians wheeled around and rode back. Crouching in the undergrowth, I might have escaped in the darkness, were it not for their cunning. Forming in a line of forty or fifty abreast, they actually covered the ground as they rode past me.

The horses themselves betrayed me. Frightened at my crouching form, they stopped and reared, informing the Indians of my hiding place.

With great presence of mind I arose the moment I found myself discovered. I told them the child had fallen asleep and dropped from the horse; that I had tried to call their attention to it but no one had heard. Fearing I would be unable to find her if we rode further, I had jumped down and attempted the search alone.

The Indians used great violence toward me. They assured me that if I made any further attempts to escape, my punishment would be even more severe. Then they promised to send a party out in search of the child when it became light.

The cool air and the sound of rippling water warned us of our nearness to a river. Soon the savages turned their horses down a steep incline that, like a mighty wall, closed in the great bed of the North Platte. The river was rapid and deep, but we plunged in and braved the current.

As the horses plunged into the swelling river, I secretly dropped another letter that, I prayed, might be a clue for my husband to the labyrinth through which we were being led.

I could see by all the Indians' precautions that their plan was to mislead any who should attempt to follow and rescue us. They had taken paths inaccessible to white men, and made their crossing at a point where it would be impossible for wagon trains to pass, so that they might avoid meeting emigrants.

Having reached the opposite bank, they separated into squads and started in every direction, except southward, so as to mislead or confuse pursuers. The band that surrounded us kept to the northward a little by west. I tried to keep the points of the compass clear in my mind because it seemed part of the hope that sustained me.

When we camped that night I was ordered to lie down on the ground near a wounded Indian. A circle of them guarded me, and three fierce warriors sat near me with drawn tomahawks.

At early dawn I was aroused by the war chief, who sent me out to catch the horses. As the animals were those belonging to our wagon train, it was supposed that I could do so readily.

Upon returning, I saw my fellow prisoner, Mrs. Larimer. She was seated with her boy upon the ground, eating buffalo meat and crackers. I went immediately to her and we conversed in low tones. I told her of my intention to escape at the first opportunity. She seemed much depressed. I tried to reassure her.

We proceeded on our journey until near noon. I was obliged to carry the gun and bow and arrows of the chief, and my arms became very tired. Then we halted in a valley not far north of Deer Creek Station, and I met Mrs. Larimer again. We rested until the scorching rays of the sun had faded in the horizon. I pleaded with the Indians to camp here all night. I had good reasons. One was that we might be overtaken by friends sent to rescue us—another, that the distance of return would be less if I should be successful in my next attempt to escape.

But the savages were determined to go forward, and we were soon mounted and started onward. We traveled until sunset, then camped in a secluded valley.

I was securely fastened for the night. But before this I told my fellow prisoner I was determined to escape that night even if my life were the forfeit, as in every wind I fancied I could hear the voice of little Mary calling me. Mrs. Larimer entreated me not to leave her. I promised help to her should I be fortunate enough to get free.

In the morning, when permitted to rise, I learned that she and her boy were gone—an Indian had helped them to escape. A terrible sense of isolation closed around me. I had been desolate before, but now that I knew myself separated from my only white companions, the feeling increased tenfold.

We were soon once more on our march. Another burden had been added to my almost worn-out frame, the leading of an unruly horse. My arms were so full of the implements I was forced to carry for the old chief that I dropped one. It was his pipe, a tube nearly three feet long. It broke and I threw it away.

The country we passed over was high, dry, and barren. When evening came we stopped to rest in a grove of great timber, where there was a dry creek bed. Water was obtained by digging in the sand, but the supply was meager and I was allowed none.

Night had begun to darken. A large fire had been built, and they all danced around it. I stood trembling. I did not know but that I was destined to be burned to death in the flames the savages were capering about.

*"Chopachanopa!"* The chief was demanding something of me in a voice of thunder. He accompanied his words with gestures whose meaning was too threatening to be mistaken.

I looked in dismay around me. I was utterly at a loss to know what was expected—yet I dreaded what would happen if I failed to obey.

Wechela, the Indian boy who had been so kind to me, now came up. He made the motion of puffing with his lips. Then I remembered the pipe. At that time I was ignorant of their veneration for the pipe and of its value as a peace offering.

The chief declared that I should die for having caused the loss of his pipe. An untamed horse was brought, and they told me I would be tied on it and used as a target for their arrows.

Helpless, and almost dying with terror, I sank on a rock. Anxiously they awaited the signal. They were all armed with pistols, bows, and spears. Some stooped and raised blazing firebrands to frighten the pawing beast that was to bear me to death.

In what I felt was almost my final breath, I prayed for my salvation and the forgiveness of my enemies. Then I remembered a purse of money in my pocket. Knowing that it would decay with my body in the wilderness, I drew it out and divided it among them, though my hands were growing powerless and my sight failing. I gave them one hundred and twenty dollars in notes, telling them its value as I did so.

To my astonishment a change came over their faces. They laid their weapons on the ground, seemingly pleased. They requested me to explain the worth of each note by holding up my fingers.

Eagerly I tried to obey, perceiving the hope their milder manner held out. But my cold hands fell powerless by my side. I sank to the ground unconscious.

When I returned to my senses I was still on the ground where I had fallen. But preparations for the deadly scene were gone, and the savages slumbered on the ground near me by the faint firelight. Crawling into a sitting posture. I surveyed the camp. Hundreds of sleeping forms lay in groups around me. The sentinels were in their places. There was no opportunity to escape.

I lay silent till daybreak, when the camp was again put in motion. At their bidding, I mounted one horse and led another as I had done on the day previous.

This was no easy task. The packhorse had not been broken and it would frequently pull back so violently as to bring me to the ground. At this the chief would become fearfully angry, threatening to kill me at once. Practicing great caution, and using strong effort, I would strive to remain in the saddle to avoid his cuffs and blows.

I felt I had forfeited the good will of the Indians and I dared make no complaint, although hunger and thirst devoured me.

The way still led through dry and sandy hills. The sun glared down. Nothing but burning sand and withering sagebrush or thorny cactus was to be seen. The terrible heat of that long day's ride increased my thirst, which was driving me to frenzy.

I thought of all I had been separated from, perhaps forever. My torment mounted. I wished to die, feeling that nothing could be worse than this living death. My voice was almost gone. I maintained my seat in the saddle with difficulty.

I turned my eyes despairingly to my captors. *"Minne"* (water) I said, and kept repeating it imploringly at intervals. They seemed to hurry forward and, just at sunset, came in sight of a grassy valley through which flowed a river.

A little brook from the hills above found its way into this greater stream. Here they dismounted and, lifting me from my horse, laid me in its shallow bed. I had become almost unconscious and the cool, delightful waters revived me.

The stream by which the Indians camped that night was Powder

River. Here, in 1866, Fort Conner was built, which in the following year was named Fort Reno.

Leaving Powder River, we passed through large pine forests and valleys rich with beautiful grasses and clear springs. I continued to drop papers by the way, hoping they might lead to my rescue. I was not aware that it would have proved fatal had anyone attempted to pursue us. The Indians prefer to kill their captives rather than give them up.

My feet were covered with a pair of good shoes, and the chief's brother-in-law gave me a pair of stockings from his stores. I gladly accepted them, never suspecting that I was outraging a custom of the people among whom I was.

The chief saw the gift. He made no remark at the time, but soon afterward he shot one of his brother-in-law's horses. A quarrel flared up.

I realized I was the cause of the disagreement. Trembling, I watched the contest. I was unable to conciliate either Indian and dreaded the wrath of both.

The chief would not offer any reparation for the wrong he had inflicted. His brother-in-law, enraged, drew his bow and aimed his arrow at my heart, determined to have satisfaction for the loss of his horse.

I could only cry to God for mercy, and prepare to meet the death which had long hung over my head.

Then a young Blackfoot, whose name was Jumping Bear, snatched the bow from the savage and hurled it to the earth.

The Indian did not draw his bow again, and the chief gave him a horse, which calmed his fury.

The terrible heat of the days continued, and the road the Indians took was singularly barren of water. After drinking plentifully before starting, they carry little sticks in their mouths, which they chew constantly, thus creating saliva. But I did not know this and suffered dreadfully from thirst.

The seventh night they entered a canyon apparently well known to them. They found horses there, which evidently had been left on a former visit. The Indians had killed an antelope that day, and a piece of the raw flesh was allotted me for a meal.

On the 21st of July we left camp early, the day being cool and favorable for traveling. A few miles brought us to a high, broken ridge. As we ascended it we came in sight of a large herd of buffalo quietly feeding upon the grass. These animals are short-sighted, and scent the approach of an enemy before they can see him. When they had made us out, they lost no time in increasing the distance between us.

But the Indians and their horses both are trained buffalo hunters and soon succeeded in surrounding a number. They ride alongside their victim and, leveling their guns or arrows, send their shot in the region of the heart. Then they ride off to a safe distance, to avoid the desperate lunge which a wounded buffalo seldom fails to make. Shaking his shaggy head, crowned with horns of most formidable strength, he stands at bay with eyes darting, savage and defiant. Soon the blood begins to spurt from his mouth and choke him as it comes. The hunters do not shoot again, but wait patiently until their victim grows weak from loss of blood. Staggering, he falls upon his knees, makes a desperate effort to regain his feet and get at his slayer, then falls once more and rolls over on his side, dead.

The Indians had a plentiful feast of *ta-tonka,* as they call buffalo meat. They gave me a knife and motioned me to help myself. I did not accept, thinking then it would never be possible for me to eat uncooked meat.

They remained here overnight, starting early next morning. We were now nearing the village where the Indians belonged.

Jumping Bear, the young Indian who had shown me so many marks of good will, again made his appearance. He had a sad expression on his face, and that day rode in silence by my side. It was an act of great condescension on his part, for these men rarely ride with women, but go in advance.

We had traveled nearly three hundred miles. Despite my fears, I began to rejoice at the prospect of arriving among women, even though they were savages. Perhaps I might be able to find one sympathetic enough to aid me to escape. I became hopeful, and almost forgot my terror of my captors.

We were now nearing a river where we found refreshing drink. Here my captors paused to dress, to make a gay appearance and imposing entrance into the village. Except when in full dress, an Indian's wearing apparel consists mainly of a buffalo robe, which is also part of a fine toilet. It is very inconveniently wrapped about the person, and must be held in position with the hands.

At this place the clothing taken from our train was in great demand. Each warrior fortunate enough to possess any article of our dress now arrayed himself to the best advantage that the garments and his limited ideas of civilization permitted.

The Indians' peculiar ideas of tasteful dress rendered them grotesque in appearance. One brawny face appeared under the shade of my hat, smiling with satisfaction at the superiority of his decorations. Another was shaded from the scorching rays of the sun by a tiny parasol. The brown hand that held it aloft was thinly covered by a silk glove—about the only article of clothing that the warrior wore, except for the invariable breechclout.

Vests and other garments were put on with the lower part upward. The Indians all displayed remarkable ingenuity in the arrangement of their decorations. They seemed to think much of their stolen goods, some of which were frivolous and others worthless. Each noble warrior endeavored to outdo the other in splendor. Their horses were also decked in the most ridiculous manner.

Ottawa, or Silver Horn, the war chief, was arrayed in full costume. He was over seventy-five, partially blind, and a little below medium height. He was very savage looking and now, when in costume, looked frightful. His face was red, with stripes of black, and around each eye a circlet of bright yellow. His long black hair was divided into two braids, with a scalp lock on top of the head. His ears held great brass wire rings, and chains and bead necklaces were suspended from his neck; armlets and bracelets of brass, together with a string of bears' claws, completed his jewelry. He wore leggings of deerskin, and a shirt of the same material, beautifully ornamented with beads and fringed with scalp locks that he claimed to have taken from his enemies, both red and white. Over his shoulders hung a great, bright-colored quilt taken from our stores. He wore a crown of eagle feathers; also a plume of feathers hanging from the back of the crown.

His horse, a noble-looking animal, was no less gorgeously arrayed. His ears were pierced, like his master's, and his neck was encircled by a wreath of bears' claws, taken from animals the chief had slain. Some bells and a human scalp hung from his mane.

When all was arranged, the chief mounted his horse and rode on in triumph toward the village.

The entire Indian village poured forth to meet us, amid song and wild dancing, flourishing flags and weapons of war in frenzied joy as we entered. The village stretched for miles along the banks of a stream and resembled a vast military encampment. The wigwams, covered with white skins, were arranged without order but faced one point of the compass.

We penetrated through the settlement over a mile, accompanied by the enthusiastic escort of men, women, and children. We rode in the center of a double column of Indians and directly in the rear of the chief, till we reached the door of his lodge. His wives came out to meet him—he had six—but the senior one remained in the tent. The women crossed their arms on the chief's breast and smiled.

They met me in silence, but with looks of great astonishment.

I got down as directed and followed the chief into the great lodge. It was decorated with brilliantly colored porcupine quills and a terrible fringe of human scalp locks, taken in battle from the Pawnees. I was shown a seat on a buffalo skin opposite the entrance.

The chief's spoil was brought in for division by his elderly spouse. As it was spread out before them, the women gathered admiringly round it. Eagerly they watched every new article displayed, grunting their approval, until the senior wife seized a piece of cloth, declaring that she meant to keep it for herself.

A squabble broke out. Each tried to grab a share of the goods. The elder matron caught her knife from her belt and sprang in among them. She vowed that she was the oldest and had the right to govern, and threatened to kill everyone if there was the least objection offered to her decrees. I had so hoped to find sympathy and pity among these women of the forest, but instead I sat cowed and trembling, scarcely daring to breathe.

The chief noticed my fear and smiled. Then he rose and made a speech. The women became quiet. Presently an invitation arrived for the chief to go to a feast, and he left.

I was sorry to see him go. Terrible as he and his men had been, the women seemed still more formidable. I feared to be left alone with them—especially with the hot temper and ready knife of the elder squaw.

Great crowds of curious Indians came flocking in to stare at me. The women brought their children. Some of them, whose fair complexion astonished me, I afterward learned were the offspring of fort marriages.

One fair little boy, who, with his mother, had just returned from

Fort Laramie, came close to me. I found the squaw could speak a few words in English. She informed me that she had been the wife of a captain there. When his white wife arrived from the East, his Indian wife was told to return to her people; she did so, taking her child with her. The little boy was dressed completely in military clothes, even to the stripe on his pantaloons, and was a very bright, attractive child of about four years.

I saw many other fair-faced little children, and heard the same sad story from their mothers. I was deeply pained to see their pale, pinched features as they cried for food when there was none to be had. They are sometimes cruelly treated by the full-blooded and larger children on account of their unfortunate birth.

Now that the question of property was decided between the women of the chief's family, they seemed kindly disposed toward me. One of them brought me a dish of meat. Many others, even from the neighboring lodges, followed her example. They really seemed to pity me, and tried to express their sympathy in signs. They examined me all over and over again—my dress, hands and feet particularly. Then they discovered my bruised limbs, which had almost been broken when I was first taken, and proceeded to dress my wounds.

I was just beginning to rejoice in the kindness that seemed to soften their swarthy faces when a messenger from the war chief arrived. He was accompanied by a small party of young warriors and had been sent to conduct me to the chief's presence.

This summons awakened new fears within me. Seeing my hesitation, the senior wife allowed a little daughter of the chief's—her name was Yellow Bird—to accompany me. I was conducted to several feasts. At each I was received with kindness and promised good will and protection. It was here that the chief himself first condescended to speak kindly to me. He told me that henceforth I could call Yellow Bird my own, to take the place of my little girl that had been killed. I did not at once understand all of his meaning, but his changed manner and the companionship of Yellow Bird, who approached me with a trust and freedom unlike the scared shyness of Indian children generally, filled me with hope.

At nightfall we returned to the lodge. They told me I must henceforth regard it as home. The old squaw put a kettle on the fire and brewed a tea, of which she gave me a portion. She assured me it would cure my weary feeling and secure me a good rest.

Soon a deep drowsiness began to steal over me. My bed of furs was shown me. Yellow Bird was told to share my couch with me, and from this time on she was my constant attendant. I lay down, and the wife of the chief removed my moccasins. I slept sweetly—the first true sleep I had enjoyed in many weary nights.

The following day my labors began. I readily adapted myself to my new position. The chief's three sisters shared the lodge with us, and his old wife seemed to feel a protecting interest in me.

The day of the 25th of July was observed by continual feasting in honor of the safe return of the braves. There was a large tent made by putting several together, and here all the chiefs, medicine men, and great warriors met for consultation and feasting. I was invited to attend and was given an elevated seat. The rest of the company all sat upon the ground, mostly cross-legged.

In the center of the circle was erected a pole, with many scalps, trophies, and ornaments fastened to it. Near the foot of the pole several large kettles were placed in a row on the ground. In these the feast was prepared.

Thousands climbed and crowded around for a peep at me. At length the chief arose, in a very handsome costume. He addressed the audience and often pointed to me. I could understand but little of his meaning.

Several others also made speeches. They all sounded the same to me. I sat trembling with fear. I thought they were deliberating upon a plan of putting me to some cruel death to finish their amusement.

Soon a handsome pipe was lit and brought to the chief to smoke. He took it and presented the stem to the north, the south, the east, and the west, and to the sun overhead. Then he uttered a few words, drew a few whiffs, and passed it around through the whole group, who all smoked. The feast throughout was conducted in silence.

The lids were raised from the kettles, which were all filled with dog's meat, made into a sort of stew. My dish was given me, and the absolute necessity of eating it was painful to contemplate. After much urging I tasted it a few times and then resigned my dish. It was passed around with others to every part of the group, who all ate heartily. In this way the feast ended, and all left silently.

By looks and gestures the women told me that I should feel highly honored by being called to feast with chiefs and great warriors and, seeing the spirit in which it was given, I could not but treat it respectfully.

As far as I could understand, the dog feast seems to be a truly religious ceremony. In it the superstitious Indian sacrifices his faithful companion to bear testimony to the sacredness of his vows of friendship for the Great Spirit. He always offers up a portion of the meat to his deity.

That night was spent in dancing. It all seemed wild and furious to me. I was led into the center of the circle and assigned the painful duty of holding above my head human scalps fastened to a little pole. The dance was kept up until near morning, when all returned to their lodges. The three kind sisters of the chief were there to lead me to mine.

The next morning the whole village was in motion. The warriors were going to battle against a white enemy, and old men, women, and children were sent out in another direction to a place of safety. The tent poles were lowered and the tents rolled up. The cooking utensils were put together, and laid on cross-beams connecting the lower ends of the poles as they trailed the ground from the horses' sides, to which they were attached. Dogs, too, were made useful, and started off with smaller burdens dragging after them, in the same manner as the horses.

The whole village was in commotion. Children screamed or laughed. Dogs barked or growled under their heavy burdens. Squaws ran hither and thither, pulling down tepee poles, packing up everything and leading horses and dogs with huge burdens.

This caravan was immensely large, nearly the whole Sioux nation having concentrated there for the purpose of war. The chief's sisters brought me a saddled horse and told me to mount it and accompany the already moving column, which spread far over the hills to the northward. We toiled onward all day. Late in the afternoon we arrived at the ground of encampment. Here we waited for orders from the warriors, who had gone to battle. I afterward learned that General Sully's army [2] was pursuing the Sioux, and that the engagement was with his men.

In three days the Indians returned to camp. Their feasting and rejoicing caused me to believe they had suffered very little loss in the battle. Here I first saw the scalp dance, a ceremonial which did not increase my confidence in the tender mercies of my captors.

This performance is only gone through at night, by the light of torches. It appears all the more terrible by the fantastic gleam of the lighted brands.

The women, too, took part in the dance, and I was forced to play a role. I was painted and dressed for the occasion, and held a staff from the top of which hung several scalps.

The braves came forth, with the most extravagant boasts of their wonderful prowess in war. A number of young women came with them, carrying the trophies of their friends, which they held aloft. The warriors jumped around in a circle, brandishing their weapons and whooping and yelling the war cry in a most frightful manner. All jumped upon both feet at the same time, with simultaneous stamping and motions with their weapons, keeping exact time. Their gestures impressed me as if they were actually cutting and carving each other to pieces as they uttered their fearful, sharp yells.

They became furious as they grew more excited, until their faces were distorted to the utmost. Their glaring eyes protruded fiendishly, while they ground their teeth and tried to imitate the hissing, gurgling sound of death in battle. Furious and faster grew the stamping, until the sight was like a picture of fiends in a carnival of battle.

This country seemed scarred by countless trails, where the Indian ponies have dragged lodge poles, in the savages' change of camp or hunting. The hatred of the Indian for its occupation by the white man is very bitter. The felling of timber, killing of buffalo, traveling of a wagon train, or any signs of permanent possession by the white man excite deadly hostility. It is the Indians' last hope; if they yield and give up this, they will have to die or ever after be governed by the white man's laws. Consequently they lose no opportunity to kill or steal from and harass the whites.

The game still clings to its favorite haunts, and the Indian must press upon the steps of the white man or lose all hope of independence. Herds of elk proudly stand with erect antlers; the mountain sheep look down from crags that skirt the northern face of the mountains. The black and white-tail deer and antelope are ever present, while the hare and the rabbit, the sage hen, and the prairie chicken are nearly trodden down before they yield to the intrusion of the stranger.

The buffalo, in numberless herds, with tens of thousands in a herd, sweep back and forth, filling the valley as far as the eye can reach;

they are valued by the red man because they yield him food, a covering for his tepee, fuel, and clothing. The Big Horn River and mountains and streams beyond are plentifully supplied with various kinds of fish. The country seems to be filled with wolves, which pierce the night air with their howls.

The Indians felt that the nearness of the troops and their inroads through their best hunting grounds would prove disastrous to them, and soon they were making preparations for battle again. On the 8th of August the warriors set forth on the warpath.

Presently I could hear the sound of battle. The echoes of the guns in the distant hills warned me of the near approach of my own people. The Indians hurried on in great desperation. They forbade me to turn my head and look in the direction of the battle. Once I broke the rule and was severely punished. They kept their eyes upon me and were very cross.

General Sully's soldiers appeared near by, and I could see them charging the Indians, who skulked behind trees, sending their bullets and arrows vigorously into the enemy's ranks. I was kept in advance of the moving column of women and children, who were hurrying on, crying and famishing for water, trying to keep out of the line of firing.

It was late at night before we stopped on the lofty bank of a river. We had traveled far and fast all day through clouds of smoke and dust, and been parched by a scorching sun. My face was blistered from the burning rays, as I had been compelled to go with my head uncovered, after the fashion of the Indian women.

Reluctant to leave the river, they all lay down under the tall willows on its bank and slept. The horses lingered near, nipping the tender grass that bordered the stream.

It was not until next morning that I thought of how they should cross the river, which I suppose to have been the Missouri. It was not very wide, but it seemed deep and quite rapid. They did not risk swimming at that place, but went further down and plunged in and swam across, leading my horse. I was very much frightened.

That morning we entered a gorge full of huge fragments which had fallen from the mountains above. The Indians led my horse and followed each other closely with as much speed as possible, as we were still pursued by the troops. During the day some two or three warriors were brought in wounded. I was called to assist in dressing their wounds. This being my first experience of the kind, I was at some loss to know what was best to do. But, seeing in it a good opportunity to rise in their estimation, I endeavored to impress them with my knowledge of surgery and as nurse or medicine woman. From their gestures and meaningful looks I felt that my life was not safe, since we were so closely pursued.

On and still on. We were forced to flee to a place known among them as the Bad Lands—a wildly desolate and barren section of country. Here great boulders of blasted rock are piled round, with hard, dry sand among the crevices. Everything has a ruined look, as if vegetation and life had formerly existed but had been suddenly interrupted by some violent commotion of nature. A choking wind blows continually and fills the air with blinding dust.

The terrible scarcity of water and grass urged us forward, and General Sully's army in the rear gave us no rest. The following day or two we were driven so far northward, and became so imperiled by the pursuing forces that the Indians were obliged to leave all their possessions behind and swim the Yellowstone River for life. By this time the ponies were famished for want of food and water. It was only with great difficulty and hard blows that we could urge them on at all.

When Indians are pursued closely, they evince a desperate desire to save themselves, without regard to property or provisions. They throw away everything that will impede flight, and all natural instinct seems lost in fear. We had left, in our haste, immense quantities of plunder, even lodges standing, which proved of immediate help, but in the end a terrible loss.

General Sully with his whole troop stopped to destroy the property. This gave us an opportunity to escape. Otherwise we would inevitably have fallen into his hands.

After the attack of General Sully was over, an Indian came to me with a letter to read, taken from a soldier killed by him. The letter stated that the topographical engineer was killed, and that General Sully's men had caught the red devils responsible, cut their heads off, and stuck them upon poles. The soldier had written a friendly letter to his people, but before it was mailed he was numbered with the dead.

As soon as we were safe, the warriors returned home. A scene of terrible mourning over the killed took place among the women. Sometimes the practice of cutting the flesh is carried to a horrible extent.

They inflict gashes an inch in length on their bodies and limbs. Some cut off their hair, blacken their faces, and march through the village in procession, wailing and torturing their bodies.

Hunger followed in the track of grief. All our food was gone, and there was no game in that portion of the country.

The Indians were terribly enraged. They seemed to have sustained a great loss, which made them feel very revengeful toward me. They threatened me with death almost hourly, and in every form.

The next morning I could see that something unusual was about to happen. The sun had scarcely appeared above the horizon when the principal chiefs and warriors assembled in council.

Soon they sent an Indian to me. He asked me if I was ready to die —to be burned at the stake. I told him whenever Wakon-Tonka (the Great Spirit) was ready, he would call for me, and I would be willing to go. He said he had been sent from the council to warn me that it had become necessary to put me to death because my white brothers had killed so many of their young men.

Now the chiefs sat silently around the council fire. The pipe carrier entered the circle, holding in his hand the pipe ready lighted. When all the chiefs and men had smoked, one after another, the pipe bearer emptied the ashes into the fire.

"Chiefs of the great Dakota nation, Wakon-Tonka give you wisdom so that whatever you decide may be just," he said. He bowed respectfully and left the circle.

A moment of silence followed. One of the most aged of the chiefs, whose body was furrowed with the scars of innumerable wounds, arose.

"The palefaces, our eternal persecutors, pursue and harass us relentlessly," he said. "They force us to abandon to them, one by one, our best hunting grounds, and we are compelled to seek a refuge in these Bad Lands. Shall we allow ourselves to be slaughtered like timid Assiniboines, without seeking to avenge ourselves? Does not the law of the Dakotas say, Justice to our own nation and death to all palefaces?" He pointed to the stake that was being prepared for me. "Let my brothers say if that is just."

"Vengeance is allowable," remarked Mahpeah, an old chief.

Chief Ottawa arose. "Vengeance is the right of the weak and oppressed—and yet it ought to be no greater than the injury received. Why should we put this young, innocent woman to death? Has she not always been kind to us, smiled upon us, and sung for us? Do not all our children love her as a sister? Why, then, should we put her to so cruel a death for the crimes of others, because they are of her nation? Why should we punish the innocent for the guilty?"

How thankful I was when I knew their decision was to spare me. Though my life was miserable, it always became sweet when I felt I was about to part with it.

A terrible time followed. Many dogs and horses died of starvation. Their bodies were eaten immediately. The slow but constant march was kept up daily, in hope of finding game, fish, and fruit.

Many days in succession I tasted no food, save what I could gather on my way. A few rose leaves and blossoms was all I could find, except the grass I would gather and chew for nourishment.

One day, as I was pursuing what seemed an endless journey, an Indian rode up beside me. I did not remember having seen him before.

At his saddle hung a bright and well-known little shawl, and from the other side was suspended a child's scalp of long, fair hair.

As my eyes rested on this frightful sight I trembled in my saddle and grasped the air for support. A blood-red cloud seemed to come between me and the outer world.

I dropped from the saddle as if dead, and rolled upon the ground at the horse's feet.

When I regained consciousness, I raised my eyes to the fearful sight. It was gone. The Indian had suspected the cause of my emotion and removed it.

They placed me in the saddle once more. I protested wildly against their touch. I implored them to kill me.

When they camped, I had not the power to seek my own tent, but fell down in the sun. The chief, returning with a scouting party, found me lying there. He asked who had abused me.

"No one," I replied. "I want to see my dear mother, my poor mother who loves me and longs for her unhappy child."

I had found by experience that the only grief with which this red nation had any sympathy was the sorrow one might feel for a separation from a mother.

Leaving for a few moments, he brought back some ripe wild plums. They were deliciously cooling to my fever-parched lips.

Hunger and thirst, sorrow and fear, with unusual fatigue and labor, had weakened me in mind and body. The days that followed found me ill and delirious, and it was some time before I was able to recall events clearly. I began to waver in my knowledge of the frightful vision that had almost deprived me of my senses.

About this time there was another battle. It lasted for three days and many warriors fell. The camp was gloomy and hopeless in the extreme. The Indians discovered I was skillful in dressing wounds, and I was called to the relief of the wounded brought into camp.

Except when encamped for rest, the tribe pursued their wanderings constantly, sometimes fleeing before the enemy. We were always hungry and tired.

One very hot day a dark cloud seemed suddenly to pass before the sun and threaten a great storm. The wind rose, and the cloud became still darker.

A few drops sprinkled the earth—and then, in a heavy, blinding shower, there fell a countless swarm of grasshoppers, covering everything and rendering the air almost black.

They seemed to rival Pharaoh's locusts in number. No doubt they would have done damage to the food of the savages had they not fallen victims themselves to their keen appetites.

To catch the grasshoppers, large holes were dug in the ground and heated by fires. Then the fires were removed and the insects were driven into these holes. The heated earth baked them. They were considered good food, and were greedily devoured by the famished Sioux. Although the grasshoppers only remained two days, and went as suddenly as they had come, the Indians seemed refreshed by feasting on such small game, and continued to move forward.

One day we halted beside good water. I had grown so weak that motion of any kind was exhausting and I could scarcely walk. I felt that I must soon die of starvation and sorrow. But, mechanically, I tried to fulfill my tasks inside the chief's tepee, to secure the continued protection of the old squaw.

My strength failed me. I almost fell as I tried to move around.

Better fed than myself, she could not sympathize with my want of strength. She became cross and left the lodge, threatening me with her vengeance.

Presently an Indian woman, who pitied me, ran into the tepee. She said her husband had got some deer meat and she had cooked it for a feast. She begged me to share it. As she spoke, she drew me toward her tent.

The chief saw us go and, not disdaining a good dinner, he followed. The old squaw came flying into the lodge like an enraged fury, flourishing her knife and vowing she would kill me.

I arose immediately and fled. The squaw pursued me. The chief attempted to interfere, but her rage was too great and he struck her. She sprang like an infuriated tiger upon him, stabbing him in several places.

Her brother beheld the fight. He judged me responsible and, determining to kill me, fired six shots. All of them missed me, but one lodged in the arm of the chief, breaking it near the shoulder.

I ran until I reached the outskirts of the village. Here I was captured by some Indians who saw me running. They dragged me back to the tent, brandishing their tomahawks.

After half an hour some squaws came and took me to the lodge of the chief, who was waiting for me to dress his wounds. He was very weak from loss of blood. A doctor of the tribe had pierced his arm with a long knife, probing in search of the ball, and the hole, thus enlarged, had to be healed. The wound of the chief was severe It was my task to bathe and dress it and prepare his food.

I never saw the old wife of the chief again.


Hunting and fishing were now out of the question for Chief Ottawa. He sent his wives to work for themselves, keeping the sisters and myself to attend him.

War with our soldiers seemed to have decreased his power to a great extent. As he lay ill, he meditated on some plan of strengthening his forces. Finally he decided to send an offer of marriage to the daughter of a war chief of another band.

General Sully's destructive attack had deprived Chief Ottawa of all ready offerings. His eyes fell on my shoes, which happened to be particularly good. Reducing me to moccasins, he sent my shoes as a gift to the expected bride. She evidently received them graciously, for she came to his lodge almost every day and sat chatting at his side, to his satisfaction.

The chief's romance was very trying to me as he continued to show his favor to his betrothed by giving her articles of my clothing.

The marriage of the chief was to be celebrated with all due ceremony when his arm got well.

(But his arm never recovered. I have been told that he still remains crippled and unable to carry out any of his wicked designs. He is now living in the forts along the Missouri River, gladly claiming support from the Government.)

Before we left this camping ground, there arrived an Indian called Porcupine. He was well dressed, mounted on a fine horse, and brought with him presents that insured him a cordial reception.

After he had been a few days in the village, he gave me a letter from Captain Marshall, of the Eleventh Ohio Cavalry. It detailed the unsuccessful attempts that had been made to rescue me, and stated that this friendly Indian had undertaken to bring me back, for which he would be rewarded. The letter further said he had received a horse and provisions for the journey, and had left his three wives, with thirteen others, at the fort, as hostages.

My heart leaped with hope. But the next instant I knew this messenger would not be true to his promise, since he had joined the Sioux, immediately after his arrival, in a battle against the whites.

My fears were not unfounded. Porcupine prepared to go back to the fort without me, disregarding my earnest prayers and entreaties.

Porcupine said he should report me as dead or impossible to find.

I reminded him of the possible vengeance of the soldiers on his wives, whom they had threatened to kill if he did not bring me back. He laughed.

"The white soldiers are cowards. They never kill women. I will deceive them as I have done before."

Saying this, he took his departure. Nor could my most urgent entreaties induce the chief to allow me to send a message to my friends. The chief found me useful and had determined to keep me. He believed that a woman who had seen so much of the Indians' deceitfulness and cruelty could do them injury at the fort, and might prevent their receiving annuities.

All hope of rescue departed. Sadly I turned again to the wearisome drudgery of my captive life.

The young betrothed bride of the old chief was very gracious to me. On one occasion she invited me to join her in a walk.

"Down there," she said, pointing to a deep ravine. "Come and walk there. It is cool and shady."

I looked in the direction she indicated, and then at the Indian girl. She became very mysterious in her manner.

"There are white people down there," she whispered.

"How far?" I asked eagerly.

"About fifty miles. They have great guns, and men dressed in much buttons. Their wagons are drawn by horses with long ears."

A fort, I thought. But remembering the treacherous nature of the people I was among, I repressed every sign of emotion.

"Should you like to see them?" questioned Egosegalonicha, as she was called.

"They are strangers to me," I said quietly. "I do not know them."

"Are you sorry to live with us?"

"You do not have such bread as I would like to eat," I replied cautiously.

"And are you dissatisfied with our home?"

"You have some meat now. It is better than it was at the other camping ground. There we had no food and I suffered."

"But your eyes are swollen and red," she hinted. "You do not weep for bread."

These questions made me suspicious. I pretended not to hear her. "Just see how green that wood is," I said.

"But you do not say you are content. Will you stay here always, willingly?"

"Come and listen to the birds." I drew my companion toward the grove.

I did not trust her. I feared to utter a single word, lest it might be used against me with the chief.

Neither was I mistaken. When we returned to the lodge, I overheard Egosegalonicha relating to the chief the amusement she had enjoyed in lying to the white woman. She repeated what she had said about the fort, and invented entreaties which she pretended I had used, urging her to allow me to flee to my white friends.

Instantly I resolved to take advantage of the affair as a joke. I approached the chief.

"It was Egosegalonicha who implored *me* to go with her to the white man's fort," I said, "and find her a white warrior for a husband. But, true to my faith with the Indians, I refused."

The wily squaw, finding her weapons turned against herself, appeared confused and suddenly left the tent. The old chief smiled grimly.

One of the occupations given me was to prepare the bark of a red willow called *killikinnick* for smoking instead of tobacco. Groups of idle warriors would gather around me before the tent, urging me to sing as I worked. It was a dreary task, chanting to please my savage companions while I rubbed and prepared the bark of the willow, my heart ready to burst with grief.

On the 5th of September they went to battle, and surprised a portion of Captain Fisk's men escorting an emigrant train. They killed fourteen, and captured two wagons loaded with whiskey, wines, and valuable articles. There was a quantity of silverware and stationery also taken.

Among the articles brought into camp were a number of pickles in glass jars, which the Indians tasted. The result was comical in the extreme, for there is nothing that an Indian abhors more than a strong acid. The faces they made can be imagined. Thinking the pickles might be improved by cooking, they placed the jars in the fire. Of course they exploded, very much to the disgust of the Indians for the "white man's kettles."

They determined to go out again and capture a quantity of horses corralled in the neighborhood, and massacre the train and soldiers. But they feared the white man's cannon, and deliberated on a means of surprising him by ambush.

For two days I implored and begged on my knees to be allowed to go with them. At last I persuaded them to allow me to write a letter to Captain Fisk, but they dictated it. In the letter they assured him they were weary of fighting and advised him to go on in peace and safety.

Knowing their malicious designs, I set to work to make them fail. Although the wily chief counted every word as it was marked on paper, I contrived, by joining words together and condensing the information I gave, to warn the officer of the intentions of the savages, and tell him briefly of my unhappy captivity.

The letter was carefully examined by the chief and the number of its apparent words recounted. At length, appearing satisfied with its contents, he had it carried to a hill in sight of the soldiers' camp and stuck on a pole.

In due time the reply arrived. In it the captain said that he distrusted all among the savages and had great reason to. His distrust even extended to me—he did not appear entirely convinced I was a white woman. His words seemed to crush my hopes of rescue.

Again my ingenuity was tasked to make the answer correspond with the number of words, so it would not condemn me. I told the Indians that the captain doubted their friendliness, and I explained the contents of the letter as I thought best.

The next day I was entrusted with the task of writing again, to solemnly reassure the white men of the Indians' good faith and friendship. This time I told the soldiers I would find an excuse for standing on the hills in the afternoon, that they might see for themselves that I was what I represented myself to be—a white woman held in bondage.

The opportunity I desired was gained. I had a chance of standing so as to be seen by the soldiers' camp. Captain Fisk proceeded to treat quietly with the savages on the subject of a ransom. He offered to deliver in their village three wagonloads of stores as the price of my liberty.

To this the Indians pretended to agree. But I, understanding their language, heard them making fun of the white soldiers for believing their promises. The Indians planned to kill the soldiers who were to bring the stores to the village. I wrote to Captain Fisk of the futility of ransoming me in that way and warned him of the treachery intended.

Captain Fisk and his companions were sadly disappointed. After a hopeless attempt at obtaining my release, he spread far and wide the news that I was a prisoner.

In October, we were overtaken by a prairie fire. At this season of the year the plants and grass, parched by a hot sun, are ready to blaze in a moment if ignited by the least spark, which is often borne on the wind from some of the many camp fires.

With frightful rapidity we saw the fire extend in all directions. The Indians ran like wild animals from the flames, uttering yells like demons. Great walls of fire advanced toward us from the right and left, hissing, crackling, and threatening to unite and swallow us up in their raging fury.

We were amid charred trees, which fell with a thundering crash, blinding us with clouds of smoke. We were burned by the showers of sparks which poured upon us from all directions.

The forest shrank in the terrible grasp of the flames. The prairie was one sheet of fire, in the midst of which the wild animals, driven from their hiding places by this unexpected catastrophe, ran about, mad with terror.

The sky gleamed with blood-red reflection, and the impetuous wind swept both flames and smoke before it.

The Indians were terrified on seeing around them the mountain heights lighted up like beacons, showing the entire destruction. The earth became hot. Immense troops of buffalo made the ground tremble with their furious tread, and their bellowings of despair would fill with terror the hearts of the bravest men.

Everyone was frightened, running about the camp as if struck by insanity.

The fire continued to advance majestically, swallowing up everything in its way. It was preceded by countless animals of various kinds, bounding along with howls of fear, pursued by the scourge, which threatened to overtake them at every step.

The Indians had been deprived of all self-possession by our imminent peril. The flames formed an immense circle around our camp. Thick smoke, laden with sparks, was already passing over it.

Ten minutes more and all will be over with us, I thought, when I saw the squaws pressing the children to their bosoms.

But then the strong breeze, which up to that moment had been fanning the fire, suddenly died down. There was not a breath of air stirring. The progress of the fire slackened.

The Indians, old and young, male and female, began to pull up the grass by the roots all about the camp, then lassoed the horses and hobbled them in the center. In a few moments a large space was cleared where the herbs and grass had been pulled up.

Some of the Indians went to the edge of this space and formed a pile of grass and plants. Then, with their flints, they set fire to the mass and thus caused "fire to fight fire," as they called it. This was done in different directions. A curtain of flames rose rapidly around us, and for some time the camp was almost concealed beneath a vault of fire.

It was a moment of intense and awful anxiety. But, by degrees, the flames became less fierce, the smoke dispersed, and the roaring diminished. At length we were able to recognize each other in this horrible chaos.

A sigh of relief burst from every throat. Our camp was saved! After the first moments of joy were over, the camp was put in order. Then we all lay down to rest. We were very much in need of it after the terrible anxieties of the preceding hours. Besides, we had to give the ground time enough to cool, so that it might be traveled over by people and horses.

The next day we prepared for departure. Tents were folded and packages were placed upon the ponies, and our caravan was soon pursuing its journey.

The prairie was much changed since the previous evening. In many places the black and burnt earth was a heap of smoking ashes. Scarred and charred trees displayed their skeletons. The fire still roared at a distance and the horizon was obscured by smoke.

The horses advanced with caution over the uneven ground, constantly stumbling over the bones of animals that had fallen victim to the flames.

At evening we again camped in a plain absolutely bare. But in the distance we could see an appearance of green. We were about to enter a spot spared by the flames.

At sunrise, next morning, we were on the march toward this oasis in the desert.

Captain Fisk had made known to General Sully the fact of my being among the Indians, and the efforts he had made for my release. When the Blackfeet,[3] anxious to purchase arms, ammunition, and necessaries for the approaching winter, presented themselves before the General, asking for peace and avowing their weariness of hostility, he replied:

"I want no peace with you. You hold in captivity a white woman. Deliver her up to us and we will believe what you say. But, unless you do, we will raise an army of soldiers as numerous as the trees on the Missouri River and exterminate the Indians."

The Blackfeet assured General Sully that they held no white woman in their possession, but that I was among the Ogallalas.

"As you are friendly with them," said the General, "go to them and secure her, and we will then reward you for so doing."

The Blackfeet warriors appeared openly in our village a few days afterward. They repeated General Sully's threat and declared they intended to take me to him.

The Ogallalas said they were not afraid and refused to let me go. They held solemn council for two days, and at last resolved that the Blackfeet should take me as a ruse, to enable them to enter the fort and slaughter all the soldiers.

While they were deliberating—part of them willing, the other half refusing to let me go—Hunkiapa, a warrior, came into the lodge and ordered me out. He led me into a lodge where there were fifty warriors, painted and armed—their bows strung and their quivers full of arrows.

The whole party, including three squaws, who, noting my extreme fear, accompanied me, started toward a creek, where there were five horses and warriors to escort us to the Blackfoot village. They placed me on a horse. We were rapidly pursuing our way when a party of the Ogallalas caught up with us. They were unwilling to have me go with the Blackfeet and had come to reclaim me.

They parleyed for a time. One of the warriors ordered me to alight from the horse and pointed a pistol to my breast. Many of them clamored for my life. Finally, after a solemn promise on the part of my new captors that I should be kindly treated and should be returned safely, we were allowed to proceed. The Blackfeet left three of their best horses as a guarantee for my safe return.

When I heard the pledge given by the Blackfeet my fears abated. Hope sprang buoyant at the thought of again being within the reach of my own people. I felt confident that, once in the fort, I could frustrate the Indians' plans by warning the officers of their intentions.

The Blackfeet are a band of the Sioux nation; consequently, they are allies in battle. On this account the chief had not dared to refuse; besides, he was wounded badly and an invalid. He had expressed the desire, if the Great Spirit should summon him away, that I might be killed, to become his attendant to the spirit land.

The Blackfoot village was one hundred and fifty miles from the Ogallalas. Often the way lay over the tops of bare and sandy hills. The journey completely exhausted me, and I suffered from the intensely cold weather.

Approaching their village, they entered it with loud singing and whooping. I was received with great joy, and even marks of distinction were shown me. That night there was a feast, and everything denoted a time of rejoicing.

My life was now changed—instead of my waiting upon others, they waited upon me.

Still, the day of my arrival in the Blackfoot village was a sad one. It was the first anniversary of my wedding. The Indians' songs and shouts of exultation seemed like a bitter mockery of my misery and helplessness.

Soon after my arrival, Egosegalonicha came to see me. She inquired how I was treated, and particularly wished to know if the Blackfeet were respectful to me. She told me that she was sent to inquire for my safety and that any mistreatment by the Blackfeet would be avenged. She said her people mourned my absence. From others I learned the same.

Next morning there was great commotion in the camp. A delegation had arrived from the Yankton Sioux with a handsome horse and saddle as a present for me.

The Yanktons desired to purchase me, offering five of their finest horses for me. The Blackfeet were quite indignant, replying that they also had fine horses. They deemed it an insult, and returned the horse and its saddle. However, fearing my disappointment, in council that night they decided to present me with something as worthy as the Yanktons had sent.

Accordingly, at the door of the tent next morning were four of their best animals. Eight beautiful robes were brought in by the young men and given me also.

The Yanktons were told to return to their tribe and that, if such a message was again sent, the hatchet would be painted and given to them. This closed the negotiation, but not their efforts to obtain me.

The large reward which had been offered for my recovery caused the Blackfeet much trouble. Frequently large parties from other tribes would come in, offering to purchase me. I was removed at different times to various lodges, as a sort of concealment. I learned the Yanktons had not yet given up the idea of securing me.

One night I awoke to behold an Indian bending over me. He had made a long slit in the tent, by which he had entered, and was cutting through the robes which covered me. Fearing to move, I reached out my hand to the squaw who slept near me and pinched her. She immediately arose and gave the alarm, at which the Indian fled. This caused great excitement in the camp, and many threats were made against the Yanktons.

The intense cold and furious storms that followed my arrival among the Blackfeet made it impossible for them to set out immediately on the journey to Fort Sully. The snowdrifts had blocked the mountain passes and the chief, Tall Soldier, informed me the Indians must wait until the way was free from danger.

One day, Jumping Bear appeared in the Blackfoot village. It was he who had saved me from the vengeful arrow of the Indian whose horse the chief shot when I was first captured. He reminded me of my debt to him for preserving my life.

Trembling with fear, I listened to his avowal of more than ordinary feeling. He assured me that I had no cause to fear him—that he had always liked me and wished to be more than a friend to me.

I replied that I did not fear him—that I felt grateful to him for his kindness and protection, but that unless he proved his friendship for me, no persuasion could induce me to listen.

"Will you carry a letter to my people at the fort and deliver it into the hands of the great chief there? They will reward you for your kindness to their sister and you will return rich."

"I dare not go," he replied. "Nor could I get back before the warriors came to our village."

"My people will give you a fast horse," I said, "and you may return speedily. Go now, and prove your friendship by taking the letter and returning with your prizes."

I assured him the letter contained nothing that would harm him or his people; that I had written of him and his kindness, and his good will toward the white soldiers. After many long interviews—with the women of the lodge also using their influence—I at last persuaded him to go.

The contents of the letter were a warning to the "Big Chief" and the soldiers that the Indians intended to attack the fort and massacre the garrison, using me as a ruse to enable them to get inside. I begged the soldiers to rescue me if possible.

I passed many days of intense anxiety after Jumping Bear's departure. The squaws, fearing I had done wrong in sending him, were continually asking questions. It was difficult, but I succeeded in allaying their anxiety and preventing them from disclosing the secret to the other women.

I never saw Jumping Bear again. Early in December the Indians decided they could make the journey to the fort in safety.

The night before our departure, I was lying awake and heard the chief address his men about their wrongs at the hands of the whites. I now spoke the Indian tongue readily, and so understood his speech. It was as follows:

"Friends and sons, listen to my words. You are a great and powerful band of our people. The inferior race, who have encroached on our rights and territories, justly deserve hatred and destruction. These intruders came among us, and we took them by the hand. We believed them to be friends and true speakers; they have shown us how false and cruel they can be.

"They build forts to live in and shoot from with their big guns. Our people fall before them. Our game is chased from the hills. Our women are taken from us or won to forsake our lodges, and wronged and deceived.

"It has only been four or five moons since they drove us to desperation, killed our brothers and burned our tepees. The Indian cries for vengeance! There is no truth or friendship in the white man. Deceit and bitterness are in his words.

"Meet them with equal cunning. Show them no mercy. They are but few, we are many. Whet your knives and string your bows—sharpen the tomahawk and load the rifle!

"Let the wretches die, who have stolen our lands, and we will be free to roam over the soil that was our fathers'! We will come home bravely from battle. Our songs shall rise among the hills, and every tepee shall be hung with the scalp locks of our foes."

The savages grunted their approval. Then they made their war preparations silently, that I might not know the evil design hidden beneath the mask of friendship.

The next morning the savages were all ready for the road. Mounting in haste, they set up their farewell chant as they wound in a long column, a thousand strong, out of the village.

My dress, as I rode out of the Indian village that morning, consisted of a narrow white cotton gown reaching below the knee and fastened at the waist with a red scarf. Moccasins, embroidered with beads and porcupine quills, covered my feet. A robe over my shoulders completed my wardrobe.

While with the Ogallalas, I wore on my arms great brass rings that had been forced on me. Some of them fitted so tight that they lacerated my arms severely, leaving scars that I shall keep for ever. I was also painted as the squaws were, but never voluntarily applied the paint.

The ground was covered with snow. It was so cold that the horses' feet did not break through the hard, glittering surface except occasionally in the deep gullies.

It was two hundred miles from the Blackfoot village to Fort Sully. My ill-clad body suffered severely from the intense cold. I was forced to walk a great part of the way to keep from freezing. I struggled on, hoping for deliverance, yet dreading lest the plans of the Indians for the capture of the fort and massacre of its garrison might prove successful. My great fear was that my letter had not fallen into the right hands.

On our journey we came in sight of a few lodges among the timber and here we camped for the night. While I was in one of the lodges, to my surprise a gentlemanly figure dressed in modern style approached me. It astonished me to meet this well-mannered gentleman under such peculiar circumstances. He addressed me courteously.

"This is cold weather for traveling. Don't you find it so?"

"Not when I find myself going in the right direction," I replied.

I asked him if he lived in that vicinity, supposing that we must be near some white settlement.

He smiled. "I am a dweller in the hills. Civilized life has no charms for me. I find in freedom and nature all I need for happiness."

I had been separated from the knowledge of national affairs just when the war between the States was at its height. So I asked:

"Has Richmond been taken?"

"No, nor ever will be," was the reply.

Further conversation on national affairs convinced me that he was a rank rebel.

We held a long conversation on various topics. He informed me he had lived with the Indians fourteen years, had an Indian wife and several children, of whom he was very proud. He seemed to be perfectly satisfied with his mode of living. This man traded with the Indians, disposing of his goods in St. Louis and in eastern cities, and

was then on his way to his home, near the mouth of the Yellowstone
River.

Early in the forenoon of December 12th, my eager and anxious
eyes beheld the fort. The Indians paused and dismounted to arrange
their dress and see to their arms. Bows were strung and guns examined
carefully. They then divided into squads of fifty. Several of these
squads remained in ambush among the hills, for the purpose of capturing any who might escape the massacre at the fort. The others then
rode on, taking me with them.

During the journey, whenever an opportunity offered I would use
a handful of snow to cleanse my cheeks from savage adornment. Now,
as we drew nearer the fort and I could see the chiefs arranging themselves for effect, my heart beat fast. My excitement became so intense
as to be painful.

Eight chiefs rode in advance, one leading my horse by the bridle,
and the warriors rode in the rear. The cavalcade was imposing. As we
neared the fort, they raised the war song loud and wild, on the still,
wintry air. As if in answer to its notes, the glorious flag of our country
was run up, and floated bravely from the tall flagstaff within the fort.

My heart gave a wild bound of joy. Something seemed to rise in
my throat and choke my breathing. I saw the roofs of the buildings
within the fort covered by the brave men who composed that little
garrison.

An Indian hanger-on of the fort had sauntered carelessly forward
a few minutes previous, as if out of curiosity, but in reality to inform
his fellow-savages of the state of the fort and its defenses.

Then the gate was opened and Major House appeared, accompanied
by several officers and an interpreter, and received the chiefs, who
rode in advance.

Captain Logan (the officer of the day) approached me. Now that
I felt myself so close to safety my emotions overcame me. I had borne
grief and terror and privation, but the delight of being once more
among my people was overpowering. I almost lost the power of speech
or motion.

"Am I free, indeed free?" I murmured.

Captain Logan's tears answered me as well as his softly uttered
"Yes."

As soon as the chiefs who accompanied me had entered the fort,
the commandant's voice thundered the order for the gates to be closed.

Jumping Bear had delivered my letter! The Blackfeet were shut out,[4] and I was beyond their power to recapture.

After a bondage lasting more than five months, during which I had endured every torture, I once more stood free, among people of my own race, all ready to assist me and restore me to my husband's arms.

# NOTES

## Prisoner of the Caughnawagas

1. Probably these were German-speaking soldiers. There were Europeans of various nationalities among the French forces in Canada.

2. Detroit was founded in 1701 by the French, who built a fort there. At the time that Smith visited it, Detroit had been a prosperous fur-trading post for many years. Not long afterward, in 1760, as the French and Indian War drew to a close, it was taken by the English, under Major Robert Rogers.

3. A carrying place was a portage or land route over which travelers carried their goods and canoes from one waterway to another in frontier days. These routes were extensively used by both the Indians and the early settlers.

4. Crown Point in Essex County, New York, is on the west shore of Lake Champlain. It was an important French fort in the French and Indian Wars. In 1759 it was taken by the British, under General Amherst.

## Massacre at Michilimackinac

1. Henry, writing his account many years after the actual events, misremembered some of the details. There were only about thirty-five men in the garrison, according to a letter which Captain (not Major) Etherington wrote to Major Gladwyn, commanding officer at Detroit, soon after the massacre. Despite minor slips such as these in Henry's work, "the authenticity of this little book has never been questioned," as Francis Parkman states in his *Conspiracy of Pontiac*.

2. It was actually June 2, 1763.

3. According to Captain Etherington's letter of June 12, 1763, already mentioned, the Indians "rushed into the Fort, where they found their squaws, whom they had previously planted there, with their hatchets hid under their blankets, which they took, and in an instant killed Lieut. Jamet and fifteen rank and file, and a trader named Tracy. They wounded two, and took the rest of the garrison prisoners, five of whom they have since killed."

4. Although Henry has little to say in favor of Langlade, the Canadian was highly praised by Captain Etherington for his aid at the time of the massacre. He appears to have been instrumental in saving the lives of many of the English; according to Etherington, Langlade and another Canadian sent for the Ottawas, who took all but five Englishmen away from the Chippewas.

Charles Michel de Langlade was born in 1729 at Mackinac, and lived there as a trader. His mother was an Ottawa, his father a French-Canadian of good family. Langlade fought in many battles of the French and Indian War, often at the head of bands of Indians from the Mackinac region. He was at Braddock's defeat in 1755 and took part in the defense of Quebec in 1759. After the surrender of New France he supported the British, and fought on their side with his Indian allies in the American Revolution. Because he was one of Wisconsin's early settlers, he has often been called the "Father of Wisconsin."

5. The final result of the deliberations was that Henry and four soldiers were allotted to the Chippewas. The other two surviving traders, eleven soldiers, Etherington, and Lesslie were given to the Ottawas, who took them to L'Arbre Croche, where they were kindly treated. They were soon joined by soldiers from Fort Edward Augustus, and then, escorted by a fleet of Indian canoes, made their way to Montreal, arriving there on August 13, 1763. The only British fort that had not fallen in the region was Detroit, which was under heavy attack from Pontiac, but was never taken.

6. Special strings or belts of wampum were often used by the Indians to convey messages. The details of the message were symbolized by dark and light beads in varying sequences. The messenger memorized the message by associating its various parts with the various beads. When he reached his destination he would study the wampum and use it to recall the details of the message. Treaties and other documents, as well as tribal histories, were also preserved in wampum this way.

7. Sir William Johnson at this time was the Superintendent of Indian Affairs, a major post in British America. Irish-born, Johnson settled in the Mohawk valley and went into the fur trade, in which he accumulated a large fortune. He wielded great influence among the Iroquois, and played an important role in the French and Indian War, capturing Fort Niagara from the French in 1759 and taking part in the capture of Montreal. In 1766 he concluded a treaty of peace with Chief Pontiac. He was the founder of Johnstown, New York, where his mansion, Johnson Hall, still stands.

8. The Six Nations were the Seneca, Cayuga, Mohawk, Oneida, Onondaga, and Tuscarora tribes, collectively known as the Iroquois, or the Iroquois Confederacy. They were among the most warlike of the American Indians and were

greatly feared by other tribes. (The name "Iroquois," in Algonquin, means "real adders.")

9. The Great Turtle was the guardian spirit of the Chippewas.

## An Inch of Ground to Fight On

1. In 1778 the Wyoming Valley, on the Susquehanna River in Pennsylvania, was invaded by Loyalist troops and their Iroquois allies under Colonel John Butler. The raiders killed more than half of the force of four hundred patriots defending the settlements. Many prisoners were tortured by the Indians, whom Butler was unable to restrain. In retaliation for this and other massacres, Generals John Sullivan and James Clinton led the punitive expedition in which Van Campen took part against the Indians in New York.

2. Almost sixty years had passed between this exploit of Van Campen's and the writing of his narrative. During the interim he seems to have enlarged the entire incident, including the part he played in it. There is still extant what appears to be a more factual account of the adventure, written in Van Campen's own hand and dated November 15, 1780—about seven months after the actual event. It is a petition for a scalp bounty, addressed to the Council of Pennsylvania. In it Van Campen states that he and other citizens of the state were captured by ten Indians at the beginning of April and carried to a point near Tioga, on the East Branch of the Susquehanna.

"Your petitioner," Van Campen wrote, "preconcerted measures with his fellow prisoners to attack the said Indians in the night . . . accordingly his plan was adopted and succeeded so far as to deliver himself and fellow prisoners. Your petitioner . . . exerted himself with such effect as to leave two of the savages dead on the spot. The scalps of them he is ready to produce as testimonials of the fact, but is now informed that the time of killing them is too early to entitle him to the reward granted by government for Indian scalps." (The council had announced, on April 8, 1780, a bounty of one thousand dollars each for the scalps of hostile Indians.)

Van Campen went on to plead that a difference of a few days could not alter the merit of his actions, and suggested to the council that he should be entitled to consideration because "a number of prisoners were rescued from captivity besides himself, the whole of the Indians were put to flight, all naked and several wounded, so that both the damages done the enemy and the benefit accruing to his fellow citizens are greater than in the case of simply taking two scalps."

Fully twenty signatures are appended to Van Campen's petition, endorsing it. These include such names as Colonel Samuel Hunter and John Kelly, which readers of Van Campen's narrative will recognize. This document is in the possession of the New York Public Library.

The curious reader is invited to compare this account with still another entitled *A Narrative of the Capture of Certain Americans at Westmoreland by Savages,* published at Hartford in 1780, by an anonymous writer, whose sources of information are not given. This account repeats the basic facts given in Van

Campen's petition without indicating who killed the two Indians. It asserts that both Pike and Pence freed themselves with knives they had obtained from the Indians.

3. The two boys with the party—young Rogers and Van Campen's cousin—had hidden during the fight but now they rejoined the group, according to the account of this incident that Van Campen gave his grandson, J. Niles Hubbard. The boys were present during the rest of the adventure, although they are hardly mentioned. Hubbard retells this story in detail in a biography he wrote of his grandfather in 1841 (*Sketches of Border Adventure in the Life and Times of Major Moses Van Campen*).

4. This was Captain Horatio Jones, who was adopted by the Iroquois and after the Revolution served as a government interpreter. Jones and Van Campen became lifelong friends, and Jones supplied an endorsement for Van Campen's petition for a pension, which is referred to in the introduction to this narrative. The "one besides himself there that knew me," mentioned a little earlier in the story, was a Dutchman named Houser, who was also present. Houser had learned Van Campen's identity and the part he had played in the Indian "massacre" of April, 1780, from a soldier in Van Campen's party. Jones warned both the soldier and the Dutchman to be silent or their own lives would be endangered. J. Niles Hubbard relates this incident at considerable length in his biography of Van Campen.

5. This is the same Colonel Butler who took part in the Wyoming Valley raid. His son, Walter, in whose place Van Campen was adopted, had been an officer in his father's troop, Butler's Rangers.

6. From Joseph Pritts' *Incidents of Border Life*, Chambersburg, Pennsylvania, 1839.

### That Is Your Great Captain

1. Simon Girty, a native of Pennsylvania, was captured by the Indians in 1756 and lived with them for three years. During the Revolution he first served the Continentals, then went over to the British, who employed him in their Indian Department. He was the leader of many savage Indian raids on the border settlements, which knew him as "the white renegade." Crawford had been acquainted with Girty in earlier days.

### To Eat Fire Tomorrow

1. It was no lie, of course. General Cornwallis had surrendered in October, 1781, at Yorktown, Virginia, bringing the formal fighting of the Revolution to a close. Matthew Elliott, born in Ireland, was an Indian trader. During the Revolution he was captured by Wyandots and taken to Detroit, an English outpost. He entered the British service and was active as an agent on the frontier. James Girty, like his brothers George and Simon, was a native of Pennsylvania who went over to the British during the Revolution.

2. Alexander McKee, a native of Pennsylvania, had a trading house on the Maumee River. He was an agent of the British Indian Department during the

Revolution and, like Simon Girty, lived among the Indians and led them in many attacks against the American settlements.

3. See note 6 of the selection *Massacre at Michilimackinac,* page 373.

4. A combination pipe-and-tomahawk, sold by the traders, was popular with the Indians. The bowl was at the same end as the blade, but on the opposite side of the handle. The handle was bored, so that it also served as a pipestem.

### White Indian

1. According to Havelock Ellis, in his work *Sexual Inversion* (*Studies in the Psychology of Sex,* volume one, page 16, Random House, 1942), "among the American Indians, from the Eskimo of Alaska downward to Brazil and still farther south, homosexual customs have been very frequently observed. Sometimes they are regarded by the tribe with honor, sometimes with contempt, but they appear to be always tolerated." Oliver La Farge also discusses sexual inverts in his fine book *A Pictorial History of the American Indian* (page 100, Crown Publishers, Inc., 1956). He observes that "at the age at which a normal youth began the full activities of man and warrior, these special individuals . . . formally donned women's clothes, and from that time forth worked, and were classed, as women. . . . The custom provided a useful place for persons who otherwise would have been hopelessly misfitted." The word *berdache* was used in some tribes to describe a sexual invert. Even in ancient Mexico, Bernal Diaz observed young men dressed as women and following this custom.

2. Dreams were regarded with great seriousness by the American Indians, as they are by all primitive peoples. The Indians believed that dreams foretold the future or conveyed warnings or guidance from the spirit world or the Great Spirit. Tanner's attitude toward such visions is exactly the same as that of Wawatam or his wife in the Alexander Henry narrative.

3. The "medicine" of an Indian was the power or spirit ("manito") to which he turned for guidance or help, especially to control the forces of nature or his own destiny. In other instances the "medicine" might be relics or objects associated with the spirit and used by the Indian to influence it.

### Three Came Back

1. The Indians perform the process of scalping without regard to the size of the portion of skin taken from the crown of the head. If, in their haste to cut it off, they take more than they need for their purpose, they afterwards pare it down in a round shape to the diameter of about two inches. Doctor Robertson, in a note to his history of America, says: "It was originally the practice of the Americans, as well as of other savage nations, to cut off the heads of the enemies they slew, and to carry them away as trophies. But as they found these cumbersome in their retreat, which they always made very rapidly, and often through a vast extent of country, they became satisfied with tearing off their scalps." [*Note in original*]

2. In 1826, Johnston learned through his friend Duchouquet what became of the most important of these Indians in later life.

Chickatommo died in an encounter with a detachment of General Anthony Wayne's army in 1795 near Fort Defiance.

Messhawa became one of the followers of the great Shawnee chief Tecumseh and his brother, the Prophet. Duchouquet believed he had fallen in a battle against the Americans, or else gone west of the Mississippi.

Tom Lewis, who had lent Johnston his blanket, fought on the American side in the War of 1812. He became a chief, but later lost the confidence of his people and went west of the Mississippi. He was reported to be still alive in 1826.

3. According to Duchouquet, Whitaker fought against the Americans when General Wayne defeated the Indians at the rapids of the Maumee River. In 1826, he had been dead for many years. King Crane also fought against Wayne, but supported the Americans later in the War of 1812, fighting on their side at the Battle of the Thames. He died in 1818.

4. General Arthur St. Clair was commander-in-chief of the American forces sent to put down the Indians in the Ohio region in 1791. His army was surprised and beaten on the Wabash River in what was considered one of the great defeats of the young republic.

5. Chief Justice John Jay was sent to England in 1794 by President Washington to settle problems arising from violations of the Treaty of 1783, which concluded the Revolutionary War. By Jay's treaty the British agreed to evacuate the forts on the American side of the Canadian border. These forts had enabled the British not only to control much of the very profitable fur trade of this region, but to encourage the Indians in their hostilities against the Americans, which lasted long after the end of the Revolution.

## The Headhunters of Nootka

1. Nootka became a favorite port of call of traders fairly soon after Captain James Cook landed there in March, 1778. Cook obtained sea-otter skins from the Nootkans, and these were later sold at a handsome price in China. His reports of the abundance of furs and the prospects of a profitable trade with China led British and American traders to the Northwest Coast. By Jewitt's time it was a standard practice to bring inexpensive goods, such as those Captain Salter carried, trade them to the Indians for furs, particularly sea otter, and then make a very advantageous exchange of the furs in China for tea and other products in demand in the New World. (Captain James Hanna, who obtained 585 sea-otter skins from Maquina and his tribe in 1785, reported that they brought $20,600 in Canton!) Before many years, the sea otter had almost been hunted to extinction.

So many of the early fur traders were from Boston that American traders were universally known among the northwestern Indians as "Boston" men.

2. According to Dr. Robert Brown, one of the early map-makers of Vancouver Island as well as Jewitt's annotator, the Indians of the Northwest Coast and the wooded region of the great rivers always took heads as trophies. The heads were later set on poles in front of their cedar-board lodges. By contrast,

the prairie tribes and the Indians east of the Rockies took scalps, presumably because heads were too cumbersome to carry. This, however, presented no obstacle to fighting men traveling in canoes, and according to Dr. Brown the heads were often fastened to the bows while the warriors were returning from a hostile expedition.

3. Dr. Brown observed that there is no "Wickinninish" tribe; this was the name of an individual, probably the chief of the Klahoquahts. The name of Nootka Indians is applied to these and close to twenty other related small tribes. The "Nootkans" proper of Friendly Cove are known as Mooachahts among themselves. The Nootka Indians are related, linguistically, to the Kwakiutl Indians, a much better-known group living to the north.

## Remember the River Raisin!

1. From *A Journal Containing an Interesting and Accurate Account of the Hardships, Sufferings, Battles, Defeat, and Captivity of Those Heroic Kentucky Volunteers and Regulars, Commanded by General Winchester, in the Year 1812-1813*, Paris, Kentucky, 1813. Elias Darnell (or Darnall), the author, appears to have been a schoolteacher. He died in 1861 at Bethany, West Virginia.

## Ambush

1. Many fugitive Negroes lived among the Seminoles in comparative freedom, paying them tribute in corn and intermarrying with them. Morning Dew, wife of Osceola, had a trace of Negro blood, and was carried off by white settlers as a slave, after she had borne her husband four children. This was one of the reasons for his deep hatred of the Americans.

## The Attack on the Lighthouse

1. Coontie or coonty root (Seminole *kunti*) is a name applied to various tough woody plants of Florida and tropical America. The half-buried stems and the roots of the plants are peeled and reduced to a starchy white meal. It is still used today in various recipes, especially for invalids and children.

2. A tail block is a pulley block having a loose tail of rope by which it may be fastened to a stationary object.

## Revolt of the Sioux

1. The later fortunes of Lavina Eastlick and others who appear in her narrative may be of some interest:

After the Civil War, Lavina was married to Smith, who had run away before the slaughter in the swamp began. Later they were divorced.

Rhodes, who had run off at the same time as Smith, also made good his escape. Charles Hatch (brother of Mrs. Everett) and Mr. Everett both lived through the massacre. Laura Duley and her remaining children were taken into Dakota Territory by the Indians and freed near the end of 1862.

Pawn, like many of the other leaders in the massacre, escaped, perhaps to Canada. However, large numbers of Sioux who had played only a minor role surrendered or were captured by the troops and tried before a military tribunal. The court's procedure of verifying evidence was irregular and the atmosphere heavy with prejudice. In the end, 306 Sioux and half-breeds were sentenced to death. President Lincoln reviewed their cases and reduced the number to thirty-eight. They were hanged in a mass execution at Mankato on December 26, 1862. William J. Duley, father of little William, whom Lavina had seen dying, was selected to cut the rope that plunged the condemned Indians to their death. There is an excellent account of the revolt in C. M. Oehler's book *The Great Sioux Uprising* (Oxford University Press, 1959).

Lavina's story was originally published in *A History of the Great Massacre by the Sioux Indians,* by Charles A. Bryant and Abel B. Murch (Rickey & Carroll, Cincinnati, 1864).

### *Ho for Idaho!*

1. The Sioux were made up of seven major tribes. The largest was the Teton Sioux, and the most populous band among the Teton was the Ogallalas, or Oglalas. The Yanktons were another tribe which Fanny was to meet later on.

2. General Alfred Sully and General H. H. Sibley led expeditions into the Dakota Territory from 1863 to 1865 to punish the Sioux for the Minnesota uprising in 1862, described in the preceding narrative.

3. The Blackfeet here referred to were a small band of the Teton Sioux. They should not be confused with the Blackfeet proper (Siksika), who were an entirely different tribe and not related to the Sioux.

4. Another version of this story, entirely from an Indian point of view, is told by Stanley Vestal in his book *Sitting Bull* (University of Oklahoma Press, 1957). According to Vestal, Fanny was the prisoner of Brings-Plenty, an Ogallala, who "used her as his wife" and gave her the highly respectful name of Real Woman. Later, with the encouragement of Sitting Bull, the Blackfoot Sioux leader Crawler took her from Brings-Plenty at pistol point. The Blackfoot Sioux then brought Fanny to Fort Sully. Sitting Bull, who appears as their guiding spirit in this version, rode with them and was locked out with them. Vestal says they had no intention of attacking the soldiers, but merely wished to be feasted and rewarded for their service. Fanny, however, did not understand their language well, and thought they meant to massacre the soldiers.

Jumping Bear, the young Indian who bore Fanny's letter of warning to the fort, is reported by Vestal to have later become famous as Chief John Grass, and to have had an important part in deciding the fortunes of his people.

Vestal's version apparently was obtained from relatives and associates of Sitting Bull, and in part from a statement made by Crawler over forty years after these events, to a South Dakota historian. On the other hand, Fanny's story was supported by sworn statements from officers stationed at the fort when she was brought in.

Fanny's book, *Narrative of My Captivity Among the Sioux Indians,* was published in 1871.

# A CATALOGUE OF
# SELECTED DOVER BOOKS
# IN ALL FIELDS OF INTEREST

# A CATALOG OF SELECTED DOVER
# BOOKS IN ALL FIELDS OF INTEREST

LASERS AND HOLOGRAPHY, Winston E. Kock. Sound introduction to burgeoning field, expanded (1981) for second edition. 84 illustrations. 160pp. 5⅜ × 8¼. (EUK) 24041-X Pa. $3.50

FLORAL STAINED GLASS PATTERN BOOK, Ed Sibbett, Jr. 96 exquisite floral patterns—irises, poppie, lilies, tulips, geometrics, abstracts, etc.—adaptable to innumerable stained glass projects. 64pp. 8¼ × 11. 24259-5 Pa. $3.50

THE HISTORY OF THE LEWIS AND CLARK EXPEDITION, Meriwether Lewis and William Clark. Edited by Eliott Coues. Great classic edition of Lewis and Clark's day-by-day journals. Complete 1893 edition, edited by Eliott Coues from Biddle's authorized 1814 history. 1508pp. 5⅜ × 8½.
21268-8, 21269-6, 21270-X Pa. Three-vol. set $22.50

ORLEY FARM, Anthony Trollope. Three-dimensional tale of great criminal case. Original Millais illustrations illuminate marvelous panorama of Victorian society. Plot was author's favorite. 736pp. 5⅜ × 8½. 24181-5 Pa. $8.95

THE CLAVERINGS, Anthony Trollope. Major novel, chronicling aspects of British Victorian society, personalities. 16 plates by M. Edwards; first reprint of full text. 412pp. 5⅜ × 8½. 23464-9 Pa. $6.00

EINSTEIN'S THEORY OF RELATIVITY, Max Born. Finest semi-technical account; much explanation of ideas and math not readily available elsewhere on this level. 376pp. 5⅜ × 8½. 60769-0 Pa. $5.00

COMPUTABILITY AND UNSOLVABILITY, Martin Davis. Classic graduate-level introduction th theory of computability, usually referred to as theory of recurrent functions. New preface and appendix. 288pp. 5⅜ × 8½. 61471-9 Pa. $6.50

THE GODS OF THE EGYPTIANS, E.A. Wallis Budge. Never excelled for richness, fullness: all gods, goddesses, demons, mythical figures of Ancient Egypt; their legends, rites, incarnations, etc. Over 225 illustrations, plus 6 color plates. 988pp. 6⅛ × 9¼. (EBE) 22055-9, 22056-7 Pa., Two-vol. set $20.00

THE I CHING (THE BOOK OF CHANGES), translated by James Legge. Most penetrating divination manual ever prepared. Indispensable to study of early Oriental civilizations, to modern inquiring reader. 448pp. 5⅜ × 8½.
21062-6 Pa. $6.50

THE CRAFTSMAN'S HANDBOOK, Cennino Cennini. 15th-century handbook, school of Giotto, explains applying gold, silver leaf; gesso; fresco painting, grinding pigments, etc. 142pp. 6⅛ × 9¼. 20054-X Pa. $3.50

AN ATLAS OF ANATOMY FOR ARTISTS, Fritz Schider. Finest text, working book. Full text, plus anatomical illustrations; plates by great artists showing anatomy. 593 illustrations. 192pp. 7⅞ × 10¼. 20241-0 Pa. $6.00

EASY-TO-MAKE STAINED GLASS LIGHTCATCHERS, Ed Sibbett, Jr. 67 designs for most enjoyable ornaments: fruits, birds, teddy bears, trumpet, etc. Full size templates. 64pp. 8¼ × 11. 24081-9 Pa. $3.95

TRIAD OPTICAL ILLUSIONS AND HOW TO DESIGN THEM, Harry Turner. Triad explained in 32 pages of text, with 32 pages of Escher-like patterns on coloring stock. 92 figures. 32 plates. 64pp. 8¼ × 11. 23549-1 Pa. $2.50

SURREAL STICKERS AND UNREAL STAMPS, William Rowe. 224 haunting, hilarious stamps on gummed, perforated stock, with images of elephants, geisha girls, George Washington, etc. 16pp. one side. 8¼ × 11.    24371-0 Pa. $3.50

GOURMET KITCHEN LABELS, Ed Sibbett, Jr. 112 full-color labels (4 copies each of 28 designs). Fruit, bread, other culinary motifs. Gummed and perforated. 16pp. 8¼ × 11.    24087-8 Pa. $2.95

PATTERNS AND INSTRUCTIONS FOR CARVING AUTHENTIC BIRDS, H.D. Green. Detailed instructions, 27 diagrams, 85 photographs for carving 15 species of birds so life-like, they'll seem ready to fly! 8¼ × 11.    24222-6 Pa. $2.75

FLATLAND, E.A. Abbott. Science-fiction classic explores life of 2-D being in 3-D world. 16 illustrations. 103pp. 5⅜ × 8.    20001-9 Pa. $2.00

DRIED FLOWERS, Sarah Whitlock and Martha Rankin. Concise, clear, practical guide to dehydration, glycerinizing, pressing plant material, and more. Covers use of silica gel. 12 drawings. 32pp. 5⅜ × 8½.    21802-3 Pa. $1.00

EASY-TO-MAKE CANDLES, Gary V. Guy. Learn how easy it is to make all kinds of decorative candles. Step-by-step instructions. 82 illustrations. 48pp. 8¼ × 11.
23881-4 Pa. $2.50

SUPER STICKERS FOR KIDS, Carolyn Bracken. 128 gummed and perforated full-color stickers: GIRL WANTED, KEEP OUT, BORED OF EDUCATION, X-RATED, COMBAT ZONE, many others. 16pp. 8¼ × 11.    24092-4 Pa. $2.50

CUT AND COLOR PAPER MASKS, Michael Grater. Clowns, animals, funny faces...simply color them in, cut them out, and put them together, and you have 9 paper masks to play with and enjoy. 32pp. 8¼ × 11.    23171-2 Pa. $2.25

A CHRISTMAS CAROL: THE ORIGINAL MANUSCRIPT, Charles Dickens. Clear facsimile of Dickens manuscript, on facing pages with final printed text. 8 illustrations by John Leech, 4 in color on covers. 144pp. 8⅜ × 11¼.
20980-6 Pa. $5.95

CARVING SHOREBIRDS, Harry V. Shourds & Anthony Hillman. 16 full-size patterns (all double-page spreads) for 19 North American shorebirds with step-by-step instructions. 72pp. 9¼ × 12¼.    24287-0 Pa. $4.95

THE GENTLE ART OF MATHEMATICS, Dan Pedoe. Mathematical games, probability, the question of infinity, topology, how the laws of algebra work, problems of irrational numbers, and more. 42 figures. 143pp. 5⅜ × 8½. (EBE)
22949-1 Pa. $3.00

READY-TO-USE DOLLHOUSE WALLPAPER, Katzenbach & Warren, Inc. Stripe, 2 floral stripes, 2 allover florals, polka dot; all in full color. 4 sheets (350 sq. in.) of each, enough for average room. 48pp. 8¼ × 11.    23495-9 Pa. $2.95

MINIATURE IRON-ON TRANSFER PATTERNS FOR DOLLHOUSES, DOLLS, AND SMALL PROJECTS, Rita Weiss and Frank Fontana. Over 100 miniature patterns: rugs, bedspreads, quilts, chair seats, etc. In standard dollhouse size. 48pp. 8¼ × 11.    23741-9 Pa. $1.95

THE DINOSAUR COLORING BOOK, Anthony Rao. 45 renderings of dinosaurs, fossil birds, turtles, other creatures of Mesozoic Era. Scientifically accurate. Captions. 48pp. 8¼ × 11.    24022-3 Pa. $2.25

# CATALOG OF DOVER BOOKS

25 KITES THAT FLY, Leslie Hunt. Full, easy-to-follow instructions for kites made from inexpensive materials. Many novelties. 70 illustrations. 110pp. 5⅜ × 8½.
22550-X Pa. $1.95

PIANO TUNING, J. Cree Fischer. Clearest, best book for beginner, amateur. Simple repairs, raising dropped notes, tuning by easy method of flattened fifths. No previous skills needed. 4 illustrations. 201pp. 5⅜ × 8½.
23267-0 Pa. $3.50

EARLY AMERICAN IRON-ON TRANSFER PATTERNS, edited by Rita Weiss. 75 designs, borders, alphabets, from traditional American sources. 48pp. 8¼ × 11.
23162-3 Pa. $1.95

CROCHETING EDGINGS, edited by Rita Weiss. Over 100 of the best designs for these lovely trims for a host of household items. Complete instructions, illustrations. 48pp. 8¼ × 11.
24031-2 Pa. $2.00

FINGER PLAYS FOR NURSERY AND KINDERGARTEN, Emilie Poulsson. 18 finger plays with music (voice and piano); entertaining, instructive. Counting, nature lore, etc. Victorian classic. 53 illustrations. 80pp. 6½ × 9¼. 22588-7 Pa. $1.95

BOSTON THEN AND NOW, Peter Vanderwarker. Here in 59 side-by-side views are photographic documentations of the city's past and present. 119 photographs. Full captions. 122pp. 8¼ × 11.
24312-5 Pa. $6.95

CROCHETING BEDSPREADS, edited by Rita Weiss. 22 patterns, originally published in three instruction books 1939-41. 39 photos, 8 charts. Instructions. 48pp. 8¼ × 11.
23610-2 Pa. $2.00

HAWTHORNE ON PAINTING, Charles W. Hawthorne. Collected from notes taken by students at famous Cape Cod School; hundreds of direct, personal *apercus*, ideas, suggestions. 91pp. 5⅜ × 8½.
20653-X Pa. $2.50

THERMODYNAMICS, Enrico Fermi. A classic of modern science. Clear, organized treatment of systems, first and second laws, entropy, thermodynamic potentials, etc. Calculus required. 160pp. 5⅜ × 8½.
60361-X Pa. $4.00

TEN BOOKS ON ARCHITECTURE, Vitruvius. The most important book ever written on architecture. Early Roman aesthetics, technology, classical orders, site selection, all other aspects. Morgan translation. 331pp. 5⅜ × 8½. 20645-9 Pa. $5.50

THE CORNELL BREAD BOOK, Clive M. McCay and Jeanette B. McCay. Famed high-protein recipe incorporated into breads, rolls, buns, coffee cakes, pizza, pie crusts, more. Nearly 50 illustrations. 48pp. 8¼ × 11.
23995-0 Pa. $2.00

THE CRAFTSMAN'S HANDBOOK, Cennino Cennini. 15th-century handbook, school of Giotto, explains applying gold, silver leaf; gesso; fresco painting, grinding pigments, etc. 142pp. 6⅛ × 9¼.
20054-X Pa. $3.50

FRANK LLOYD WRIGHT'S FALLINGWATER, Donald Hoffmann. Full story of Wright's masterwork at Bear Run, Pa. 100 photographs of site, construction, and details of completed structure. 112pp. 9¼ × 10.
23671-4 Pa. $6.50

OVAL STAINED GLASS PATTERN BOOK, C. Eaton. 60 new designs framed in shape of an oval. Greater complexity, challenge with sinuous cats, birds, mandalas framed in antique shape. 64pp. 8¼ × 11.
24519-5 Pa. $3.50

**READY-TO-USE BORDERS**, Ted Menten. Both traditional and unusual inter-changeable borders in a tremendous array of sizes, shapes, and styles. 32 plates. 64pp. 8¼ × 11. 23782-6 Pa. $2.95

**THE WHOLE CRAFT OF SPINNING**, Carol Kroll. Preparing fiber, drop spindle, treadle wheel, other fibers, more. Highly creative, yet simple. 43 illus-trations. 48pp. 8¼ × 11. 23968-3 Pa. $2.50

**HIDDEN PICTURE PUZZLE COLORING BOOK**, Anna Pomaska. 31 delightful pictures to color with dozens of objects, people and animals hidden away to find. Captions. Solutions. 48pp. 8¼ × 11. 23909-8 Pa. $2.25

**QUILTING WITH STRIPS AND STRINGS**, H.W. Rose. Quickest, easiest way to turn left-over fabric into handsome quilt. 46 patchwork quilts; 31 full-size templates. 48pp. 8¼ × 11. 24357-5 Pa. $3.25

**NATURAL DYES AND HOME DYEING**, Rita J. Adrosko. Over 135 specific recipes from historical sources for cotton, wool, other fabrics. Genuine premodern handicrafts. 12 illustrations. 160pp. 5⅜ × 8½. 22688-3 Pa. $2.95

**CARVING REALISTIC BIRDS**, H.D. Green. Full-sized patterns, step-by-step instructions for robins, jays, cardinals, finches, etc. 97 illustrations. 80pp. 8¼ × 11. 23484-3 Pa. $3.00

**GEOMETRY, RELATIVITY AND THE FOURTH DIMENSION**, Rudolf Rucker. Exposition of fourth dimension, concepts of relativity as Flatland characters continue adventures. Popular, easily followed yet accurate, profound. 141 illustrations. 133pp. 5⅜ × 8½. 23400-2 Pa. $2.75

**READY-TO-USE SMALL FRAMES AND BORDERS**, Carol B. Grafton. Graphic message? Frame it graphically with 373 new frames and borders in many styles: Art Nouveau, Art Deco, Op Art. 64pp. 8¼ × 11. 24375-3 Pa. $2.95

**CELTIC ART: THE METHODS OF CONSTRUCTION**, George Bain. Simple geometric techniques for making Celtic interlacements, spirals, Kellstype initials, animals, humans, etc. Over 500 illustrations. 160pp. 9 × 12. (Available in U.S. only) 22923-8 Pa. $6.00

**THE TALE OF TOM KITTEN**, Beatrix Potter. Exciting text and all 27 vivid, full-color illustrations to charming tale of naughty little Tom getting into mischief again. 58pp. 4¼ × 5½. 24502-0 Pa. $1.50

**WOODEN PUZZLE TOYS**, Ed Sibbett, Jr. Transfer patterns and instructions for 24 easy-to-do projects: fish, butterflies, cats, acrobats, Humpty Dumpty, 19 others. 48pp. 8¼ × 11. 23713-3 Pa. $2.50

**MY FAMILY TREE WORKBOOK**, Rosemary A. Chorzempa. Enjoyable, easy-to-use introduction to genealogy designed specially for children. Data pages plus text. Instructive, educational, valuable. 64pp. 8¼ × 11. 24229-3 Pa. $2.25

*Prices subject to change without notice.*

Available at your book dealer or write for free catalog to Dept. GI, Dover Publications, Inc., 31 East 2nd St. Mineola, N.Y. 11501. Dover publishes more than 175 books each year on science, elementary and advanced mathematics, biology, music, art, literary history, social sciences and other areas